SACRED TIME

The Sabbath as a Perpetual Covenant

Edited by Gaye Strathearn

RSC BYU

DESERET BOOK

Published by the Religious Studies Center, Brigham Young University, Provo, Utah, in cooperation with Deseret Book Company, Salt Lake City, Utah.
Visit us at rsc.byu.edu.

Printed in the United States of America by Sheridan Books, Inc.

Interior layout by Alex Socarras
Cover image: *In Remembrance of Me*, Walter Rane. Courtesy of Intellectual Reserve, Inc.
ISBN: 978-1-9503-0437-0

Library of Congress Cataloging-in-Publication Data

Names: Strathearn, Gaye, editor.
Title: Sacred time: the Sabbath as a perpetual covenant / edited by Gaye Strathearn.
Description: Provo, Utah : Religious Studies Center, Brigham Young University ; Salt Lake City, Utah : Deseret Book, [2023] | Includes index. | Summary: "How does a person live the commandment to keep the Sabbath day holy in a world that is vastly different from the commandment's original context with Moses on Mount Sinai? Chapters in this volume explore the Sabbath throughout time, from both the Old Testament and the New Testament, the post-New Testament Christian Church during the second through the fourth centuries, the rabbinic teachings, and modern efforts to keep the Sabbath relevant, including the Restoration and other Christian and Jewish efforts"-- Provided by publisher.
Identifiers: LCCN 2022046143 | ISBN 9781950304370 (hardback)
Subjects: LCSH: Church of Jesus Christ of Latter-day Saints--Doctrines. | Sabbath. | Sunday.
Classification: LCC BX8643.S2 S23 2023 | DDC 263/.2--dc23/eng/20221125
LC record available at https://lccn.loc.gov/2022046143

Contents

Contents

Introduction

Sacred Time:
The Sabbath as a Perpetual Covenant

Gaye Strathearn

Time: sixty seconds in a minute, sixty minutes in an hour, twenty-four hours in a day, seven days in a week. Time is a precious commodity. In mortality it is finite and, if we're not careful, it ticks away almost imperceptibly. Even so, the demands on our time are many and trying to balance them all can sometimes feel overwhelming. These demands include family time, work time, sleep time, leisure time, service to our community time, and a multitude of other "times." For the religious there is also a desire to include sacred time. Sacred time is different from the other "times" that compete for our attention. It is when individuals and communities intentionally create moments of set-apart time that transcends the hustle and bustle demanded by our busy mortal lives and that instead encourages us to slow down and spiritually "smell the roses." Although this time is part of our mortal time, it also transcends it as we shift our focus from worrying about the things of this world and instead find time to learn about and better understand the possibilities of eternity. It is a time to create and strengthen our vertical connections with God. Many religious traditions encourage their followers to engage in some form of sacred time.

For Christians and Jews alike, sacred time is centered on the Sabbath day. The Lord commanded Moses on Mount Sinai that the Israelites were to "remember the sabbath day, to keep it holy. Six days shalt thou labour, and do all thy work: But the seventh day is the sabbath of the Lord thy God; in it thou shalt not do any work" (Exodus 20:8–10). Later the Lord taught that the Sabbaths were meant to be a "perpetual covenant. . . . A sign between me and the children of Israel for ever" (Exodus 31:16–17). In the ensuing three millennia since these commandments were first given, Jews and Christians have sought to keep the Sabbath alive in both their communal and individual lives.

The purpose of this collection of essays is to help modern Latter-day Saint readers better understand how the Sabbath day was understood and practiced throughout the centuries leading up to and including the modern day.

One of the difficulties that people have recurringly struggled with throughout the centuries is the question of how to interpret the Sabbath command for *their* particular time and circumstances. Commandments usually teach principles rather than provide direct and specific applications. For example, Jesus reiterated the importance of the two Mosaic commands to "love the Lord thy God with all thine heart, and with all thy soul, and with all thy might" and to "love thy neighbour as thyself" (Mark 12:29–31 and parallels; see also Deuteronomy 6:5; Leviticus 19:18), but Jesus did not immediately follow up those commands with specific directions on how to apply them. For the most part he left the hearers with the responsibility of working out how to make them relevant in their lives, just as he did with the command to keep or remember the Sabbath day. As we will see in the chapters that follow, although the importance of the Sabbath command was well established in the Old Testament, there is limited evidence of specific direction on how it should have been applied, especially for regular Israelites who did not perform the Sabbath sacrifices at the temple. By the time of Jesus, some of those directions were no longer even applicable for Jews (such as not collecting manna on the Sabbath).

Therefore, over time people have had to consciously work to find meaning in and apply the Sabbath command in a world that is very different from the one in which Moses first received it. Efforts by the ancients are sometimes viewed negatively when modern readers encounter the Sabbath controversies between Jesus and the Pharisees and other Jewish groups. But it is important to remember that like us, in many ways, ancient Jews and Christians were trying to figure out how to keep the Sabbath day alive and relevant in a world where, if they were not careful, it could be consumed by the political, social, and religious environments where they lived. Jews and Christians were asking questions about how to live the Sabbath precisely because they understood its central place in maintaining their covenantal identity. In doing so they began to discuss the Sabbath commandment and to find ways to apply it to *their* situations. Much of our modern understanding of these applications is filtered through the lens of Rabbinic Judaism, where they eventually became codified. But it is important for modern readers to understand that during the New Testament period, these applications were still in a state of flux. They were not yet set in stone, and some groups interpreted them differently than others did. So it was with Jesus. Sometimes he agreed with Jewish interpretations, but other times he used his authority as "Lord . . . of the Sabbath" (Mark 2:28) to raise the bar for the people's understanding of the ongoing eternal purposes of the Sabbath.

The earliest Christians also found themselves struggling to understand and apply the Sabbath. Initially, like Jesus, they joined with their Jewish counterparts and continued to celebrate the Sabbath on Saturday. They attended additional Christian meetings to partake of the sacrament (see 1 Corinthians 11:20–22) and, presumably, to read the scriptures through the lens of Jesus's teachings. But as Christianity began to split from Judaism towards the end of the first century, and as Christians sought to establish their own identity, some Christians continued to worship on the Jewish Sabbath while others began to distance themselves from it. As we shall see, only over time did Christianity transfer to Sunday many of the familiar aspects of "keeping the Sabbath": Sunday as the Sabbath, Sunday as a day of rest, Sunday as a time of Church worship services, and so forth.

In recent years, the emphasis on the Sabbath as a holy day distinct from the other days of the week has been on the decline in western culture. A 2016 *Deseret News* poll found that in the 38 years from 1978 to 2016, "the personal importance of the Sabbath Day to Americans has dropped by 24 percentage points." Only 50 percent of the US adults surveyed said that the Sabbath has personal spiritual meaning for them, which is down from 74 percent in a corresponding 1978 Gallup poll. Further, the 2016 poll found that only 41 percent of millennials consider Sunday to have any religious meaning.[1] In contrast, the poll indicated that 83 percent of members of The Church of Jesus Christ of Latter-day Saints (identified as "Mormons" in the survey) answered that Sunday does have particular religious or spiritual meaning for them. At the other end of the spectrum, only 38 percent of Jews answered the question affirmatively (with Sunday being replaced with Saturday in the question).[2]

These statistics reinforce what many already know: the sacrality of the modern Sabbath is increasingly being marginalized and secularized in favor of work, sports, shopping, and leisure activities. Even so, not everyone considers this decline inevitable, and many have sounded calls to reemphasize the Sabbath in both Jewish and Christian circles.[3] Walter Brueggemann has described these calls as attempts to maintain "'mindfulness' in a society that is increasingly mindless" about the place and importance of the Sabbath in the modern age.[4]

Even though Latter-day Saints "are 28 percentage points more likely than average to spend time in religious meditation [on the Sabbath] and more than 40 percentage points more likely to attend church,"[5] Church leaders have still sought to reemphasize the Sabbath as a cornerstone of both public and family worship. Church members around the world have been urged "to improve their observance of the Sabbath day," particularly regarding individual and family "worship at Church and in the home."[6]

But how does one live a three-millennia-old commandment in the modern world? Life today is admittedly different. The command was given long before the industrial revolution, and long before inventions such as air and space travel, twenty-four-hour shopping, televisions, computers, smart phones, smart watches, Sunday sports, and Amazon's seven-day-a-week delivery. While the Sabbath command may have originally been written on stone tablets, it has survived because of the fluidity whereby generations have continued to engage in the command within the context of their own needs and circumstances.

Latter-day Restoration scripture reinforces the biblical emphasis on observing the Sabbath (see Jarom 1:5; Mosiah 13:16–19; 18:23; Doctrine and Covenants 59:9–14; 68:29), and Church leaders have asked members to strengthen their Sabbath worship both at church and in the home. President Russell M. Nelson reminds us that Exodus 31's description of the Sabbath as a perpetual sign of the covenant between God and humans (see vv. 13, 16) continues to be relevant in the modern world,[7] and he has urged members to "keep on the covenant path."[8] The recent changes to the Latter-day Saint meeting schedule and curriculum were designed, in part, to honor "the Sabbath day, with a focus on the ordinance of the sacrament" and to enable Saints to use the Sabbath as a time of "gospel learning and teaching at church and in the home."[9] These changes place greater emphasis on the increased responsibility of both individuals and families to determine how they will remember and keep the Sabbath day as a sign of their covenant loyalty.

While the specific cultural and economic circumstances that modern Saints face are different from those in the ancient world, the chapters in this book argue that there is still a sense of shared experience. Latter-day Saints, along with other Christians and Jews, also face the challenges of determining what constitutes work in their modern context and of discovering ways to find meaning in the Sabbath day.

At its heart the Sabbath is meant to help people connect with God by strengthening their covenantal relationship with him and rejoicing in that relationship. Jonathan Edwards, one of America's greatest philosophical theologians, reminded his congregants that "if [the Sabbath] be the day on which God requires us especially to seek him, we may argue, that it is a day on which especially he [God] will be found." Further, "The Sabbath-day is an accepted time, a day of salvation, a time wherein God especially loves to be sought, and loves to be found."[10]

The motivation for this book is to help modern Saints increase their understanding of how people across time have worked to incorporate and utilize the Sabbath to make the most of this gift that God has extended to us. For the Sabbath to remain vibrant and meaningful across time, no generation can passively live it based on another generation's interpretations of it. The command has always compelled people to actively find ways to understand it and live it within their own circumstances. Ironically, that takes work; journalist Judith Shulevitz wrote:

> Most people mistakenly believe that all you have to do to stop working is not work. The inventors of the Sabbath [rules] understood that it was a much more complicated undertaking. You cannot downshift casually and easily, the way you might slip into bed at the end of a long day. . . . The [Sabbath] rules did not exist to torture the faithful. They were meant to communicate the insight that interrupting the ceaseless round of striving requires a surprisingly strenuous act of will, one that has to be bolstered by habit as well as by social sanction. . . . Only a Sabbath that you have to work for will appear worth keeping.[11]

This volume is aimed at helping modern readers learn the value and significance of participating in sacred time, even in our very busy lives. I am grateful for my friends and colleagues who have willingly contributed their areas of expertise on the Sabbath. It is our hope that as readers learn how people throughout time have labored to remember and protect the Sabbath, they will desire even more deeply to invest their time, energy and, yes, their "work," to discover anew its value in their lives. We have faith that this generation will continue to keep the Sabbath command alive and relevant in the twenty-first century and beyond.

Endnotes

1. The poll was conducted by YouGov from April 13 to April 15, 2016, and analyzed by Y2 Analytics, and "the results carry a margin of error of +/– 3.1 percentage points." "Sabbath Day Observance in the U.S.," *Deseret News*, 2016, 1, https://www.deseretnews.com/media/misc/pdf/DNN-Ten-Today-Sabbath.pdf.
2. Additionally, a 2013 Pew poll of Jews living in America reported that 94 percent of participants believed that a person could be Jewish if he or she worked on the Sabbath. The phone poll questioned "3,475 Jews across the country from Feb. 20–June 13, 2013, with a statistical margin of error for the full Jewish sample of plus or minus 3.0 percentage points." "A Portrait of Jewish Americans," Pew Research Center, October 1, 2013, http://www.pewforum.org/2013/10/01/jewish-american-beliefs-attitudes-culture-survey.
3. Judith Shulevitz, "Bring Back the Sabbath," *New York Times*, March 2, 2003, http://www.nytimes.com/2003/03/02/magazine/bring-back-the-sabbath.html; Richard Louv, "Sacred Time for a Family Sabbath," *Baltimore Sun*, January 8, 1993, https://www.baltimoresun.com/news/bs-xpm-1993-01-08-1993008188-story.html; and Adrienne Scrima, "Why You Need a Sabbath," *Relevant*, published June 18, 2014, updated September 20, 2019, https://relevantmagazine.com/god/practical-faith/why-you-need-sabbath. Even without the religious aspect, some people are now advocating a "secular Sabbath." See Pico Iyer, "Why We Need to Slow Down Our Lives," November 4, 2014, https://ideas.ted.com/why-we-need-a-secular-sabbath.
4. Walter Brueggemann, *Sabbath as Resistance: Saying No to The Culture of Now* (Louisville, KY: Westminster John Knox Press, 2014), x; see also Michael Fishbane, *Sacred Attunement: A Jewish Theology* (Chicago: University of Chicago Press, 2008), 124–28.
5. Kelsey Dallas, "New Poll Finds Americans Less Likely to Keep Sabbath Than in 1978, But Majority Still Say It's Important to Society," *Deseret News*, April 27, 2016, https://www.deseret.com/2016/4/27/20587346/new-poll-finds-americans-less-likely-to-keep-sabbath-than-in-1978-but-majority-still-say-it-s-import.
6. "Church Leaders Call for Better Observance of Sabbath Day," *Church News*, July 15, 2015, https://www.lds.org/church/news/church-leaders-call-for-better-observance-of-sabbath-day. See also Henry B. Eyring, "Gratitude on the Sabbath Day," *Ensign*, November 2016, 99–102; and Linda K. Burton, "Our Sabbath Day Gifts," in *At the Pulpit: 185 Years of Discourses by Latter-day Saint Women*, ed.

Jennifer Reeder and Kate Holbrook (Salt Lake City: Church Historian's Press, 2017), 323–30. For more examples of this imperative to better observe the Sabbath, see the fourth Sunday lessons for January through April in the 2018 curriculum for Priesthood and Relief Society.

7. Russell M. Nelson, "The Sabbath is a Delight," *Ensign*, May 2015, 129–30.
8. Nelson, "A Message from the First Presidency" (worldwide broadcast, Salt Lake City, January 16, 2018), https://www.lds.org/bc/content/ldsorg/church/news/2018/01/19/2018-01-1000-a-message-from-the-first-presidency.pdf.
9. Quentin L. Cook, "Deep and Lasting Conversion to Heavenly Father and the Lord Jesus Christ," *Ensign*, November 2018, 9–11.
10. Jonathan Edwards, "Sermon XV, The Perpetuity and Change of the Sabbath Day," in *Works of President Edwards, in Four Volumes* (New York: Leavitt and Allen, 1852), 4:634.
11. Shulevitz, "Bring Back the Sabbath."

Chapter One

"And God Blessed the Seventh Day, and Sanctified It": The Sabbath at Creation, Dedications, and Christ's Theophany in 3 Nephi

Daniel L. Belnap

The Creation narrative, found in various places within the canon of scripture of The Church of Jesus Christ of Latter-day Saints, describes the institution of two different types of time.[1] The first type of time is established in the "fourth day" with the placement of the astronomical bodies, which act as markers "for signs, and for seasons, and for days, and for years"—that is, common time (Genesis 1:14; Moses 2:14). The second type of time is established in the "seventh day," when the Lord rests from his labors. Situated as it was at the conclusion of the physical creation and marking what could be considered the beginning of the social creation (such as the naming of the animals, the institution of marriage, and the production of clothing), this event is described as a day of divine rest and represents the institution of sacred time (see Genesis 2:2–3; Moses 3:2–3; Abraham 5:2–3).[2] The Lord's rest is often interpreted as a cessation of work or activity, but this is not fully accurate. At least two activities were associated with this restful period, or sacred time—namely, the Lord's blessing and sanctifying of the earth—with a third activity, that of assembly, implied.

It is from the day of rest that the Sabbath emerged. Yet the activities associated with the day of rest, as well as its liminal, or "in-between," nature, suggest a relationship with another type of sacred time—the time of dedications (that is, dedicatory events such as temple dedications). In fact, the similarities that exist between these two events, the day of rest and dedications, may suggest that the day of rest in the Creation, and in subsequent Sabbaths, may be understood as dedicatory time. By noting the characteristics of these two types of times, the day of rest established in the Creation and dedicatory events, we can recognize the presence of sacred time even when it is not explicitly designated by any known source—for example, during the time surrounding Christ's ministry in the New World.

The Sabbath as a Dedication

As noted above, one way to better understand the Sabbath as a dedicatory event is to recognize its liminal nature. So named from the Latin *limen*, meaning "doorway" or "threshold," liminality describes those places (or in this case times) that are not meant to be permanent but that instead act as transition points where individuals can interact with other members of the given community in ways not possible in "regular" space or time. In other words, liminality refers to an "in-between" state in which one has the time and space to transform into new states while engaging with others who may be in other social or community contexts that one does not normally engage with directly.[3] With this definition in mind, two characteristics of the Sabbath—its unique placement within the scheme of creation and its temporary nature—suggest that the Sabbath may be understood as a liminality.[4] Dedicatory events are also liminal in that they too are temporary, an "in-between" time: they simultaneously culminate one period and inaugurate another, and they are enacted to facilitate the transformation of an object or a place into a state in which that object or place can function as designed. In light of the similarities in liminality between the Sabbath and dedications, specifically temple dedications, it may not be surprising to see that the three activities associated with the creation Sabbath—namely assembly, blessing, and sanctification—may also define the dedicatory experience.

One of the challenges to understanding the role of the Sabbath in the Creation narrative is that the final version of that narrative, Genesis 1–3, appears to be an amalgamation of two Creation narratives that later editors spliced together. Similarities between Genesis 1 and the tabernacle texts in Exodus and Leviticus have led some scholars to suggest that Genesis 1 is a product of one or more "priestly" authors or redactors.[5] Because of differences in narrative, setting, and even terminology between Genesis 1 and Genesis 2–3, it has been presumed that chapters 2 and 3 of Genesis have been written by another author or redactor to represent a different Creation narrative.[6] For Latter-day Saints, the differences between the two narratives have been understood to reflect two different temporal periods of the Creation: (1) a premortal organization by which the spiritual reality and relationship of all things were established prior to their physical creation and arrangement, and (2) the subsequent physical creation.[7] Whether or not this interpretation of these two narratives is the correct one, it does highlight the intended relationship between them, namely that the final redactor clearly believed them to harmonize with one another and therefore put them next to each other. And in fact, the narrative elements mentioned above do not so much highlight a different physical creation as they highlight the creation of the social cosmos, in which the social aspects of the Creation are emphasized.[8]

The creation of this social cosmos begins in Eden, God's earthly garden. Further geographical areas are designated by the four rivers that flow from Eden, which may be understood as social space—that is, space that indicates a social function. In this case, the social function is found in the inhabited areas of the ancient Near East.[9] The designation of a garden in Eden suggests that it too may be understood as social space, in that gardens are artificially planned environments that indicate prestige or other social dynamics.[10] In similar fashion, while Genesis 1 emphasizes the physical creation of the animals, Genesis 2 emphasizes the naming of the animals, thereby showing that the social act of naming takes place in the second creative period. Later comes the differentiation of the moral principles that can sustain a society, such as right and wrong; obedience and disobedience; guilt and innocence; and correct and incorrect—polarities that are at the foundation of a sociolegal tradition and are essential to a functioning society. These examples demonstrate the continuity between the first creative event and the second, yet they also show a change in focus. The institution of the Sabbath separated the two periods, acting as a transitory mechanism from one to the other.

Key to understanding this transitioning function of the Sabbath is understanding what exactly is meant by "he rested" (Genesis 2:2). Though often understood to mean "ceasing activity," the verb *shavat* (from which the term *Sabbath* derives) actually reflects "the coming to an end" of an activity; therefore, the verb is particularly appropriate when a specific activity is finished or completed, not merely stopped.[11] The verb's usage and placement in the Creation narrative suggests that the specific completed activity from which God rested was the physical creation of the cosmos, as highlighted in Genesis 2:1. Having finished physically creating the cosmos, God was now ready to dedicate it for its ultimate use.

The association of the Sabbath rest with inauguration or dedication has been noted elsewhere, specifically highlighting the similarities between the Creation narrative and the dedication of other sacred spaces such as temples. S. Dean McBride Jr., who sees the newly formed earth as a templelike space, suggests that "this day of silent divine rest is a consummation of all that has gone before because it inaugurates God's residence within the cosmic temple."[12] Likewise, John H. Walton highlights the relationship between the Sabbath as dedication and the dedication of Solomon's temple:

> When the house was complete, however, all that existed was a structure, not a temple. It was ready to be a temple, but it was not yet functioning like a temple, and God was not dwelling in it . . . what constituted the transition from a structure that was ready to be a temple to an actual functioning temple? . . . This is an important question because there is a comparison to be drawn if Genesis 1 is indeed a temple text. We find that in both the Bible and the ancient Near East there is an inauguration ceremony that formally and ceremonially marks the transition from physical structure to functioning temple. [13]

As for what was being dedicated, it is possible that the earth itself was inaugurated, reflecting its function for all humankind; however, a more specific location may be the Garden of Eden. The Garden of Eden's similarity to and possible function as a temple space has been noted elsewhere, and in light of its cultic function, the suggestion that the institution of the Sabbath acted as the garden's dedication is not unfeasible.[14] Regardless, the dedicatory nature of the Sabbath would indicate not a cessation from activity but rather an introduction to another set of activities specifically designed to inaugurate the functioning of creation.

For Latter-day Saints, the act of dedicating has been historically related to the completion of a temple. Though the first temple was built six years after the official organization of the Church itself in 1830, Joseph Smith had been receiving revelation concerning its construction and usage as early as 1831. On March 27, 1836, the dedicatory events for the Kirtland Temple began. The dedication process itself was relatively simple. It was a communal experience in which the Church members gathered to receive instruction from Church leaders. This was then followed by the dedicatory prayer, in which Joseph Smith prayed that God would accept their labors and requested requisite blessings by virtue of the temple's completion. The dedicatory prayer suggests that the dedication process acted as part of the construction and that the building was now ready for God's divine presence, which would denote the building as a functional temple (Doctrine and Covenants 109:4, 10–13). The dedication, at least those elements performed by the Church members, concluded with the Hosanna Shout, consisting of the congregation speaking aloud in unison, "Hosanna, Hosanna, Hosanna, to God and the Lamb" three times. While there is no official explanation as to why they did this, the use of the term hosanna, derived from the Hebrew *hôšîʿāh-nāʾ*, meaning "save us, please," suggests that it was an official invitation to turn the building into a functioning house of God, so noted by God's presence.

Since then, every one of the 162 temples now in operation[15] has been dedicated in similar fashion, with the dedication marking the point at which the building becomes a sacred space used to further humanity's salvation. Though no Church leader has explicitly associated these events of dedication with the inauguration of the Sabbath, at least one has suggested that the Creation contained a dedicatory event: Lorenzo Snow, the fifth prophet of the Church, remarked in 1899 that the Job 38:7 reference in which "the morning stars sang together and all the sons of God shouted for joy" referred to the "the first shout of 'Hosanna'" given at the Creation.[16] Thus, from President Snow's perspective, every Latter-day Saint who engages in a temple dedication reenacts one of the earliest events of all creation.

As noted earlier, corresponding to the overall function of the creation Sabbath as a dedicatory event, three specific activities within Genesis 2:1–3 completed the Creation and prepared it for further creative action.

The first of these is assembly. Genesis 2:1 sums up the creative process thus far by stating that heaven and earth were finished "and all the host of them." Though the first two elements, heaven and earth, can be understood as a reference to the totality of the physical creation, the word "host" (*ṣevāʾām*) is often used in the Hebrew Bible to refer to the assembly of heaven or, when in reference to Israel, the congregation.[17]

Who exactly this assembly comprises in Genesis 2 is less clear, but many have noted the role of the divine assembly in the creative process.[18] Though Job 38 has already been noted in a Latter-day Saint context specifically in regard to the Hosanna Shout, the verses themselves seem to place the shouting of the sons of God within the Creation narrative: "Where wast thou when I laid the foundations of the earth . . . Who hath laid the measures thereof . . . or who hath stretched the line upon it? Whereupon are the foundations thereof fastened? Or who laid the cornerstone thereof, when the morning stars sang together, and all the sons of God shouted for joy?" (vv. 4–7). If this reading is correct, then the creation Sabbath can be characterized as a time of assembly during which the hosts of heaven came together at this pivotal moment in the Creation (see also Abraham 3:21–26). Though somewhat outside the purview of this paper, the Israelite practice of the Sabbath also incorporated assembly as part of its praxis.[19]

The second specific activity was that of blessing. As to the nature of the blessing, that is less clear, but Norman Habel suggests that this particular activity was "a key factor in sustaining the creation process. To bless (*barak*) is to impart power. In this instance, that power activates a capacity to procreate and 'multiply on *Erets* [earth].'"[20] In other words, while all living things were potentially able to "be fruitful and multiply" and were even expected to do so, they could not perform their function until God blessed them. The created cosmos remained in a state of potentiality until God's blessing, which allowed for the elements of the Creation to begin doing what they were designed to do. This appears to be the case regarding Adam; though his spirit had already been made in the image of God, his physical body was not enlivened until after the divine blessing on the Sabbath (Genesis 2:3, 7). Latter-day Saint scripture may add another perspective to the blessing activity. In the book of Moses, a revelation given to Joseph Smith that included a version of the Creation, chapter 3 contains an additional phrase at the point where God looks over his completed works in the seventh day: "and I, God, saw that they were good" (v. 2). In the biblical version, this phrase is found at the end of the preceding chapter, as God concludes the physical creation in Genesis 1 on the sixth day. However, it is not found in the seventh-day narrative of Genesis 2:1–3. The Moses version makes it clear that the Sabbath activities are directly associated with the pronouncement found throughout the narrative. More than merely an acknowledgment of what has happened, the declaration that the aspects of the Creation, including the Sabbath, were "good" represents a fundamental and crucial observation as well as a promise that the objects noted are fulfilling their divine purpose and function.[21] This declaration represents the intrinsic integrity making up the cosmic entities and thereby the underlying order and organization of the cosmos as a whole.[22] Thus it is possible that the declaration itself is the blessing.

The final activity was that of sanctification. The act of sanctification, based on the term *q-d-š*, is often understood as a "setting apart" in which sanctified objects are assigned a new position or function apart from similar objects. However, the adjectival form is often translated as "holy," an English word related to the similar terms "whole" and "hale." This implies that sanctification is not just the setting apart of an object, but that it is the act through which the object set apart becomes "complete."[23] Moreover, the Hebrew term itself has variants, thus the meaning or usage of the term in any scriptural passage depends upon which variant of *q-d-š* was used. The most common form is *qōdeš*, which is used to describe a number of things, such as the clothing of the priests, the animals offered for sacrifice, and the instruments in the tabernacle. The term *qadōš*, on the other hand, is rarer and used to describe objects or individuals that are not just holy themselves but also have the dynamic ability to move objects into a divine, or completed, state. Not surprisingly, God is the number one entity described as *qadōš*, but Israel too is expected to be *qadōš*, like their God (Leviticus 11:44–45; 19:2).[24]

In light of the above, the assembly, blessing, and sanctifying actions taken by both the "host" of heaven and by God (actions that are associated in other contexts with dedications of sacred spaces) suggest that the creation Sabbath too can be viewed as a dedication, a liminal state and time in which the completed physical creation is now made functional.[25] Moreover, as the prototype to historical Sabbaths, or those Sabbaths experienced within human history (as opposed to the prehistorical period of the Creation), it is possible that these three same activities of assembly, blessing, and sanctification are to be part of all Sabbaths—that is, that these acts may be crucial elements in any Sabbath worship, with the Sabbath itself being a liminal state completing one week and inaugurating the next. Finally, as the prototype of any sacred time (at least biblically), the Creation's dedicatory Sabbath may act as a template for other sacred times that are not explicitly referenced as Sabbaths, such as Christ's theophany in 3 Nephi 8–26.

Christ's Theophany as a Dedicatory Sabbath

The events surrounding the theophany of Christ as depicted in 3 Nephi 8–26 suggest a transition from one period of Nephite history to another. Considering this, it may not be surprising to recognize Creation narrative elements within this record. Two aspects are particularly suggestive of a parallel between Christ's arrival and the Creation: (1) the darkness, and (2) the unorganized nature of the physical landscape.

Genesis 1 begins with a setting that is familiar to those who know ancient Near Eastern cosmology. According to verse 2, the pre-creative state was one of darkness, in which the earth had no distinctive shape and was "without form, and [was] void." The corresponding Hebrew phrase, *tohû wābohû*, does not mean "nothing" or indicate an absence, as the English translation suggests, but instead refers to a state that was often associated with water, in which material was present yet unorganized and unformed.[26]

In 3 Nephi 8, after Christ's crucifixion, the reader is told that following hours of physical devastation "there was thick darkness upon all the face of the land" (v. 19). Some scholars have provided possible, even plausible, scientific and geological explanations for the nature of this darkness;[27] regardless of the exact cause, Mormon's descriptions of this event appear to parallel the pre-creative state of the cosmos as described in Genesis. According to Mormon, the preternatural darkness preceding the arrival of Christ in the Americas was a "vapor" that could be felt (3 Nephi 8:20); two verses later, he refers to it as "the mists of darkness . . . upon the face of the land." The darkness was so pervasive that "there could be no light, because of the darkness, neither candles, neither torches; neither could there be fire kindled . . . there was not any light seen, neither fire, nor glimmer, neither the sun, nor the moon, nor the stars" (vv. 21–22).

The fluidic aspect of this period may also be seen in the ever-changing geological landscape. Throughout chapter 8, the reader is told that the whole earth shook "as if it was about to divide asunder" (v. 6); that the "whole face of the land was changed" (v. 12); that some cities were sunk and others were replaced by mountains (vv. 9–10); and that the "face of the whole earth became deformed" as the "rocks were rent in twain; they were broken up upon the face of the whole earth, insomuch that they were found in broken fragments, and in seams and in cracks, upon all the face of the land" (vv. 17–18). Though this geological unrest initially took place during the first three hours of destruction, 3 Nephi 10:9–10 suggests that it continued for the next three days: "And it came to pass that thus did the three days pass away. And it was in the morning, and the darkness dispersed from off the face of the land, and the earth did cease to tremble, and the rocks did cease to rend, and the dreadful groanings did cease, and all the tumultuous noises did pass away. And the earth did cleave together again, that it stood."[28] These verses describe a dark, ever-changing, and fluid landscape, in which the very earth itself was under continuous change—an environment that perfectly reflects the precreative state in Genesis 1.[29]

Paralleling the physical chaos, the social system in 3 Nephi could also be described as precreative. Prior to the physical destruction of the cities, Nephite (and apparently Lamanite) social structure had fractured into tribal circles, "every man according to his family and his kindred and friends; and thus they did destroy the government of the land . . . and the regulations of the government were destroyed . . . [until] the more part of the people had turned from their righteousness, like the dog to his vomit, or like the sow to her wallowing in the mire" (3 Nephi 7:2, 6, 8). Thus, by the time the physical calamities took place, society had already been effectively destroyed. Like the earth itself (in both Genesis 1 and in 3 Nephi), society was ready to be remade into something new.[30]

As noted above, in 3 Nephi 10 we read that the darkness lifted after three days, and the earth settled into a new form; yet this "new" creation remained incomplete, with the social structure completely undefined until Christ's arrival. Interestingly, Mormon provides no time frame between the lifting of the darkness and the arrival of Christ, an omission that appears to be deliberate. It is clear that Mormon can provide very specific information on times and dates, but he chooses not to do so here, perhaps highlighting the symbolic nature of the events rather than the literal, sequential occurrences.[31] Thus, instead of providing only a description of existence during this stasis period, Mormon also anticipates Christ's coming, which will complete this new creation and establish a new society.

Regarding the above, it is not surprising to see aspects of the Creation narrative in Christ's arrival, particularly the formation or presence of light. Christ himself had used some of this imagery when speaking to the survivors of the cataclysmic events who were still experiencing the mists of darkness. Noting that he was the creator of the heavens and the earth, he also referred to himself as "the light and life of the world" (3 Nephi 9:18) suggestive of God's first creative work in Genesis 1.

According to the text of 3 Nephi 9, a few hours later Christ spoke again, this time likening his work to "a hen who gathereth her chickens" (vv. 4–6). While this latter imagery is seemingly pastoral, it is also reminiscent of God's creative labors. In Genesis 1:2, prior to the creative acts by which the cosmos is brought into being, the reader is told that "the Spirit of God moved upon the face of the waters." The verb translated as "moved," *rāḥap*, is also used to describe the hovering of an eagle's wings over her young in Deuteronomy 32:11, suggesting then a similar action taken by God in the Creation. If this is the case, then Christ not only used terminology and imagery that reflected the survivors' covenantal relationship with God but also incorporated creation imagery to show them that his creative powers were still available even in their current state. Just as the spirit had hovered over the nascent creation in the precosmic darkness, so too did Christ spread his "wings" over his children as they stood in the mists of darkness.[32]

Yet it isn't the creative acts per se that suggest Christ's theophany may be understood as a Sabbath; rather, it is the three activities that have been associated with dedications and that were present in the creation Sabbath: assembly, blessing, and sanctification. Assuming that the criteria for a dedication were similar to those for dedications performed today, the need for a dedication would have been present following the destruction of civilization in 3 Nephi. For instance, as the text makes clear, entire cities were destroyed by fire, drowned in the sea, or swallowed up by the earth. Sacred sites would have needed to be rebuilt and therefore rededicated for use. Even those sites that survived the cataclysmic events would have required a rededication since their designs reflected praxis under the law of Moses, and when he spoke in the darkness Christ had explicitly stated that this law was fulfilled (3 Nephi 9:16–20). In any case, we can see that the three dedication activities played essential roles in Christ's visit.

The first activity, assembly, is the primary setting for the entirety of Christ's ministry in 3 Nephi. According to 3 Nephi 11:1, prior to Christ's immediate arrival but after the darkness had lifted, "a great multitude gathered together" at the temple in Bountiful. We are not told why they gathered at this specific place, nor are we given the date of when this gathering took place; however, this gathering may suggest that Christ's arrival coincided with one of the festivals associated with temple assembly. Regardless of the reasons, the text makes it clear that there was an assembly and that the activities and teachings associated with Christ's ministry are to be understood within the context of an assembly. In fact, of the 104 references to "multitudes" in the Book of Mormon, almost half of them are found in 3 Nephi 11–26, clearly emphasizing the communal nature of the events.

At least three different assemblies took place during the theophany. The first was the initial assembly noted above in 3 Nephi 11:1. This multitude witnessed Christ's arrival and participated in the physical experience of handling Christ's resurrected body. This initiatory event is described in verses 14–16, concluding with those assembled crying, "Hosanna! Blessed be the name of the Most High God!" in verse 17. The meaning of the term "hosanna" has been explained above; based on the root *yasa'* meaning "to save" with a suffixal ending "*-nah*," most often understood as a precative particle, it results in a term that has the basic meaning of "save us, please." Although the meaning is clear, the origin of the term is less certain. It is only found once in the Old Testament in Psalm 118:25, a psalm that has been historically associated with entrance to the temple. However, many scholars connect the usage of the term with Christ's triumphal entry into Jerusalem at the beginning of the last week of his mortal ministry (see Matthew 21:15; Mark 11:10; John 12:13). Its place in this gospel narrative is often assumed to be messianic in nature, with its usage denoting the desire for those gathered to be delivered by the incoming Son of David, thus indicating Christ's royal status.[33]

In the Book of Mormon, the Hosanna Shout is found three times. The first instance is in 1 Nephi 11. The Spirit of the Lord proclaims: "Hosanna to the Lord, the most high God; for he is God over all the earth, yea, even above all" (v. 6). Then he blesses Nephi with his desired vision. The second instance is in 3 Nephi 4:32, concluding a sequence of events in which the Gadianton chief, Zemnarihah, is executed by hanging. Following his death and the cutting down of the tree, those gathered are reputed to have collectively shouted three declarations. The first was a plea that the Lord preserve the community by "felling" all who sought power through secret combinations, just as Zemnarihah had been felled. The second declaration immediately followed the first: the people rejoiced and cried again, "May the God of Abraham, and the God of Isaac, and the God of Jacob, protect this people in righteousness, so long as they shall call on the name of their God for protection" (v. 30). The final communal declaration was the Hosanna Shout: "Hosanna to the Most High God" (v. 32). The final usage of hosanna is during Christ's appearance in 3 Nephi 11, as noted earlier.

Though each one of the three usages occurred in completely different circumstances, they all mark a transition, in which one event is concluded and another is about to begin. In the case of 1 Nephi 11, the divine usage marks the conclusion of the angel's preliminary worthiness questions to Nephi and the beginning of the vision proper; in 3 Nephi 4, the usage marks the end of the conflict with the Gadianton robbers; and finally, the usage in 3 Nephi 11 marks the conclusion of the initiatory events and the beginning of Christ's sermons. Thus, the exclamation of hosanna appears as an element of transition, a liminal experience in which God's protective power is requested specifically as the individual or community transits from one state to another.

Yet the creation Sabbath specified a particular type of assembly, namely one in which both the divine and the mortal hosts ("heaven and earth") interacted. While we do not have records of an incident in which both mortal and divine communities cried aloud together, 3 Nephi 17 does record interaction between the two. According to verse 24, following a round of blessing, those gathered "cast their eyes towards heaven, and they saw the heavens open, and they saw angels descending out of heaven as it were in the midst of fire." A similar event is described in 3 Nephi 19: following the baptism of the twelve disciples Christ had chosen, "angels did come down out of heaven and did minister unto them" (v. 14). As the angels were ministering, Christ himself appeared among them and also ministered. What is unclear in both events is how long the divine community remained with the multitude following their respective ministering. In 3 Nephi 17 the angels appeared following Christ's healing of the sick and his blessing of the children but before his institution of the sacrament, his blessing of the disciples, and his ascension into heaven. In 3 Nephi 19 the angelic visitations took place after the baptism of the disciples but preceded all the events described in 3 Nephi 19–26. In neither case is mention given concerning the leaving of the angelic hosts, perhaps suggesting that this mixed assembly of mortal and divine beings remained together throughout all the events that followed their conjoining. In any case, the event of assembly, even an assembly of the hosts of heaven and of earth, was present during Christ's theophany.

The second activity associated with dedications and the creation Sabbath is that of blessing. According to Genesis 2, having instituted or designated the time of the Sabbath, God then blessed it as well as the nascent creation to that point. Not surprisingly, the act of blessing also played a prominent role in Christ's ministry to the New World, especially in the assembly depicted in 3 Nephi 17. Following a sermon that included the blessed sequence of Christ's "sermon on the mount," Christ requested all who were sick or "lame, or blind, or halt, or maimed, or leprous, or that [were] withered, or that [were] deaf, or that [were] afflicted in any manner" to come and be healed by him (v. 7). This was followed by his pronouncing that they were "blessed" because of their faith, whereupon he took the children of the assembled and "one by one . . . blessed them, and prayed unto the Father for them" (v. 21). In chapter 18, we learn that Christ introduced a new ordinance: the sacrament, which was characterized by the blessing of wine and bread. Christ promised that those who partook of this ordinance would be blessed (see vv. 1–14).

Blessing continued to play an important part of the proceedings on the second day of Christ's ministry as well. The latter part of 3 Nephi 19 bears record to Christ's praying on behalf of the disciples and the multitude gathered. The next chapter describes another sacramental observance and then Christ's primary sermon of the day. The sermon began with Christ discussing the land itself: "The Father hath commanded me that I should give unto you this land, for your inheritance" (3 Nephi 20:14). This may seem to be simply reinforcing what had already been promised to the people as far back as Lehi, but it is possible that this supposed reiteration of the promise concerning the land as a land of inheritance may in fact have been referring to the new landscape that followed the physical destruction described earlier. If this is the case, then Christ's pronouncement might not have been a reiteration or a renewal, but a new declaration or dedication of the land to those who were righteous. Regardless, Christ promised, "It shall be a New Jerusalem. And the powers of heaven shall be in the midst of this people; yea, even I will be in the midst of you" (v. 22), as characterized by the divine–mortal interaction. The declaration was followed by Christ announcing that those gathered were the fulfillment of the covenant made to Abraham, by which he and his seed would bless all the nations of the earth. Thus, part of the sermon includes announcing that the people themselves were a blessing. This was then followed by Christ declaring that blessing the multitude was one of the primary purposes of his visit: "The Father having raised me up unto you first, and sent me to bless you in turning away every one of you from his iniquities; and this because ye are the children of the covenant—and after that ye were blessed then fulfilleth the Father the covenant which he made with Abraham, saying: In thy seed shall all the kindreds of the earth be blessed—unto the pouring out of the Holy Ghost through me upon the Gentiles, which blessing upon the Gentiles shall make them mighty above all" (vv. 25–27).

The rest of the sermon details how those assembled would experience the fulfilling of God the Father's covenants, resulting in a peaceful, prosperous society (3 Nephi 22:13–17). Though this promise will ultimately be fulfilled during Christ's millennial reign, it was also fulfilled by the official reinstitution of the Church (3 Nephi 27; 4 Nephi 1) and the establishment of a Zion society immediately following Christ's visit (3 Nephi 26:19–20; 4 Nephi). Just as the dedicatory blessing of the Creation formally acknowledged that the cosmos could now function as designed, so too did Christ's blessing reinforce the multitude's covenant relationship with God, the newly formed land, and themselves.

The final activity associated with dedications and the creation Sabbath was that of sanctification. As noted above, one of the consequences of blessing is a resulting sanctification of the person or object being blessed. In the case of the Creation narrative in Genesis, the sanctified object was the Sabbath time itself, which was "set apart" from the rest of the cosmos and specifically identified as separate in function from other times and spaces. In Christ's theophany, sanctification was also present, yet unlike in the Creation narrative, in 3 Nephi it is not a time or space that is sanctified, but a people. According to 3 Nephi 19, after having been baptized, the disciples of Christ were then "filled with the Holy Ghost and with fire" (v. 13). When Christ arrived he prayed, thanking the Father for "giving" to him the disciples, suggesting a separation from the greater community (see v. 20). While the disciples continued to pray, Christ blessed them, "and the light of his countenance did shine upon them, and behold they were as white as the countenance and also the garments of Jesus; and behold the whiteness thereof did exceed all the whiteness, yea, even there could be nothing upon earth so white as the whiteness thereof" (v. 25). In this case, the sanctification that took place affected the physiology of the disciples, thus transfiguring them into a state similar to that of divine beings.

Christ acknowledged the transformation with a second prayer:

> Father, I thank thee that thou hast purified those whom I have chosen, . . . and I pray for them, and also for them who shall believe on their words, that they may be purified in me, . . . even as they [the disciples] are purified in me. Father, I pray not for the world, but for those whom

> thou hast given me out of the world, because of their faith, that they may be purified in men, that I may be in them as thou, Father, art in me, that we may be one, that I may be glorified in them (vv. 28–29).

While similar to the first prayer, the second prayer now acknowledges that those who have been transfigured have also been purified. Moreover, the prayer requests that all who heed the words of the sanctified disciples would themselves become sanctified so that the purified can become one with God. This consequence of becoming one with God may in fact give insight into the purpose or function of sanctification: instead of simply denoting the separateness of the divine world from the mortal world, sanctification as described in 3 Nephi 19 may be the process by which the divine and the mortal are brought together. In other words, the primary function of sanctification is to facilitate the union of the divine and mortal communities. If this is the case, then it follows that the purpose of God's sanctifying the Sabbath at creation was for the same purpose—namely, to facilitate the unity between God and the cosmos. Moreover, it may further suggest that, like the disciples who were transfigured, humankind now has the primary function to accelerate that unity as much as possible. Finally, it may also provide insight into the function of all Sabbaths (or even all sacred times in general) by demonstrating the infinite mercy of God, who from the beginning set apart a liminal, dedicatory time in which transformations could be enacted that allowed for direct interaction between the mortal and divine realms.

Conclusion

As interesting as the Sabbath's function as dedication may be within a scholastic setting, the impetus of this study lies in the possible application of this perspective in modern worship. Beginning in 2015, Latter-day Saint Church leadership embarked on a worldwide effort to emphasize the Sabbath, with the hope that doing so would increase faith among the membership, thus preparing them for future trials.[34] The Church's concern is not unique, as other denominations have also recognized a need to renew the Sabbath as an integral part of one's religious experience.[35] Part of this renewal entails understanding the nature of the Sabbath within the scriptural canon.

This study provides a new perspective on the relationship between the Sabbath and the Creation and the relationship between Sabbaths and dedications. In turn, it allows for a new understanding of Christ's theophany as an example of such sacred time. Moreover, it is hoped that this study will also allow for a reconsideration of our own Sabbaths. When we understand the Sabbath as a liminal, dedicatory event, it can become a time of personal commitment in which we are blessed and sanctified before reentering the common time and space of the world. The Sabbath thereby becomes a sacred time in which everyday social interactions that once separated an individual from his or her fellows, or even from God, can be suspended, allowing unity between heaven and earth, thus finally fulfilling the paramount purpose of the Creation itself.

Endnotes

1. There are three primary Creation accounts: Genesis 1–3; Moses 2–4; and Abraham 4–5. A fourth account with which Latter-day Saints may be familiar is the narrative given during the temple endowment.
2. The production of clothing and the investiture of Adam and Eve take place after Adam and Eve partake of the fruit but before they are expelled from the Garden of Eden, which allows us to place the production of clothing as part of the second stage of Creation, as the social elements above suggest.
3. Anthropologist Arnold van Gennep was the first to coin this term in his seminal study concerning rituals and ritual space, *Les rites de passage* (Paris: Librairie Critique, 1909). But it was Victor Turner in his seminal work, *The Ritual Process: Structure and Anti-Structure* (Ithaca, NY: Cornell University Press, 1969), who suggested that liminal space created what he called "communitas," or the creation of or engagement with social relationships that would not be possible outside of the liminal space.
4. See S. Dean McBride Jr., "Divine Protocol: Genesis 1:1–2:3 as Prologue to the Pentateuch," in *God Who Creates: Essays in Honor of W. Sibley Towner*, ed. William P. Brown and S. Dean McBride Jr. (Grand Rapids, MI: Eerdmans, 2000), 3–41. John H. Walton further expands on the idea of temples as dedicatory institutions:

   > Solomon spent seven years building the house to be used as the temple of God in Jerusalem. When the house was complete, however, all that existed was a structure, not a temple. It was ready to be a temple, but it was not yet functioning like a temple, and God was not dwelling in it. . . . What constituted the transition from a structure that was ready to be a temple to an actual functioning temple? How did the house become a home? This is an important question because there is a comparison to be drawn if Genesis 1 is indeed a temple text. We find that in both the Bible and the ancient Near East there is an inauguration ceremony that formally and ceremonially marks the transition from physical structure to functioning temple. . . . In that inauguration ceremony, the functions of the temple are proclaimed, the functionaries are installed and rituals are begun as God comes down to inhabit the place that has been prepared by his instruction.

The Lost World of Adam and Eve: Genesis 2–3 and the Human Origins Debate (Downers Grove, IL: InterVarsity Press, 2015), 50.

5. See Robert B. Coote, *In the Beginning: Creation and the Priestly History* (Minneapolis: Fortress Press, 1991). For sake of convenience, biblical scholars often refer to those texts that may have been redacted or edited by priests as "P," and they refer to the presumed writers as "P" as well. For more on "P," see also Suzanne Boorer, *The Vision of the Priestly Narrative: Its Genre and Hermeneutics of Time* (Atlanta: SBL Press, 2016). For specific studies on the relationship of "P" and the tabernacle and creation, see Gordon J. Wenham, "Sanctuary Symbolism in the Garden of Eden Story," in *I Studied Inscriptions from before the Flood: Ancient Near Eastern, Literary, and Linguistic Approaches to Genesis 1–11*, vol. 4 of Sources for Biblical and Theological Study, ed. Richard S. Hess and David Toshio Tsumura (Winona Lake, IN: Eisenbrauns, 1994), 399–404; and Moshe Weinfeld, "Sabbath, Temple and the Enthronement of the Lord: The Problem of the Sitz im Leben of Genesis 1:1–2:3," in *Melanges bibliques et orientaux en l'honneur de M. Henri Cazelles*, ed. André Caquot and M. Delcor, in Alter Orient und Altes Testament 212 (Kevelaer, DE: Butzon & Bercker; Neukirchen-Vluyn, DE: Neukirchener Verlag, 1981), 501–12. For a more recent study engaging in more contemporary methodologies, see G. Geoffrey Harper, *"I Will Walk Among You": The Rhetorical Function of Allusion to Genesis 1–3 in the Book of Leviticus* (University Park, PA: Eisenbrauns, 2018).
6. The editor/redactor of Genesis 2-3 is often referred to as "J" because of the prominent use of Yahweh (Jehovah) in the narratives presumed to have been edited or redacted by this individual (or individuals). Narratives presumed to have been written by "J" are, therefore, referred to as "J" narratives. For more on the nature of the J narrative, see Albert de Pury, "Yahwist ('J') Source," in *Anchor Bible Dictionary*, ed. David Noel Freedman (New York: Doubleday, 1992), 6:1012–20; and John Van Seters, *The Yahwist: A Historian of Israelite Origins* (Winona Lake, IN: Eisenbrauns, 2013).
7. The Latter-day Saint reading is influenced directly by additional scripture found in Moses 3:5–9, which presents a different version of the material found in Genesis 2. While Genesis 2:4–5 may imply a level of creation prior to the physical creation, it is not explicit: "These are the generations of the heavens and of the earth when they were created, in the day that the Lord God made the earth and the heavens, and every plant of the field before it was in the earth, and every herb of the field before it grew." Chapter 3 of the Moses version expands on the possible existence of the plant prior to its physical creation, noting that all things were made spiritually first, "every plant of the field before it was in the earth, and every herb of the field before it grew. For I, the Lord God, created all things, of which I have spoken, spiritually, before they were naturally upon the face of the earth" (v. 5). This concept is repeated later, when discussing the physical formation of humans: "And I, the Lord God, formed man from the dust of the ground, and breathed into his nostrils the breath of life; and man became a living soul, the first flesh upon the earth, the first man also; nevertheless, all things were before created; but spiritually were they created and made according to my word" (v. 7). For more on the Latter-day Saint reading of the spiritual creation, see

Jeffrey M. Bradshaw, *In God's Image and Likeness: Creation, Fall, and the Story of Adam and Eve* (Salt Lake City: Eborn Books, 2014), 1:135–45.

8. Many scholars have noted the social cosmos element. Eckart Otto explains that "not only is Genesis 2:7 terminologically tied to Genesis 1, Genesis 1:27 contains the 'fact' of the creation of man, whereas following up on Genesis 2:7 the "how" is developed." Otto, "Paradieserzählung Genesis 2–3, Eine nachpriesterschriftliche Lehrerzählung in ihrem religionshistorischen Kontext," in *Jedes Ding hat seine Zeit*, ed. Otto Kaiser, Beihefte zur Zeitschrift für die alttestamentliche Wissenschaft 241 (Berlin: de Gruyter, 1996), 183–84. Seth D. Postell agrees: "Otto's words point to overriding compositional intentions that go beyond any putative and contradictory sources. Moreover, the fact that Genesis 2–3 is aware of the 'priestly' materials and even includes vocabulary classically assigned to 'P' undermines Wellhausen's theory both in terms of his understanding of the chronological relationship of 'J' to 'P' and in terms of the notion of clearly identifiable and distinguishable literary criteria used to distinguish one hypothetical source from another." Postell, *Adam as Israel: Genesis 1–3 as the Introduction to the Torah and Tanakh* (Cambridge, MA: James Clarke, 2012), 18. Similarly, Walton states the following: "In Genesis 1:2, an inchoate cosmos is described, whereas an inchoate earth is described in Genesis 2:5–6. . . . Genesis 2 explains how humans function in sacred space and on its behalf (in contrast to Genesis 1, which addressed how sacred space functioned for humanity)." *Lost World*, 69. John Day offers further clarification: "The account in Gen. 2.4b–3.24 is often spoken of as the second Creation account in Genesis, following on that of P in Gen. 1:1–2.4a. This is true, but the second account very much centres on the Garden of Eden and the first man and woman, and apart from that there is very little on the creation of the world." Day, *From Creation to Babel: Studies in Genesis 1–11* (London: Bloomsbury, 2013), 24–25. In all these cases, there is an awareness that Genesis 2 does not describe merely another tradition. Instead, it describes the next stage of the creation event: the creation of society.
9. The focus on socially recognized spaces has led some to note the relationship between the Genesis 2–3 narrative and those of the patriarchs. As Postell points out, "Scholars have noticed inner-textual parallels between Adam and Abraham. Not only does the text thematically link Abram to Adam, but Genesis 15–16 appears to be an intentional recapitulation of Adam's story in Genesis 2–3. . . . First, in both passages the central figure undergoes a deep and divinely induced slumber. Second, both passages provide homogenous geographical information regarding the boundaries of a divinely provided land. Third, while Genesis 2 does not mention a covenant as does Genesis 15, it is clearly covenantal in nature." *Adam as Israel*, 90–91. For Latter-day Saints, the use of ancient Near Eastern geographical nomenclature may clash with modern-day insight in which the Garden of Eden has been presumably located in Missouri. One possible answer is that the texts in question, Genesis 1 and Moses 3, both reflect their ancient Near Eastern (and Israelite) audiences. Interestingly, in the Book of Abraham no geographical nomenclature is mentioned (see Abraham 5:10), perhaps reflecting its earlier, pre-Israelite origin.
10. Ziony Zevit explains this nuance:

> In biblical Hebrew, *gan*, 'garden,' refers to a plantation of trees, fruit-bearing, aromatic, decorative, or in some aesthetic mix (Isa 1:30; Ezek 31:4–9; Song of Songs 4:16; 5:1; 6:2), as well as to a green garden for raising vegetables (1 Kings 21:2). The Hebrew word is related to the verbal root *g-n-n* used to generate verbs referring to protecting and sheltering. It is distinguished from *śādeh*, 'open field,' where cereals were raised, and *kerem*, 'orchard,' where grape vines and olives trees were cultivated. Elements of an orchard might have been imagined in a garden, but not fields. . . . Gardens are civilized artifacts. Manufactured and controlled, they are usually created for some mix of utilitarian and aesthetic purposes.

What Really Happened in the Garden of Eden? (New Haven, CT: Yale University Press, 2013), 89–90.

11. G. Johannes Botterweck, Helmer Ringgren, and Heinz-Joseph Fabry, eds., *Theological Dictionary of the Old Testament* (hereafter *TDOT*), trans. Douglas W. Scott (Grand Rapids, MI: Eerdmans, 2004), s.v. "*shavat*," 14:382–86. Norman Habel notes that God resting "apparently does not mean inaction or taking a vacation," as the event described "in Gen. 2.3 indicates continued divine action." *The Birth, the Curse and the Greening of Earth: An Ecological Reading of Genesis 1–11*, Earth Bible Commentary Series (Sheffield, MA: Sheffield Phoenix Press, 2011), 40. Carol L. Meyers gives fuller context on the meaning of divine rest:

> What is the nature of divine rest in the Hebrew Bible? In the ancient Near Eastern literature, we have noted a range of activities (and inactivity) that were involved in rest: from peaceful sleep, to leisure time for entertainment and banquets, to sovereign rule. Some have interpreted the rest in Genesis 1 as representing disengagement and the enjoyment of relaxation. Thus, Levenson comments that the text "leaves us with an impression of the deity in a state of mellow euphoria, benignly fading out the world that he has finished and pronounced 'very good' [J. Levenson, *Creation and the Persistence of Evil*, 109]. It should be noted, however, that the 'disengagement' form of rest in the ancient Near East is consistently based either in polytheism (e.g., social activities among and entertainment with other gods) or in the belief that the gods had humanlike needs and desires (e.g., sleep or sexual activity). . . . In fact, however, although the idea of divine rest in the ancient Near Eastern (sic.) includes retirement as one possibility, other texts examined above showed rest as the freedom to rule. In the Hebrew Bible, Psalm 132 provides a key passage, in which not only is the temple identified as the resting place of Yahweh but we also find rest identified with rue, for in the temple he sits enthroned. In this sense, divine rest is not primarily an act of disengagement but an act of engagement. No other divine rest occurs in the Hebrew bible than the rest that is associated with his presence in his temple.

The Tabernacle Menorah: A Synthetic Study of a Symbol from the Biblical Cult, American Schools of Oriental Research Dissertation Series 2, ed. David Noel

Freedman (Missoula, MT: Scholars Press for the American Schools of Oriental Research, 1976), 179–80.

12. McBride, "Divine Protocol," 14.
13. Walton, *Lost World, 50.*
14. For more on the relationship between the building of the temple and the creation, see Donald W. Parry, ed., "Garden of Eden: Prototype Sanctuary," in *Temples of the Ancient World: Ritual and Symbolism* (Salt Lake City and Provo, UT: Deseret Book Company and Foundation for Ancient Research and Mormon Studies, 1994), 126–51. See also Victor Hurowitz, *I Have Built You an Exalted House: Temple Building in the Bible in Light of Mesopotamian and North-West Semitic Writings* (Sheffield, GB: JSOT Press, 1992), 235–42. Weinfeld makes a salient point on the connection between the Creation and the temple: "The fact that with the completion of the instructions for the building the Tabernacle in P. there appears a commandment on the Sabbath (Ex. 31:12–17), shows also the connection which existed between Creation and the Building of the Temple. Indeed, this connection is well expressed in the congruence which is found between the description of the completion of the Tabernacle in Exodus. Gen. 1:1–2:3 and Ex. 39:1–40:33 are typologically identical. Both describe the satisfactory completion of the enterprise commanded by God, its inspection and approval, the blessing and the sanctification which are connected with it." "Sabbath, Temple and the Enthronement," 502–3. Similarly, Postell creates a link between the Garden of Eden and the temple: "In one real sense, the garden serves as the prototypical reality of which the tabernacle serves only as a copy or a type. The tabernacle and its operation are permeated with an aroma of Eden. A link is forged between God's creation purposes and the construction of the tabernacle, whereby the Mosaic tabernacle and its priesthood perpetuate, albeit imperfectly, the 'sanctuary' in Eden and its 'priesthood.'" Postell, *Adam as Israel,* 113.
15. As of March 25, 2022, with 44 others in states of construction, 8 undergoing renovation, and another 51 announced on which construction has not yet begun. See https://www.churchofjesuschrist.org/temples/list for the most recent updates.
16. See Jacob W. Olmstead, "From Pentecost to Administration: A Reappraisal of the History of the Hosanna Shout," *Mormon Historical Studies* 2, no. 2 (Fall 2001): 7–37, specifically 28.
17. *TDOT,* s.v. "*ṣevāʾām,*" 12:211–15. See also *The Anchor Bible Dictionary,* ed. David Noel Freedman (New York: Doubleday, 1992), s.v. "Hosts, Host of Heaven," by E. Theodore Mullen Jr., 3:301–304; and Karel Van Der Toorn, Bob Becking, Pieter W. Van Der Horst, eds., *Dictionary of Deities and Demons in the Bible,* 2nd ed. (Leiden, NLD; Grand Rapids, MI: Eerdmans, 1999), s.v. "Yahweh Zebaoth," by T. N. D. Mettinger, 920–24.
18. Day offers an interesting insight on the divine assembly:

> The dominant view nowadays is that there is a reference to the heavenly court which God addressed (cf. Job 38.7, where 'all the sons of God shouted for joy' at the time of the creation, though admittedly it does not say that God consulted them). . . . It might be objected that in Gen. 1.28 it was only God, not the heavenly court, who actually created humanity. However, it is arguable that the momentous decision to create humanity is envisaged as a joint

> act between God and his heavenly council, even if it was only God himself who finally enacted the decision.

From Creation to Babel, 12–13.

19. See Pike, "The Sabbath in the Old Testament," in this volume.
20. Habel, *Birth, Curse and Greening*, 34.
21. Thus this process (differentiating, naming, and declaring as good) may also be understood as a revelatory one. As Habel points out, the infinitive verb "to appear" in the clause "cause dry land to appear" may also be translated as "to be revealed": "The Niphal form of this verb used here is used elsewhere when God or an angel of God is revealed or 'appears'. In Gen. 18.1, 'Yhwh appeared to Abraham (cf. Gen 12.7; 35:1). The language of God's theophanic appearances to humans is here, in Gen. 1.9–10, associated with the appearance of Erets, highlighting the climactic significance of the event." *Birth, Curse and Greening*, 31–32.
22. Rolf P. Knierim gives further clarification on the meaning of "good" in this context:

> The created world order has certain qualitative notions which explicate Yahweh's relationship to and presence in it. The fact of creation out of chaos alone represents more than a merely quantitative event. It is a *good event*. The priestly formulation, according to which the whole creation is *very good* in God's judgment [see Genesis 1:31] is not superficial because the word 'good' is a common word. It is the most profound formulation which in essence includes all else that can be said. It cannot be said any better. It is a fundamental theological statement about the world. This goodness is not only true for the order of creation in the beginning. It is also true for the entire time in which this order exists in accordance with its beginning.

The Task of Old Testament Theology: Substance, Method, and Cases (Grand Rapids, MI; Cambridge, GBR: Eerdmans, 1995), 199. Similarly, Walton explains the following:

> The recurring formula in Genesis 1—"it was good"—offers this same assessment of the creative acts that brought order to the cosmos: the cosmos now functioned well. The evidence that this is the nuance of the Hebrew word *tob* (which admittedly has a wide semantic range) comes from the context. Contextually, it is useful to consider the nuance that the word has by asking what it would look like for something not to be good. Fortunately, the context does indicate something that is not good: "It is not good for man to be alone" (Gen. 2:18). The word *tob* in this good concerns proper functioning: it is not a negative assessment of craftsmanship or moral purity. We can therefore infer that the recurring assessment that things were good in Genesis 1 does not refer to the absence of corruption or flaw. It instead is an affirmation that the functions were set to operate according to their design.

Genesis 1 as Ancient Cosmology (Winona Lake, IN: Eisenbrauns, 2011), 169–70. Habel suggests a more intimate aspect as well: "The 'good' that Elohim sees in 'Erets' is not 'good' in some dualistic or moral sense. 'Good' is Elohim's response to what is seen, experienced in the moment of its appearance. A similar idiom is used to describe the response of Moses' mother when he is born. When she first bonds with the child 'she sees he is good' (Ex. 2.1). Elohim beholds Earth emerge from the waters below and 'sees Earth is good.'" *Birth, Curse and Greening*, 32.

23. "We conclude that holiness is exemplified by completeness." Mary Douglas, *Purity and Danger: An Analysis of Concepts of Pollution and Taboo* (London: Routledge Classics, 2002), 67. For a review of the use of Douglas's model, see Saul M. Olyan, "Mary Douglas's Holiness/Wholeness Paradigm: Its Potential for Insight and its Limitations," *Journal of Hebrew Scriptures* 8 (2008): 2–9.
24. E. Jan Wilson, *"Holiness" and "Purity" in Mesopotamia and Ancient Israel,* Alter Orient und Altes Testament 237 (Kevelaer, DE: Butzon & Bercker; Neukirchen-Vluyn, DE: Neukirchener Verlag, 1994), 87–88. For more discussion on the distinction of these terms, see Gaye Strathearn, "'Holiness to the Lord' and Personal Temple Worship," in *The Gospel of Jesus Christ in the Old Testament,* The 38th Annual BYU Sidney B. Sperry Symposium, ed. D. Kelly Ogden, Jared W. Ludlow, and Kerry Muhlestein (Provo, UT: Religious Studies Center, Brigham Young University; Salt Lake City: Deseret Book, 2009), 219–32.
25. Habel gives a full explanation of this completed state:

> The cosmos is now complete and Elohim can rest (shabat) with creation. But that rest apparently does not mean inaction or taking a vacation: the use of bara in Gen. 2.3 indicates continued divine action. And, as van Wolde suggests, this verse means that God made the seventh day by 'separating' it and setting it apart of the other days[. . .]. Elohim also blesses and sanctifies the day that celebrates completion—Elohim invests that day with a power comparable to the power of procreation given to living creatures of Erets. . . . Prior to that day, blessing has been dispensed to activate life as such. Now time is blessed with the inherent capacity to initiate, sustain, and restore life.

Birth, Curse and Greening, 41. See also Ellen van Wolde, "Why the Verb ברא Does Not Mean 'to Create' in Genesis 1.1–2.4a," *Journal for the Study of the Old Testament* 34, no. 1 (2009): 3–23.

26. Walton, *Genesis 1*, 145–46. See also *TDOT*, s.v. "*tehôm*," by Leonhard Waschke, 15:577–81, which discusses the Hebrew term for the "deep," or the waters upon which was *tohû wābohû* (see note 30).
27. For a review of the literature concerning this event, see Brant A. Gardner, *Helaman through 3 Nephi,* Second Witness: Analytical & Contextual Commentary on the Book of Mormon 5, (Salt Lake City: Kofford Books, 2007), 301–12.
28. Gardner makes reference to 3 Nephi 8:19: "Mormon records Nephi as saying, 'it was said by some . . . ,' a clear indication that Nephi is integrating reports by others into his account. Despite the apparent precision of "three hours" and "three days," it would have been difficult if not impossible to determine either duration. There were no clocks for the hours, and the darkness would have made it impossible to differentiate day from night." *Helaman through 3 Nephi*, 5:308.

29. Walton gives clarification about this precreative state:

> In [*tohû's*] twenty occurrences (more than half in Isaiah), we find that it often describes a wilderness or wasteland (e.g., Deut 32:10; Job 12:24 ;6:18; Ps 107:40). It can describe the results of destruction (Jer 4:23). It is used to convey things that have no purpose or meaning (e.g., idols, Is 41:29, and those who make them, Is 44:9). All its uses can be consolidated in the notion of things that are of no purpose or worth. They lack order and function. It now becomes clear that the starting condition in Genesis 1:2, the precreation situation that describes nonexistence, is a condition that is not lacking material. Rather, it is a situation that is lacking order and purpose.

Lost World, 29. Day gives further insight on the 'emptiness' in the precreative world:

> It is clear that the word's connotations in Biblical Hebrew range from the concrete "desert" to the abstract "non-entity," the central meaning uniting these being that of 'empty' or 'nothing'. 'Empty' seems to be the meaning we have in Gen. 1.2. . . . Of course the world was not completely empty, since it was covered in water. What is meant is that the earth existed only in an inchoate state and was devoid of all its familiar features and inhabitants which are subsequently created in Genesis 1. D.T. Tsumura and Terry Fenton are right in saying that *tohû wābohû* in Gen. 1.2 has sometimes been wrongly understood as chaos. However, the term chaos is surely not inappropriately used of the raging waters that God has to do battle within some parts of the Old Testament at the time of creation (e.g., Ps. 104.6–9) and which ultimately lies behind the waters of the deep in Gen. 1.2.

From Creation, 8–9.

30. The actual creative process involving the shaping or organizing of the preexisting material begins as God speaks light into existence, thereby delineating the elemental states of light and dark. This act typifies the Creation process, as God takes the undifferentiated and unformed precosmic material and organizes or arranges the material via separation. Walton explains that "'to bārā' something brings it into existence by giving it a role and function in an ordered system . . . in this view, the result of bara is order. The roles and functions are established by separating and naming. These are the acts of creation." *Lost World*, 30. Don Michael Hudson gives an explanation for sacred space: "Sacred space, according to Eliade and others, is space that is separated from the sameness of the creative order by differentiating a place that is symbolically or ritually different from any place like it . . . the introduction of sacred space into a predominantly profane world reflects the possibility for orientation. . . . the symbolic means to distinguish in the midst of sameness, orient himself or herself in the midst of potential wastelands, and thereby communicate ritually with the sacred world in which the gods resided." "From Chaos to Cosmos: Sacred Space in Genesis," *Zeitschrift für die Alttestamentliche Wissenschaft* 108 (1996): 90–91.
31. Grant Hardy notes the same; see *Understanding the Book of Mormon: A Reader's Guide* (New York: Oxford University Press, 2010), 191–92.

32. See Jane Allis-Pike, "'How Oft Would I Have Gathered You as a Hen Gathereth Her Chickens': The Power of the Hen Metaphor in 3 Nephi 10:4–7," in *Third Nephi: An Incomparable Scripture*, ed. Andrew C. Skinner and Gaye Strathearn (Salt Lake City and Provo, UT: Deseret Book and Neal A. Maxwell Institute, Brigham Young University, 2012), 57–74. Though Allis-Pike does not examine this passage through Genesis 1:2 imagery, she does explore the passage with the symbolism of the hen as creator and mother. See also Daniel Becerra, *3rd, 4th Nephi: A Brief Theological Interpretation* (Provo, UT: Neal A. Maxwell Institute, Brigham Young University, 2020), 17–19, who also explores the imagery of Christ as mother and hen.
33. See Marvin H. Pope, "Hosanna: What It Really Means," *Bible Review* 4, no. 2 (1988): 16–25; and Daniel L. Belnap, "'They Did Fell The Tree': The Hanging of Zemnarihah as a Ritual Resolution for Nephite Trauma," in *They Shall Grow Together: The Bible in the Book of Mormon*, ed. Charles Swift and Nicholas J. Frederick (Provo, UT: Religious Studies Center, Brigham Young University; Salt Lake City: Deseret Book, 2022), 143–177.
34. "We all need more faith. The Brethren are looking ahead and they are seeing what is coming." Elder Kim B. Clark, quoted in Sarah Jane Weaver, "Leaders Hope Emphasis on Sabbath Observance Increases Faith in God," *Church News*, December 30, 2015, https://www.churchofjesuschrist.org/church/news/leaders-hope-emphasis-on-sabbath-observance-increases-faith-in-god.
35. See Brent L. Top, "The Decline of Sabbath Observance in an Increasingly Secular Society: Twenty-First Century Efforts to Reclaim the Lord's Day," and Andrew C. Reed, "'The Erosion of Sabbath Worship is now Extensive': The Imperative to Learn Holiness from Other Religious Traditions," both of which are in this volume.

Chapter Two

The Sabbath in the Old Testament

Dana M. Pike

The scriptures consistently depict the significance of sacred space and sacred time in the lives of the Lord's covenant people. Sacred time is still experienced today, as in the past, through commemorations and celebrations on specific days that are dedicated to God and thus regarded as holy. These days punctuate the passing of ordinary or common time and are intended to help bring focus and clarity to relationships with the divine.

Moving from the broad topic of sacred time discussed in the previous chapter, this chapter focuses on what we learn about one particular dimension of sacred time, the Sabbath day, as found in the oldest scriptures currently available to us: the Hebrew Bible, which Christians call the Old Testament. Just as the Old Testament is foundational to the whole of the Latter-day Saint canon of scripture in general, so too it contains the earliest and some of the most important and oft-quoted passages about the Sabbath.[1]

Because there is debate about when the various books in the Old Testament reached their final form, it is possible that some passages and books that appear to be chronologically early may have actually reached their final form, as we have them, at a time later than other passages or books.[2] However, this uncertainty does not adversely impact the overall purpose of this paper, which is to assess the contribution of the Old Testament as a whole to a Latter-day Saint understanding of the Sabbath in ancient Israel, and how these scriptures set the pattern for Sabbath beliefs and practices that continue to our day.

The following study overviews the word "sabbath," examines passages in the Old Testament that provide evidence for Sabbath observance in ancient Israel, and then discusses pertinent Sabbath-related topics, concluding with a brief look at how Latter-day Saints have used these Old Testament passages to teach about the Sabbath in this dispensation.

Sabbath: The Word and the Concept[3]

In scripture, names, titles, and other specific terms are often intended to teach and remind us of important concepts. The word "sabbath" is a good example of this pattern. Our English word "sabbath" is a transliteration of the Hebrew noun *šabbāt* (pronounced *shah-BAHT*),[4] which occurs over one hundred times in the Hebrew Bible. This noun is likely related to the verbal root *š-b-t*.

The primary sense of the verbal root *š-b-t* is "to cease, stop," emphasizing the act or process of stopping, of coming to an end, although such stopping did not necessarily lead to "rest" (the Hebrew lexical root *n-w-ḥ* specifically means "to rest").[5] So, for example, "the manna ceased [*š-b-t*] on the morrow" (Joshua 5:12), and "behold, I will cause to cease [*š-b-t*] out of this place . . . the voice of gladness" (Jeremiah 16:9).[6]

Of course, resting *can* be a byproduct of ceasing work. And Bible readers' perceptions of the meaning of *š-b-t* are very much dependent upon translators and their choices in rendering Hebrew words into English or some other language. For example, the KJV renders the Hebrew of Exodus 23:12 as, "Six days thou shalt do thy work, and on the seventh day thou shalt rest [*š-b-t*]: that thine ox and thine ass may rest [*n-w-ḥ*]." However, in the NET Bible this same verse reads, "but on the seventh day you must cease [*š-b-t*], in order that your ox and your donkey may rest [*n-w-ḥ*]."[7]

The issue of translating verbal forms of *š-b-t* raises the question of how best to translate the noun *šabbāt*. Actually, as noted above, it is usually not translated, but rendered in transliteration as "sabbath" in English versions of the Bible. And the predominant use of *šabbāt* or sabbath in the Hebrew

Bible involves not only the sense of "ceasing" work, but also the sense of some sort of "resting."[8]

Besides the word *šabbāt* itself, the historical development of the Sabbath concept and practice has been much debated by scholars, with many suggesting the Sabbath was not institutionalized as a recurring seventh day of rest in ancient Israel until the Babylonian Exile (6th century BC) or the subsequent Persian period, both of which were long after Moses.[9] Likewise debated is the original impetus for a Sabbath day, since the weekly Sabbath as presented in the Old Testament was unique in the ancient world.[10] And theories on Sabbath origins range from proposing the Israelites adopted and adapted a monthly full-moon festival from the Canaanites or Babylonians, to a Kenite connection, to early socioeconomic impulses to provide greater equality.[11] Of course, most of these non-revelation-based theories regarding the Sabbath's origins and Israelite practices relating to it are at variance with what little is preserved in the Bible regarding such matters.

Based on this introductory overview, it is not surprising that the noun *šabbāt* came to designate a day of "rest," because one ceased from working on that day. Of course, "ceasing" and "resting" can relate to many activities, including rest from servitude, rest from travel, and rest from war, as well as rest from life's wearisome labors. And although resting could be construed to mean doing nothing, in ancient Israel the weekly Sabbath day was considered sacred time, which meant, by definition, doing something different from one's regular weekday labors, something more focused on holy things—something dedicated to God and what *he* considered sacred. Thus, the Israelite weekly day of "rest" encompassed physical, emotional, and spiritual components—acts and attitudes of worship—designed to bring "rest" to one's body and soul.[12]

The Sabbath in Genesis–Deuteronomy

The following comments on occurrences of the noun *šabbāt* deal first with Sabbath passages in the Pentateuch or Torah, designations given to the biblical books comprising Genesis–Deuteronomy. Not surprisingly, most of these passages occur in texts with a priestly orientation. Generally speaking, priestly texts deal with activity related to cultic or ritual matters, such as the calendar; holy days; holiness and purity; and sacrificial rituals and other activities associated with the tabernacle and later the temple in Jerusalem.[13] As James Kugel (and others) have observed, the Sabbath "was a subject dear to priests, . . . [and] the proper observance of the Sabbath is stressed [in priest-oriented texts] in a way not found elsewhere [in the Bible]."[14] This priestly focus was, at least in part, because the Sabbath day was the most basic and oft-recurring holy day in the Israelite calendar.

Surprisingly, the noun *šabbāt* does not occur in the Bible until Exodus 16, although verbal forms of *š-b-t* do occur occasionally before Exodus 16. This means there is no information in the Old Testament, nor in the rest of Latter-day Saint scripture, on any peoples' observance of the Sabbath day in early human history.

Genesis

Although the noun *šabbāt* does not occur in the book of Genesis, the Bible *does* present sacred time as dating back to the creation of the earth. Genesis 2:2–3 is of major importance for understanding the biblical Sabbath, for after the six creative periods summarized in Genesis 1, "on the seventh day God ended his work which he had made; and he rested [*š-b-t*] on the seventh day from all his work which he had made. And God blessed the seventh day, and sanctified it: because that in it he had rested [*š-b-t*] from all his work" (KJV).[15] Pursuant to the discussion above, some modern translations render *š-b-t* in these verses as "ceased."[16]

Regardless of how the verb in question is translated, several pertinent points can be made about the content of this passage, including the following:

- As presented in the Bible, the cosmic rhythm portrayed in the creation account in Genesis 1:1–2:4—the act of working six "days," or time periods, then ceasing and resting on the seventh—becomes the paradigm for a seven-day week of human time.
- Genesis 2:2–3 recounts that "God blessed the seventh day, and sanctified it," or made it holy (by divine decree), because on this day he ceased or rested from his creative activities. The seventh "day" of the creation process was thus designated as separate and distinct, different from the other six days, and as the culmination of what preceded it. As one commentator has expressed, the "sabbath belongs to the created order; it cannot be legislated or abrogated by human beings. . . . Creation thus has to do, not simply with spatial order, but with temporal order [that is, time itself] as well."[17]
- Genesis 2:2–3 presents the *concept* of work followed by ceasing and resting on the seventh "day," a divine Sabbath, but neither it nor what follows in Genesis contain any instruction about humans following suit. In the Bible *as we have it*, there is no Sabbath law or commandment given to Adam and Eve or their posterity to "go and do" as God did regarding the cessation of work on the seventh day until the time of Moses, when the Lord gave the Israelites the Sabbath command at Mount Sinai (Exodus 20).[18]

- Based on this biblical depiction, most scholars assume that Sabbath observance was not the norm until at least the time of Moses, and many scholars assume that the practice developed centuries later than that (see comments above).[19] Latter-day Saints tend to disagree, as discussed next.

Given the general Latter-day Saint understanding that the principles and practices of the gospel of Jesus Christ were on the earth from the very beginning of human activity, it is not surprising that Latter-day Saint leaders and publications have taught that the Sabbath was observed from the time of Adam and Eve onwards. Speaking of this general perspective, Spencer W. Kimball taught, "Moses . . . brought to the wandering children of Israel the Ten Commandments, fundamental rules for the conduct of life. These commandments [which include keeping the Sabbath day holy], however, were not new. They had been known to Adam and his posterity, who had been commanded to live them from the beginning, and were merely reiterated by the Lord to Moses."[20] And more specifically, the Latter-day Saint Bible Dictionary claims that "the Sabbath was a holy day before the giving of the law [to Moses], even from the earliest times . . . but we have no evidence of its observance in patriarchal times. This is no doubt due to the scantiness of the record, for the Sabbath is an eternal principle and would have existed from the days of Adam, whenever the gospel was on the earth among men."[21] Thus, for Latter-day Saints with a Restoration perspective, the lack of biblical information about the Sabbath from Adam and Eve to Moses is not a barrier to believing in Sabbath-day practice prior to the time of Moses, despite its lack of occurrence in our surviving scriptural records.[22]

Exodus

As mentioned above, the first time the noun *šabbāt* occurs in the Bible is in Exodus 16, which recounts some of the Israelites' experiences after fleeing Egypt (see Exodus 12) but before arriving at Mount Sinai (see Exodus 18–19). In particular, Exodus 16:22–30 narrates Moses's instructions to the Israelites about gathering manna to eat: "To day is a sabbath [*šabbāt*] unto the Lord: to day ye shall not find it [manna] in the field. Six days ye shall gather it; but on the seventh day, which is the sabbath, in it there shall be none. . . . the Lord hath given you the sabbath, therefore he giveth you on the sixth day the bread of two days. . . . So the people rested [*š-b-t*] on the seventh day" (16:23–30).[23]

This account presents a coherent "six days–seventh day" approach to the work of gathering manna in the wilderness, reminiscent of the report of the divine cessation from work in Genesis 2:2–3. Just as God did not work on the seventh day after creating the earth, he likewise ceased working on the seventh day of each week by not providing the Israelites with manna on that day. And the Israelites were to follow this model. They would not be working to gather and prepare manna on the seventh day. They thus practiced a *šabbāt* of sorts.

But at this point in the narrative, the Bible as we have it has not yet related a commandment or an explanation about the Sabbath day in general. That first comes with the Ten Commandments in Exodus 20. In fact, Exodus 16:29 is understood by some scholars as introducing the Sabbath concept to Israelites for the first time—"See, for that the Lord hath given you the sabbath"—with a humanitarian as opposed to a religious emphasis, as preparation for the command that comes in Exodus 20.[24] However, most Latter-day Saints would tend to see this as a continuation of an unattested but age-old Sabbath practice, not as a new innovation.

The Israelites' arrival and stay at Mount Sinai provided a period of rest and spiritual focus for them after their time in and exodus from Egypt. Exodus 19–20 recounts a dramatic theophany in which Jehovah declared the Ten Commandments. As indicated in Exodus 19 and 20, with support from Deuteronomy 4 and 5 (see below), Jehovah spoke the Ten Commandments, or the Decalogue, to *all* the Israelites gathered at the base of the mountain. Each Israelite heard the voice of God declaring these standards, collectively to all but individually to each of them.[25]

The very fact that Jehovah gave the Sabbath commandment (see Exodus 20:8–11), the fourth of the ten, as part of the Decalogue signals its gravity in the Israelites' relationship with him (and in our relationship with him as well). This commandment formally introduces and grounds the Sabbath law in the Bible. And in contrast to the first three of the Ten Commandments (and most of the subsequent commandments), this commandment is not a prohibition against a certain action but a positive command to *do* something.

Thus, Exodus 20:8 states, "Remember the sabbath day, to keep it holy."[26] This command immediately requires two conjoined responses from the Israelites. First, they are to "remember" the day of *šabbāt*. As commentators usually stress, "remembering" in the Bible often means more than merely recalling something. It involves paying attention to and considering, which leads to commitment and action.[27]

This proper "remembering" of the Sabbath leads to the second needed response, "to keep it [the Sabbath] holy." As presented in Genesis 2:3, God "sanctified" the seventh day—that is, he made it holy, which made it separate and different from the other six days of the week. The Sabbath belongs to God; it originated with him. Now in Exodus 20:8 the charge comes to *maintain* the divinely sanctioned holiness of the day. Thus, every week the Sabbath came to the Israelites, and comes to each of us, as a holy day. As we keep or maintain its holiness, it has the power to help us become holy. This transformation correlates with Jehovah's greater charge to his covenant people: "Ye shall be holy: for I the Lord your God am holy" (Leviticus 19:2).[28]

After the command is given, Exodus 20:9–10 provides instructions about the Sabbath. Ancient Israelites did not have the luxury of a four- or five-day work week, so the mention of working six days per week was essentially a given. What is unique here is that the Israelites were commanded to *not* do *any* work every seventh day. And remarkably, *everyone* was to cease working: each Israelite family; their entire household, meaning all slaves or servants; every *gēr*, translated variously as "stranger/sojourner/resident alien"; and all animals (vv. 9–10; compare Exodus 23:12).[29] This all-encompassing *šabbāt* concept is extraordinary, and was intended, at least in this context, to provide a status-leveling dimension to Israelite society—every person and animal was expected to cease working and experience rest on the Sabbath. Thus, as expressed by Bernard White, "Before God, we stand as equals: all are his servants, all are his creatures, all are recipients of his tender care."[30]

Exodus 20:11 summarizes the content of Genesis 1:1–2:3 and provides the basis for this powerful Sabbath commandment: God created the earth in six days, and then he "blessed the sabbath day, and hallowed it." This divine cosmic rhythm was presented as the foundation for a weekly human rhythm of work followed by rest, thereby refocusing the Lord's covenant people on the divine. This explanation loops back to the initial injunctions in verse 8: "Remember the sabbath day, to keep it holy." Thus, remembering the Sabbath and maintaining its holiness involves recalling what God did during and after six days of creation; why he did it; and what one's relationship is to him and to his purposes.

However, some things are left unsaid in this passage, such as what constitutes work. There is no defined list in the Old Testament of what

Israelites were expected to do on the Sabbath and what "work" they were to cease doing. Their regular occupational work and their subsistence labors were obvious activities to cease, and this seems to be the focus of the instructions in verses 9–10. In this regard, observing the Sabbath required the exercise of great faith by the Israelites. Given their agrarian-based society, not working one day of the week displayed trust in Jehovah and in his willingness to provide. (Other activities that came to be considered "work" to be avoided on the Sabbath are discussed in a separate section below.)

A few chapters later, Exodus 31 further emphasizes Jehovah's view of the sacred nature of the Sabbath day. Following revelation to Moses on Mount Sinai about the design of the tabernacle, its cultic items, and the ordaining of Aaron and his sons as priests (see Exodus 25:1–31:11), Jehovah instructed: "Verily my sabbaths [*šabbĕtōt*, plural] ye shall keep [*š-m-r*]: for it is a sign [*ʾôt*] between me and you throughout your generations; that ye may know that I am the Lord that doth sanctify you. . . . It is a sign [*ʾôt*] between me and the children of Israel for ever: for in six days the Lord made heaven and earth, and on the seventh day he rested [*š-b-t*]" (Exodus 31:13, 17). Thus, the Israelites' keeping the Sabbath day holy was meant not only to provide them rest but also to act as an individual and group marker—a sign—of their covenant relationship with Jehovah (see Exodus 24) and of their recognition that he alone had the power to make them holy like he is. God's work-then-rest paradigm from the earth's creation is again emphasized as the basis for this Sabbath practice.

The Sabbath as a sign in Exodus 31 parallels the purpose of the sign of circumcision given to Abraham in Genesis 17—"circumcise the flesh of your foreskin; and it shall be a token [*ʾôt*] of the covenant betwixt me and you" (v. 11)[31]—in that Jehovah intended it to function as a human demonstration of obedience to and covenant relationship with the divine.[32] However, "unlike circumcision, it [Sabbath observance] is not a single act but an attitude to be consistently maintained" by all covenant Israelites.[33]

Lastly, Exodus 31 is the first biblical passage that mentions a consequence for Israelite violation of the Sabbath. Exodus 31:14–15 explicitly presents Jehovah's words: whoever profanes the Sabbath (that is, treats it as a regular, common, and therefore *un*holy day) by doing work on it "shall surely be put to death." Although situated in a different time period and cultural context, this penalty for profaning the Sabbath seems harsh to our modern sensibilities. The Old Testament does not specifically state a reason for this severe penalty, but by way of context, capital punishment in ancient Israel was associated with violations of the first seven of the Ten Commandments, plus with other social violations such as kidnapping and rape.[34]

The Old Testament contains only one example of capital punishment applied to Sabbath-day violation. Numbers 15:32–36 recounts the case of a man gathering sticks on the Sabbath. Since this passage follows others dealing with unintentional sins (vv. 22–29) and sins committed "presumptuously" (KJV) or with "a high hand" (ESV, NRSV; vv. 30–31), it may be that the stick gatherer was acting defiantly as well as publicly in violation of the Sabbath commandment. Moses inquires of Jehovah what should be done, and Jehovah instructs Moses that the Israelites should stone the person to death outside the camp.[35] This concise passage in Numbers 15 asserts a penalty for the man's actions, but it does not answer most questions about the incident or its outcome.[36] It is not clear how often death was inflicted for profaning the Sabbath, since there are other instances of Sabbath violation recounted in the Old Testament in which death was *not* the outcome (for example, see Amos 8:5; Nehemiah 13:15–18). Thus many scholars think it was rare for Israelite Sabbath violation to result in capital punishment, and the capital consequence prescribed in Exodus 31:14–15 is understood as a biblical tradition that emphasizes how sacred the Sabbath was to Jehovah.[37]

At the very least, violation of the Sabbath demonstrated a disrespect for one's promises to and relationship with God on a larger scale. After the Israelites formally accepted and entered into a covenant with Jehovah at Mount Sinai—thereby indicating they would do all that he had commanded them (see Exodus 24:3–8)—profaning the Sabbath, the day that Jehovah had made holy, not only violated a direct commandment from him but also undermined the efficacy of the *sign* of their covenant with him.[38] An underlying biblical principle is that God's holiness, and by extension the holiness of things made holy by God (such as the Sabbath day), inherently has greater and more powerful dimensions than many people realize.[39]

The last Sabbath passage in Exodus discussed herein is Exodus 35:1–3, which repeats and adds to the Sabbath commands already given: "Six days shall work be done, but on the seventh day there shall be to you an holy day, a sabbath of rest [*šabbat šabbātôn*] to the Lord: whosoever doeth work therein shall be put to death. Ye shall kindle no fire throughout your habitations upon the sabbath day." Not only are the work-rest paradigm and the death penalty repeated here, but a new proscription is added—that kindling fires on the Sabbath constitutes work and must be avoided (hinted at in Exodus 16:23; again, a discussion of "work" is provided below).[40]

These passages in Exodus 20, 31, and 35 powerfully inform the rest of the Sabbath passages in the Old Testament. The majority of the remaining Sabbath passages in the Pentateuch are also in priestly oriented passages, with the exception of Deuteronomy 5 (discussed below).

Leviticus

With its focus on sacrifice, holiness, and other priestly matters, Leviticus depicts the Israelites while they are still camped at Mount Sinai. Major Sabbath-day commandments and instructions occur in Leviticus 19 and 24.[41] But the largest concentration of references to the Sabbath in Leviticus is found in chapters 23 and 25–26. Leviticus 23 outlines annual holy-day feasts in the Israelite calendar, but it actually begins with a reemphasis of the weekly Sabbath: "it is the sabbath of the Lord in all your dwellings" (v. 3; the Sabbath is also mentioned in verses 11, 15, 16, 32, and 38).

The significance of the Sabbath principle was illustrated not only by observing the seventh day of each week as holy. Ancient Israelites were also taught to observe a seven-year cycle and a fifty-year Jubilee cycle—that is, a cycle of seven periods of seven years plus one—with practices that brought "rest" to their agricultural lands and to those in debt and debt slavery. Space does not allow further discussion here, but for example, Leviticus 25:2–7 presents the concept of a Sabbath *year* for land.[42] It is not clear to what extent these Sabbath-year laws were actually practiced, but such passages demonstrate the broad significance of the Sabbath principle in Israelite theology, further reinforcing the rationale for rest and release from the burdens of ordinary life and providing an expansive view of recurring sacred time.

Further reaffirmation of the Sabbath-day command occurs in Leviticus 26. Preceding a list of blessings Jehovah would provide if the Israelites were righteous and curses if they were disobedient are the reminders to not worship other deities and to keep the Sabbath holy: "Ye shall keep my sabbaths, and reverence my sanctuary: I am the Lord" (v. 2). As the listing of curses concludes, Jehovah promises the Israelites he will "scatter [them] among the heathen" if they break their covenant with him (v. 33), stating that "then shall the land enjoy her sabbaths" by lying at rest when the Israelites are exiled elsewhere (vv. 33–34; compare vv. 35, 43).

Numbers

There are only sporadic references to the Sabbath in texts recounting the Israelites' experiences after leaving Mount Sinai (see Numbers 10). The incident of the man gathering sticks on the Sabbath, outlined in Numbers 15, was mentioned above in connection with Exodus 31. Numbers 28–29 contain a sacrificial calendar of sorts, indicating what "sacrifices [should be] made by fire" on the altar at the tabernacle (and later at the Jerusalem temple) on various holy days. Numbers 28:9–10 indicates that every Sabbath day, the regular morning and evening sacrifices should be doubled (see 28:1–8 for the daily offerings, which are first mentioned in Exodus 29:38–39). Thus, two additional lambs were to be offered as whole burnt offerings each Sabbath (one extra in the morning and in the evening), along with doubled grain and drink offerings. These additional offerings highlight the special status of the Sabbath day.

Deuteronomy

The book of Deuteronomy primarily presents Moses's last teachings to the Israelites in the plains of Moab, east of the Jordan River, before his departure and their entrance into the land of Canaan. Although Deuteronomy reviews laws, as did the previously discussed books in the Pentateuch, it is *not* priestly literature. Much of its language, tone, and interests are different, emphasizing covenant loyalty; faithfulness to and love for Jehovah alone; and the chosen status of the Israelites.

Deuteronomy's early chapters present Moses's review of his experiences with the Israelites, including their reception of the Ten Commandments at Mount Sinai. Although the Sabbath command as presented in Deuteronomy 5:12–15 is similar to what is recounted in Exodus 20:8–11, these verses also contain important differences. These include the following:

- Deuteronomy 5:12: "Keep [*š-m-r*] the sabbath day to sanctify it, as the Lord thy God hath commanded thee." In Exodus 20:8, the command is to "remember the sabbath day" to sanctify it, while here the Hebrew verb is *š-m-r*, meaning "to keep, observe, watch over, protect, guard."[43] Although there is no good explanation for the difference in wording—especially since the verse ends with Moses saying "as the Lord thy God hath commanded thee," referring back to the giving of the Decalogue at Mount Sinai—the variants to "remember" (Exodus 20:8) and to "keep, guard" (Deuteronomy 5:12) the Sabbath day to maintain its holiness are best seen as complementary injunctions. Properly remembering the Sabbath leads one to protect its holy status.

- Deuteronomy 5:14 ends with an additional reminder not found in Exodus 20: "Thy manservant and thy maidservant may rest as well as thou." This clause emphasizes the divine ideal of the need for *all* people in Israel to cease their labors on the Sabbath, no matter what their social status.[44]
- Deuteronomy 5:15 concludes this version of the Sabbath command by providing a markedly different reason for observing the day than the reason given in earlier scripture. In Exodus 20:11, the basis for the Israelite Sabbath observance was that God had created the earth in six days, after which he ceased or "rested the seventh day: wherefore the Lord blessed the sabbath day, and hallowed it;" thus the Israelites were expected to emulate Jehovah's pattern by doing likewise every week. However, Deuteronomy 5:15 explains that "the Lord thy God commanded thee to keep the sabbath day" to help Israelites "remember that thou wast a servant in the land of Egypt, and that the Lord thy God brought thee out thence through a mighty hand and by a stretched out arm." As with the difference between "remember" and "keep" at the beginning of the Sabbath command (Exodus 20:8; Deuteronomy 5:12), these motivations for Sabbath observance are not mutually exclusive. The version in Deuteronomy 5:15 presumably assumes knowledge of the contents of Genesis 2 and Exodus 20 but, by picking up on a thread in Exodus 20:2, it also exhorts the Israelites to "remember" that, by providing the Israelites with release and rest from Egyptian bondage and engaging with them at Mount Sinai, Jehovah had created, as it were, a newly constituted covenant people. Therefore the Israelites should also rest on the Sabbath day in commemoration of God's goodness and his power to deliver them.[45]

These two versions of the Sabbath command—Exodus 20:8–11 and Deuteronomy 5:12–15—connect the Sabbath with two different great acts of God: (1) creating the earth and designating a holy day (see Genesis 2:2–3), and (2) fulfilling a promise to redeem the Israelites from Egyptian servitude and offering them a covenant opportunity (see Exodus 1–24). These two passages complement each other by restating Jehovah's expectations for Israelite Sabbath compliance (and our own Sabbath compliance by extension) and by calling attention to Jehovah's power to create and to deliver.

As just reviewed, passages in the Torah or Pentateuch introduce and explain the nature of the weekly commemoration known biblically as the Sabbath day. These Sabbath passages appear primarily in priestly-oriented content and comprise the foundational texts for all Sabbath-related activity in the rest of the Old Testament. These Torah texts are part of the Israelites' binding covenant with Jehovah and prescribe what was *supposed* to happen regarding the Sabbath, rather than describing what actually *did* happen (with the exception of Numbers 15:32–36).

Moving beyond the Pentateuch, there is no general discussion of the Sabbath in the remainder of the Old Testament, but there are several narrative passages that mention the Sabbath in passing, and several prophetic books that present critiques of Israelite behavior in relation to the Sabbath.[46] Some of these passages will now be considered, followed by discussions of what the Israelites were to do and not do on the Sabbath day and how Latter-day Saints have employed these Old Testament teachings about the Sabbath.

Sabbath: Practice and Reproof after Moses

Mention of the Sabbath in Narrative Texts

Following Moses's departure, the Bible narrates that Joshua led the Israelites into the land of Canaan, which then became known as the land of Israel. The noun *šabbāt* does not occur anywhere in the books of Joshua, Judges, Ruth, 1 and 2 Samuel, or 1 Kings, although one can assume that at least some Israelites observed the Sabbath during the centuries overviewed by these books.[47] Scattered references to the Sabbath in other narrative texts say little *about* the Sabbath itself, but they do indicate awareness of the day and its related practices, as well as abuses thereof.

One passage worth highlighting occurs in 2 Kings 4.[48] A son in an Israelite family living in the northern kingdom of Israel in the mid-800s BC died. The boy's mother instructed her husband to prepare a donkey and a servant so she could ride to find "the man of God," meaning the prophet Elisha. Her husband responded, "Wherefore wilt thou go to him to day? it is neither new moon, nor sabbath. And she said, It shall be well" (v. 23). The monthly new moon was a day of sacrifice and rest, similar to the weekly Sabbath day in some ways (compare Numbers 28:11–15). The husband's response suggests that people would gather around prophets on worship days, such as the New Moon and the weekly Sabbath, and further assumes at least some degree of observance of the Sabbath by Israelites in that region at that time.[49]

Other important narrative passages relating to Sabbath expectations occur in Nehemiah 10 and 13. The reported events took place in Jerusalem in the mid-400s BC, in what is called the postexilic period—that is, the period following the Babylonian destruction of the Jerusalem Temple, the subsequent deportation of Israelites to Babylonia, and the ensuing return from exile and rebuilding of the temple in the Persian era.[50]

Nehemiah 10 recounts that many Israelites in Jerusalem pledged to keep "all the commandments of the Lord our Lord" (v. 29), the stipulations of which included that "if the people of the land bring ware[s] or any victuals [grain] on the sabbath day to sell, that [the Israelites] would not buy it of them on the sabbath, or on the holy day" (v. 31).[51] As recounted in Nehemiah 13:15–22, Nehemiah's efforts to rebuild Jerusalem physically and spiritually included eliminating the production and transportation of goods by Israelites and foreigners by securing the gates of Jerusalem on the Sabbath day. Many of Nehemiah's people had not learned this important lesson from the past: a major reason for the divine judgments which culminated in the Babylonian destruction of Jerusalem was the violation of Sabbath law (compare Jeremiah 17:21–27; Lamentations 2:6; compare Amos 8:5; these passages are discussed below). Thus, based on Nehemiah 13, the issue of profaning the Sabbath in preexilic times continued among some postexilic Israelites.

The accounts in 1 and 2 Chronicles, produced in the postexilic period, assert (among other things) the significance of Jerusalem, the temple, and priestly and Levitical activities. With this priestly orientation, it is no surprise that the word *šabbāt* occurs ten times therein: twice in 1 Chronicles 9:32 in reference to preparation of showbread for the Sabbath, and the remaining eight times (in both singular and plural forms) in connection with sacrificial offerings or other priestly service on the Sabbath day.[52]

Mention of the Sabbath in Prophetic Texts—Critiques

Many of the occurrences of the noun *šabbāt* in the prophetic books appear in critiques of some Israelites' lack of compliance with prophetic expectations regarding the Sabbath day. Each has its own context, important for understanding the full dimensions of the prophetic critique. However, space limitations necessitate limiting most context in what follows.

Prophesying that various covenant violations would result in the coming destruction of the northern kingdom of Israel, Amos portrays some Israelites as saying, "When will the new moon be gone, that we may sell corn? and the sabbath, that we may set forth wheat, making the ephah small, and the shekel great" (Amos 8:5). These people were not really celebrating the Sabbath but rather enduring it so they could return to their business practices. Although not providing much description of actual Sabbath-day activities, this passage affirms an ongoing Sabbath-day tradition in the northern kingdom of Israel in the mid-700s BC.[53]

Likewise, Isaiah 58 relates Jehovah's condemnation of Israelites who engaged in fasting for selfish rather than compassionate reasons (see vv. 1–4).[54] Following instructions on what constitutes an acceptable fast (see vv. 5–12), this Sabbath-related encouragement is given: "If thou turn away thy foot from the sabbath, from doing thy pleasure on my holy day; and call the sabbath a delight, the holy [day] of the Lord, honourable; and shalt honour him, not doing thine own ways, nor finding thine own pleasure, nor speaking thine own words: Then shalt thou delight thyself in the Lord" (vv. 13–14). Here, again, proper observance of the Sabbath serves as a sign of one's focus on and commitment to Jehovah and his will. And again, an Israelite prophet was calling at least some people to repent of their abuses of the Sabbath day.

Sometime before the Babylonian destruction of Jerusalem (586 BC), Jehovah instructed Jeremiah to publicly declare this message in Jerusalem: "Thus saith the Lord; Take heed to yourselves, and bear no burden on the sabbath day, nor bring it in by the gates of Jerusalem; Neither carry forth a burden out of your houses on the sabbath day, neither do ye any work, but hallow ye the sabbath day, as I commanded your fathers. But they obeyed not" (Jeremiah 17:21–23). This rebuke is followed by a conditional promise of spiritual and political blessings (see vv. 24–26), which would all be voided if the Israelites in Jerusalem did not keep the Sabbath day holy: "But if ye will not hearken unto me to hallow the sabbath day, and not to bear a burden, even entering in at the gates of Jerusalem on the sabbath day; then will I kindle a fire in the gates thereof, and it shall devour the palaces of Jerusalem, and it shall not be quenched" (17:27).[55] The passage in Nehemiah 13 dealing with closing the gates of Jerusalem on the Sabbath, cited above, draws on the content of this Jeremiah passage. By doing so, Nehemiah 13 encourages postexilic Israelites, those living in Jerusalem a century and a half after the time of Jeremiah, to honor the Sabbath more faithfully than their preexilic ancestors had done.

Just as the Lord warned in Jeremiah 17, Jerusalem *was* destroyed by the Babylonians in 586 BC, resulting in death, destruction, and the deportation of thousands of Israelites (see 2 Kings 25; Jeremiah 39; 52; and Lamentations 2). The destruction of the temple ended the special sacrifices offered there on the Sabbath day for the next seventy years, thus eliminating that institutional ritual aspect of Sabbath worship until the Jerusalem temple was rebuilt and dedicated in 515 BC.

Turning now to the book of Ezekiel, Ezekiel was an Aaronic priest deported to Babylonia in 597 BC. He was called while in exile as a prophet to represent Jehovah to others who had also been deported. The book of Ezekiel, which displays a definite priestly tone and focus, contains several passages mentioning the Sabbath day in a context of judgement. For example, chapter 20 references the Israelite exodus-era experiences, and includes denouncements such as: "I gave them my sabbaths, to be a sign between me and them, that they might know that I am the LORD that sanctify them. But the house of Israel rebelled against me in the wilderness: . . . and my sabbaths they greatly polluted" (20:12–13; compare 20:16, 20–21, 24; and Nehemiah 9:13–17). Thus we can see that centuries after Moses, Israelite prophets were utilizing teachings in Exodus 20 and 31 to emphasize Sabbath observance as a covenant sign between Jehovah and the Israelites and as a conduit to sanctification. Ten of the fifteen occurrences in the Old Testament of the phrase "my sabbaths," meaning Jehovah's Sabbaths, are in the book of Ezekiel.[56] This phrase emphasizes that Jehovah set the Sabbath and certain other days apart as holy. The Sabbath day belongs to him, and his covenant people are expected to keep it holy.

The book of Ezekiel also states that the profaning of the Sabbath by Ezekiel's contemporary Israelites, including priests and princes, was a key factor in Jehovah's willingness to allow the Babylonians to destroy Jerusalem in 586 BC (see 22:8, 26, 31; 23:38). Powerfully, Ezekiel 22:26 ends with this claim: "they [the priests] have put no difference between the holy and profane, . . . and have hid their eyes from my sabbaths, and *I am profaned among them*" (emphasis added). Regarding this final phrase, Old Testament scholar Daniel Block has observed that "the priests' betrayal of their calling ultimately affects Yahweh himself. Their irresponsibility reflects not only on his character, since he had appointed them to this office, it also inhibits the nation as a group in its performance of his will."[57] Although profaning the Sabbath (and other occasions of "sacred time") was not Israel's only covenant infraction that provoked divine judgment ending in destruction, passages in Jeremiah and Ezekiel clearly indicate that it was a major factor.

Collectively, the strong response from some biblical prophets to Sabbath violations among Israelites living in the kingdoms of Israel and Judah serves many purposes: it emphasizes the significance of the Sabbath day in Jehovah's relationship with his people; it recounts an ongoing disregard for approved Sabbath observance; and it provides, at least in part, justification for divine judgments against the Israelites. Sadly, as scholar Ronald Clements has observed, the language in the Sabbath command in Deuteronomy 5:13–15 "serve[s] to confirm a perspective corroborated elsewhere in the OT that this particular commandment [of Sabbath observance] was especially vulnerable to indifference and neglect."[58]

Mention of the Sabbath in Prophetic Texts—Future Observance

In addition to reproof for Israelite Sabbath-day violations, prophetic texts in the Old Testament also contain a few passages presenting a future vision of peace and harmony that includes ideal Sabbath-day observance. For example, Isaiah 56:1–8 contains a remarkable set of promises from Jehovah in the context of the claim that "my salvation is near to come, and my righteousness [is soon] to be revealed" (v. 1). All people, Israelites *and* foreigners (*nēkār*; KJV, "stranger"), who abide by God's law are promised blessings. Although commentators differ on when this was or will be fulfilled (and likely it will not completely be fulfilled until the Millennium), the emphasis on honoring the Sabbath is important here. Happiness is promised to each faithful person "who keeps [*š-m-r*] the sabbath, not profaning it, and keeps his hand from doing any evil" (v. 2, ESV; see also vv. 4, 6).

Additionally, Isaiah 66 looks forward to an ideal age when those in Jerusalem would all worship Jehovah in truth and harmony, including the prophecy that "it shall come to pass, that from one new moon to another, and from one sabbath to another, shall all flesh come to worship before me, saith the Lord" (Isaiah 66:23). This view of an ideal future stands in stark contrast to ongoing calls in such prophetic books as Amos, Isaiah, and Jeremiah for Israelites to repent and keep the Sabbath day holy.[59]

This concludes the overview and assessment of important Sabbath passages in the Old Testament. The following two sections deal with specific issues relating to the Sabbath.

Ancient Israelite Sabbath Activities

The biblical laws, teachings, and practices reviewed above emphatically attest that Jehovah expected Israelites to cease their weekly labors as part of their Sabbath observation. However, as many commentators have stated, the Bible contains little description about what constituted the "work" that should be avoided. Similarly, there is no specific list of activities Israelites were expected to do on the Sabbath.[60] This situation is likely due, at least in part, to the focus and purpose of the Old Testament texts in general: they usually do not report the details of day-to-day life. Additionally, ancient prophets and scripture compilers may have taken an approach similar to many Latter-day Saint prophets, who have typically emphasized Sabbath principles over lists of what is acceptable or objectionable for the Sabbath day.[61] Therefore, the following comments provide a brief overview of the biblical passages that contribute to our understanding of Sabbath practice in ancient Israel.

"Work" to be Avoided on the Sabbath

As indicated above, Exodus 20:10 and Deuteronomy 5:14 are quite specific that the Israelites—along with everyone in their household, sojourners, and animals—should "not do any work" on the Sabbath. Thus, occupational and subsistence labor was to cease each Sabbath day as part of maintaining the day's holiness.

Additional passages, *if* they are broadly representative, help illustrate what, beyond occupational and agricultural activity (see Exodus 34:21), was considered "work" that was to cease on the Sabbath. For example, gathering food (see Exodus 16:23–30), gathering wood (see Numbers 15:32–36), kindling fire (see Exodus 35:3), and engaging in commercial activities (see Nehemiah 10:31; 13:15–22) all desecrated the Sabbath day.[62]

Specific accusations of commercial activities as Sabbath violations are found in Amos 8:5; Jeremiah 17:19–27; and Nehemiah 10:31; 13:15–18 (all of which are mentioned above). This shows us that, according to Jeremiah's and Nehemiah's accounts, "profaning the Sabbath" included the acts of buying and selling on the day that Jehovah had set apart as sacred.

Additionally, Isaiah 58:13 prompts Israelites to "call the sabbath a delight, the holy of the Lord, . . . not doing thine own ways, nor finding thine own pleasure, nor speaking thine own words." This admonition clearly indicates that personal interests and pleasures commonly pursued during the week had replaced the divinely focused perspective Jehovah desired on the Sabbath. Reverence for God and his holy day was being subverted by the Israelites' own mundane activities on the Sabbath; the Israelites were thus profaning or making common that holy day.

It is not currently possible to know if these stipulations were all in effect during the whole of Israelite history, but cumulatively these few passages have certainly shaped the post–Old Testament understanding of Sabbath practice.[63] With these guidelines and restrictions in mind, the next subsection examines what the Israelites did on the Sabbath day, again based only on what is preserved in the Old Testament.

What the Israelites Did on the Sabbath

Just as with the issue of what "work" was to be avoided on the Sabbath, scholar Harold P. Dressler's claim that "the actual celebration of the Sabbath is not described in detail" in the Old Testament is accurate but also greatly understated.[64] The Sabbath is not only "not described in detail"; no description whatsoever is provided. However, returning to Exodus 20:8 provides the framework of the Sabbath principle: to keep the Sabbath day holy. This means that things which contributed to the holiness or uncommonness of the day were and are acceptable to Jehovah. Things that detracted from the holiness of the Sabbath—work and other activities that made it common—were to be excluded.

The few Old Testament passages available to us that depict acceptable Sabbath activities fall into two categories: (1) ritual actions prescribed for Aaronic priests, and (2) what nonpriestly "regular" Israelites did. Regarding priestly activity, the daily morning and evening sacrifice of lamb, grain, and drink offerings at the tabernacle, and later at the Jerusalem temple, were doubled on the Sabbath day (see Numbers 28:9–10).[65] The offering of these extra sacrifices emphasized the importance of the Sabbath. These sacrifices were not considered "work"; instead they were considered priestly activity directed towards Jehovah in worship rather than towards one's own self-interest.[66]

Additionally, the priests who entered the tabernacle every morning to burn incense and ensure that the oil lamps on the menorah were still burning would, on the Sabbath, eat "in the holy place" the twelve "loaves" (ESV) or "cakes" (KJV) of flat bread that had rested on the table of showbread during the week, replacing them with twelve fresh loaves that were placed before Jehovah for the coming week (see Leviticus 24:5–9; compare Exodus 25:25–30). These twelve loaves represented the twelve tribes of Israel and their gratitude for the blessings of life Jehovah had given them, a worshipful offering renewed by the priests on behalf of the people each Sabbath day.[67] These priestly and related activities on the Sabbath, occurring in the sacred space of the tabernacle or temple area, emphasize the magnitude of this weekly sacred time.

Segueing to what the majority of Israelites (the nonpriestly ones) did on the Sabbath, Ezekiel 46:3 states that at the future temple in Jerusalem, "the people of the land shall worship at the door of this [eastern] gate before the LORD in the sabbaths and in the new moons." Such prophesied Sabbath worship at the temple likely reflects actual practice in Jerusalem in Ezekiel's time and probably earlier, and this worship was presumably led by priests with Levitical assistance (see also Isaiah 1:13, which contains an implication of worshipful assemblies on the Sabbath).

However, many Israelites lived beyond practical travelling distance to the tabernacle or temple. Again, based on only the few passages in the Old Testament, it appears that those Israelites who could not go to the tabernacle or temple on the Sabbath worshipped at or near their home.[68] This notion of home-based Sabbath worship is implied in the Ten Commandments, with the specification that the entire household was to cease work and rest on the Sabbath (see Exodus 20:10; 23:12), and in the injunction to "kindle no fire throughout your habitations upon the sabbath day" (Exodus 35:3).

Further affirming this perspective, Leviticus 23:3 states that "the seventh day is the sabbath of rest . . . ; ye shall do no work therein: it is the sabbath of the LORD in all your dwellings." The phrase "in all your dwellings" indicates that many Israelites would celebrate the Sabbath locally or regionally (usually in kin-based groups), not at the tabernacle.[69] Because of this, resting from weekday labors provided time for special meals, praying, teaching, and service, which likely took place in an immediate- or extended-family context.

Furthermore, this locally based worship appears to have included gatherings (at least sometimes) with a religious authority figure, as suggested by the account in 2 Kings 4, in which a mother's insistence on finding the prophet Elisha and securing his help to revive her deceased son is met with this response from her husband: "Wherefore wilt thou go to him [Elisha] to day? it is neither new moon, nor sabbath" (v. 23). This supports the notion that some Israelites gathered around a prophet or perhaps some other leader, such as a priest or patriarch, on Sabbaths and other holy days for worship and instruction. Finally, Psalm 92, a "song for the sabbath day" (superscription), recounts praise and gratitude that many Israelites likely expressed in Sabbath worship, whether at home or at the temple.

Given the conjoined commands to cease weekday work and to keep the Sabbath day holy, we can confidently assume, aided by these few biblical clues, that what Jehovah expected Israelites to do on the Sabbath day was to worship and praise him; to teach and learn about him, including remembering his great acts of creating, delivering, and covenanting; to bless the lives of family members and neighbors; and to demonstrate in desire and deed that the Sabbath was a sign or symbol of their covenant relationship with him—that this one day of their week was distinct from the other six days of the week, a holy day. Doctrine and Covenants 59:10 reiterates this general approach to Sabbath observance in this dispensation: "This is a day appointed unto you to rest from your labors, and to pay thy devotions unto the Most High."

Latter-day Saint Use of Old Testament Sabbath Teachings

Given that the Old Testament contains such foundational scriptures commanding Sabbath worship, it is no surprise that Latter-day Saint leaders and Church materials often utilize these scriptures in teaching about the Sabbath day in this dispensation. Later chapters in this volume more thoroughly focus on Latter-day Saints and the Sabbath. Here it is sufficient to briefly illustrate the use of Old Testament passages in recent teachings about the Sabbath.

There are, of course, comments on the Sabbath in Church manuals and other media, and these deal with such major passages as Genesis 2, Exodus 20, and Isaiah 58 (as well as Mark 2 and Doctrine and Covenants 59). For the sake of brief illustration, the following comments deal with the employment of Old Testament Sabbath passages in recent general conference addresses.

Passing encouragements to keep the Sabbath day holy from one or more speakers occur in most general conferences of the Church, and these encouragements often cite Exodus 20:8 as support.[70] Additionally, every few years there has been a major conference address focusing on observing the Sabbath day, and these have drawn heavily on passages in the Old Testament.

Examples of this include Elder H. Aldridge Gillespie's October 2000 conference address entitled "The Blessing of Keeping the Sabbath Day Holy," in which he quoted from Exodus 20:8, Leviticus 26:2–12, and Isaiah 58:13–14.[71] In an April 2011 conference address entitled "The Sabbath and the Sacrament," Elder L. Tom Perry quoted Genesis 2:3 and Exodus 20:8–11.[72] And in an address in the April 2015 General Conference entitled "The Sabbath Is a Delight"—the title of which derives from Isaiah 58:13—then-Elder Russell M. Nelson explained the meaning of the Hebrew word *šabbāt* and referenced a wide variety of Sabbath passages, including Genesis 2:2–3; Exodus 20:8 and 31:13, 16; Deuteronomy 5:12; Leviticus 19:3, 30, and 26:2–4; Ezekiel 20:20 and 44:24; and Isaiah 58:13–14—all of which have also been cited in this chapter.[73]

The citing of Old Testament verses has not been confined to recent general conference addresses. The January 1978 issue of the *Ensign* magazine had a Sabbath-day focus, beginning with a First Presidency message from President Spencer W. Kimball entitled "The Sabbath—A Delight."[74] Additionally, on September 28, 1992, the First Presidency of the Church released a letter entitled "Sabbath Day Observance" that was to be read in sacrament meetings throughout the Church.[75] Although no Old Testament passages were quoted in this letter, "observance of the Sabbath" is mentioned as "one of the Ten Commandments" (see Exodus 20:8). Finally, Church emphasis on keeping the Sabbath day holy in 2015 and 2016 included passages from the Old Testament as well as a media campaign that encouraged Latter-day Saints "of all ages and living around the world to share their photos and thoughts as they honor the Sabbath day—#HisDay."[76]

Hopefully, these few examples are sufficient to illustrate the significant role that Sabbath-day passages from the Old Testament have had, and continue to have, on The Church of Jesus Christ of Latter-day Saints, as prophets and apostles have reaffirmed the importance of the Sabbath during the past few decades of this dispensation.[77]

Conclusion

Much has been said and could yet be said about the principle and practice of the Sabbath in the Old Testament. The Old Testament presents the Sabbath as a great gift from God, holy and sacred time in an unholy world, designed to assist each of us in our transformation to becoming true saints—that is, holy people.[78] In conclusion, these few points are offered by way of review and application.

First, the Old Testament teaches that humans properly observing the Sabbath are paralleling God and the pattern he established, with six days of creative activity followed by a day for ceasing work, resting, and finding spiritual refreshment (see Genesis 1:3–2:3). God's designating a holy day says something about his nature, since holiness is a divine attribute. And our keeping the Sabbath day holy says something about our desire to accept his invitation to develop this attribute of holiness in ourselves (see Leviticus 19:2). In this way, "sanctifying the Sabbath is part of our imitation of God, but it also becomes a way to find God's presence."[79]

Second, the command to honor the Sabbath day is introduced in both Exodus 20 and Deuteronomy 5 with a connection to an event—respectively, the creation of the earth and Jehovah's deliverance of the Israelites from Egypt. Recognizing and remembering these and other great acts of God invokes a sense of awe and gratitude. Severing Sabbath-day observance from this commemorative dimension diminishes the power that commemoration has: the power to direct and sustain a worshipful focus and the pursuit of holiness. This diminishment of power that happens when the Sabbath is not kept then negatively impacts one's future possibilities. This is because "the setting aside of one day when human beings attend, not to their own responsibilities and freedoms, but to God's ordering of life honors the larger creative purposes of God and integrating oneself into them. It acknowledges that God is indeed the Creator and provider of all things,"[80] as well as the one who has power to redeem his covenant people from all things.

Third, God declared the Sabbath day holy and indicated that keeping the Sabbath day holy is a sign of our active covenant relationship with him (see Exodus 31). Sabbath observance was intended to reflect Israel's orientation— what the Israelites valued and to whom they looked. Sabbath observance was about their *relationship* with God. The Israelites' view of Jehovah and the significance he had in their lives was signified by the value the Sabbath day had in their lives, and likewise for us. As has been aptly stated, "observing the Sabbath is one of the quintessential expressions of loyalty to God."[81]

Fourth, in the Old Testament as we have it, the Pentateuch contains the command to keep the Sabbath day holy but provides little by way of promised blessings.[82] However, a few of the Sabbath passages in the prophetic books contain related promises, especially Isaiah 58, which states that those who will honor and "delight in the sabbath" will "delight [themselves] in the LORD; and I [Jehovah] will cause thee to ride upon the high places of the earth, and feed thee with the heritage of Jacob thy father: for the mouth of the LORD hath spoken it" (58:14; see also 56:1–6).[83] This Sabbath blessing promises ultimate victory and security through Jehovah for all faithful, Sabbath-observing saints.

Fifth, in the scriptures, sacred time is presented as being at least as important as sacred space. As was likely the case with ancient Israelites, Latter-day Saints would not think of desecrating the sacred space of a temple. But "many Latter-day Saints have become lax in their observation of the Sabbath day," participating in "activities that now commonly desecrate the Sabbath," which is sacred time.[84] By setting the Sabbath apart from the other days of the week, to and for God, we receive a regularly recurring opportunity to benefit from the blessings of sacred time.

Finally, the seventh day of the week functioned as the Sabbath or day of rest during the Old Testament time period prior to the institution of Christian worship on Sunday, "the Lord's Day." This day is meant to commemorate Jesus's resurrection from the dead, another great act of God. It also serves as a symbolic foreshadowing of a future "ultimate rest for the people of God."[85] As God created the earth and then ceased and rested, so is that pattern utilized in Restoration scripture to present the history of the earth in its fallen condition, after which Jehovah—the resurrected Lord—will conclude the salvation of his people and join with them in the great millennial "day of peace and rest."[86]

Endnotes

* I express my gratitude to Daniel L. Belnap, Gaye Strathearn, two anonymous reviewers, and my wife, Jane Allis-Pike, for reading and providing helpful comments on earlier drafts of this paper.

1. For interesting thoughts on the relationship between space and time, including the sacred time of the Sabbath, see Abraham Joshua Heschel, *The Sabbath: Its Meaning for Modern Man*, paperback ed. (New York: Farrar, Straus, and Giroux, 2005), 21. Heschel states that the Sabbath day "is like a palace in time with a kingdom for all."
2. Given the uncertainty about many questions of textual composition and final form, those reading this paper will likely find other publications that claim, for example, that Sabbath laws in Exodus are late developments interjected into earlier times. Latter-day Saints, in general, tend to conservatively accept the biblical texts, their presentations, and their claims at face value. This is not inherently bad but may sometimes lead to missing other real possibilities of textual development. For the purposes of this paper, I am taking a generally canonical approach.
3. Many studies on the Sabbath day have been published, and many commentaries deal with the Old Testament passages that mention the Sabbath, far too many to list here. I have utilized some of these and cite them below, but readers should be aware that other resources are also available, some better than others. Also, much more could be said about the passages mentioned below, but space does not allow this.
4. For further discussion of the word "sabbath," see Dana M. Pike, "Biblical Hebrew Words You Already Know, and Why They are Important," *Religious Educator* 7, no. 3 (2006): 101–3. Transliterated words are different from translated words. Translated words are ones in which the *meaning* of a word crosses (hence the root "trans") from one language to another without necessarily retaining the sound of

the original word. On the other hand, transliterated words are ones in which the general *sound* of a word in one language crosses into another language, creating a new word in the second language.

5. See the entry *š-b-t* in Ludwig Koehler and Walter Baumgartner, *The Hebrew and Aramaic Lexicon of the Old Testament*, trans. and ed. under the supervision of M.E.J. Richardson (Leiden: Brill, 2000), 4:1407–9; hereafter abbreviated *HALOT*. See also the comments of E. Haag, "*š-b-t*," in *Theological Dictionary of the Old Testament*, ed. G. Johannes Botterweck, Helmer Ringgren, and Heinz-Josef Fabry, trans. David E. Green (Grand Rapids, MI: Eerdmans, 2004), 14:381–86; hereafter abbreviated *TDOT*. See also Andreas Schuele, "Sabbath," in *The New Interpreter's Dictionary of the Bible*, ed. Katharine Doob Sakenfeld et al. (Nashville: Abingdon, 2006–2009), 5:3; hereafter abbreviated *NIDB*. And see Harold H. P. Dressler, "The Sabbath in the Old Testament," in *From Sabbath to Lord's Day: A Biblical, Historical, and Theological Investigation*, ed. D. A. Carson (Grand Rapids, MI: Zondervan, 1982), 23–24.
6. Quotations of biblical passages cited in this paper are from the King James Version (KJV) unless otherwise indicated. Other translations cited herein are the New Revised Standard Version (NRSV; 1989); the English Standard Version (ESV; 2016); the New English Translation, 2nd ed. (NET; 2019); and the Schocken Bible (SB; 2019), translated by Everett Fox. These quotations derive from their current versions in Accordance Bible Software.
7. For a more complete discussion of the concept of "rest" in the Old Testament, especially as connected to the lexical root *n-w-ḥ*, see, for example, *HALOT*, s.v. "*n-w-ḥ*"; and the chapter entitled, "The Rest Motif in the Old Testament," in Jon Laansma, *"I Will Give You Rest": The Rest Motif in the New Testament, with Special Reference to Mt 11 and Heb 3–4* (Tübingen: Mohr Siebeck, 1997), 17–76.
8. Some scholars have asserted that the Sabbath day was originally intended as a day on which one ceased working, but not necessarily for the purpose or benefit of "rest." See, for example, Dressler, "Sabbath in the Old Testament," 23–24, 37n30; and Niels-Erik A. Andreasen, *The Old Testament Sabbath: A Tradition-Historical Investigation*, SBLDS 7 (Missoula, MT: Society of Biblical Literature, 1972), both of whom cite earlier scholars on this issue.
9. These theories are beyond the scope of this paper, but see, for example, Oded Tammuz, "The Sabbath as the Seventh Day of the Week and a Day of Rest: Since When?," *Zeitschrift für die alttestamentliche Wissenschaft* 131, no. 2 (2019): 288–89, and the many citations provided there.
10. For this assessment, see, for example, Dressler, "Sabbath in the Old Testament," 23; and Carol Meyers, "Feast Days and Foodways: Religious Dimensions of Household Life," in *Family and Household Religion: Toward a Synthesis of Old Testament Studies, Archaeology, Epigraphy, and Cultural Studies*, ed. Rainer Albertz et al. (Winona Lake, IN: Eisenbrauns, 2014), 234.
11. For further discussion, see, for example, Tammuz, "Sabbath as the Seventh Day," 287–88; Dressler, "Sabbath in the Old Testament," 22–23, 27; and the previous studies they both cite. Dressler, 22, quotes Andreasen's claim that "the origin and early history of the sabbath . . . continue to lie in the dark." *Old Testament Sabbath*, 8. See also Schuele, "Sabbath," 3–4.

12. It is also worth noting that the Hebrew word *šabbātôn* is related to the noun *šabbāt*, but its distinction is no longer clear. So, for example, it is described in *HALOT*, s.v. "*šabbātôn*," as "a sabbath that is markedly different . . . inasmuch as it is to be observed strictly and to be celebrated in a special way" (several other explanations for the meaning of this word are also given). See also Nahum M. Sarna, *Exodus*, JPS Torah Commentary (Philadelphia: Jewish Publication Society, 1991), 90. Translators have taken various approaches to rendering this word. Occurring only eleven times in the Hebrew Bible, *šabbātôn* appears with *šabbāt* in some of the passages discussed below. It is not discussed further herein, but it attests to an extra dimension of sacred Sabbath time that is no longer well understood.
13. In this paper I broadly designate passages and texts as having a priestly orientation or perspective, without dealing with the academic conceptions of a specific priestly source (P) in the books of the Pentateuch or the dating of such texts. As noted above, I am taking a more canonical approach to this topic.
14. James L. Kugel, *How to Read the Bible: A Guide to Scripture, Then and Now* (New York: Free Press, 2007), 54.
15. The NRSV and ESV read similarly.
16. See, for example: "Then he ceased [*š-b-t*], on the seventh day, from all his work that he had made. God gave the seventh day his blessing, and he hallowed it, for on it he ceased [*š-b-t*] from all his work" (SB; NET reads similarly).
17. Terence E. Fretheim, "The Book of Genesis," in *The New Interpreter's Bible—Old Testament and Apocrypha* (Nashville: Abingdon, 2015), 1:346. Similarly, Sarna stated that the seventh day in the creation sequence is an "integral part of the divinely ordained cosmic order. . . . Its blessed and sacred character is a cosmic reality entirely independent of human effort." *Genesis*, JPS Torah Commentary (Philadelphia: Jewish Publication Society, 1989), 14. See also the comments and quotations included in Jeffrey M. Bradshaw, "The Seventh Day," Book of Moses Essay #52, https://www.pearlofgreatpricecentral.org/the-seventh-day.
18. See, for example, Sarna, *Genesis*, 14; and Dressler, "Sabbath in the Old Testament," 28.
19. Sarna, for example, claimed that "the Sabbath is a distinctively Israelite ordinance" (*Genesis*, 14), so one would not expect to read about the Sabbath prior to the Israelite exodus account or about non-Israelites observing it.
20. Spencer W. Kimball, "The Sabbath—A Delight," *Ensign*, January 1978, 2. See also the comments and quotations provided in Kerry Muhlestein, Joshua M. Sears, and Avram R. Shannon, "New and Everlasting: The Relationship of Gospel Covenants in History," *Religious Educator* 21, no. 2 (2020): 26–27.
21. Bible Dictionary, "Sabbath." Similarly, Robert J. Matthews claimed, "No doubt the sacredness of the Sabbath day was known to the true believers from the time of Adam, although the Bible is not very clear on this point." "Why do we observe the Sabbath on Sunday when the biblical Sabbath seems to have been on the seventh day?," *Ensign*, January 1978, 15.
22. As a corollary to the claim of "the scantiness of the [biblical] record," consider also the fact that the word "sabbath" occurs a total of five times in the Book of Mormon. Three of these five occurrences are in one recitation of the Ten Commandments (see Mosiah 13:16–19), which leaves only *two* other references

to the Sabbath day in a record dealing with about one thousand years of time (not counting the redacted Jaredite record, which contains no mention of the Sabbath; see Jarom 1:5; Mosiah 18:23). Thus, the focus and/or purpose of any document or collection of texts plays a major role in what is included and what is excluded.

23. The phrase "the Lord" is the English substitution for the divine name *yhwh*, which in Hebrew is thought to have been pronounced "Yahweh," and which is sometimes written YHWH. "Jehovah" is a hybrid form of the consonants *yhwh* and the vowels of the Hebrew word translated "lord." For the purposes of this chapter, the term has been capitalized, as it appears in the KJV, to remind readers that it represents the divine name Yahweh/Jehovah. For a fuller discussion of these matters, see, for example, Dana M. Pike, "The Name and Titles of God in the Old Testament," *Religious Educator* 11, no. 1 (2010): 17–31, especially 19–21.
24. This notion is not so odd, given the received canon of the Bible. For example, see the comments of Dressler, "Sabbath in the Old Testament," 16, 22, 27–28, 37n39.
25. See, in particular, Exodus 19:9; 20:18–22; Deuteronomy 4:10, 12–13, 33, 36; 5:4, 22–25; and Hebrews 12:19.
26. Significantly, Doctrine and Covenants 59 introduces the reaffirmation to observe "the Lord's day" (v. 12), also called "my holy day" (v. 9), with "a commandment" to love God, love one's neighbors, and to "not steal, neither commit adultery, nor kill nor do anything like unto it" (vv. 5–6). This is a powerful way of tying the sabbath concept back to the Ten Commandments, first articulated in scripture as we have it in Exodus 20.
27. See, for example, the comments of Sarna, *Exodus*, 13, 112. In this light, consider the promise Latter-day Saints renew whenever participating in the weekly sacrament ordinance, to "always remember" Jesus (Doctrine and Covenants 20:77, 79).
28. See similarly in Leviticus 20:7, 26; 1 Peter 1:15–16; and Doctrine and Covenants 59:9.
29. On *gēr*, see, for example, *HALOT*, s.v. "*gēr*"; and David Jobling, "Sojourner," *NIDB*, 5:314–16. On animals resting on the Sabbath, see Bernard White, "The Sabbath: A Surprising Boon for Animals," *Academia Letters*, Article 175 (January 2021), 1–5; and Jeffrey H. Tigay, *Deuteronomy*, JPS Torah Commentary (Philadelphia: Jewish Publication Society, 1996), 69, 357n93.
30. White, "Sabbath: A Surprising Boon," 5.
31. Although the KJV translates the Hebrew word *ʾôt* in Genesis 17:11 as "token" (as also, for example, in Genesis 9:12, 13, 17 [rainbow], and Exodus 12:13 [Passover lamb]), *ʾôt* is the standard Hebrew word for "sign." It is the word the KJV translates as "sign" in Exodus 31:13 and dozens of times elsewhere in the Old Testament. So, as far as the Hebrew text is concerned, there is no distinction made between "token" and "sign" in these various promise passages. In fact, every time the word "token(s)" occurs in the KJV Old Testament (not counting the three italicized instances that were added by the translators), it is the KJV rendition of *ʾôt* in the Hebrew Bible.

32. See the previous footnote. For further discussion of signs in the Old Testament, see, for example, Patricia K. Tull, "Signs in the OT," *NIDB*, 5:254.
33. John H. Walton, Victor H. Matthews and Mark W. Chavalas, eds., *The IVP Bible Background Commentary: Old Testament* (Downers Grove, IL: IVP Academic, 2000), 114.
34. For passages that proscribe capital punishment for the violation of various religious and societal laws given to Israelites through Moses, see, for example, Roy E. Gane, *Old Testament Law for Christians: Original Context and Enduring Application* (Grand Rapids, MI: Baker Academic, 2017), 326–32.
35. For further discussion of this passage and of Moses's questions (Was stick gathering work? How should the man be put to death? Was the Sabbath law applicable only in the land of Israel or everywhere?), see, for example, Jacob Milgrom, *Numbers*, JPS Torah Commentary (Philadelphia: Jewish Publication Society, 1990), 126, and especially 408–410; Timothy R. Ashley, *The Book of Numbers*, New International Commentary on the Old Testament (Grand Rapids, MI: Eerdmans, 1993), 290–92; and Thomas B. Dozeman, "The Book of Numbers," in *New Interpreter's Bible*, 2:128.
36. In this stick-gathering incident in Numbers 15:32–36, this unnamed man became a life-and-death object lesson to the Israelites of the realities of covenanting with a holy being. It seems *to me* that the scriptures report such "object lessons" early in most, if not all, gospel dispensations. See, for example, the consequence received by Ananias and Sapphira in Acts 5, early in the New Testament Christian dispensation. Such people can presumably repent in the spirit world, even though their mortal life was cut short through their disobedience.
37. Many scholars would agree with this statement from Ronald E. Clements: "That it was ever customary to enforce it [that is, the Sabbath-day commandment to cease work] by imposing capital punishment (cf. Num 15:32–36) appears very unlikely." "The Book of Deuteronomy," in *New Interpreter's Bible*, 2:332. The passage at the end of Exodus 31:14, "every one that defileth it shall surely be put to death: for whosoever doeth any work therein, that soul shall be cut off from among his people," seems to diminish the severity of the consequence for profaning the Sabbath, but then the death penalty is repeated in the next verse. A similar consequence is stated in Numbers 15:31, and elsewhere in the Old Testament, for intentional sins. See, for example, Milgrom, *Numbers*, 125, 405–8; and Gerhard F. Hasel, "*kārat*," in *TDOT*, 7:339–52, especially 345–49.
38. See similarly, for example, Ganes, *Old Testament Law for Christians*, 326, who writes: "Zero tolerance for breaking these commandments [including the sabbath] accords with the fact that they constituted stipulations of the covenant between YHWH and Israel, which had to be preserved for the well-being of all Israelites."
39. For examples of instances in the Old Testament in which disrespecting the holiness of the Ark of the Covenant had serious consequences, see 1 Samuel 6:19–20; 2 Samuel 6:6–11.
40. Some commentators suggest that the literary location of these two Sabbath reminders— Exodus 31:13–17 at the end of the "how-to" revelation about building the tabernacle and Exodus 35:1–3 at the beginning of the report about the construction of the tabernacle (with the golden-calf and covenant-

renewal incidents in between; see Exodus 32–34)—further emphasizes that the seventh day would be a day of ceasing and rest even during the construction of the tabernacle. This further underscores the nature of the Sabbath day and the importance of keeping it holy. See, for example, Adele Berlin and Marc Zvi Brettler, *The Jewish Study Bible*, 2nd ed. (New York: Oxford, 2014), 173.

41. It is worth noting that Leviticus 16 introduces the most solemn and sacred annual holy day in the Israelite calendar: *yom kippur*, the Day of Atonement. In addition to fasting and prayer by the Israelites, the Aaronic High Priest led various ceremonial activities, which were intended to ritually remove the accumulated uncleanliness from the people and everything associated with the tabernacle (see v. 16). Reminiscent of the Sabbath day instructions, on *yom kippur* the Israelites were to "do no work at all, whether it be one of your own country, or a stranger [*gēr*] that sojourneth among you. . . . It shall be a sabbath of rest [*šabbat šabbātôn*] unto you, and ye shall afflict your souls" (vv. 29, 31). Thus it is clear that this annual holy day and the weekly Sabbath day shared important aspects of sacred time.

42. Just as Israelites were to work six days then cease on the seventh, so did laws prescribe that they work their agricultural lands for six years and then let them lie fallow during the seventh (see Exodus 23:10–11). Additionally, Exodus 21:2–6 and Deuteronomy 15:12–18 stipulate that Israelite debt slaves were to be released after six years and their debts were to be forgiven at that time, and Deuteronomy 15:1–11 specifies that Israelites should be released from their debts every seventh year. Thus the principle of seventh-year rest also provided rest from poverty and societal injustice. For a discussion of all aspects of the sabbatical year, see, for example, Michael LeFebvre, *The Liturgy of Creation: Understanding Calendars in Old Testament Context* (Downers Grove, IL: InterVarsity, 2019), 30–32; and Mark W. Hamilton, "Sabbatical Year," in *NIDB*, 5:11–13. Finally, Leviticus 25:8–18 indicates that after seven cycles of Sabbath years (7×7), the fiftieth year should be celebrated as a Jubilee, in which no agricultural activity was to take place, debt slaves were to be released, and family land lost due to debts was to be returned (compare Leviticus 25:39–46; Isaiah 61:1). For comments on the jubilee year, see for example, LeFebvre, *Liturgy of Creation*, 33–36; and Sharon H. Ringe, "Jubilee, Year of," in *NIDB*, 3:418–19. Although the various Sabbath-year prescriptions are not completely in harmony with each other, and there are theories about their development in relation to each other, it is sufficient here to mention these practices.

43. See *HALOT*, s.v. "*š-m-r*." The Hebrew verb *š-m-r* does not occur in Exodus 20:8, despite the KJV rendition "to keep it holy."

44. Note also that Deuteronomy 5:14 expands on the general mention of "cattle" (*bĕhēmāh*; NRSV and ESV: "livestock") in Exodus 20:10, stating, "thine ox, nor thine ass, nor any of thy cattle [*bĕhēmāh*]." This functions as a more explicit reminder that all animals belonging to Israelites were to cease working on the Sabbath day.

45. Tigay notes that this command to the Israelites to remember they had previously been slaves in Egypt is additionally found in Deuteronomy 15:15; 16:12; and 24:18, 22. *Deuteronomy*, 69.

46. Readers who are less familiar with the Old Testament may find it helpful to consult a general resource such as Richard Neitzel Holzapfel, Dana M. Pike, and David Rolph Seely, *Jehovah and the World of the Old Testament* (Salt Lake City: Deseret Book, 2009).
47. See again the comment in note 22 about the paucity of the word "sabbath" in the Book of Mormon.
48. Joshua, Judges, to a lesser extent 1 and 2 Samuel, and 1 and 2 Kings all exhibit a clear connection with the language and perspectives of Deuteronomy and are often referred to collectively as the Deuteronomistic History.
49. Elsewhere in 2 Kings the Sabbath is mentioned in 11:1–20 and 16:17–18.
50. The term "preexilic" refers to Israelite history before the Babylonian conquest of Judah and Jerusalem in the early 500s BC, while the term "postexilic" refers to the time period beginning with the Persian allowance of Israelites to return to the land of Israel, beginning about 538 BC.
51. The "people of the land" in this passage may have been non-Israelites. See, for example, F. Charles Fensham, *The Books of Ezra and Nehemiah: New International Commentary on the Old Testament* (Grand Rapids, MI: Eerdmans, 1982), 239–40.
52. For more on Chronicles and its relationship to other biblical priestly literature, see, for example, Jaeyoung Jeon and Louis C. Jonker, eds., *Chronicles and the Priestly Literature of the Hebrew Bible* (Boston: De Gruyter, 2021).
53. See also Hosea 2:11 (2:13 in Heb.).
54. For centuries now, scholars have debated when various portions of the book of Isaiah were initially written. The historical Isaiah prophesied primarily during the time of kings Ahaz and Hezekiah, who reigned in Jerusalem from ca. 735–687 BC, and traditionally all 66 chapters of the book of Isaiah have been attributed to him. However, for multiple reasons chapters 40–55 appear to most scholars to have been written in the sixth century BC. These are attributed to an anonymous "Second Isaiah," and some posit that a different anonymous "Third Isaiah" wrote chapters 56–66. Thus, it is possible, depending on one's views, that some of the teachings of "Isaiah" about the Sabbath are from more than one person and from more than one century. This chapter deals with Sabbath passages as found in the canonical book of Isaiah without further specification. For examples of how some Latter-day Saints have recently dealt with this issue, see Sears, "Deutero-Isaiah in the Book of Mormon: Latter-day Saint Approaches," in *They Shall Grow Together: The Bible in the Book of Mormon*, ed. Charles Swift and Nicholas J. Frederick (Provo, UT: Religious Studies Center, Brigham Young University; Salt Lake City: Deseret Book, 2022), 365–91; and Kent P. Jackson, "Isaiah in the Book of Mormon," in *A Reason for Faith: Navigating LDS Doctrine and Church History*, ed. Laura Harris Hales (Provo, UT: Religious Studies Center, Brigham Young University; Salt Lake City: Deseret Book, 2016), 69–78; see also the additional citations these two authors provide.
55. Although Jeremiah was of priestly lineage, the book of Jeremiah is strongly Deuteronomistic in language and focus.
56. There is also one occurrence of this phrase in Exodus 31, three total in Leviticus 19 and 26, and one in Isaiah 56. Ezekiel's priestly orientation likely accounts, at least in part, for the higher number of occurrences of this phrase in the book that

bears his name, given the occurrences in Exodus and Leviticus. In the Hebrew Bible, "my sabbaths" is written *šabbĕtōtay* and *šabbĕtôtay*. Some scholars have asserted that the plural form, "sabbaths," came to designate not just the ongoing observation of the weekly Sabbath, but also the other holy days on which work was to cease, such as in the aforementioned case of *yom kippur*. On this plausible claim, see, for example, Daniel I. Block, *Ezekiel 1–24: New International Commentary on the Old Testament* (Grand Rapids, MI: Eerdmans, 1997), 632, and note 95.

57. Block, *Ezekiel 1–24*, 726.
58. Clements, "Book of Deuteronomy," 332.
59. Also, Ezekiel 40–48 include prophecies concerning the building of a (still future) temple and the return of Jehovah's glory to it. Chapters 44–46 focus largely on priests and Levites, their temple service, the role of a future "prince," and the celebration of holy days and their attendant sacrifices, including Sabbath-day observance (see 44:24; 45:17; 46:1–4, 12). As with the prophetic texts in Isaiah 56 and 66, these passages in Ezekiel claim that the future age will not be complete without Sabbath-day worship that is acceptable to Jehovah.
60. As illustrations, the seven-day marriage festival of Samson (see Judges 14:10–17) and the week- or two-week-long festival celebrating Solomon's dedication of the Jerusalem temple (see 1 Kings 8:65–66) both must have included Sabbath days, but nothing is mentioned about the Sabbath in these contexts. Note that there is a challenge with the Hebrew text for 1 Kings 8:65–66, since it says the feasting was fourteen days (v. 65), but that Solomon sent everyone home on the eighth day (v. 66). Modern translations attempt to rectify this situation differently, often using the Septuagint, which states the feast was seven days, not fourteen.
61. Russell M. Nelson had this to say: "I learned from the scriptures that my conduct and my attitude on the Sabbath constituted a sign between me and my Heavenly Father. With that understanding, I no longer needed lists of dos and don'ts. When I had to make a decision whether or not an activity was appropriate for the Sabbath, I simply asked myself, 'What sign do I want to give to God?' That question made my choices about the Sabbath day crystal clear." "The Sabbath is a Delight," *Ensign*, May 2015, 130. In a similar vein, see Dallin H. Oaks, "Gospel Teaching," *Ensign*, November 1999, 79.
62. Similar lists of biblical passages are cited in, for example, Sarna, *Exodus*, 112; and Tigay, *Deuteronomy*, 68, 357n91.
63. See especially the tractate "Shabbath" in the Jewish Mishnah for an illustration of the increasing specification of "work" in later time periods. In addition, see the chapter by Avram Shannon in this volume. Note, for example, that Exodus 16:29 states, "let no man go out of his place on the seventh day." Given in conjunction with the instructions about manna gathering in the wilderness, this verse, quoted above, later became the basis for the idea that one should only walk or travel a certain distance on the Sabbath, which was eventually referred to as a "sabbath day's journey" (Acts 1:12). It is not likely that this impacted Sabbath observance in the land of Israel during Old Testament times, but our records are silent on the matter.
64. Dressler, "Sabbath in the Old Testament," 33.

65. For an even larger Sabbath-day offering by "the prince" in the future Jerusalem temple, see Ezekiel 46:4–5.
66. See similarly the comments of Tigay, *Deuteronomy*, 68.
67. Additionally, at least at one point in time, the changing of the temple guards occurred on the Sabbath day (2 Kings 11:5–9).
68. See, for example, Meyers, "Feast Days and Foodways," 234–35.
69. For this view, see also Baruch A. Levine, *Leviticus*, JPS Torah Commentary (Philadelphia: Jewish Publication Society, 1989), 155.
70. See, for example, David A. Bednar, "Exceeding Great and Precious Promises," *Ensign*, November 2017, 92.
71. H. Aldridge Gillespie, "The Blessing of Keeping the Sabbath Day Holy," *Ensign*, November 2000, 79–80. Three other examples of Sabbath-focused general conference addresses in the previous decades, most of which include multiple Old Testament citations, help illustrate this pattern: Earl C. Tingey, "The Sabbath Day and Sunday Shopping," *Ensign*, May 1996, 10; John H. Groberg, "The Power of Keeping the Sabbath Day Holy," *Ensign*, November 1984, 79; and Sterling W. Sill, "Remember the Sabbath," in Conference Report, October 1969, 16–18.
72. L. Tom Perry, "The Sabbath and the Sacrament," *Ensign*, May 2011, 6–9. His main focus was on Jesus and several New Testament passages. On page 9 he states, "Sometimes we think of resting from our labors as merely letting the hay baler stand idle in the field or putting a Closed sign on the business door. Yet in today's world, labor includes the every-day work of our lives. This could mean business activities we may accomplish from home, athletic competitions, and other pursuits that take us away from Sabbath day worship and the opportunity to minister to others."
73. Nelson, "Sabbath Is a Delight," 129–132.
74. Kimball, "Sabbath—A Delight," 2–5. In this message, President Kimball quotes Exodus 20:3, 8–11; Leviticus 26:2–6; and Isaiah 58:13–14, along with other Sabbath passages, including Doctrine and Covenants 59.
75. A copy of this letter is in the author's possession. The First Presidency at the time was Ezra Taft Benson, Gordon B. Hinckley, and Thomas S. Monson.
76. See https://www.churchofjesuschrist.org/church/news/church-invites-members-to-share-how-they-honor-hisday.
77. It would be easy to conclude that all this prophetic emphasis on the Sabbath indicates that many latter-day covenant Israelites, like their ancient counterparts, struggle with a full and true observance of this holy day.
78. The English word "saint" derives from the Latin *sanctus*, which means holy. So, a true Latter-day "Saint" is a person striving to become holy through the power of Christ's redeeming sacrifice and the influence of the Holy Spirit, recognizing that it is not possible to obtain this status without their assistance nor fully in this mortal life.
79. Susannah Heschel, "Introduction," in Abraham Heschel, *Sabbath*, xiii.
80. Fretheim, "Book of Genesis," 348.
81. Tigay, *Deuteronomy*, 68.
82. Although Leviticus 26:2–13 is sometimes used to teach that Sabbath observance will bring a multitude of blessings, the Sabbath command in verse 2 is actually

separated from the promise of blessings that begins in verse 3 with this conditional statement, "If ye walk in my statutes, and keep my commandments, and do them; Then . . . " (the curses for disobedience begin in verse 14). Note the plural forms of "commandments" and "statutes," followed by "them." So, while honoring the Sabbath is certainly one of Jehovah's commandments and will bring many blessings, this whole passage is not explicitly about Sabbath-specific blessings but rather about the promise of a variety of blessings for keeping all the Lord's commands (plural).

83. See, for example, "Line upon Line: Isaiah 58:13–14," *New Era,* February 2016, 40.
84. The quoted phrases are from the 1992 First Presidency letter, "Sabbath Day Observance," referenced above.
85. Dressler, "Sabbath in the Old Testament," 29.
86. Joseph L. Townsend, "The Day Dawn is Breaking," *Hymns* (Salt Lake City: The Church of Jesus Christ of Latter-day Saints, 1985), no. 52; see also Doctrine and Covenants 77:7, 12; 29:11.

Chapter Three

Keeping the Sabbath Relevant in Some Late Second Temple Jewish Texts

Gaye Strathearn

How do people live a commandment that was given over a thousand years before their time? This is a question with which many religious people might struggle today. How do those commandments continue to have relevance over time, especially when political, social, cultural, and religious climates are in a state of constant flux? Although divine principles are eternal, their specific application in people's lives sometimes changes over time. For example, the principle of sacrifice is eternal, but the way sacrifice is practiced has changed. Beginning with Adam and continuing up until the destruction of Herod's temple in AD 70, animal sacrifices were performed. In modern times, however, members of The Church of Jesus Christ of Latter-day Saints generally focus their performance of sacrifices through offering a "broken heart and a contrite spirit" (3 Nephi 9:19–20; Doctrine and Covenant 59:8)[1] and through the paying of tithes (Doctrine and Covenants 64:23). Similarly, the Lord taught Moses that the Sabbath is "a perpetual covenant. . . . A sign between me and the children of Israel for ever" (Exodus 31:16–17). Just as modern saints today endeavor to find ways to reemphasize the Sabbath day in their communal and family lives, so too did Jews living in the late Second Temple period (200 BC–AD 70).[2]

The late Second Temple period was a time when Jews were faced with colliding political, religious, and cultural forces that pressed their communities to reexamine the Sabbath in light of their circumstances. Their intent was not only to "remember" the Sabbath day (Exodus 20:8), but also to "keep" (Hebrew *šāmôr*) it (Deuteronomy 5:12). *Šāmôr* is the same root word used to describe a guard or a watchman and emphasizes the Israelites' responsibility to actively guard, preserve, and protect the Sabbath and its holiness.[3] They wanted to make sure that it didn't become lost to the modernizing influences of the Greek and Roman worlds in which they lived. This was also a time that coincided with the Sabbath controversies recorded in the New Testament, which will be covered in greater detail in other chapters in this volume. Here it is sufficient to note that those controversies were part of this ongoing discussion on how to keep and protect the Sabbath day.

We are fortunate to have a variety of contemporary sources that document Sabbath observance in this period. These sources, such as the writings of Philo, a Jewish-Hellenistic philosopher (ca. 20 BC–ca. AD 50), and Josephus, a Jewish historian (AD 37–ca. AD 100), as well as Jewish texts such as Jubilees (mid second century BC),[4] 1 and 2 Maccabees (second century BC), the Damascus Document (ca. 175 BC–AD 70), and others[5] have survived to give modern readers an important lens through which to view and interpret some facets of this discussion.

At the outset, it is important to note that these texts do not manifest any normative, unified Sabbath interpretation or praxis during this time period. Rather, what we find is different communities in different geographical areas engaging with the question of Sabbath observance and often coming up with different answers. Nevertheless, the Sabbath had clearly become an important marker that distinguished the Jewish community in an increasingly pluralistic society. John M. G. Barclay's observation about Jews in the diaspora is probably also true for Jews living under foreign rule in the Holy Land: "Of all the festivals celebrated by Diaspora Jews, the Sabbath was, in social terms, by far the most important, since its observance was so regular, so noticeable and so socially problematic, affecting . . . not only personal but also financial, legal and political relationships."[6] As a result, ongoing communal discussions developed over how to interpret and apply the Sabbath command in the various religious and political environments in which they lived. It appears that these discussions enabled the communities to find meaning in the Sabbath command—something that could also provide a helpful model for modern Sabbath observers as they likewise engage in similar tensions and seek to protect, guard, and preserve the Sabbath day in the present world. The communities during this period engaged the Sabbath in three such ways:

1. They reemphasized the Sabbath as a central focus of their covenantal lives.
2. The Sabbath became a marker of their religious identity at a time when many outsiders mocked them and their Sabbath observance.
3. They sought for meaningful ways to apply the Sabbath-day commandment in their family and communal lives since, as noted in the previous chapter, outside of the Sabbath sacrifices at the temple, the Hebrew Bible gave very little practical direction for how the non-priestly Israelites should act on the Sabbath.

To help modern readers better appreciate and understand the Jews' efforts to keep the Sabbath day relevant, this chapter will first examine the political and religious climate the Jews found themselves in during the late Second Temple period. This was very different from the environment in which the Israelites first received the Sabbath commandment, and it impacted Jewish religious life in powerful ways. With that background in place, we will then be prepared to examine some of the Jewish texts that provide evidence of Jews grappling with the Sabbath commandment in *their* world. It is hoped that this discussion will help modern readers in three ways: First, to help them develop a better understanding of some of the circumstances that prompted the variety of interpretations that Jewish groups applied to the Sabbath. Second, to provide a background for, and a more nuanced understanding of, the Sabbath controversies in the New Testament gospels that will be discussed in subsequent chapters. Lastly, to offer some models for ways that Saints today might navigate similar struggles in our modern world.

Living the Sabbath in the Late Second Temple Period

During the time that the temple stood and Israel controlled their own government and religion, the Sabbath directives in the Hebrew Bible were apparently sufficient.[7] But as Jews found themselves living in increasingly pluralistic societies, either because of foreign rule, exile, or the fact that they lived in satellite communities spread throughout the eastern Mediterranean, the rise in religious tension was inevitable. On the one hand, "religious tradition and observance assumed an ever greater role in maintaining distinctive identity"[8] and covenantal loyalty; but on the other hand, some of that religious tradition and observance had to be adapted to enable the community to survive. In other words, they had to find ways to thrive in the world they lived in without letting their religious identity become absorbed by it.[9] Observing the Sabbath seems to have straddled both ends of this continuum.

For Jews who focused on covenant loyalty in the late Second Temple period, the Sabbath became one of the important markers in a process that scholar Tom Holmén calls "covenant path searching." By this phrase he means that Jews were actively seeking for "concrete meaning of the divine covenant in a human life." It was about looking for ways to "learn how to be loyal to the covenant."[10] Although many Jewish groups of the time participated in covenant path searching, not everyone did it in the same way with the same focus, which led to some variety in Sabbath interpretations.

Applying the Sabbath Commandment to Rest

Throughout the late Second Temple period, during the political reign of the Greek Seleucids and the Romans, the impact of Exodus 31's designation of the Sabbath day as a sign of the perpetual covenant was at the fore politically as well as religiously. Josephus viewed profaning the Sabbath as an example of "covenant disloyalty,"[11] and both those inside and outside of the Jewish community recognized the Sabbath as one of the central identifying markers of Judaism.[12] For example, Josephus claims that a Greek historian and geographer named Agatharchides wrote about Jewish Sabbath practice in this way: "There are a people called Jews, who dwell in a city the strongest of all other cities, which the inhabitants call Jerusalem, and are accustomed to rest on every seventh day; on which times they make no use of arms, nor meddle with husbandry, nor take care of any affairs of life, but spread out their hands in their holy places, and pray until evening."[13] Josephus further states, perhaps with some exaggeration, that "there is not any city of the Grecians, nor any of the barbarians, nor any nation whatsoever, whither our custom of resting on the seventh day hath not come."[14] By the Roman period, Sabbath-day rest was one of the few things that Roman writers knew about Jewish belief,[15] and many of those writers used it to condemn the Jews for "idleness." The Stoic philosopher Seneca "found fault with the sacred things of the Jews, and especially the Sabbaths, affirming that they act uselessly in keeping those seventh days, whereby they lose through idleness about the seventh part of their life."[16]

While it is true that some Roman political leaders made concessions for Jewish Sabbath observance,[17] at times they viewed it as a stumbling block against the peace and stability of their empires. As a result, some Romans attacked Jews during the Sabbath. According to the author of 1 and 2 Maccabees, the Seleucid ruler Antiochus Epiphanes IV declared it unlawful "for a man to keep sabbath days or ancient feasts, or to profess himself at all to be a Jew" (2 Maccabees 6:6).[18] Apparently some Jews welcomed the new Hellenistic way of life that Antiochus IV promoted (see 1 Maccabees 1:11–15) and "consented to his religion, and sacrificed unto idols, and profaned the sabbath" (1 Maccabees 1:43); however, 2 Maccabees glorifies those who instead refused to capitulate and conform. For example, it describes a group who refused to accept Antiochus's ban and continued to meet secretly in a cave on the Sabbath. When they were discovered, they refused to defend themselves from the ensuing attack because of "their respect for the most holy day" and, as a result, were burned to death (2 Maccabees 6:11). Additionally, Jutta Leonhardt explains that, according to Philo, a Roman governor "attempted to destroy Judaism by interfering with its most prominent customs, beginning with the Sabbath rest from work."[19]

Such political antagonism combined with the increasing pressure of cultural and religious assimilation may have been behind the flurry of Jewish texts in the late Second Temple period that sought to promote and understand the meaning of the Sabbath commandment.[20] The author of Jubilees reemphasizes the Deuteronomic command to not only "remember" but also "guard" the Sabbath: "Command the children of Israel, and let them *guard* this day so that they might sanctify it and not do any work therein, and not defile it because it is more holy than any day" (Jubilees 2:26; italics added).

The question, though, was *how* the Jews were to maintain the Sabbath in their pluralistic society. Not only were there pressures from Gentile neighbors and overlords, but there was also a wide range of Sabbath interpretations within the Jewish community. Philo, for one, was keenly aware of this wide spectrum. He describes one group, whom he characterizes as living on the theological periphery of the community, "as if they were mere souls unconnected with the body,"[21] who viewed the "written laws as symbols" and therefore saw no value in living the Sabbath laws.[22] He also knew of those who used the Sabbath rest as license for "devoting their leisure . . . to sports, or exhibitions of actors and dancers, . . . run[ning] madly after theatrical amusements."[23] Although Philo acknowledged the importance of Sabbath symbols, he argued to defend the Sabbath laws: "It does not follow that on that account we may abrogate the laws which are established respecting [the Sabbath]."[24] The difficulty was, however, that not everyone agreed on what those laws were.

As we have seen in the previous chapter, the Hebrew Bible, which gives only limited guidance on how to live the Sabbath, occasionally referred to activities associated with the temple but primarily emphasized that it was a day of rest and focused on a short list of prohibitions of certain types of work. It is clear that by the late Second Temple period, this biblical list of prohibitions was inadequate for the community's needs. Three texts, Philo's *On the Migration of Abraham* 91; Jubilees 2:25–33; 50:8–13; and the Damascus Document (CD X, 14–XII, 6; 4Q*D*[e] 10 V, 1–21),[25] are evidence of their need for further clarification. Each text sought to define the work prohibited on the Sabbath by developing lists that both expanded and reinterpreted the biblical proscriptions. Each of these lists provide important windows into the variety of ways the respective authors and their communities were interpreting the Sabbath commandment. Both Jubilees and the Damascus Document seem to be written by those living within the holy land, whereas Philo represents those living in the diaspora.[26] Of the three lists, the one found in the Damascus Document is the most expansive.

In these lists, only two of the biblical prohibitions are specifically mentioned: plowing and carrying burdens. Both Philo[27] and Jubilees include the biblical prohibition against plowing a field (Jubilees 50:12), but neither list makes any mention of harvesting. The Damascus Document, however, uses a more generic prohibition of "walking in a field to do work" (CD X, 20).[28] The type of work is not specified, but could reasonably include both plowing and harvesting. The act of walking should also be recognized as part of the prohibition, since it is immediately followed by the injunction against walking more than one thousand cubits (approximately 0.3 miles) outside of the city on the Sabbath (CD X, 21; see also 4Q264a 1 I, 1).

Philo prohibits the carrying of all burdens, which has broader ramifications than Jeremiah's injunction against carrying burdens in or out of the city or the home. In their lists of prohibitions, Jubilees and the Damascus Document omit Jeremiah's ban on carrying in and out of the city and focus instead on carrying things in or out of a house or carrying them from house to house, or even to their tents (Jubilees 2:29–30; 50:8;

CD XI, 7–9; 4Q265 2 I, 4–5). Thus the emphasis on commercial concerns has been omitted in favor of domestic ones. The Damascus Document extends the prohibited actions even further than those found in Jubilees, expanding the prohibition to include a wet nurse lifting a baby to go out or come into the house, helping an animal give birth, and helping an animal that has fallen into a well or a pit (CD XI, 7–14; 4Q*D*[e] 10 V, 16–18; 4Q265 2 I, 5).[29] We know that not all Jews agreed with the last of these injunctions because it was not included in the Jubilees list of prohibitions, and in Luke 14:1–6, Jesus assumes—with the apparent agreement of the Pharisees—that rescuing an animal in a well is acceptable on the Sabbath. If, however, a person rather than an animal fell into water on the Sabbath, it was possible for a rescuer to use his own garment to lift the person up, but "no one should carry a vessel" (4Q265 2 I, 6–8).

In addition, Jubilees and the Damascus Document both reinterpret the biblical directive about gathering manna. A reinterpretation was clearly needed because by the late Second Temple period, no Israelite or Jew had eaten manna for over a thousand years—since the time they had entered the promised land (Joshua 5:12). The issue was further complicated by the question of whether the directive to prepare manna before the Sabbath was specific to the manna and thus not applicable after entering Canaan, or whether it should be metaphorically applied to all food. Even more complicating is the fact that manna was not the only food that the Israelites consumed while in the wilderness—they also ate quail. But the biblical text says nothing about them hunting and preparing quail on the Sabbath (Exodus 16:13; Numbers 11:31–32; Psalm 105:40).

Nevertheless, both Jubilees and the Damascus Document interpret the directive about manna to include all food. They both prohibit eating anything on the Sabbath that has not been prepared the previous day (Jubilees 2:29; 50:9; CD X, 22). They also expand the directive to include specific directions about drinking water, and Jubilees goes even further and forbids the act of drawing water on the Sabbath (2:29). Like the biblical manna instructions, it only permits drinking water that was drawn the previous day (Jubilees 50.8; see also 4Q251 1). The Damascus Document prohibits drinking any water that has come from outside the camp (probably in accordance with their restriction on walking more than a thousand cubits) or water that was collected in a vessel (CD X, 23–XI, 2). If a person was bathing, however, then he was permitted to "drink where he stands" (CD XI, 1).

Both Jubilees and Philo also include the Exodus 35 ban on kindling fires (vv. 2–3). The content of the Exodus passage is interesting. It paraphrases and combines the Exodus 20:9–10 declaration that the seventh day is a day of rest with the Exodus 31:14 penalty of death for those who defile it by doing any kind of work. Then it follows with just one example of the type of defiling work: "Ye shall kindle no fire throughout your habitations upon the sabbath day" (35:3). The biblical text gives no indication why kindling fire was singled out as the sole example of work. Clearly this prohibition did not apply to the temple sacrifices performed on the Sabbath because of the command that the fire on the altar "shall ever be burning upon the altar; it shall never go out" (Leviticus 6:12–13). Jubilees also includes this biblical directive against lighting a fire in its list of prohibitions but does not elaborate on it any further (50:12). Nevertheless, it does not seem to have the same priority afforded to it in Exodus 35 because, rather than being singled out, it is simply included along with several other prohibitions.

Philo also includes the lighting of fire in his list,[30] but unlike either Exodus 35 or the Jubilees list, he attempts to explain *why* lighting a fire is prohibited. He argues that lighting a fire is a precursor to breaking many of the other Sabbath prohibitions:

> Why [the prohibition against lighting fires]? Because, not only mere handicraft trades, but also nearly all other acts and businesses, and especially all such as have reference to any providing or of seeking for the means of life, are either carried on by means of first themselves, or, at all events, not without those instruments which are made by fire. On which account Moses, in many places, forbids any one to handle a fire on the sabbath day, inasmuch as that is the most primary and efficient source of things and the most ancient and important work; and if that is reduced to a state of tranquility, he thought that it would be probable that all particular works would be at a stand-still likewise.[31]

Both Jubilees and the Damascus Document lists forbid three actions that are not included in the biblical prohibitions. The first is an injunction against striking an animal, which probably refers to the goading of work animals and is a reminder that even animals were to rest on the Sabbath (see Exodus 20:10; Jubilees 50:12; CD XI, 6).[32] The second is a prohibition against fasting on the Sabbath (see Jubilees 50:13, CD XI, 4–5), which may have been viewed as a practice contrary to Isaiah's description of the Sabbath as "a delight" (Isaiah 58:13). The third is a sanction against speaking of secular matters. Jubilees specifically bans talking on the Sabbath about going on a journey to buy or sell (50:8). The Damascus Document prohibits talking about "riches or gain," discussing "matters of work or of the task to be carried out on the following day" (CD X, 18; see also 4Q*D*ᵉ 10 V, 4; 4Q264a I, 5–8), and even prohibits anyone from saying "a useless or stupid word" (X, 17–21; see also 4Q*D*ᵉ 10 V, 3). These prohibitions may have been formulated to ensure that not just deeds but also conversations were focused on matters of holiness.[33]

While there are some commonalities in these intertestamental sources, they each have prohibitions that are unique to their individual lists. Philo includes bringing accusations, conducting suits at law, demanding a restoration of a deposit, or exacting the repayment of a debt. He also includes "any other of the things which are usually permitted at times which are not days of festival."[34] Jubilees includes proscriptions on lying with a spouse (50:8); riding on an animal; traveling on the sea in a boat; killing anything, including cattle, birds, or fish (50:12); and making war (15:13). The Damascus Document forbids lending anything to another person, sending a foreigner to perform a person's wishes (probably prohibited Sabbath activities), wearing clothing that has not been properly laundered with water and incense, raising a hand to strike with a fist, wearing perfumes, and staying in a place close to a Gentile (CD X, 18; XI, 2, 3–4, 9–10, 14–15).[35]

All of the variations in these three lists of Sabbath prohibitions are evidence of the fluid nature of interpreting and applying the Sabbath commandment during this period. While these expansions of the biblical injunctions may seem extreme to modern readers, it is important to remember that these laws reflect each community's ongoing engagement in trying to keep the Sabbath commandment relevant in their lives. Modern readers are reminded that during the late Second Temple period, Jews saw the Sabbath day not as an outdated institution to be ignored and relegated to the distant past but as something that was living and vibrant and important across both time and space.[36]

These differing lists are also important tangible evidence for the beginnings of the halakic debate within Judaism. In this debate over how to apply the Sabbath commandment, we find the heart of the Sabbath controversies detailed in the New Testament Gospels. The primary intent of the Jews of this period was not to create complicated legal lists but rather to understand how to apply the principle of the Sabbath. The various lists explore the implications of practical questions, such as "how does the Sabbath command apply to the specific situations that our community encounters?" One example of such a situation—going to war on the Sabbath—shows the fluidity of Sabbath interpretations and how one community came to their interpretation. Given the political climate in Judea, this was not simply a theoretical or philosophical discussion, but one that would have very real implications for the continued existence of their community.

The Hebrew scriptures are not helpful in this case because they do not address issues of war on the Sabbath. By the late Second Temple period, however, the community behind Jubilees had determined that engaging in war violated Sabbath rest and thus included it in its expanded list of prohibitions (50:13). This interpretation may explain why some of their enemies specifically attacked Jewish settlements on the Sabbath.[37] However, it is important to note that a similar prohibition is *not* included in the Damascus Document's list of Sabbath prohibitions—thus reminding us again of the variety of interpretations.[38]

But it is in the Maccabean literature where we most fully see the fluidity of another community's application of the Sabbath commandment in times of war. During the Maccabean Revolt (163–160 BC), Jewish soldiers initially refused to "profane the Sabbath day" and defend themselves when attacked (1 Maccabees 2:32–34).[39] They declared, "Let us die all in our innocency: heaven and earth shall testify for us, that ye put us to death wrongfully" (v. 37). The result of their interpretation was that one thousand men, women, and children were slaughtered when they refused to defend themselves (v. 38). These heavy losses created both a practical and theological quandary for the Maccabean leaders: "If we all do as our brethren have done, and fight not for our lives and laws against the heathen, they will now quickly root us out of the earth" (v. 40). If this pattern continued, soon no one would be left to either remember or keep the Sabbath. How would the Sabbath be a "perpetual covenant" or a "sign between [Jehovah] and the children of Israel for ever" (Exodus 31:16–17) if everyone was slaughtered? Thus the Jewish leaders rethought their position: "Whosoever shall come to make battle with us on the sabbath day, we will fight against him; neither will we die all, as our brethren that were murdered in the secret places" (1 Maccabees 2:41). Their interpretation seems to have been limited to defensive battles, because at least some continued to refrain from offensive forays on the Sabbath (see 2 Maccabees 8:24–28; 12:38).

This example is significant because it allows us to see a community who acknowledged and respected the Sabbath command grappling with its application. As Heather McKay has noted, "The Sabbath law had to be discussed by the community, and then be interpreted, or re-interpreted, to exclude fighting from classes of work forbidden on the sabbath. Such an interpretation would [then] aid the survival of those who wished to keep the Sabbath week by week, thus guaranteeing the continued observance of the Sabbath."[40]

Sabbath Worship during the Late Second Temple Period

Thus far our discussion has focused on some of the different interpretations about the prohibition of Sabbath work during the late Second Temple period. Yet stopping our discussion here would skew our view of Jewish Sabbath practice. Here we will examine the few texts that shed light on the positive activities Jews engaged in on the Sabbath.

In the Hebrew Bible the Sabbath was considered one of the holy assemblies appointed by God (see Leviticus 23:2–3) and, as we have noted, the activities of that day often focused on priestly sacrifices performed in the temple. During the late Second Temple period, however, there were different interpretations about which sacrifices should be performed on the Sabbath. Jubilees, for example, permitted all sacrifices—both the daily and the Sabbath burnt offerings (Jubilees 50:9–11)—while the Damascus Document sanctioned only the latter (CD XI, 17–18).

Yet these texts again give no indication of how those who were not priests "remembered" or "kept" the Sabbath. McKay argues that Jews did not participate in any weekly Sabbath worship until the second century AD.[41] While it is true that there is not much evidence of nontemple worship practices in the Second Temple period, McKay's assessment seems extreme. Surely the Jews who defied Antiochus IV's ban on keeping the Sabbath day and met secretly in the cave (2 Maccabees 6:11) were gathered to *do something* that warranted their deaths. Jutta Leonhardt argues that "most Second Temple Jews . . . would have been surprised by [McKay's] conclusion."[42]

The question then is, what did Jews *do* on the Sabbath day? The author of Jubilees simply states that it was a day to "eat, drink, and bless the creator of all things" (2:21), although there is no explanation of those activities, each of which could be performed in the home. But according to Philo, Jews in Rome were also "in the habit of visiting [synagogues], . . . most especially on the sacred sabbath days."[43] As we will see below, Philo and texts from the Dead Sea Scrolls indicate that in at least some communities, such Sabbath gatherings were designed for two communal activities: (1) reading and teaching from sacred scrolls, and (2) participating in communal Sabbath prayers.

In contrast to McKay's assessment of Sabbath worship, Shemaryahu Talmon has argued that "the liturgical reading from the Law . . . [goes] back to the times of Ezra and Nehemiah . . . [and is] one of the earliest components of synagogue worship."[44] A few texts from the late Second Temple period support such a practice. From Qumran, 4Q264a 1 I, 4–5 reads:

4. [a scro]ll of a book [to rea]d what is written in it on the day of [Sabbath.]
5. [ ] they [will re]ad and teach them. One should not plan [aloud]
6. [or speak] about all matters of work or about wealth or [gain]
7. [ ] on the day of Sa[bba]th. And one should not sp[eak a w]ord except to [speak words of]
8. [holiness. In accordance with the decree one shall sp]eak to praise God. Indeed, one may speak [a word] regarding eating and dri[nking rest].[45]

Although the text is fragmentary, the context clearly deals with Sabbath halakah, and the plural pronouns ("they will read and teach them") suggest the communal nature of the reading.

Philo confirms that the reading and discussing of scrolls was also an important part of Sabbath synagogue activity in both Alexandria and Rome. In his description of the Sabbath assemblies in Egypt, Philo observes that their gathering was for "reading [their] sacred volumes and explaining whatever is not quite clear."[46] Elsewhere, he also writes that Jews in Rome "were in the habit of visiting [synagogues] . . . most especially on the sacred sabbath . . . assembling for the interpretation of the law." Philo claims that these gatherings had both theological and more practical purposes. They were a time when "human and divine things [were] appreciated, and placed upon a proper footing."[47] As such, they were also a time for self-reflection: a time to evaluate activities from the previous week in the context of the law, to correct any errors, and to make efforts to guard against repeating them in the future.[48] These gatherings were also a time to "publically cultivate their national philosophy,"[49] reemphasizing that the Sabbath was a means by which Jews sought to identify and establish their boundaries in their pluralistic society.

In one of Philo's most detailed descriptions of Sabbath activity, he argues that Jewish reading and discussing of the scrolls was simply a continuation of the directions that Moses himself had given:

> What then did he [Moses] do on this sabbath day? He commanded all the people to assemble together in the same place, and sitting down with one another, to listen to the laws with order and reverence, in order that no one should be ignorant of anything that is contained in them; and, in fact, they do constantly assemble together, and they do sit down one with another, the multitude in general in silence, except when it is customary to say any words of good omen, by way of assent to what is being read. And then some priest who is present, or some one of the elders, reads the sacred laws to them, and interprets each of them separately till eventide; and then when separate they depart, having gained some skill in the sacred laws, and having made great advances towards piety.[50]

This Sabbath activity of reading from the scrolls is consistent with New Testament descriptions of Sabbath activities in the synagogue. Both Jesus and Paul participated in the Sabbath synagogue by reading and/or commenting on passages from the scrolls (see Luke 4:16–21; Acts 13:14–16).[51]

A second purpose for Sabbath gatherings was to participate in liturgical, or communal, prayers. Although we do not know when Jewish liturgical prayers began, by the late Second Temple period, the practice seems to have been sufficiently entrenched in the Sabbath activities that it was known to outsiders.[52] Liturgical prayers function differently from individual prayers. While an individual's prayers are generally intermittent and spontaneous acts meant to express awe and thanksgiving to deity, usually in response to a specific circumstance, liturgical prayers are instead fixed, standardized, and regularly repeated.[53] According to Talmon, "they do not aim at bringing about an immediate response from deity with regard to a specific situation, but rather at safeguarding the continuous, slow-flowing relationship between the worshipper and his [or her] God." He further notes, "By its standardization, its fixity, and its recurrence, institutionalized prayer serves as an expression of what is common to a congregation (or to mankind), not of what determines the individuality of man. Thus the very institutionalization of prayer reveals a communal spirit and at the same time strengthens the spirit."[54]

In examining the communal role of liturgical prayers, we see that the Dead Sea Scrolls provide examples of prayers used both by those within the community as well as by those outside of it.[55] For the Qumran community, who rejected the temple in Jerusalem, these liturgical prayers may have functioned as a substitute for sacrificial forms of worship.[56] For example, in 1QS IX, 3–5, we see that sacrificial language is explicitly applied to prayer and, as Esther Glickler Chazon argues, is the "preferred instrument for atonement and service to God":

> When there exist in Israel in accordance with these rules in order to establish the spirit of holiness in truth eternal, in order to atone for the fault of the transgression and for the guilt of sin and for approval for the earth, without the flesh of burnt offerings and without the fats of sacrifice—the offering of the lips in compliance with the decree will be like the pleasant aroma of justice and the correctness of behavior will be acceptable like a freewill offering (see also CD XI, 18–21).[57]

Here we will focus on just one of the Sabbath liturgical texts—the Songs of the Sabbath Sacrifice—with brief references to other texts.[58]

The Songs of the Sabbath Sacrifice consist of a series of texts that were found primarily in cave 4 at Qumran (4Q400–401, 403–407), but copies were also found in cave 11 (11Q17) and at Masada (Mas1k). The number of copies found in caves 4 and 11 and its apparent influence on other sectarian texts[59] suggests that this was an important text for the Qumran community, though the content does not specifically point to a Qumran origin.[60] The copy found at Masada suggests that its influence was broader than just the Qumran community.

The Songs of the Sabbath Sacrifice consist of thirteen hymns that collectively describe the heavenly temple and the angelic priests who worship in it. The liturgical nature of the texts suggest that the community recited them as an opportunity "to share in the experience of heavenly worship."[61] Each of the songs begins with a formulaic statement that calls for the angels to praise God. For example, 4Q403 1 I, 30–33 reads, "Praise [Hebrew *hllw*][62] the God of the august heights, you august ones among the divinities of knowledge. . . . The chiefs of the praises of all the gods, praise the God of magnificent praises, for in the magnificence of the praises is the glory of his kingdom."[63] Although the exact wording of these praises is not recorded, we get some sense of their focus from the following passage describing the praise offered by some of the sovereign (angelic) princes for God's blessings, justice, kingdom, glory, wonders, power, and holiness:

> *1* [Psalm of celebration on the tongue of the] third of the sovereign princes. He will celebrate the God of the exalted angels seven times, with seven words of wonderful exultations.
>
> *2* Psalm of praise, on the tongue of the fourth, to the Powerful One who is above all [the gods] with his seven wonderful powers. He will praise the God
>
> *3* of the powers seven times, with seven words of [wonderful] praise. [Ps]alm of thanksgiving on the tongue of the fifth, to the King of glory,
>
> *4* with seven acts of wonderful thanks. [Psalm] of exultation
>
> *5* on the tongue of the sixth, to the God of goodness, with seven [wonderful] exultations. He will exult in the King of goodness seven times, [with seven words] of wonderful exultation.
>
> *6* Psalm of singing on the tongue of the seventh of the [sovereign] princes, a powerful song [to the God] of holiness with se[ven wonderful songs.
>
> *7* He will have to sing to the King of holiness seven times with seven words of [wonderful son]gs. Seven
>
> *8* psalms [of his blessings.] Seven psalms of glorification o[f his justice. Seven psalms] of exaltation of his kingdom.
>
> *9* [Seven] psalms [of praise of his glory. Seven psalms of thanksgiving for his wonders.] [Seven psalms of exult]ation in his power. Seven [psalms of song] of his holiness. (4Q403 1 I, 1–9)

The praising of God in this liturgy was a time for the angels, and by extension the community, to rejoice in (Hebrew *rnn*; 4Q403 1 I, 3–7) and give thanks to their God (4Q403 1 I, 38; 4Q404 4.6; see also 4Q264a 1.7–8, 4Q504 1–VII, 4–5). This focus on praising God and giving thanks is consistent with the opening to the biblical Psalm 92, which is introduced as "a Psalm or Song for the sabbath day." Chazon has argued that the focus on praise made the Sabbath prayers distinct from those performed on other days. Their focus was on petitioning God for blessings.[64]

The Sabbath Commandment and Latter-day Saints

Recent changes in Latter-day Saint practice towards a home-centered, Church-supported curriculum place greater emphasis on the increased responsibility of both individuals and families to determine how they will choose to remember and keep the Sabbath day as a sign of their covenant loyalty.

While the specific cultural and economic circumstances that modern Saints face are different from those in the late Second Temple period, I would argue that there is still a sense of shared experience. Latter-day Saints also face the challenge to determine what constitutes work in their modern context. In some cases, biblical injunctions, such as the command against Sabbath commerce, remain relevant in the modern world—perhaps even more so than when they were first given. But in other cases, some of the biblical injunctions seem less applicable. Just as the issue of collecting manna on the Sabbath was no longer relevant for the Jewish communities that we have examined and was thus reinterpreted, so too could it be argued that the issue of gathering sticks and lighting fires is likewise much less germane in the modern world. It does, however, beg the question of what might be understood as the modern equivalents for such practices.

But "remembering," "keeping," and "guarding" the Sabbath has always been more than a list of prohibitions, a list of "thou shalt not's." I would argue that, for modern saints, there is merit in also remembering the positive ways that Jews in the late Second Temple period sought to remember God and to establish ways to praise and give thanks to him. For them it was a time when they could gather together to study from their sacred texts, sing songs of praise, and give thanks to God. These activities strengthened not only their covenantal relationship with God but also their communal relationships with each other.

For the Sabbath to remain vibrant and meaningful across time, no generation can passively live it based on another generation's interpretations of it. The Sabbath commandment has always compelled people in every dispensation to actively find ways to understand it and live it within their own circumstances.

Endnotes

* This essay appeared in a longer form and was originally published as Gaye Strathearn, "Remembering and Keeping the Sabbath Day in the Late Second Temple Period," in *Seek Ye Words of Wisdom: Studies of the Book of Mormon, Bible, and Temple in Honor of Stephen D. Ricks*, ed. Donald W. Parry, Gaye Strathearn, and Shon D. Hopkin (Orem, UT: The Interpreter Foundation; Provo, UT: Religious Studies Center, Brigham Young University, 2020), 233–64.

1. Under the law of Moses, both animal sacrifice and "a broken heart and a contrite spirit" were required by the Lord. See Dana M. Pike, "3 Nephi 9:19–20: The Offering of a Broken Heart," in *Third Nephi: An Incomparable Scripture*, ed. Andrew C. Skinner and Gaye Strathearn (Provo, UT: Neal A. Maxwell Institute for Religious Scholarship; Salt Lake City: Deseret Book, 2012), 35–56.
2. The late Second Temple period was not the first time that political and religious forces combined to refocus Jews on the importance of the Sabbath command. The fall of Jerusalem and the Exile also brought about a reemphasis on the Sabbath (see Ezekiel 20:12–13, 20–21, 24; 46:1–8; Isaiah 56:2, 4, 6; 58:13–14; Nehemiah 13:15–22).
3. *Hebrew and Aramaic Lexicon of the Old Testament* (hereafter *HALOT*), s.v. שׁמר/ *sh-m-r*.
4. Scholars are agreed that it belongs to the second century BC but are divided over more precise dates. R. H. Charles argued for a dating between 134 and 104 BC; see *The Book of Jubilees* (London: A. and C. Black, 1902), lviii–lxiii. James VanderKam argued for 163–161 and 140 BC. See *Textual and Historical Studies in the Book of Jubilees* (Missoula, MT: Scholars Press, 1977), 207–85; see also O. S. Wintermute, "Jubilees: A New Translation and Introduction," in *The Old Testament Pseudepigrapha* (hereafter *OTP*), 2 vols., ed. James H. Charlesworth (Garden City, NY: Doubleday, 1983–85), 43–44. Jonathan A. Godstein argues for a dating between 175 and 167 BC; see "The Date of the Book of Jubilees," *Proceedings of the American Academy for Jewish Research* 50 (1983), 63–86.
5. One such Jewish text is the Mishnah, a compilation of Jewish oral traditions that was redacted by Judah ha-Nisi around AD 200. It contains many interpretations, including a full tractate dealing with interpretations of the Sabbath command. For a discussion, see Yehuda Brandes, "The Canonization of the Mishnah," *Journal of Ancient Judaism* 10, no. 2 (2019): 145–80. While some of the Mishnah's sayings may reflect first century teachings and interpretations, it is difficult to determine which ones do so. Therefore, this paper will focus on texts specifically from the late Second Temple period. For a discussion of the Sabbath interpretations in the Mishnah, see Avram Shannon's chapter in this volume.
6. John M. G. Barclay, *Jews in the Mediterranean Diaspora: From Alexander to Trajan (323 BCE–117 CE)* (Edinburgh: T&T Clark, 1996), 440.
7. It is possible, of course, that there was a set of guidelines that was never recorded in the Hebrew Bible, but currently we have no way of knowing what these guidelines would have included.
8. John J. Collins, *Between Athens and Jerusalem: Jewish Identity in the Hellenistic Diaspora*, 2nd ed. (Grand Rapids, MI: Eerdmans, 2000), 1.

9. Although the Book of Daniel is set during the Babylonian exile, many scholars argue that it was written during the Maccabean period, as a reaction to the "abomination of desolation" when Antiochus IV desecrated the Jerusalem temple. The text recognized that the Jews were in Babylon for a long time and therefore needed to learn how to successfully survive and thrive in that environment. There were some things that they could compromise on: they started speaking Aramaic—chapter 1 and chapters 8–12 of Daniel are written in Hebrew, while chapters 2–7 are written in Aramaic—and they started taking on Babylonian names (see Daniel 1:6–7). But the book also argues that if Jewish identity was to be maintained, three things could not be compromised: diet (Daniel 1), idolatry (Daniel 3), and prayer (Daniel 6).
10. Tom Holmén, *Jesus & Jewish Covenant Thinking* (Leiden, Netherlands: Brill, 2001), 51–57.
11. Josephus, *Antiquities of the Jews* 11.346–47 (11.8.7); James D. G. Dunn, *The Partings of the Ways: Between Christianity and Judaism and Their Significance for the Character of Christianity* (London: SCM, 2006), 40.
12. "At a time when Judaism's distinctive identity was under constant threat, Torah provided three badges in particular which marked the Jew out from the pagan: circumcision, Sabbath, and the kosher laws. . . . But, even within such [mostly-Jewish] societies, the keeping of the Sabbath was a matter of dispute: what counted and what did not. . . . Torah thus provided the vital covenant boundary-marker. . . . it was Torah, and particularly the special badges of sabbath and purity, that demarcated the covenant people and that therefore provided litmus tests of covenant loyalty and signs of covenant hope." N. T. Wright, *The New Testament and the People of God* (Minneapolis: Fortress Press, 1992), 237–38. Dunn describes the Sabbath as "a badge of ethnic identity and devotion to ancestral custom." *Partings of the Ways,* 40. There were, however, differing opinions about whether the Sabbath day was incumbent upon Gentiles. According to Jubilees, God chose the "seed of Jacob" and he made "known to them the Sabbath day so that they might observe therein a Sabbath from all work" (Jubilees 2:2; English translation in all references from Wintermute, in Charlesworth *OTP*, 2:58). Gentiles were not required to observe the Sabbath: "The Creator of all blessed it, but he did not sanctify any people of nations to keep the Sabbath thereon with the sole exception of Israel. He granted to them alone that they might eat and drink and keep the Sabbath thereon upon the earth" (Jubilees 2:31). Nevertheless, it has been argued the Elephantine papyri may imply that some Gentiles observed the Sabbath; see, for example, Bezalel Porten, "The Religion of the Jews of Elephantine in Light of the Hermopolis Papyri," *Journal of Near Eastern Studies*, 28, no. 2 (1969): 117, 121; and Sakae Kubo, "The Sabbath in the Intertestamental Period," in *The Sabbath in Scripture and History*, ed. Kenneth A. Strand (Washington, DC: Review and Herald Publishing Association, 1982), 57–58.
13. Josephus, *The Life Against Apion*, trans. H. St. J. Thackery (Cambridge, MA: Harvard University, 1926), 247–49.
14. Josephus, *Against Apion* 405–407.
15. Horace, *Satires*, trans. H. R. Fairclough (Cambridge, MA: Harvard University, 1929), 1.9.65–70; Ovid, *The Art of Love*, trans. J. H. Mozley (Cambridge, MA:

Harvard University, 1939), 1.75–78, 413–17; Persius, "Satire 5," in *Juvenal and Persius*, ed. and trans. Susanna Morton Braund (Cambridge, MA: Harvard University, 2004), 5.180–84; Plutarch, "Superstition," in *Moralia*, trans. Frank Cole Babbitt (Cambridge, MA: Harvard University, 1928), 8; Cassius Dio, *Roman History*, trans. Earnest Cary (Cambridge, MA: Harvard University, 1914), 37.17.3; Seneca, as quoted in Augustine, *City of God against the Pagans*, trans. George E. McCracken (Cambridge, MA: Harvard University, 1957), 6.11; and Josephus, *Against Apion* 1.22.205–11. See also J. Hugh Michael, "The Jewish Sabbath in the Latin Classical Writers," *American Journal of Semitic Languages and Literatures* 40, no. 2 (January 1924): 117–24. For a discussion of Pagan attacks on Jewish Sabbath observance, see Louis H. Feldman, *Jew and Gentile in the Ancient World: Attitudes and Interactions from Alexander to Justinian* (Princeton, NJ: Princeton University Press, 1996), 158–67. For further discussions on the Sabbath day, see Molly Whitaker, *Jews and Christians, vol. 6, Graeco-Roman Views* (Cambridge: Cambridge University Press, 1984), 63–73; and Heather A. McKay, *Sabbath and Synagogue: The Question of Sabbath Worship in Ancient Judaism* (Leiden: Brill, 1994), 11–131.

16. Saint Augustine, *The City of God*, trans. Marcus Dods (Peabody, MA: Hendrickson, 2009), 182. Speaking of the Jews' laws, Juvenal says in his satires, "Some happen to have been dealt a father who respects the Sabbath. . . . But it's their fathers who are to blame, taking every seventh day as a day of laziness and separate from ordinary life." *Juvenal and Persius*, 14.96, 106; translation from Loeb Classical Library, 91:466–467. See also Tacitus, *The Histories*, trans. Clifford H. Moore (Cambridge, MA: Harvard University, 1925), 5.4. In a similar vein, Cassius Dio states that "on the day of Saturn"—that is, Saturday—the Jews "refrain from doing any serious work." *Roman History* 37.17.3. Philo, however, takes exception to these charges of laziness: "And on this account too Moses calls the Sabbath, which name being interpreted means 'rest,' 'the sabbath of God.' . . . And by 'rest' I do not mean 'inaction' (since that which is by its nature energetic, that which is the cause of all things, can never desist from doing what is most excellent), but I mean an energy completely free from labour, without any feeling of suffering, and with the most perfect ease." *On the Cherubim* 2.87. All English translations for Philo are from *The Works of Philo, Complete and Unabridged*, trans. C. D. Yonge (Peabody, MA: Hendrickson, 1993). Philo also points out the significance of the Sabbath rest occurring on the seventh day. He states that the number seven is "freedom from seditions and from wars, and is of all the numbers that which is the most averse to contention." *On Abraham* 28.

17. In his *Antiquities of the Jews*, Josephus records that Jews were exempt from appearing in court on the Sabbath or Sabbath Eve (see 16.161–63; 167–68), and from military service because they could not bear arms, travel on the Sabbath, or procure food (see 14.224–26). He also records occasions when Roman officials decreed that Jews were not to be interfered with in their observance of the Sabbath (see 14.241–42, 244–46, 256–58, 262–64). Philo reminded Emperor Gaius Caligula that Augustus had made special allowance for the Jews to receive their monthly allocations of grain on the following day, whenever it fell on the Sabbath. He records the rippling effects of these kinds of concessions: "Therefore, all people in every country, even if they were not naturally well inclined towards

the Jewish nation, took great care not to violate or attack any of the Jewish customs of laws." *On the Embassy to Gaius* 158–59. For a discussion on why the Roman leaders were so accommodating, see Robert Goldenberg, "The Jewish Sabbath in the Roman World up to the Time of Constantine the Great," in *Rise and Decline of the Roman World*, ed. Hildegard Temporini-Gräfin Vitzthum and Wolfgang Haase (Berlin and New York: W. de Gruyter, 1979), 418–21.

18. Antiochus IV's persecution of Jews and repression of Judaism seems to have been a departure from the generally peaceful rule of both the Ptolemies and the Seleucids before him. For a discussion of Antiochus IV's persecution of Jews living in Judea, see Erich S. Gruen, "Hellenism and Persecution: Antiochus IV and the Jews," in *Hellenistic History and Culture*, ed. Peter Green (Berkeley: University of California Press, 1993), 238–74.
19. Jutta Leonhardt, *Jewish Worship in Philo of Alexandria*, vol. 84 of *Texts and Studies in Ancient Judaism*, ed. Martin Hengel and Peter Schäfer (Tübingen: Mohr Siebeck, 2001), 71.
20. It should be noted that there are also some Jewish texts from this period that make no mention of the Sabbath, "even where one might expect it to appear, as in the description of the piety of the young man Tobit" and in the writings of "Ben Sira who records the names of some holy days, and refers to the exalting and hallowing of certain (unspecified) days, [but] does not mention the Sabbath at all." McKay, *Sabbath and Synagogue*, 44.
21. It is important to note that the ancient Jews and Greeks did not understand the concept of "soul" in the same way that it is defined in Doctrine and Covenants 88:15—that is, as the body and spirit combined. Rather, they viewed the soul as being something very distinct from the body.
22. Philo, *On the Migration of Abraham* 89–90.
23. Philo, *On the Life of Moses* 2:211.
24. Philo, *Migration of Abraham* 91.
25. Unless noted otherwise, the English translations for all Dead Sea Scrolls documents are taken from Florentino García Martínez, *The Dead Sea Scrolls Translated: The Qumran Texts in English*, trans. Wilfred G. E. Watson (Leiden: Brill, 1994). These are the major texts, but see also 4Q264a frag. 1 and the discussion in Vered Noam and Elisha Qimron, "A Qumran Composition of Sabbath Laws and Its Contribution to the Study of Early Halakah," *Dead Sea Discoveries* 16 (2009): 55–96. By around AD 200, thirty-nine activities were prohibited in the Mishnah (*Shabbat* 7) and later incorporated into the Talmud.
26. Fragments from the book of Jubilees were found in caves 1, 2, 3, 4, and 11 at Qumran, indicating that it was an important book for the Qumran community.
27. Philo, *Migration of Abraham* 91.
28. Lines 5–12 are missing in 4QD^e 10 V, which possibly contained this prohibition.
29. Noam and Qimron reconstruct 4Q264a I, 1–4 to read that the injunction against carrying on the Sabbath extended to taking up an instrument on the Sabbath ("Qumran Composition," 65–80). Eibert Tigchelaar, however, reconstructs the passage very differently: "One should not speak a word except to speak words of holiness. In accordance with the decree one shall speak to praise God." "Sabbath Halakha and Worship in *4QWays of Righteousness: 4Q421* 11 and 13+2+8 Par *4Q264a* 1–2," *Revue de Qumrân* 18, no. 3 (June 1998): 364.

See also Richard Hidary, "Revisiting the Sabbath Laws in 4Q264a and Their Contribution to Early Halakha," *Dead Sea Discoveries* 22, no. 1 (2015): 4.

30. Philo, *Migration of Abraham* 92.
31. Philo, *Life of Moses* 2:219.
32. Ben Zion Wacholder, *The New Damascus Document. The midrash on the Eschatological Torah of the Dead Sea Scrolls: Reconstruction, Translation, and Commentary*, Studies on the Texts of the Desert of Judah 56 (Leiden: Brill, 2007), 334–35.
33. See also 4Q264 1 I, 5–8, which forbids any speech, "with the exception of that devoted to God . . . and to Sabbath needs." Noam and Qimron, "Qumran Composition," 60.
34. Philo, *Migration of Abraham* 91.
35. For the direction to wear clean clothes on the Sabbath, see also 4Q265 2 I, 1–4. Instead of "medicines" in XI, 9–10, García Martínez translates סמנים (*smnym*) as "perfumes." *Dead Sea Scrolls Translated*, 42.
36. Philo knew of some Jews who viewed the Sabbath through a symbolic lens and therefore gave no credence to living these types of laws for Sabbath day. While he agrees that there are important symbols in the Sabbath, he argues that "it does not follow that on that account we may abrogate the laws which are established respecting it, so as to light a fire, or till land, or carry burdens or bring accusations, or conduct suits at law or demand a restoration of a deposit, or exact the repayment of a debt, or do any other of the things which are usually permitted at times which are not days of festival." *Migration of Abraham* 4.91. For a discussion, see Herold Weiss, *A Day of Gladness: The Sabbath among Jews and Christians in Antiquity* (Columbia, SC: University of South Carolina Press, 2003), 32–51.
37. See 1 Maccabees 9:32–34; 2 Maccabees 5:24–26; 15:1–5; Josephus, *Against Apion* 1:209–10; Strabo, *Geography* 16.2.40; Frontinus, *Art of Strategy* 2.1.17; Plutarch, *Superstition* 8; and Cassius Dio, *Roman History* 37:16; 49:22; 65:7.
38. See also Philo, *On Abraham* 28; Josephus, *Against Apion* 1:209; *Against Jews* 14:224–26; and 2 Maccabees 6:11.
39. See also Josephus, *Against Apion* 1:209–10; Frontius, *Art of Strategy* 2.1.17; Plutarch, *Superstition* 8.35–36; Cassius Dio, *Roman History* 37.16; 49.22.
40. McKay, *Sabbath and Synagogue*, 47.
41. McKay, 251.
42. Leonhardt, *Jewish Worship in Philo*, 8.
43. Philo, *Embassy to Gaius*, 156.
44. Shemaryahu Talmon, "The Emergence of Institutionalized Prayer in Israel in Light of Qumran Literature," *The World of Qumran from Within: Collected Studies* (Leiden: Brill, 1989), 241.
45. Tigchelaar, "Sabbath Halakha," 363–64. Talmon has argued that one of the "fundamental differences in patterns of worship between the Covenanters [in the Dead Sea Scrolls] and the larger Jewish community" is "the absence of the liturgical reading from the Law," which "is usually viewed as one of the earliest components of synagogue worship." "Institutionalized Prayer," 241. 4Q264a, if it is a sectarian text, may call this assessment into some question.
46. Philo, *On Dreams* 2.127.
47. Philo, *Life of Moses* 2.216.

48. Philo, *The Decalogue* 96–98.
49. Philo, *Embassy to Gaius* 156–57.
50. Philo, *Hypothetica* 7.12–13.
51. Other New Testament passages refer only to Jesus's teaching in the synagogue (see Matthew 13:54; Mark 1:21–22; 6:2).
52. Josephus, *Against Apion* 1:209; see also Matthew 6:5.
53. Talmon, "Institutionalized Prayer," 226.
54. Talmon, "Institutionalized Prayer," 226; and Esther Glicker Chazon, "Prayers from Qumran and Their Historical Implications," *Dead Sea Discoveries* 1, no. 3 (1994): 265.
55. Chazon, "Prayers from Qumran," 267; and Chazon, "On the Special Character of Sabbath Prayer: New Data from Qumran," *Journal of Jewish Music and Liturgy* 15 (1992–93): 1–2.
56. Talmon, "Institutionalized Prayer," 226.
57. Chazon, "Prayers from Qumran," 265.
58. When it comes to identifying specific Sabbath liturgical texts from Qumran two important interpretive issues arise. First, the fragmentary nature of many of the Qumran texts makes it difficult to identify the Sabbath texts. The process is easier, of course, if the word "sabbath" is present in a surviving portion (4Q504 VII, 4; 4Q403 1 I, 30; II, 18; 4Q404 III, 2; 4Q405 VIII–IX, 1; XX–XXII, 6), but sometimes the identification relies on the inclusion of important Sabbath themes such as "rest" (4Q503 21–28 VII, 10; 37–38 XII, 15), "holiness" (4Q503 37–38 XII, 15; 40–41, 5), describing the day as a "delight" (compare Isaiah 58:13; 4Q503 21–28 VII, 10), or a focus on various aspects of creation (4Q503 21–28 VII, 14). Chazon, "Prayers from Qumran," 266–70. The second issue deals with the provenance of the Sabbath texts. Although they were found in the caves surrounding Qumran, the question is whether they were written by the community and its members and were thus reflective of unique Qumran liturgical practices, or whether, like the book of Jubilees, they were outside texts that were adopted by the community but that also reflected practices by other communities. See Carol A. Newsom, "'Sectually Explicit' Literature from Qumran," in *The Hebrew Bible and Its Interpreters*, ed. William Henry Propp, Baruch Halpern, and David Noel Freedman (Winona Lake, PA: Eisenbrauns, 1990), 167–87. Given the ritual nature of liturgical texts, which "draw upon a common liturgical heritage," such textual cross-pollination should not be surprising. See Chazon, "Special Character of Sabbath Prayer," 1; and Newsom, "Sectually Explicit," 176.
59. See, for example, the Songs of the Maśkil (4Q510 and 4Q511) and 4QBerakhot (4Q280 and 4Q286–290). See also Newsom, "Sectually Explicit," 180; and Newsom, "'He Has Established for Himself Priests': Human and Angelic Priesthood in the Qumran Sabbath *Shirot*," in *Archaeology and History in the Dead Sea Scrolls: The New York Conference in Memory of Yigael Yadin*, ed. Lawrence Schiffman (Sheffield, UK: JSOT Press, 1990), 104.
60. Yigael Yadin was the first to propose the theory that a member of the Qumran community brought the copy to Masada after the destruction of Qumran. Newsom initially agreed with this position but later argued that its presence at

Masada was evidence that the text "was known and used in circles quite distinct from the Qumran community." "Sectually Explicit," 180–85.

61. Newsom, "He Has Established for Himself Priests," 115–16.
62. For transcriptions of 4Q400–401 and 4Q403–405 see Carol Newsom, *Songs of the Sabbath Sacrifice: A Critical Edition*, Harvard Semitic Studies 27 (Atlanta: Scholars Press, 1985).
63. See also 4Q400 1 I, 1–2; 4Q400 2.1; 4Q401 1–2; 4Q403 1 I, 30–33, 41–43; 4Q403 1 II, 18–27, 32–36; 4Q404 3.2; 4Q405 6.2–5; 4Q405 8–9.2; 4Q405 20–22.6; 4Q503 29–32 VII, 9, 13; 4Q503 40–41.6; and 4Q503 51–55.9.
64. Chazon, "Special Character of Sabbath Prayer," 4–5.

Chapter Four

An Overview of the Sabbath in the Synoptic Gospels: Texts and Reflections

Jennifer C. Lane

In exploring the Sabbath in the texts of the Synoptic Gospels, we enter terrain that is both foreign and familiar. These texts were written for an ancient audience and deal with concerns and expectations that belong to a different cultural world. At the same time, with a sense of the value of the Sabbath day and the importance of honoring it, we peer into these records hoping both to understand more of those ancient people's experience and to find messages that resonate with our lives. In these texts we can see the wisdom of keeping commandments and hear a warning against resisting the one who is the Giver of the command.

The first and central part of this chapter will focus on the texts of the Synoptic Gospels and their presentation of the Sabbath, followed by reflection on what we might learn from these accounts. This is primarily a textual rather than a historical endeavor, but if we are to better understand these texts, it helps to spend a little time on context. It is important to remember that these Gospels were written in an early Christian period. While they do capture some of the experience of Judaism in the Second Temple period, those glimpses are filtered through the concerns of the early

Christians. Since most of the early Christians were Jews, their relationship to the Sabbath was shared with the Jews in many ways. Yet the depiction of the Sabbath in these texts also suggests a point of contrast between Christian and Jewish self-understanding.

The importance of the Sabbath to first-century Jews becomes clear when we recognize their context within a larger Hellenistic culture for several hundred years. Divisions among the Jews at this time were precipitated by increasing pressure from the spread of Hellenism. Some Jews were more integrated than their compatriots with the then-dominant culture of the eastern Mediterranean. Adopting the values and norms of Greek culture that took root in the wake of Alexander the Great's conquests in the fourth century BC, these Jews left behind distinctive practices such as Sabbath observance. Others, seeking to preserve their identity and covenant faithfulness to the God of Israel, paid close attention to the biblical requirements about the Sabbath and were actively thinking through how to apply the commandment to keep the Sabbath in their new cultural and political context. Many—perhaps most—of the Jews of this era were somewhere in between. They found themselves in a world shaped by both a larger Hellenistic culture and their desire to maintain their distinct identity as the covenant people who belonged to both worlds.

Even Jews who were deeply connected with Hellenistic thought, such as Philo of Alexandria in the first century BC, used Sabbath observance as an identity marker.[1] Although there were differences in interpretation as to how to apply the biblical regulations, Yonatan S. Miller observes that "Jewish writers in the Second Temple period accorded the Sabbath the sanctity with which it is consistently recorded in Scripture, and they understood the profaning/defiling of the Sabbath as an offense that violated the day's sacred/pure nature."[2] It is important, however, to recognize that the intertestamental period was characterized by a wide range of views within Judaism and a debate over what was appropriate on the Sabbath. As discussed elsewhere in this volume, these views are represented in different texts that include Josephus, 1–2 Maccabees, the Damascus Document of the Qumran community, Jubilees, and Philo.[3]

Given this variety, the teachings of Jesus about the Sabbath as found in the Synoptic Gospels are now seen to fit within the intertestamental "range of views" about Sabbath observance. This is in contrast to John's Gospel, in which Christ's command for a healed man to carry a burden (his bed) would have been understood by all to be a command for the man to work on the Sabbath (see John 5:8).[4] In the Synoptic Gospels, Jesus's similar actions on the Sabbath day generally elicited some controversy, but the focus in those accounts does not seem to directly challenge the shared religious expectations of the Sabbath. However, the early Christian communities for whom these texts were important may, like their Jewish contemporaries, have been thinking through what was appropriate on the Sabbath day.[5]

Many scholars believe that "the Christian communities represented by the Synoptic Tradition" were those who were still keeping the law of Moses or who at least "held on to some Jewish observances, but did not insist on circumcision."[6] For these Christians, keeping the Sabbath and the regulations regarding Sabbath worship would not have been controversial. The accounts in the Synoptic Gospels may have helped them think through what they should do in order to keep the Sabbath as disciples of Christ.

Noncontroversial Sabbath Texts in the Synoptic Gospels

The noncontroversial Sabbath texts include accounts of ordinary life shaped by the Sabbath and accounts of Christ's passion, burial, and resurrection. The ordinary life events that are recorded in several Gospels describe Christ as following a regular Jewish pattern of gathering to a synagogue on the Sabbath. It is on these regular occasions that we find him both teaching and healing on the Sabbath. Near the beginning of the Gospel of Mark, we see that "they went into Capernaum; and straightway on the sabbath day he entered into the synagogue, and taught" (Mark 1:21). In Luke 4:16 we see Jesus joining those in his hometown for scripture study on the Sabbath: "And he came to Nazareth, where he had been brought up: and, as his custom was, he went into the synagogue on the sabbath day, and stood up for to read." After this account of his experience in Nazareth, we are told that Jesus "came down to Capernaum, a city of Galilee, and taught them on the sabbath days" (v. 31), illustrating his regular pattern of Sabbath synagogue attendance. Both Mark and Matthew also describe Christ as teaching in the synagogue in "his own country," meaning his hometown (Matthew 13:54), but only Mark mentions that this occurred on the Sabbath day: "When the sabbath day was come, he began to teach in the synagogue: and many hearing him were astonished" (Mark 6:2). It is possible that this detail was not specified in the Gospel of Matthew because Matthew's audience would have assumed that this teaching took place on the Sabbath day.

Likewise, there are times when Christ's healing ministrations on the Sabbath are mentioned in passing but are not a source of controversy. One such account is in Mark 1:21–28, where after Christ finishes his teaching on the Sabbath day, a man in the synagogue possessed by an unclean spirit cries out, "Let us alone; what have we to do with thee, thou Jesus of Nazareth? art thou come to destroy us? I know thee who thou art, the Holy One of God." In rebuke Jesus says, "Hold thy peace, and come out of him." The account continues: "When the unclean spirit had torn him, and cried with a loud voice, he came out of him" (vv. 24–26). In response to this healing, the people "[a]re all amazed" and wonder, "What thing is this? what new doctrine is this? for with authority commandeth he even the unclean spirits, and they do obey him" (v. 27). But there is no discussion or controversy about this event happening on the Sabbath. Luke 4:31–37 has a similar account of this event in the synagogue on the Sabbath, and here again the response to Christ's action seems positive: "What a word is this! for with authority and power he commandeth the unclean spirits, and they come out" (v. 36).

The role of the Sabbath in shaping Jewish life is reflected not only in accounts of Christ teaching and healing without controversy on the Sabbath, but also in texts concerning his death, burial, and resurrection. Mark emphasizes that Joseph of Arimathea asked for the body of Jesus "when the even was come, because it was the preparation, that is, the day before the sabbath" (Mark 15:42).[7] In the Gospel of Matthew, the disciples' care in keeping the Sabbath right after the Crucifixion can be seen as subtly reflecting their piety, in contrast to the piety of those who were plotting against them. As Herold Weiss observes, "the evidence reviewed thus far would seem to indicate that the Christian communities that sustained the Synoptic tradition did observe the Sabbath, and some of them probably felt they were doing it even better than the Pharisees."[8] In Matthew, the Pharisees are shown to make arrangements on the day *after* the day of preparation (i.e., on the Sabbath) to have the tomb sealed and guarded (27:62). By this means, Weiss argues, the Pharisees are seen to be "in flagrant violation of the Sabbath while, by contrast, the Christian women, who were rather anxious to anoint Jesus' body, wait until after the Sabbath to go about their business (28:1)."[9] In Luke we also see the careful observation that those same women "rested the sabbath day according to the commandment" (23:56). It was only "upon the first day of the week, very early in the morning, [that] they came unto the sepulchre, bringing the spices which they had prepared, and certain others with them" (24:1). The empty tomb on Easter morning was first witnessed by faithful women who had carefully kept the Sabbath.

Sabbath Controversy Texts

While the noncontroversial Sabbath texts do have a fair amount of overlap among the Gospels, it is notable that two striking accounts of Sabbath controversies are found in all three of the Synoptic Gospels and are given back-to-back. These accounts are (1) the story of Jesus and the Apostles picking grain on the Sabbath (Matthew 12:1–8; Mark 2:23–28; Luke 6:1–5) and (2) the story of the man with a withered hand being healed (Matthew 12:9–21; Mark 3:1–12; Luke 6:6–11). I will work through these shared controversial texts to identify nuanced differences between them. Then I will examine two additional accounts that appear only in Luke.

Plucking Grain

The Gospel of Mark records that Jesus was seen "going along on the sabbaths through the [grainfields]—and his disciples began to make a way, plucking the ears" (Mark 2:23, Young's Literal Translation).[10] The sense that reaping or plucking grain on the Sabbath would be a violation of Sabbath law "would not, in any way, be a distinctively Pharisaic rule,"[11] but rather would be a generally accepted sense of what was inappropriate on the Sabbath. Thus in each Gospel, the explanation of why Jesus permits the disciples to pluck the grain is an important statement, and in each Gospel the elements of that explanation differ.

In Mark this story does not specify that the disciples were hungry and picking food for immediate consumption—a detail that we do see in Matthew 12:1. By not mentioning eating, the text in Mark might be intended to put the emphasis on the disciples "making a way" for Jesus—a clear allusion to the beginning of Mark, which says: "Prepare ye the way of the Lord, make his paths straight" (Mark 1:3). This proclamation is actually a quotation from Isaiah, describing the followers of a king preparing the way for him.[12] The question of whether any consumption was implied in the disciples' plucking of grain might be informed by one of Jesus's statements in an earlier story. In Mark, there are two controversial stories about food back-to-back; in the earlier story, Jesus explains that his disciples do not fast because "as long as they have the bridegroom with them, they cannot fast" (Mark 2:19), and that "new wine must be put into new bottles" (v. 22).[13] This is not to say that the account of the disciples plucking grain was tied to fasting or not fasting, but the previous story might strengthen the theory that eating was a part of this account. In any case, this narrative sequence in Mark suggests that Jesus is introducing a new order of the kingdom of God.[14]

Whether or not there was eating involved in the Mark account, this action of plucking grain is clearly seen by the Pharisees as "reaping," because they ask Jesus why the disciples are doing "that which is not lawful" on the Sabbath (Mark 2:24; compare Exodus 34:21). As we shall see, in giving the analogy of David eating, Christ does not say that the Sabbath command is done away. Rather, he shows that there is a precedent for the disciples' action in David's action of eating "the shewbread, which is not lawful to eat but for the priests" (Mark 2:26).[15] So, as Robert A. Guelich notes, the Markan text, rather than being "an apology for the disciples' . . . sabbath conduct, . . . makes a Christological statement about Jesus and his ministry."[16] Mark's account shows that Jesus was a king with the Davidic authority to sanction the disciples' actions.

Luke's account of this event does mention that the disciples ate the kernels of grain as they went: "One Sabbath Jesus was going through the grainfields, and his disciples began to pick some heads of grain, rub them in their hands and eat the kernels" (6:1, NIV).[17] In Luke, as in Mark, this account directly follows the story in which Jesus explains why the disciples do not fast and introduces the metaphor about putting new wine into new bottles.

In Matthew, however, the account of plucking grain includes a mention that the disciples were hungry: "At that time Jesus went through the grainfields on the Sabbath. His disciples were hungry and began to pick some heads of grain and eat them" (12:1, NIV). Matthew's account directly follows Christ's invitation in 11:28–30: "Come unto me, all ye that labour and are heavy laden, and I will give you rest. Take my yoke upon you, and learn of me; for I am meek and lowly in heart: and ye shall find rest unto your souls. For my yoke is easy, and my burden is light." Matthew's description emphasizes the hunger of the disciples, seemingly showing that they picked the grain to ease a burden of hunger. Christ's promise of rest clearly expands beyond merely lightening the regulations around the Sabbath, but this particular story of Christ making sure the disciples were fed might connect the rest that Christ offers with the rest that the Sabbath was meant to give.

We can see another subtle difference between the Synoptic Gospels in the Pharisees' reactions to the event. In Mark and Matthew, the Pharisees ask Jesus about his *disciples'* behavior. Consider these verses: "The Pharisees said unto him, Behold, why do they on the sabbath day that which is not lawful?" (Mark 2:24); and "when the Pharisees saw it, they said unto him, Behold, thy disciples do that which is not lawful to do upon the sabbath day" (Matthew 12:2). In Luke, however, the question is asked of Jesus more directly, even though it is his disciples that are described as picking the grain: "One Sabbath Jesus was going through the grainfields, and his disciples began to pick some heads of grain, rub them in their hands and eat the kernels. Some of the Pharisees asked Jesus, 'Why are you doing what is unlawful on the Sabbath?'" (Luke 6:1–2, NIV). Herold Weiss argues that "like Matthew with his comparison of Jesus and the temple, by singling out Jesus's activity as unlawful, Luke is giving prominence to the story's secondary Christological significance."[18] François Bovon reveals another dimension to the question being addressed to Jesus: "What is presupposed is the relationship of Jesus to his disciples as a teacher to his students. He is responsible for their actions."[19] The disciples' obedience to Jesus highlights his new form of obedience to the law in which "the nearness of the kingdom and the relationship of the Sabbath to God's will at creation are the theological basis of their freedom, and of the new attitude," in contrast to the Pharisees' observance, which (in order to keep people from slipping into sin) prohibited the plucking of grains "to prevent harvesting on a Sabbath."[20]

In all three Gospels, Jesus cites the precedent of David eating temple showbread, asking, "Have ye never read what David did, when he had need, and was an hungred, he, and they that were with him? How he went into the house of God in the days of Abiathar the high priest, and did eat the shewbread, which is not lawful to eat but for the priests, and gave also to them which were with him?" (Mark 2:25–26).[21] Jesus's response points to the analogy of David eating showbread that was lawful only for the priests to eat. This response, found in all the Synoptic Gospels, does not speak to the Sabbath directly but is, as Lutz Doering notes, "an inference from the infringement of holy things (perhaps on the Sabbath) to the violation of a Sabbath regulation" and "implies a (typological?) correspondence between David and Jesus: Like David earlier, Jesus has the authority to cover for an exceptional transgression caused by hunger."[22] David had the authority to partake of food that normally would have been off-limits, and that same kingly authority is being invoked by Jesus for the disciples crossing the boundary of what would normally be considered work on the Sabbath.

Jesus's next comment explaining the action of plucking grain is found only in Mark: "And he said unto them, The sabbath was made for man, and not man for the sabbath" (2:27). This line of thinking, in which the Sabbath has the role of serving human beings, is also seen in the rabbinic tradition in a statement from the late second century attributed to Rabbi Shim'on ben Menasya in the Mekilta: "To you the Sabbath has been delivered, and not are you delivered to the Sabbath."[23] This pattern of thought emphasizes that the Sabbath is the servant of human beings and not the master of them.

It is generally understood that the Gospel of Mark was a source for the other Synoptic Gospels, but the Gospels of Matthew and Luke exclude this statement in their accounts. This exclusion has been explained as showing how later Gospels used this story "to establish the lordship of Christ, something which is tangential to the questions of lawful Sabbath conduct."[24] It has been suggested that the removal of the phrase "The sabbath was made for man, and not man for the sabbath" in Matthew and Luke also removes ambiguity from the statement about the Son of Man being Lord of the Sabbath. Doing so would avoid a potentially generalized reading in which the term "son of man" is referring to all of humanity (that is, any man) as lord of the Sabbath, instead putting the focus more directly on Jesus (the Son of Man).[25] In Luke the statement about Christ being the Lord of the Sabbath is in the very next verse after the discussion of David in the temple; in Matthew, however, two other statements expand on the principle of things taking precedence over the temple.

In only the Gospel of Matthew, Jesus's statement about David is followed by his question as to whether the Pharisees have "read in the law" that "priests in the temple profane the sabbath, and are blameless" (12:5). This question is then followed with a declaration: "But I say unto you, That in this place is one greater than the temple" (v. 6). The biblical requirement that priests work on the Sabbath would have been known to ancient readers. There was a specific sacrifice the priests performed on the Sabbath: they took "two lambs of the first year without spot, and two tenth deals of flour for a meat offering, mingled with oil, and the drink offering thereof: This [was] the burnt offering of every sabbath, beside the continual burnt offering, and his drink offering" (Numbers 28:9–10).[26] Like all of Israel, priests were to keep the Sabbath holy and not work, but they also had a particular kind of work in the temple that they were commanded to do. Thus, it could be said that on the Sabbath the "priests in the temple profane[d] the sabbath and [were] blameless." Donald A. Hagner observes, "The priests are about the work of God and thus are not bound by the normal regulations concerning the sabbath. So too it is implied by an *a fortiori* argument (or in rabbinic idiom, *qal wāḥōmer*) that Jesus and his disciples constitute a special instance and thus are not bound."[27] If the exception is allowed for something lesser (the priests who worked in the temple on the Sabbath), it would certainly be allowed for something great (Christ, who is greater than the temple and the priests and who could authorize work on the Sabbath).

Another way in which the precedent of the priests working on the Sabbath would be relevant to David eating the shewbread was that the Sabbath was the day upon which the bread in the Holy Place was changed and eaten by priests: "Every sabbath he shall set it [the bread] in order before the Lord continually, being taken from the children of Israel by an everlasting covenant. And it shall be Aaron's and his sons'; and they shall eat it in the holy place" (Leviticus 24:8–9). This verse might further explain the reference to David: he was doing what the priests did on the Sabbath.[28] These details might also illustrate Christ's lordship as both king and priest.[29]

Thus, while the idea of the temple being greater than the Sabbath finds support in the fact that its priests worked there on the Sabbath, the statement "That in this place is one greater than the temple" (Matthew 12:6) makes it clear that Christ is greater than the temple.[30] Like the rabbinic parallel of the statement in Mark about the Sabbath being made for humans and not humans for the Sabbath, there is also a rabbinic parallel for reasoning about the temple being greater than the Sabbath and something else having precedence over temple worship;[31] it is recorded that Rabbi Akiba taught, "If punishment for murder sets aside Temple worship, which in turn supersedes the Sabbath, how much more the duty of saving life supersedes the Sabbath laws."[32] In both lines of thinking, it is clearly understood that the temple is greater than the Sabbath and that something else can be seen as greater than the temple.

Matthew contains another detail not included in the other two Gospel accounts of this event. After the discussion of the priests being blameless in working on the Sabbath (Matthew 6:5), it is only in Matthew that we find the reference to Hosea 6:6: "But if ye had known what this meaneth, I will have mercy, and not sacrifice, ye would not have condemned the guiltless" (Matthew 12:7). Here again something is being put above the temple and, by extension, above regulations about the Sabbath: mercy. Elsewhere in Matthew, Jesus also uses the Hosea passage's point about mercy being above temple sacrifice to explain to the Pharisees why he is eating with people who are ritually unclean (see Matthew 9:11–13), something that the Pharisees would have seen as violating the principles of temple holiness associated with their practice of table fellowship. In this context of the disciples and the grain, Jesus implies that "had the Pharisees understood the meaning of Hosea, they would not have pronounced judgment upon the innocent (τοὺς ἀναιτίους) (12:7)"—the disciples who were as blameless (ἀναίτιοί) as the priests laboring on the Sabbath (v. 5).[33]

While each of the Synoptic Gospels takes a different route following the initial discussion of the precedent of King David eating temple showbread, they all end with the same conclusion about the lordship or kingship of Jesus: the Son of Man is Lord of the Sabbath (Mark 2:28; Matthew 12:8; Luke 6:5).[34] In the texts of Mark and Luke this statement certainly would have been "new wine" to put in a "new bottle," and it might also connect the disciples' eating of grain with the question of why Jesus's disciples did not fast—they had the Bridegroom with them, and he was changing the structure and focus of Sabbath worship. A new era can be seen, as Joel Marcus notes: "Jesus restores the compassionate aspect of the original Sabbath, which in the interim has been effaced by a human hard-heartedness that has transformed the good Sabbath into a source of destruction."[35] As the Lord and messianic king, the Son of Man "acts as the final and infallible interpreter of the will of God as expressed in Torah and sabbath commandment."[36]

In Matthew, the dimension of the Sabbath as a day of rest (see Exodus 16:23) brings another aspect to this concluding statement that the "Son of man is Lord even of the sabbath day" (Matthew 12:8). Just as we saw in Mark, the text before this story in Matthew may help us understand its meaning. Given the Matthew 11 text that precedes this story of the disciples plucking the grain, this statement of Jesus's messianic lordship over the Sabbath can be seen as connecting the rest given by the Sabbath to the rest that Jesus promises to give to those who come unto him and learn of him (Matthew 11:28–30).[37] Donald A. Hagner summarizes this connection well: "The rest and rejoicing symbolized by the sabbath find fulfillment in the kingdom brought by Jesus."[38]

It has also been argued that in the Gospel of Matthew these accounts of Sabbath controversies are strategically placed after the Sermon on the Mount, in which Christ states that instead of destroying the law, he is asking for greater righteousness (see Matthew 5:17–20).[39] Thus the Gospel of Matthew declares Christ as the Lord of the Sabbath, fulfilling the law and the prophets and asking for greater righteousness in how the Sabbath is observed. From this perspective, the Hosea 6:6 reference, with its emphasis on mercy over temple sacrifice, points to that "greater righteousness" and clarifies the purpose of the Sabbath as a day of rest in allowing those who are hungry to eat.

Unlike Mark and Matthew, the Gospel of Luke includes no commentary between the comparison to David and the statement that "the Son of man is Lord also of the sabbath" (Luke 6:5). Lutz Doering gives a possible explanation for this difference: "The justification of the disciples' transgression, more directly [in Luke] than in Matthew, focuses on the sovereign authority of the Son of Man, who is presented as the divinely authorized Lord (κύριος) of the Sabbath."[40] All three Synoptic Gospels end with this point, but because there is variation in the rhetorical journey that each Gospel takes from the statement about David in the temple to this final point, the nuances of the message are unique in each of these texts.

Man with a Withered Hand

Like the account of the disciples plucking grain on the Sabbath, the account of Christ healing the man with a withered hand is found in all Synoptic Gospels directly after the previous controversy account (Matthew 12:9–21; Mark 3:1–12; Luke 6:6–11). This story is framed with Jesus being watched to see "whether he would heal [the man with the withered hand] on the sabbath day; that they might accuse him" (Mark 3:2). This act seems to have been viewed as helping someone with a chronic condition rather than as saving life on the Sabbath, the latter of which would have been unquestionably acceptable. The early Jewish sources are not clear on the broader context for how healing those with chronic conditions was understood in those times. There are no pre-Tannaitic sources other than the Gospels that say healing per se was forbidden on the Sabbath, but it is also not clear that it was an approved Sabbath activity.[41] Doering concludes that "it is very likely that Pharisees in the first century would have considered healing such ailments forbidden on the Sabbath, no matter how they were carried out in detail."[42]

In Mark, explaining his invitation to the man with the withered hand to rise and be healed, Jesus seems to be expanding the sense of "lifesaving" to include changing the quality of life of one with a chronic condition. He asks the broader question, "Is it lawful to do good on the sabbath days, or to do evil? to save life, or to kill?" (Mark 3:4). Guelich notes that "Jesus' question and the opponents' response only become intelligible when set against the broader scope of Jesus' ministry" of proclaiming the coming of the kingdom of God (1:15). "'To do good' and 'to save a life' takes on the eschatological ring of the coming of the day of salvation, the fulfillment of God's promised activity in history, . . . which Jesus came to announce and effect."[43] In the Markan account there is no response to Jesus's question from those in the synagogue who are opposed to his action. We read that Jesus tells the man in need of healing to stretch forth his hand, and as he does so "his hand [is] restored whole as the other" (3:5). It is a sad irony that the Pharisees respond to Jesus's doing good and saving a life by counseling with the Herodians on how to destroy him.

In Matthew, rather than focusing on Jesus's explanation first, the story is framed with the *onlookers* asking Jesus the narrower question, "Is it lawful to heal on the sabbath days? that they might accuse him" (12:10). Jesus draws a parallel between the man's need and an animal falling into a pit on the Sabbath day. His response echoes a view that saving life on the Sabbath would be acceptable, a belief shared by those who followed the Pharisees.[44] The stricter, isolationist group associated with the Damascus Document would have had a more extreme view in which leaving animals or perhaps even people in pits would be required to keep the Sabbath, but Jesus's listeners likely would not have condoned this practice.[45] Doering suggests that this more widely shared attitude toward animals (and people) in pits on the Sabbath "might reflect pragmatic rural legal practice, perhaps of Galilean provenance."[46]

In the Matthean account, Jesus then completes his explanation with a broad conclusion: "Wherefore it is lawful to do well on the sabbath days" (12:12). This expansion of the idea of saving life to include helping those in need might be seen as an extension of the earlier discussion about the plucking of grain on the Sabbath day, driving home the principle of mercy overriding exact obedience to the law.[47] Keeping the Sabbath is still expected, but this interpretation broadens the sense of lawfulness to include helping and caring for those in need, demonstrated here in the healing of the man with the withered hand.[48]

In Luke's account it is stated that this was "another sabbath" (that is, not the same day as the grain controversy) when Jesus met the man with the withered hand in the synagogue, and this Gospel specifies that the man's right hand was the withered one (6:6). Here again Jesus asks a question before the healing takes place: "I will ask you one thing; Is it lawful on the sabbath days to do good, or to do evil? to save life, or to destroy it?" (v. 9). Doering notes that in Luke's account, the responses of those opposed to Jesus have been seen as "more moderate and less violent than in the other synoptics, thereby remaining closer to likely reactions to Sabbath infringement in ancient Judaism."[49] To be fair, however, the scribes and Pharisees as depicted in Luke were still seeking to find an accusation against Jesus before the healing (see v. 7), and after he healed the man, we are told that the Pharisees and the teachers of the law "were furious and began to discuss with one another what they might do to Jesus" (v. 11, NIV). François Bovon suggests that in Luke's account "Jesus is not satisfied with the mere healing of the sick man, because the attention of his opponents is an expression of a counterfeit faithfulness to the law: an observance of the Sabbath that incites people to wait for their neighbor to stumble is no longer obedience to the will of God."[50]

Two Additional Controversy Stories in Luke

Luke includes two stories of Sabbath controversy over healing on the Sabbath that are not found in either of the other Synoptic Gospels: the stories of the bent woman (13:10–17) and the man with dropsy (14:1–6). In the story of the woman healed in the synagogue, Jesus is there teaching when he encounters this woman, who is bent and cannot lift herself up. Jesus proclaims that she is "loosed" from her infirmity, lays hands on her, and "immediately she [is] made straight, and glorifie[s] God" (13:13). The controversy begins because the *archisynagogus*, the head of the synagogue, speaks to the people, applying the Sabbath-day prohibition of work to condemn what Jesus has done: "There are six days in which men ought to work: in them therefore come and be healed, and not on the sabbath day" (v. 14). In defense of his healing, Jesus asks the people, "Doth not each one of you on the sabbath loose his ox or his ass from the stall, and lead him away to watering?" (v. 15) Then he asks, "Ought not this woman, being a daughter of Abraham, whom Satan hath bound, lo, these eighteen years, be loosed from this bond on the sabbath day?" (v. 16).

James G. Crossley observes that Jesus's explanation provides a kind of halakic argument, first framing the woman as being in bondage of Satan and needing to be loosed, then comparing that to "untying animals and leading them to water [and] assum[ing] a position which was held by legal interpreters from different perspectives."[51] While there was debate in Jewish law about how far cattle should be allowed to travel on the Sabbath, the premise of loosing them to lead them to water was accepted even by the strict provisions found in the Damascus Document.[52] This "loosing" of the woman can be seen as a fulfilment of the messianic role of Jesus: "The Spirit of the Lord is on me, because he has anointed me to preach good news to the poor. He has sent me to proclaim freedom for the prisoners and recovery of sight for the blind, to release the oppressed" (Luke 4:18, NIV).[53]

In the story of healing the man with dropsy (a medical condition involving retention of a large amount of fluids), Jesus is carefully observed by the Pharisees while eating at one of their houses on the Sabbath. Here again, as in the Lukan account of the healing of the withered hand, Jesus asks a question before performing the healing: "Is it lawful to heal on the sabbath day?" (Luke 14:3). After receiving no response, Jesus "t[akes] him, and heal[s] him, and let[s] him go" (v. 4), then continues to explain his actions with reference to the analogy of how people would treat their animals: "Which of you shall have an ass [or son] or an ox fallen into a pit, and will not straightway pull him out on the sabbath day?" (v. 5).[54] And again, "they could not answer him again to these things" (v. 6). Some texts have a reading of *υἱός* (son) in this verse, making it an even stronger case for intervention in such a circumstance. But since having a chronic condition was not life-threatening, the comparison between saving a life and helping someone who could be helped on another day is not a direct parallel. Lutz Doering suggests that one could read Jesus's explanation "with its emphasis on loss and rescue" in the context of the parables in Luke 15, "reflecting God's salvific attention to the 'lost ones' of Israel."[55]

Conclusion: Relevance for Our Lives

In this chapter we have looked at the Sabbath texts in the Synoptic Gospels, texts that were written for ancient audiences about early events.[56] Even though they describe elements of the life of Christ and the context for his death, burial, and resurrection, these expectations and debate belong to a world that we can only partly reconstruct. So what do they have to tell us about our lives and the world we live in? What can we learn from them?

First, from the Jews of that era we can learn the importance of being faithful and keeping the commandments as we have them. Covenant faithfulness, specifically with respect to keeping the Sabbath, is a "sign" between us and God, as President Russell M. Nelson has reminded us.[57] The Jews in the late Second Temple period were aware of how powerful their contemporary cultural forces were. They realized how easily they could be moved away from God and a life of covenant faithfulness. Their desire to be obedient to the command to keep the Sabbath day holy shows great wisdom in prioritizing their covenant relationship with God. This is true for both the Pharisees and the disciples of Christ. We can learn from all the Jews of this time who made the Sabbath a priority. The women disciples who wanted more than anything to finish preparing the Savior's body for burial waited until Sunday morning when the Sabbath was over, at which time "they returned, and prepared spices and ointments; and rested the sabbath day according to the commandment" (Luke 23:56). Commandments provide boundaries, and our obedience in staying within those boundaries shows God that we remember him and are faithful to him and to our covenants. Even if the specifics of a commandment may later change, we are responsible to keep the commandments we are given right now. In time, the Sabbath for Christians would be observed on Sunday rather than on Saturday, but the followers of Jesus were faithful to what they were given at that time.

Second, we can recognize the importance of other people and their needs as we think about what we choose to do on the Sabbath. In his actions and explanations, Christ was not saying that the command not to work was lifted. Instead he shifted the priority from the rule itself to the careful consideration of each person's situation. The Jewish range of interpretation of how to properly keep the Sabbath in the late Second Temple period also recognized human needs as justification for actions that might normally be considered work, and so in some ways, Jesus's actions and explanations in the Synoptic Gospels are not out of place. At the same time, these texts show a consistent interpretive pattern. Christ's interpretation of what is lawful is always in relation to the needs of the people with him. Whether it was the disciples in the field, the man with the withered hand, the bent woman, or the man with dropsy, Christ proritized their well-being in his actions and in his proclamations about what was permissible on the Sabbath. His interpretive standard of "doing good" on the Sabbath (Matthew 12:12; Mark 3:4) showed that both sustaining and improving human life were part of his work of salvation, rather than the narrower standard of only preserving life. As the lawgiver, Christ was the one to determine how the law should be interpreted and followed in each situation.

Finally, I would suggest that the principle of mercy that informed Jesus's actions did not become a new rule replacing the need for the Sabbath and its boundaries. Instead, this principle shows us Jesus's nature and disposition. To find the rest that he offers, Jesus invites us to take his yoke upon us and learn of him (see Matthew 11:29). He models a way of being in which a compassionate and helpful disposition toward other people informs our choices. Rather than extracting the above principle and making it our lord, part of taking Jesus's yoke upon us is learning to watch ourselves and to beware of putting rules and principles above the authority of Christ, as this could diminish our ability to learn of him. Loving our neighbor does not eliminate the need to love God. We show God our love both by keeping the commandment of the Sabbath and by being loving and aware of others' needs on that day.

In finding our way through the complexities of living a faithful life, we can develop or adopt a range of principles that enable us to live up to our ideals. Determining how to keep the law of Moses in a Hellenistic cultural context was difficult for ancient Jews, and they adopted many different strategies, splitting off into partisan groups. In the first century, these partisan groups included the Pharisees, who wanted to keep themselves separate from the uncleanliness of the world by establishing many rules and regulations for personal conduct; the Sadducees, who navigated being in power and collaborating with political oppressors while still retaining their heritage and temple worship; the Zealots, who believed that only political independence would allow them to truly be the people of God; and those in the Qumran community, who took themselves out of society and rejected all the other Jews, whom they saw as collaborators with worldly influences and powers.

We can recognize the good that each group sought, but we must also look back and see the limitations and shortcomings of each of these religious perspectives. Just as different groups of Jews during the intertestamental period settled on a variety of different approaches to keeping covenants and being faithful to God, we also adopt and can potentially get locked into partisan perspectives. Those in each ancient group listened to different leaders who offered them a way to be confident about how they were living. Their confidence in their own interpretation of what was appropriate to do on the Sabbath led the Jewish leaders in the Synoptic Gospels to criticize the Savior and his disciples. In our day, the same confidence—based on political affiliation or social principles—can sometimes lead us to criticize the Lord's apostles and Church when what is taught does not match what we are hearing from partisan voices.

One of the most powerful messages for me in these encounters between Christ and those who criticized his actions based on external principles is the ease with which these Jewish leaders became convinced that having principles and regulations made them the judges, thereby forgetting where real authority lies. Christ's response to each individual and each situation was varied and personal, ultimately showing that he is the standard—the only true judge. Those who criticized Jesus for his actions on the Sabbath wanted to be right. They were convinced they *were* right because of rules and principles they had developed.

Similarly, having principles in our lives can make us feel that we are the masters and judges of any given situation. But these records of encounters with Jesus reveal that he sees more than we can see, and he will judge more rightly that we can judge. Making ourselves "judges" of him and his work through his ordained servants is a misguided effort to find the truth somewhere other than in the one who is "the way, the truth, and the life" (John 14:6) of the world. As we become willing to leave behind our prideful confidence in partisan systems of belief built up into ideological "temples" at which so many people worship today, we will find that "in this place [where Christ is in his Church] is one greater than the temple" (Matthew 12:6). Recognizing that his authority has been bestowed upon his servants can give us confidence to accept their judgment of a situation, even—perhaps especially—when it does not match our own.

Endnotes

1. James G. Crossley, *The New Testament and Jewish Law: A Guide for the Perplexed* (London: T&T Clark, 2010), 20. While Philo saw the law of the Sabbath allegorically, he also believed it needed to be observed with the body:

   > For although the seventh day is a lesson to teach us the power which exists in the uncreated God, and also that the creature is entitled to rest from his labours, it does not follow that on that account we may abrogate the laws which are established respecting it, so as to light a fire, or till land, or carry burdens, or bring accusations, or conduct suits at law, or demand a restoration of a deposit, or exact the repayment of a debt, or do any other of the things which are usually permitted at times which are not days of festival. . . . But it

> is right to think that this class of things resembles the body, and the other class the soul; therefore, just as we take care of the body because it is the abode of the soul, so also must we take care of the laws that are enacted in plain terms: for while they are regarded, those other things also will be more clearly understood, of which these laws are the symbols.

On the Migration of Abraham, 89–93.

2. Yonatan S. Miller, "Sabbath-Temple-Eden: Purity Rituals at the Intersection of Sacred Time and Space," *Journal of Ancient Judaism* 9, no. 1 (January 2018): 136. Miller argues that the sectarian Jews had an even stronger sense of the Sabbath as a parallel in holiness to the temple and that later the rabbis moved away from this: "For the rabbis, the connection between Sabbath and Temple only went so far as generating lists of forbidden labors. Ironically, the notion—so artfully spoken of by theologians—of the rabbinic Sabbath as a 'Temple in time' best belongs to the world of the sectarians." Miller, "Sabbath-Temple-Eden," 138.
3. See Gaye Strathearn, "Keeping the Sabbath Relevant in Some Late Second Temple Jewish Texts," in this volume.
4. Crossley, *New Testament and Jewish Law*, 43.
5. Herold Weiss, "The Sabbath in the Synoptic Gospels," *Journal for the Study of the New Testament* 38 (1990): 22.
6. Weiss, "Sabbath in the Synoptic Gospels," 24.
7. Joel Marcus observes that the term for "evening," *opsia*, can designate late afternoon: a time when it is evening but not yet dark and therefore not yet the Sabbath. *Mark 8–16: A New Translation with Introduction and Commentary*, The Anchor Yale Bible (New Haven: Yale University Press, 2009), 1070.
8. Herold Weiss, *A Day of Gladness: The Sabbath among Jews and Christians in Antiquity* (Columbia: University of South Carolina Press, 2003), 90.
9. Weiss, *Day of Gladness*, 89.
10. There is a provision in the law that "if you enter your neighbor's grainfield, you may pick kernels with your hands, but you must not put a sickle to their standing grain" (Deuteronomy 23:25, NIV). This would not, however, have been seen as a permissible Sabbath activity.
11. Lutz Doering, "Sabbath Laws in the New Testament Gospels," in *The New Testament and Rabbinic Literature*, ed. Reimund Bieringer et al. (Leiden: Brill, 2010), 213. While some commentaries have focused on later classifications seen in the rabbinic sources, Doering argues that this sense of reaping or plucking being unlawful would have been a widely shared perception.
12. Marcus notes that the term for the disciples "making their way" through the field, *hodon poiein*, "usually signifies 'to create a road.' Mark may wish to play on this meaning. . . . If so, the disciples' action would become a partial fulfillment of the prophecy of Isaiah that is cited in 1:3: they are preparing the way of the Lord. . . . It is appropriate in a pericope that hints at Jesus' royal authority, since royal visits were often prepared for by roadworks." *Mark 1–8*, 239.
13. Marcus observes that "Mark 2:23–28 thus continues the eating motif of the last two passages, but an escalation of tension is evident: Jesus' disciples are implicitly accused not just of a break with Pharisaic traditions of table fellowship and

fasting but of a violation of the written Law's injunction against working on the Sabbath," *Mark 1–8*, 243.

14. Robert A. Guelich notes that "the thrust of this pericope is clearly Christological. . . . The nature of Jesus' ministry sets implicit claim to the presence of something new, the new age of salvation. . . . This theme continues in the following story of [the disciples'] behavior on the Sabbath." *Word Biblical Commentary: Mark 1–8:26* (Nashville: Thomas Nelson, 1989), 117.
15. Adela Yarbro Collins notes the emphasis that the Markan Jesus puts on the transgression of David to show that this is not rejecting the commandment, but rather providing "a criterion for interpreting that [biblical] prohibition." *Mark: A Commentary*, ed. Harold W. Attridge (Minneapolis: Fortress, 2007), 202–3.
16. Guelich, *Mark 1–8:26*, 123.
17. For a helpful discussion on the manuscript variations as to whether this was the second Sabbath, see François Bovon, *Luke 1: A Commentary on the Gospel of Luke 1:1–9:50*, ed. Helmut Koester, trans. Christine M. Thomas (Minneapolis: Fortress, 2002), 196.
18. Weiss, *Day of Gladness*, 91–92.
19. Bovon, *Luke 1*, 198.
20. Bovon, 199.
21. Bovon offers a very interesting reading of Luke's version, suggesting that Luke frames this occurrence "from a eucharistic perspective: from the old temple comes forth the new Christian meal." He notes that the language in Luke 6:4 (namely, that David "did take and eat . . . and gave") "sounds liturgical; the old restriction, 'the priests alone,' has been lifted, and it is now permissible to eat the bread." *Luke 1*, 200.
22. Doering, "Sabbath Laws," 215.
23. Šabbta Mek. Y., Ki tissa 1, on Exodus 31:12, 14; Horovitz-Rabin 341, line 3f, 14f, in Doering, "Sabbath Laws," 216.
24. Weiss, *Day of Gladness*, 92; see Bovon, *Luke 1*, 197.
25. Crossley, *New Testament and Jewish Law*, 30.
26. Crossley, 36–37. It is possible that the use of fire was the part of the sacrifices considered "work," as making fires normally would be prohibited on the Sabbath.
27. Donald A. Hagner, *Word Biblical Commentary: Matthew 14–28* (Nashville: Thomas Nelson, 2000), 329.
28. This connection between David and the priests was also mentioned in rabbinic literature (Yalq. to 1 Samuel 21:5 [§130]; b. Menaḥ. 95b). See Doering, "Sabbath Laws," 214–15.
29. Crossley, *New Testament and Jewish Law*, 37.
30. There is another reading of these texts that sees this argument setting mercy as greater than the temple. This leans heavily on the connection with the following verse (Matthew 12:7) from Hosea. See Ulrich Luz, *Matthew 8–20: A Commentary on the Gospel of Matthew*, ed. Helmut Koester, trans. James E. Crouch (Minneapolis: Fortress, 2001), 181–83. Luz notes: "Matthew's entire argumentation is in its depth very Jewish, but it has a new foundation. It is based on the reality that through the *Son of Man* Jesus the biblical command of mercy becomes the greatest command—greater than the temple" (183).
31. Weiss, *Day of Gladness*, 91.

32. *Mekhilta de-Rabbi Ishamel*, ed. Jacob Z. Lauterbach (Philadelphia: Jewish Publication Society, 2004), 2:494. See Weiss, *Day of Gladness*, 91; and Géza Vermès, *Jesus the Jew: A Historian's Reading of the Gospels* (New York: Macmillan Press, 1974), 181.
33. Hagner, *Matthew 1–13*, 331.
34. Guelich works through a possible reading of an original play on words between "man" in "the Sabbath is made for man" and "Son of man" in Mark 2:27–28. "By referring to the order of creation in 2:27, Jesus affirms the value of both 'man' and the 'sabbath' in light of creation but places the sabbath in the service of humanity." In referring to himself in the third person "in 2:28 by virtue of the order of creation ('so'), he, the 'Son of man,' claims the authority over the sabbath not for humanity in general ('son of man' meaning 'man') but for himself ('Son of man' meaning 'I')." *Mark 1–8:26*, 129.
35. Marcus, *Mark 1–8*, 246.
36. Hagner, *Matthew 14–28*, 331.
37. François P. Viljoen, "Sabbath Controversy in Matthew," *Verbum et Ecclesia* 32, no. 1 (2011): 4.
38. Hagner, *Matthew 14–28*, 331.
39. Viljoen, "Sabbath Controversy in Matthew," 1–2.
40. Doering, "Sabbath Laws," 226.
41. Doering, 228.
42. Doering, 229.
43. Guelich, *Mark 1–8:26*, 136. Guelich further states: "Rather than a casuistic justification for healing on the Sabbath or a programmatic annulment or reinterpretation of the sabbath law, Jesus' question called for a decision regarding his person and ministry. Once again the focus of the pericope was ultimately Christological" (136–37).
44. The background to saving a life as reason to justify breaking the Sabbath goes back to the Maccabean period, in which not fighting on the Sabbath proved disastrous, and so the decision was made to fight anyone who attacked on the Sabbath. This position to act defensively was not universally supported, but it seems to have been in force when the Romans attacked Jerusalem in 63 BC. See Crossley, *New Testament and Jewish Law*, 38–39; 1 Maccabees 2:29–41; and E. P. Sanders, *Jewish Law from Jesus to the Mishna: Five Studies* (London: SCM Press, 1990), 13.
45. On the Damascus Document (a Dead Sea Scrolls text abbreviated *CD*) preserving a radical view on this point, see Crossley, *New Testament and Jewish Law*, 33. With regards to leaving an animal in a pit: "(. . .) and if it (sc. the animal) falls into a cistern (14) or a pit, he may not raise it up (or: "sustain it"—see below) on the Sabbath" (CD 11:13f.), quoted in Doering, "Sabbath Laws," 232. Similarly, people were to be left in a hole if saving them could only be done with a ladder or rope (see CD 11:16–17).
46. Doering, "Sabbath Laws," 234; see Luz, *Matthew 8–20*, 187.
47. Doering, "Sabbath Laws," 235; see Luz, *Matthew 8–20*, 188.
48. "While rabbinically saving a life is a boundary for the Sabbath commandment, in Matthew love becomes the commandment's center. For Matthew this center is not something that is foreign to Jewish law." Luz, *Matthew 8–20*, 188.

49. Doering, "Sabbath Laws," 237.
50. Bovon, *Luke 1*, 203.
51. Crossley, *New Testament and Jewish Law*, 39.
52. "The various positions relating to cattle going out on the Sabbath [are] recorded in some detail (*m. Shab.* 5.1–4; *m. 'Erub.* 2.1–4). In such passages we get mention or assumption of the reference to the Sabbath limit, which is mentioned elsewhere in *'Erubin* (4.5), and is 2000 cubits, approximately the equivalent of 1000 yards or 915 metres. . . . Even the stricter views from the Dead Sea Scrolls provide scope for cattle within the Sabbath limit: 'No-one should go after an animal to pasture it outside his city, except for two-thousand cubits' (CD 11.5–6)." Crossley, *New Testament and Jewish Law*, 40.
53. John Nolland, *Word Biblical Commentary: Luke 9:21–18:34* (Nashville: Word Books, 1993): 724.
54. "It does assume a position with which Pharisees would have agreed. Here we are back in the realm of saving life overruling the Sabbath and how Jesus is presented as seeing his healings as a development of this principle." Crossley, *New Testament and Jewish Law*, 41.
55. Doering, "Sabbath Laws," 238.
56. While much of New Testament scholarship has moved away from seeing the Gospels as texts describing historical events, a helpful case for seeing eyewitness testimony in the Gospels is found in Richard J. Bauckham's "The Gospels as Testimony to Jesus Christ: A Contemporary View of Their Historical Value," in *The Oxford Handbook of Christology*, ed. Francesca Aran Murphy (Oxford: Oxford University Press, 2015), 55–71. He observes: "These eyewitness testimonies speak to us from the inside of events, experienced by those who recognized the disclosure of God in them. Beyond the dichotomy of the Jesus of history and the Christ of faith, they offer us the Jesus of testimony" (69). A fuller discussion can be found in Bauckham's volume *Jesus and the Eyewitnesses: The Gospels as Testimony* (Grand Rapids, MI: Eerdmans, 2017).
57. Russell M. Nelson, "The Sabbath Is a Delight," *Ensign* or *Liahona*, May 2015, 129–32.

Chapter Five

Bringing Forth a New Creation: The Sabbath in the Gospel of John

Eric D. Huntsman

When it comes to treating Jesus and his relationship with the Sabbath, the Gospel of John, as is so often the case, presents material that is unique and not found in the Synoptic accounts.[1] On one level, some of Jesus's miracles are controversial because he performs them on the Sabbath. Though different incidents, on the surface these Johannine miracles are similar to those found in one or more of the Synoptics. Just as Jesus restores a man with a withered hand (Mark 3:1–6; parallels Matthew 12:1–8; Luke 6:1–5), releases a woman bent over from a long infirmity (Luke 13:10–17), and heals a man with "dropsy," a case of severe edema perhaps suggestive of congestive heart failure (Luke 14:1–6), in the Fourth Gospel he heals an invalid at the Pool of Bethesda (John 5:1–15) and gives sight to a man who had been blind from birth (John 9:1–7).[2] Perhaps more effectively than Mark or Matthew and much like Luke, rather than demonstrating an abolition of the principles of the Sabbath, the incidents in John instead present a "clarification," illustrating that this holy day should instead be used for the work of salvation and redemption.[3] Likewise, much as Jesus makes a pronouncement to justify his disciples' gleaning grain on the

Sabbath by appealing to scriptural precedent (Mark 2:23–28; parallels Matthew 12:1–8; Luke 6:1–5), in John's Gospel he explains his own "work" on the Sabbath by drawing on parallels in the law and sacred practice (John 7:19–24). In these instances, the Johannine material provides additional attestation demonstrating that the historical Jesus deliberately performed miracles and otherwise acted in ways that sought to demonstrate a new understanding of the Sabbath day and his relationship to it.[4]

On another, deeper level, however, John's treatment of the Sabbath is subordinated to the Fourth Gospel's higher Christology.[5] Rather than simply being "powerful deeds" (Greek *dynameis*), the miraculous Sabbath healings are, like all Johannine miracles, first and foremost "signs" (Greek *sēmeia*) that reveal who Jesus truly is and what his greater work is.[6] Additionally, each of the miracles is followed by typically Johannine teaching in which Jesus speaks about himself, his divine identity, and his saving and exalting mission.[7] First, following the healing at Bethesda, Jesus engages in a sharp exchange with "the Jews" (John 5:16–18), his opponents among the Jewish leadership,[8] after which he delivers a discourse on how he is in fact the Divine Son (vv. 19–47). Similarly, after the healing of the blind man, the efforts of the Pharisees to undermine the miracle and cast aspersions on Jesus (19:8–34) lead Jesus to confront them about the difference between physical and spiritual blindness, underscoring that he is the true Light of the World and that rejecting him results in the persistence of sin (9:39–41). Although commentators have noted how these dialogues coordinate Jesus's "works" (Greek *erga*)[9] with those of the Father, Jesus's seeming transgression of the Sabbath arguably says something even more specific about his atoning mission, which in this Gospel results in a new creation. Whereas the original creation, which the premortal Divine Word accomplished under the direction of the Father (John 1:3), was completed on the seventh "day,"[10] the Incarnate Word's work of atonement, healing, and exaltation is ongoing. While it is in many ways realized for some people now, it will not be experienced generally until a future, eschatological Sabbath. In other words, whereas the Father's initial work was in some sense complete, the Son's work of "re-creation" is not. Finally, a foretaste of the completion of this new creation is seen in Jesus's own resurrection on the first day of the week, making Sunday, "the Lord's Day," the new Christian Sabbath.[11]

Healing at the Pool of Bethesda

The Sabbath healings are two of the seven miraculous signs featured in John 2–11, a section of the Fourth Gospel also known as the "Book of Signs" because of the prominence of such signs in this portion of the narrative and the way they dramatically illustrate who Jesus is and what he came to do.[12] These Johannine Sabbath miracles also fall within a subsection of the Book of Signs that illustrates how Jesus fulfilled the meaning of various Jewish festivals such as Passover, Tabernacles, and Dedication.[13] In the case of the first Sabbath miracle, the healing at Bethesda, the story is set during "*a* feast of the Jews" (John 5:1; emphasis added) without specifying which one it was. Although many later Byzantine manuscripts read "*the* feast" (Greek *hē heortē*),[14] perhaps suggesting Passover, older and arguably more secure manuscripts lack the definite article, and without clear seasonal references, any of the annual feasts, such as Tabernacles, might have been meant.[15] Although the Feast of Trumpets, or Rosh Hashanah, was not one of the pilgrimage festivals that would have likely drawn Jesus to Jerusalem, the surprisingly later notice that the healing took place on the Sabbath (v. 9) might suggest that the Johannine source or author also had some of the imagery of this feast in mind.[16] Rosh Hashanah, later known as "the birthday of the world," was associated with the Creation, and the Sabbath was a weekly commemoration of creation's completion. The creation and re-creation images then figure prominently in the symbolism of both the miraculous sign and its following discourse.

The man whom Jesus healed was one of many sick people who gathered at the Pool of Bethesda (possibly meaning "House of Mercy"), a double pool north of the temple complex. Water from the upper pool was periodically released into the lower through a sluice gate in the dike between the two pools,[17] perhaps to meet the requirements of making the water ritually pure. The pool or pools were thought to be a place of healing when the water was disturbed, either because of intermittent springs that fed it from below or perhaps from water flowing periodically through the sluice gate. This movement of water was subsequently explained by the curious story of an angel coming down to trouble the waters (John 5:4), an explanation that was inserted into later versions of the text.[18]

Nevertheless, the moving of the water, from whatever cause, that preceded healing may have been part of the original story. It certainly contributes to the symbolism of the miracle that Jesus performs given its resonance with the opening lines of the Creation story: "darkness was upon the face of *the deep*. And the Spirit of God *moved upon the face of the waters*" (Genesis 1:2; emphasis added). Primordial waters were a symbol of uncreated chaos; God's spirit sweeping across them anticipated the first acts of creative organization.[19] This allusion to the first creation ties this, the third miraculous sign in John, to the first: the miracle at Cana (John 2:1–11), where the Incarnate Word's ability to change water into fine wine symbolized, among other things, that he was in fact the Divine Word, who under the direction of the Father brought forth all things. For Latter-day Saints, who understand that creation is in fact an act of organization rather than production *ex nihilo*, this symbolism is even more clear: as the premortal Jehovah he had organized the heavens and the earth; now, as the man Jesus he reorganized elements to fit the moment's need.[20]

If we see healing as the act of restoring a disordered body back into its proper form and function, then it, too, is an act of re-creation. Whereas the Incarnate Word had reorganized inanimate matter in the first sign, with the second miraculous sign, the healing of the nobleman's son, he reordered the ill body of the boy, restoring him to health (John 4:46–54).[21] The second sign thus serves as a bridge from the first to the third, so that Jesus's appearance at the water's edge signals the beginning of yet another new creative event. Just as the Lord had created when his spirit moved upon the first waters, Jesus, as Jehovah made flesh, engaged in an act of re-creation by restoring the health and ability of the invalid waiting by Bethesda's waters. This man had suffered with his infirmity for thirty-eight years, the same period of time during which rebellious Israel wandered in the wilderness between Kadesh-barnea and Wadi Zereb (see Deuteronomy 2:14). Because journeys through the wilderness can symbolize our mortal probation, this invalid can be taken as a type of all of us in mortality. Much as the world had been created or organized in perfection but then fell into a state of disorder through the Fall, so all of us in mortality are physically imperfect, subject to illness and eventual death.

Jesus's injunction to the man, "*Rise*, take up thy bed, and walk" (John 5: 8; emphasis added), uses a Greek verb (*egeire*) and an image that intimates resurrection, the healing of his particular infirmity representing the full, complete healing of the body that comes at the Resurrection. Inasmuch as the man in his disability represents all of us in our fallen, mortal state, his restoration can thus symbolize our own future resurrection, when "the soul shall be restored to the body, and the body to the soul; yea, and every limb and joint shall be restored to its body; yea, even a hair of the head shall not be lost; but all things shall be restored to their proper and perfect frame" (Alma 40:23; see also 11:43).

Only at the point when the now-healed man picks up the mat (Greek *krabbaton*; KJV, "bed")[22] and begins to walk does the narrator inform readers, almost as an afterthought, that "the same day was the sabbath" (John 5:9). We will see that the same delay in informing readers that the miracle took place on the Sabbath will happen in the case of Jesus's healing the man born blind (9:14), and in both cases this might reflect purposeful narrative irony in that both Jesus and the recipients of his miracles are aware of something—that it was the Sabbath—that readers are not. Tom Thatcher sees this as "unstable irony" because it could undercut readers' expectations of Jesus, who is unexpectedly revealed as a Sabbath breaker,[23] but better understanding the symbolism of the miracles might provide a better explanation for the delay. In the case of the invalid at Bethesda, it is true that the healing takes place on the calendrical Sabbath, but that Sabbath looked back to the old creation, while the miracle itself is part of a larger process of re-creating the world, a process that was not yet finished and pointed to a future, complete restoration of all things. As a result, while it was in fact the weekly Sabbath, the *eschatological* Sabbath, toward which Jesus was working, still lay ahead.

Narratively, however, the fact that the healing takes place on the Sabbath occasions a conflict with the Jewish authorities because developing interpretations of the Jewish law may have prohibited the transport of even such a small, light item on the Sabbath.[24] Such regulations began in certain sectarian circles—in groups such as the Pharisees and the Qumran community—but do not appear to have been normative until later in the rabbinic period, so we do not know whether they were yet widely accepted and observed across the population. Additionally, in all such discussions it is important for us to remember that such regulations were not *intended* to be burdensome or hypocritical: such "hedges about the law" likely developed as sincere efforts to worship God and live his law more fully.[25] Nevertheless, because both Jesus and the invalid knew that it was the Sabbath, they probably knew that their actions might be criticized by some authorities, Jesus for healing and the man for carrying his mat. As Cornelis Bennema notes, "Perhaps the man obeyed Jesus' command because he would rather get well and violate the Sabbath than keep the law and remain ill. Willing to face the consequences, he believes Jesus' word and obeys."[26]

In any event, the Jewish leadership criticizes the newly healed man but does not seek to punish him (John 5:10). Instead, they are more concerned with discovering who performed the miracle, though the man cannot immediately tell them who healed him (v. 13), having not met Jesus before the incident. Part of this concern may have been the tendency of the Gospel authors to locate later controversies between early Christians and their Jewish competitors, Pharisees in particular, in the ministry of Jesus. But historically it might have been because the leadership in that period actually did see the healing itself as "work" prohibited on the Sabbath, a view that seems to have been increasingly the case with the depiction of Jesus's activities in the Synoptics.[27] The bigger issue, however, may have been the authority that Jesus's opponents felt he had assumed in determining what was and was not appropriate for the Sabbath, which was the case when he directed the man to carry his mat.

As for the man, Jesus finds him in the temple and calls on him to avoid sin. This does not suggest that previous sin had been the direct cause of his ailment but rather that continuing in sin might bring about something worse—spiritual death rather than a more severe illness.[28] Alternatively, in addition to symbolizing a future physical resurrection, the man's healing might represent a spiritual healing comprising forgiveness and moral restoration. In other words, Jesus healed the whole man, spirit as well as body, and is now calling on him to "retain a remission of . . . sins" by persisting in the love of God (see Mosiah 4:12). Because in John sin is primarily a function of failing to believe, Jesus's admonition that the man "stop sinning" is actually a call for him to leave his unbelief and instead place his trust in Jesus.[29]

Jesus as the Divine Son

When the newly healed man reports to "the Jews" that Jesus was the man who healed him, their anger reaches murderous proportions, suggesting that their preexisting animosity toward Jesus was the real factor in their reaction. This supports the idea that it was not the mere act of healing on the Sabbath but the fact that it was *Jesus* who performed the miracle on the Sabbath, especially since he also usurped what they felt was their authority by allowing the man to break their Sabbath regulations by carrying his mat. Jesus responded to them by declaring, "My Father *worketh hitherto*, and I work" (John 5:17; emphasis added), a declaration that both supports the creation/re-creation symbolism of the miracle and further angered his opponents.

Saying that God "worketh hitherto" (Greek *heōs arti ergazetai*) acknowledged contemporary Jewish belief that God had continued to work since the Creation through his constant nurture, sustaining, and preservation of that creation.[30] Although we do not know what wording (presumably in Aramaic) Jesus originally used, the possible force of the phrase *heōs arti* of John's Greek allows for different interpretations. The traditional interpretation of *hitherto* means "until now," suggesting constancy and continuous creation. The emphatic position of this adverbial phrase before the verb, however, could suggest culmination, meaning that God has been working "*even* until now," the time when Christ has come to bring the promised Sabbath rest to fruition. According to Samuele Bacchiocchi, after the initial rest on the first primeval Sabbath, God had resumed his work because of sin, a work that would be at last completed by the work of Jesus.[31] That is, God has finished his initial creation and found it good, but because the earth has been marred by sin, Jesus's re-creative efforts were still ongoing.[32] Indeed, in John's cosmology, creation was never fully completed and Jesus's mission is to finish it. Thus, while the Jews rested each Sabbath to commemorate the completion of the first creation, Jesus cannot rest until his new creation is finished and the true final rest can begin.[33]

Both Jesus's actions and now his words, saying that he was working even as God had been working, reignited the intent of his opponents to kill him (John 5:18). While the KJV reads "*had broken* the Sabbath," the Greek verb (*eluen*) is actually in the imperfect tense, which might suggest that their anger was not due to this single incident but because he had, in their view, repeatedly violated the Sabbath. Interestingly, this very verb can be used to mean "to loose" or "to set free,"[34] which is how Luke used it in the healing of the woman who was severely bent over by her infirmity, when Jesus asked, "And ought not this woman, being a daughter of Abraham, whom Satan hath bound, lo, these eighteen years, be loosed from this bond on the sabbath day?" (Luke 13:16). Consonant with Jesus's arguments in the Synoptics that it was permitted to do good on the Sabbath, here also Jesus may have been freeing the observance of the Sabbath from unnecessary regulations and instead performing actions that were wholly appropriate for the Sabbath.[35] By undercutting the interpretations of the Jewish leaders in Jerusalem, however, he was threatening their power.

Above all, however, it was his claiming authority and status with God that angered "the Jews," who complained that he also said that "God was his Father, making himself equal with God" (John 5:18). While always subordinating himself to the will of the Father, Jesus not only does not deny his relationship to the Father but underscores it by saying, "Verily, verily, I say unto you, The Son can do nothing of himself, but what he seeth the Father do: for what things soever he doeth, these also doeth the Son likewise" (v. 19).[36] Jesus's discourse on his identity and role as the Divine Son continues by attesting his role with judgment, life, and resurrection (vv. 21–30) and concludes with discussion of witnesses of his divinity (vv. 31–38) and the role of scripture as additional, vital witnesses of him and his saving work (vv. 39–47). Taken with the preceding miracle at the Pool of Bethesda, with its images of creation and re-creation, this discourse shows how Jesus fulfilled and deepened the meaning of the Sabbath by turning from the first Sabbath, which looked back to the initial creation, toward a new Sabbath, on which creation was renewed and restored through Christ.

A Broad Johannine Eschatology

When and how God's final purposes for humanity are accomplished is part of the larger theological question of eschatology. Literally "the study of the last things," in Christian thought eschatology concerns itself with the glorious return of Christ, the end of the world, judgment, resurrection, and the final condition of the believers in the eternities.[37] Mark, Matthew, and in most instances Luke all exhibit *future eschatology*: although Jesus defeats the powers of Satan and heals during his ministry, and his crucifixion defeats sin, the final vanquishing of evil, the vindication of God's people, and the general resurrection of humankind all lie ahead.[38] On the other hand, John frequently portrays *realized eschatology*: that is, it depicts the effects of Jesus's saving work as being already realized in the lives of believers. For instance, in the Discourse on the Divine Son, Jesus proclaims, "He that heareth my word, and believeth on him that sent me, *hath* everlasting life, and shall not come into condemnation; but *is passed* from death unto life." (John 5:24; emphasis added). Those who believe are described as already having eternal life, and they have passed from spiritual death to a new kind of spiritual life.[39] Examples elsewhere in John include Jesus giving power to those who receive him to become the children of God (1:12); his giving life to whom he will (5:21); those who eat his flesh and drink his blood already having eternal life (6:54); and his giving eternal life to those who hear him (10:27–28).

While such passages have led many to suggest that John's emphasis is largely on realized eschatology, there are nonetheless clear examples of future eschatology. Just four verses after Jesus taught that those who hear and believe already have eternal life, he went on to prophesy, "The hour is coming, in the which all that are in the graves *shall hear* his voice, and *shall come forth*; they that have done good, unto the resurrection of life; and they that have done evil, unto the resurrection of damnation" (John 5:28–29), locating these resurrections in the yet-unrealized future. Likewise, in the same Discourse on the Bread of Life, in which he had maintained that those who ate his flesh and drank his blood already have eternal life, Jesus also taught, "Every one which seeth the Son, and believeth on him, may have everlasting life: and I *will raise* him up at the last day" (6:40; italics added).

Noted Johannine scholar Raymond Brown described eschatology in the Fourth Gospel this way: "Much that is anticipated, hoped for, and expected in the future in ancient Jewish writings and other books of the New Testament is understood to be already present in a real sense in the Gospel of John. There is still the hope for the future realization of that which is not yet present, but John is distinctive in its proclamation that eternal life is already a present reality for those who believe in Jesus."[40] In the main, other than Jesus's own resurrection, the raising of the dead lies in the future, whereas forgiveness of sin, the healing of hearts and souls, and the restoration of people to a full relationship with deity can be realized now. Because Restoration teaching usually defines eternal life as the kind of immortal, exalted life that God and the risen Christ have enjoyed, Latter-day Saint readers in particular must bear in mind the way eternal life is understood in John. In his Intercessory Prayer, Jesus defines eternal life, saying, "And this is life eternal, that they might *know* thee the only true God, and Jesus Christ, whom thou hast sent" (John 17:3; emphasis added). It is this relationship, along with the fuller, more abundant spiritual life that Jesus brings to those who believe in him (see 10:10), that constitute the realized eternal life of the Fourth Gospel.

Alan Culpepper has observed, "John distinguishes eternal life from resurrection, claiming that it is the present experience of those who believe. . . . For the faithful, the experience of blessedness, the life of eternity, is not withheld until death—it is a present reality. Eternal life is the present experience of those in the Johannine community."[41] Thus, while Jesus's work was, in one sense, completed in the life of the invalid at the Pool of Bethesda, the invalid's full healing awaits the resurrection at the end of the world. It is then that Jesus's healing, atoning, and restoring work will be complete, ushering in an eschatological Sabbath. John's eschatology is accordingly broad, beginning in the life of the believer now but completed in the future.

Tabernacles, the Sabbath, and the Law

After Jesus's bold discourse to the Jewish leadership in Jerusalem, the setting of John's narrative abruptly shifts to the account of Jesus fulfilling the intent and imagery of Passover with his miracles of the feeding of the five thousand and walking on water, followed by his Discourse on the Bread of Life (John 6:1–71). The setting then returns to Jerusalem and the temple, where several discourses and another miraculous sign serve to demonstrate how Jesus fulfills the meaning of the Feast of Tabernacles (John 7:1–10:21). Originally commemorating the wandering of the children of Israel in the wilderness and the Lord's support of them in that period, Tabernacles (Hebrew *sukkôt*, "booths"; Greek *skēnopēgia*, "tent festival") had become a joyous autumn harvest festival in the Holy Land. In the Second Temple period the festival acquired other features, such as the ritual pouring of water on the altars as part of the community's prayers for winter rains (m. Sukkah 4:9–10) and the lighting of great lamps in the temple courts (5:3–4), which provided images for Jesus's teachings, such as flowing rivers of water (John 7:37–39) and the light of the world (8:12–59).[42] For "the Jews," however, behind this festival was the ever-present figure of Moses and the law that came through him and bore his name.

As a result, it was not surprising that as Jesus taught in the temple during the early part of the weeklong festival of Tabernacles, he would bring up both Moses and the law as part of his explanation of his Sabbath-day activities and what they symbolized. After declaring the divine source of his doctrine (John 7:16–18), Jesus challenged the Jewish authorities in regard to their own hypocrisy, saying, "Did not Moses give you the law, and yet none of you keepeth the law?" (v. 19). Then referring to one "work" (Greek *ergon*) that had made them marvel, probably the healing of the man at the Pool of Bethesda (v. 21), Jesus proceeded to give an example of how the law itself mandated another work, or ritual, whose performance seemed to transgress the Sabbath: "Moses therefore gave unto you circumcision; . . . and ye on the sabbath day circumcise a man" (v. 22). Jesus's observation here that the Jewish leaders allowed circumcision on the Sabbath because it was a weightier obligation[43] parallels his reference in the Matthean version to how priests regularly "broke" the Sabbath by profaning the temple (Matthew 12:5).

Noting that the sanctification of one member through circumcision affected only one part of the body, Jesus then declared, "If a man on the sabbath day receive circumcision, that the law of Moses should not be broken; are ye angry at me, because I have made a man every whit whole on the sabbath day?" (John 7:23). This was a type of *qal vahomer*, or "light to heavy," argumentation that slightly later sources suggest was common in the first century,[44] but it was about more than the physical body. Within the context of the Gospel of John, Jesus's reference to a man made "every whit *whole* on the sabbath day" (emphasis added) almost certainly refers to the recent healing of the man at Bethesda, with the reference to his becoming well or healthy (Greek *hygiēs*; KJV "whole") connecting his declaration here not only to the man's healing but also to Jesus's greater work of re-creation that it symbolized. Accordingly, if Jews redeemed an infant boy by the "work" they performed in circumcising a part of him to bring him into the covenant, even more so Jesus's healing of the whole body was a symbol of his greater work of redeeming and restoring fallen men and women.[45]

Healing Physical and Spiritual Blindness on the Sabbath

The story of Jesus's healing the man blind from birth and its aftermath (John 9:1–41) parallels and builds on the story of the man at Bethesda, following the basic outline in most of its points while simultaneously adding detail, further personalizing it, and adding an additional theological point.[46] While there were several cases of restored sight in the Synoptics (Mark 8:22–26; 10:46–52, with parallels at Matthew 20:30–34; Luke 18:35–43; Matthew 9:27–31), in typical Johannine fashion the miracle in this Gospel is greater and more momentous: "Since the world began was it not heard that any man opened the eyes of one that was born blind" (John 9:32). Both stories in John have Jesus take the initiative (5:6; 9:6); both involve the waters of pools (5:2; 9:7); both occur on the Sabbath, though this information is delayed (5:9; 9:14); both have Jewish leaders criticize Jesus for his timing (5:10; 9:16); and in neither does the man initially know Jesus or where he is (5:13; 9:12). Yet whereas the man at Bethesda was healed instantly, the blind man's restoration involved several steps, including the application of mud to his eyes, which is more reminiscent of the colorful, detailed description of miracles in Mark than those in Matthew, Luke, or usually John.[47]

In fact, the details of Jesus making mud or a paste (Greek *pēlos*; KJV "clay") by spitting on the ground, anointing the man's eyes with it, and then having him wash in the Pool of Siloam are so unusual for John that they demand some explanation. As with the reference to the moving of the water at Bethesda, the answer might be found in seeing in the making of mud a reference to the original Creation story. In Genesis 2:7 the Lord God fashioned Adam out of the dust of the ground and then made him "a living soul" by placing in him "the breath of life" (Hebrew *nišmaṯ ḥayyîm*). Because water so often serves as a symbol of spirit in John,[48] Jesus's using his saliva to mix with the dust or dirt on the ground in front of him could represent God's putting spirit in the first man. While Adam was perfect at first, since the Fall we are all mortal, imperfect, and susceptible to illness and disability. Just as the invalid at Bethesda represented all of us in a general fallen state that is overcome by Jesus, the blind man's renewal involves additional detail, namely the need to "wash" away the effects of mortality. Indeed, if we extend the washing imagery to the symbolism of baptism, we see that it is necessary for all,[49] not just for sinners.[50]

Again, the notice that the miracle took place on the Sabbath is delayed until *after* the miracle (John 9:14),[51] perhaps suggesting that the meaningful Sabbath is the eschatological Sabbath that follows the completion of Jesus's work. In any case, Jesus's opponents, who in this account are specifically identified as Pharisees, saw the simple act of making paste as a work (v. 16). The now-seeing man, however, is not dissuaded by the Pharisaic claim that Jesus is a sinner and not of God; rather he maintains that Jesus must be a prophet (v. 17) and despite threats declares that God is with him (vv. 31–33). After he is cast out by "the Jews," Jesus finds him, giving the man a chance to express faith and worship him (vv. 35–38). When we recall that this miracle took place during or soon after the Feast of Tabernacles with its association with light, the miracle takes on further symbolism. Not only was a man who once lived in physical darkness now able to see, but he has also come to know who Jesus is: the true Light of the World (8:12).

The story of the blind man ends with Jesus declaring, "For judgment I am come into this world, that they which see not might see; and that they which see might be made blind" (John 9:39). Because this leads some of the Pharisees to question whether Jesus is claiming that they are somehow blind, Jesus closes the encounter by teaching, "If ye were blind, ye should have no sin: but now ye say, We see; therefore your sin remaineth" (v. 41), indicating that rejecting Jesus means rejecting forgiveness and spiritual healing. If the healing of the invalid at the Pool of Bethesda represents the general overcoming of mortality through the Resurrection, then the more specific story of the blind man and the Pharisees represents specific cases of those who come to Christ and are baptized, thereby overcoming spiritual death, and those who refuse to see him for who he is and remain in their sins.[52]

The Resurrection and the Lord's Day

As soon as Jesus says "It is finished" and surrenders his spirit on the cross, John notes that the Sabbath was beginning (John 19:30–31), linking the completion of that part of Jesus's salvific work with the completion of the original Creation and the start of the first Sabbath.[53] While the Synoptics had stressed that Jesus's healing on the Sabbath had not abolished it but rather emphasized other productive aspects of its observance, the Fourth Gospel's motif of Jesus's working a new creation placed him and his ministry on a different calendar, one that transcended the weekly observance of the old Sabbath and was oriented forward to a new, eschatological significance.[54] Yet overcoming sin and spiritual death was only part of the saving work of Jesus. While the seven miraculous signs, including especially the two Sabbath healings, represented the Son's ongoing saving work, his resurrection, the eighth and greatest sign, signals the completion of the new creation.[55] Overcoming physical death and all the attendant effects of mortality through Christ's resurrection made the first day of the week (John 20:1) the time that best celebrates the true rest of God. Indeed, at some point early in Christian history the weekly marking of the Lord's Day (see Acts 20:7; 1 Corinthians 16:2; Revelation 1:10) led to its becoming the Christian Sabbath, a time to commemorate the completion of Christ's work and to look forward to its full application to each of us at the end of time.

Endnotes

* I am grateful for the research and editorial help of my long-time research assistant, Jackson Craig Abhau, who not only helps make my writing cleaner but also frequently provides me with important insights. Our collaboration over the past years has been stimulating and fruitful, and I wish him well as he begins graduate school. I also express appreciation for the final editing of Derek Kenton Baker.

1. Henry Sturcke, *Encountering the Rest of God: How Jesus Came to Personify the Sabbath* (Zürich: Theologischer Verlag Zürich, 2005), 204–65.
2. Some source and form critics maintain that these two Johannine healings, perhaps having been preserved first in a postulated Signs Gospel, were originally unconnected to Sabbath controversies, only later being put in a Sabbath context that allowed them to become part of a larger controversy. See, for instance, Robert T. Fortna, *The Fourth Gospel and Its Predecessor* (Philadelphia: Fortress, 1988), 115–17; and Daryl D. Schmidt, "The Sabbath Day: To Heal or Not to Heal," *Dialogue* 27, no. 4 (1994): 138–40.
3. Samuele Bacchiocchi, "The Sabbath in John," *Endtime Issues* 110, January 2004, 4–8, https://archive.org/details/Samuele-Bacchiocchi-Endtime-Issues-Newsletter-110.
4. Raymond E. Brown, *The Gospel according to John, I–XII*, Anchor Bible 29 (Garden City, NY: Doubleday, 1966), 210.
5. Sturcke, *Encountering the Rest of God*, 204.
6. Eric D. Huntsman, *The Miracles of Jesus* (Salt Lake City: Deseret Book, 2014), 3, 135–36.
7. Huntsman, "Jesus on Jesus: John 5 and 7," in *Scriptural Theology*, ed. James E. Faulconer and Joseph M. Spencer, Perspectives in Mormon Theology (Salt Lake City: Greg Kofford Books, 2015), 69, 71–72.
8. For the use of the Greek *hoi Ioudaioi* to refer to the ruling class and not to all Jewish people, see Brown, *Gospel according to John*, lxx–lxxv; Daniel Boyarin, "The *Ioudaioi* in John and the Prehistory of 'Judaism,'" in *Pauline Conversations in Context*, ed. Janice Capel Anderson, Philip Harl Sellew, and Claudia Setzer (Sheffield: Continuum, 2002), 216–40; Craig S. Keener, *Gospel of John: A Commentary*, 2 vols. (Peabody, MA: Hendrickson, 2003); and Huntsman, *Becoming the Beloved Disciple: Coming unto Christ through the Gospel of John* (Springville, UT: Cedar Fort, 2018), 78–79, 86–87n13.
9. Whereas the Johannine narrator consistently refers to and discusses Jesus's miracles as *sēmeia*, or "signs," Jesus himself simply refers to them as *erga*, or "works," making them an integral part of his overall work of redemption.
10. While English translations generally follow the Masoretic Text's reading of "on the seventh day" (*bayyôm haššəḇîʿî*), interestingly the Septuagint reads "on the *sixth* day God finished his works" (*kai synetelesen ho theos en tēi hēmerai heketēi ta erga autou*).
11. Huntsman, *Miracles of Jesus*, 145n9.
12. Raymond E. Brown, *Introduction to the Gospel of John*, ed. Francis J. Moloney (New York: Doubleday, 2003), 300–307; Ruth B. Edwards, *Discovering John: Content, Interpretations, Reception* (Grand Rapids: Eerdmans, 2015), 170–71; and Huntsman, "The Gospel of John," in *New Testament, Culture, and Society: A Background to the Texts of the New Testament*, ed. Lincoln H. Blumell (Provo, UT: Religious Studies Center, Brigham Young University, 2019), 311. The seven signs are changing water to wine at Cana (John 2:1–11), healing the son of the royal official (4:46–54), healing the invalid at Bethesda (5:1–16), feeding five thousand (6:1–15), walking on water (6:16–21), curing the man blind from birth (9:1–7), and raising Lazarus from the dead (11:34–46).

13. Brown, *Gospel according to John*, cxli, cxliv, 201–4, and *Introduction to the Gospel of John*, 301–2. Brown often wrote of Jesus "replacing" Jewish feasts, but Francis Moloney, who posthumously edited *Introduction*, suggested that today Brown would have favored using the word *fulfill*.
14. Bruce M. Metzger, *A Textual Commentary on the New Testament*, 2nd ed. (Stuttgart: United Bible Societies, 1994), 178.
15. Brown, *Gospel according to John*, 206; Leon Morris, *Gospel according to John* (Grand Rapids: Eerdmans, 1995), 265n6; and Keener, *Gospel of John*, 635–36.
16. Huntsman, "Jesus on Jesus," 72–73.
17. Jerome Murphy-O'Connor, *The Holy Land: An Oxford Archaeological Guide*, 5th ed. (Oxford: Oxford University Press, 2008), 29–30; and Keener, *Gospel of John*, 636–39.
18. Metzger, *Textual Commentary*, 179. See the competing arguments of Zane C. Hodges, "Problem Passages in the Gospel of John, Part 5: The Angel at Bethesda—John 5:4," *Bibliotheca Sacra* 136 (1979): 25−39; and Gordon D. Fee, "On the Inauthenticity of John 5:3b−4," *Evangelical Quarterly* 54 (1982): 207−18.
19. Huntsman, *Miracles of Jesus*, 52–53.
20. James E. Talmage, *Jesus the Christ* (Salt Lake City: Deseret Book, 1982), 1146–49; Bruce R. McConkie, *The Mortal Messiah*, vol. 1, *From Bethlehem to Calvary* (Salt Lake City: Deseret Book, 1979), 453–54; and Fred E. Woods, "The Water Imagery in John's Gospel: Power, Purification, and Pedagogy," in *The Lord of the Gospels*, ed. Bruce A. Van Orden and Brent L. Top (Salt Lake City: Deseret Book, 1991), 192. For this miracle as a symbol of the incarnation itself, see Huntsman, "'And the Word Was Made Flesh': A Latter-day Saint Exegesis of the Blood and Water Imagery in the Gospel of John," *Studies in Bible and Antiquity* 1 (2009): 55–57, and *Miracles of Jesus*, 15–19.
21. Huntsman, *Miracles of Jesus*, 42–44.
22. The Greek term *krabbatos* suggests a mat, camp bed, pallet, or perhaps a gurney that could be used to transport the sick. See Peter von der Osten-Sacken, "krabbatos," in *Exegetical Dictionary of the New Testament*, ed. Horst Balz and Gerhard Schneider, 3 vols. (Grand Rapids, MI.: Eerdmans, 1990–3), 2:313; and Kim Papaioannou, "John 5:18: Jesus and Sabbath Law: A Fresh Look at a Challenging Text," *Journal of the Adventist Theological Society* 20, nos. 1–2 (2009): 245.
23. Tom Thatcher, "The Sabbath Trick: Unstable Irony in the Fourth Gospel," *Journal for the Study of the New Testament* 76 (1999): 53–77.
24. The biblical foundations for the later rabbinic prohibitions seem to have involved carrying heavy loads, presumably for sale in the market, and would not have immediately applied to the man carrying his pallet (see Papaioannou, "Jesus and Sabbath Law," 247). Instead, carrying the sleeping mat might have constituted transporting an object from one domain to another, an infraction of the oral law as it was later codified in the Mishnah (see m. *Shabbat* 7:2; compare Nehemiah 13:19; Jeremiah 17:21). Stephen Westerholm and Craig A. Evans, *Dictionary of the New Testament Background* (Downers Grove, IL: InterVarsity Academic, 2000), s.v. "Sabbath"; Keener, *Gospel of John*, 641–43; and Cornelis Bennema,

Encountering Jesus: Character Studies in the Gospel of John (Minneapolis: Fortress, 2014), 190.

25. This is important for Christians, including Latter-day Saints, to keep in mind, especially because bandying about unnuanced criticism of Pharisees today can unintentionally be taken as being critical of modern Rabbinic Judaism, since post-Temple Judaism developed largely from the Pharisaic school. In fact, historically, Jesus has more in common with the Pharisees than he did with other groups in the Second Temple period, and it is worth noting that the most strident opposition to Jesus was from the Jerusalem leadership, which consisted of the chief priests and *leading* Pharisees, and not necessarily from all Pharisees. See Trevan G. Hatch, *A Stranger in Jerusalem: Seeing Jesus as a Jew* (Eugene, OR: WIPF & Stock, 2019), 168–74.
26. Bennema, *Encountering Jesus*, 189.
27. Interestingly, Jesus's first miracle in Mark, the casting out of a demon, which took place in a synagogue on the Sabbath (Mark 1:21–27), did not raise any question about violations of the Sabbath. Neither did healing Simon's mother-in-law that same afternoon (vv. 30–31), although many waited until sunset to travel to be healed by Jesus (vv. 32–24). Westerholm and Evans note, "That not every record of a sabbath healing is linked with a dispute suggests that Jesus' activities were not in flagrant transgression of existing formulations of sabbath law and that, perhaps in the initial stages of his career, public enthusiasm may have silenced whatever private compunctions may have been felt." "Sabbath," 1032.
28. Bennema, *Encountering Jesus*, 191–92.
29. "The 'something worse' than thirty-eight years of illness would be not knowing who Jesus really is, not receiving the divine life that he gives but experiencing divine judgment instead." Bennema, *Encountering Jesus*, 193.
30. Keener, *Gospel of John*, 646; and Peder Borgen, "The Sabbath Controversy in John 5:1–18 and the Analogous Controversy Reflected in Philo's Writings," in *The Gospel of John: More Light from Philo, Paul and Archaeology* (Leiden: Brill, 2014), 183–84. Philo, an important first-century Hellenized Jewish philosopher, tried to explain God's working on the Sabbath by noting that the LXX text of Genesis 2:2 noted that because God was always active and creative, he actually "caused to rest" (Greek *katepausen*), not "rested" (Greek *epausato*), on the first Sabbath (*Allegorical Interpretation* 1.5, 18; *On the Cherubim* 87). A later rabbinic commentary, which might have preserved ideas from the earlier period, explained that since the heavens and the earth are the dwelling place of God and one is permitted to move items around in his dwelling, God is permitted to work (Genesis Rabbah 30:6).
31. Bacchiocchi, "Sabbath in John," 3.
32. Huntsman, "Jesus on Jesus," 73.
33. A. J. Droge, "Sabbath Work/Sabbath Rest: Genesis, Thomas, John," *History of Religions* 47, nos. 2–3 (2007–2008): 112–41.
34. Karl Kerteleg, "lyo," in Balz and Schneider, *Exegetical Dictionary of the New Testament*, 2:368.
35. Papaioannou claims, "The resultant implication is that Jesus was setting the Sabbath free from rabbinic casuistry, 'unbinding' tedious human prohibitions, and that in doing so he was moving within the sphere of his rights as a teacher

of the law." "Jesus and Sabbath Law," 257. While we agree that Jesus in general came to set people free from bondage, including from "burdensome" systems of all sorts, Papaioannou's characterization is overly triumphalistic in its portrayal of Pharisaism.

36. This passage seems to have inspired Joseph Smith, serving as a catalyst for his King Follet discourse, which is important for Latter-day Saint theology and its Christology in particular. In it Joseph Smith is reported to have taught, "What did Jesus Christ do the same thing as I se[e] the Father do see the father do what, work out a kingdom, when I do so to I will give to the father which will add to his glory." "Discourse, 7 April 1844, as Reported by Wilford Woodruff," 135, *The Joseph Smith Papers*, https://www.josephsmithpapers.org.
37. Rather than being an ancient term, *eschatology* was a term first used in seventeenth-century Lutheran dogmatics as a way of discussing Christian scripture or doctrine "about death, the resurrection of the dead, the last judgment, the end or dissolution of the world, about hell or eternal death and, finally, about eternal life." Jörg Frey, "New Testament Eschatology—an Introduction: Classical Issues, Disputed Themes, and Current Perspectives, in *Eschatology of the New Testament and Some Related Documents*, ed. Jan G. van der Watt (Tübingen, Germany: Mohr Siebeck, 2011), 6.
38. Examples of Synoptic future eschatology include Luke 6:35; Mark 8:35 (parallels Matthew 16:25; Luke 17:33); Mark 8:38 (parallels Luke 9:26); Mark 9:1 (parallels Matthew 16:28; Luke 9:27); Mark 9:43 (parallel Matthew 18:8–9); Mark 10:30 (parallels Matthew 19:29; Luke 18:30); Luke 20:35–36; Mark 13:26 (parallels Matthew 24:30; Luke 21:27); and Mark 14:62 (parallels Matthew 26:64; Luke 22:69). Luke occasionally depicts *realized* eschatology—for instance, in Luke 11:20 and 17:21. Outside the Gospels, apocalyptic imagery is a particularly vivid manifestation of eschatology that presents a detailed imagination of the end time. See Frey, "New Testament Eschatology," 20.
39. "The verb here is perfect, indicating a completed action with continuing effects." R. Alan Culpepper, "Realized Eschatology in the Experience of the Johannine Community," in *The Resurrection of Jesus in the Gospel of John*, ed. Craig R. Koester and Reimund Bieringer (Tübingen, Germany: Mohr Siebeck, 2008), 526.
40. Brown, *Gospel according to John*, cxvi–cxxi. See also Culpepper, "Realized Eschatology," 253; Huntsman, *Becoming the Beloved Disciple*, 93.
41. Culpepper, "Realized Eschatology," 255.
42. See Brown, *Gospel according to John*, 326–27, 343–44; Keener, *Gospel of John*, 722–24, 739; and J. Ramsey Michaels, *The Gospel of John*, The International Commentary on the New Testament (Grand Rapids: Eerdmans, 2010), 423–24.
43. m. Nedarim 3:11. See Brown, *Gospel according to John*, 312; and Keener, *Gospel of John*, 716. Importantly, it was because circumcision on the eighth day was a time-bound commandment that it could supersede the weekly Sabbath; any circumcisions other than those performed on the eighth day of a boy's life were still forbidden on Sabbath (see Šabbat 19).
44. For lists of references from Tannaitic literature, see Keener, *Gospel of John*, 716–17; and Borgen, "Sabbath Controversy in John 5:1–18," 183.
45. Bacchiocchi, "Sabbath in John," 5.

46. R. Alan Culpepper, *Anatomy of the Fourth Gospel: A Study in Literary Design* (Philadelphia: Fortress, 1983), 139–40; and Keener, *Gospel of John*, 639–40.
47. Whereas the Marcan narrator seems to enjoy describing Jesus's miracles in colorful detail, including his use of words, actions, and objects, Matthew and Luke generally shy away from portraying any of Jesus's miracles in a way that would make them seem more magical than divine. Because of the even greater divinity of the Johannine Jesus, miracles in the Fourth Gospel generally just need Jesus to speak or will something for it to be done; see Huntsman, *Miracles of Jesus*, 133–36.
48. Huntsman, "'Word Was Made Flesh,'" 54–55, 57–59, 63–65.
49. Huntsman, *Miracles of Jesus*, 96–99.
50. Jesus, in fact, made it clear that this man's blindness was not the result of either his parents' or his own sin (John 9:3). Indeed, Jesus himself, though perfect, submitted to baptism "to fulfill all righteousness" (Matthew 3:15).
51. Thatcher, "Sabbath Trick," 57.
52. Huntsman, *Miracles of Jesus*, 99–100.
53. Jeannine K. Brown, "Creation's Renewal in the Gospel of John," *Catholic Biblical Quarterly* 72, no. 2 (2010): 285–86.
54. Herold Weiss, "The Sabbath in the Fourth Gospel," *Journal of Biblical Literature* 110, no. 2 (1991): 311–21.
55. Brown, "Creation's Renewal," 287–88.

Chapter Six

Sabbath and Sunday in Ancient Christianity: Second through Sixth Centuries

Jason R. Combs

The Christian practice of worshipping on Sunday may have had its origins in the first century, but it would be many more centuries before Sunday became a "Sabbath" for Christians. In the earliest centuries of Christianity, Christians were divided on the Sabbath.[1] Some early Christians believed that they should continue to worship on Saturday with their fellow (non-Christian) Jews, as Jesus and the earliest disciples had done (see Luke 4:16; Luke 23:56; Acts 13:14–15, 44; 17:2). Other Christians believed that they should not worship on Saturday. For them, the Sabbath was a part of the law of Moses that had been fulfilled in Jesus Christ (see Colossians 2: 16–17; compare Romans 14:5; Galatians 4:10–11). Some of these Christians insisted that the biblical Sabbath rest was a foreshadowing of a greater heavenly rest (see Colossians 2:16–17; Hebrews 4:4–11) or of a continual rest from sin in this life (see below). Christian understanding of the Sabbath and of a day set apart for worship was, therefore, bound up with how Christians understood their own relationship to Judaism.[2]

Christian practices of worship on the Sabbath (Saturday) and on the Lord's day (Sunday) varied across the Roman Empire and across time.[3]

The story of the Christian development of worship on Sunday can be told through the words of two Christians from the second century—Ignatius of Antioch and Justin Martyr—and a few more from the fourth and fifth centuries—John Chrysostom and the authors of the *Apostolic Constitutions* (an ancient church handbook of instruction). These ancient Christian authors ultimately represent only those practices that they themselves were familiar with and their own personal biases regarding proper Christian worship. Nevertheless, through their words we can gain insights into how Christians came to prefer Sunday as the official day for worship and how beliefs developed regarding what should and should not be done on that day.

A Saturday or a Sunday Sabbath?

Ignatius of Antioch

Christian beliefs and practices surrounding the Sabbath were influenced by Christianity's relationship with Judaism. We find an example of this as early as the start of the second century in the writings of Ignatius of Antioch, bishop of the church in Syria.[4] Around AD 110, Ignatius was arrested by Roman authorities—he said that he was bound in chains for his belief in Christ.[5] Under a ten-person military guard, Ignatius was taken to Rome, where he expected to be tortured and killed by wild beasts in an amphitheater.[6] As the convoy traveled toward Rome, they were delayed in the city of Smyrna on the west coast of modern-day Turkey. Ignatius took advantage of the opportunity to write letters to Christians who had supported him on this difficult journey.[7] One of these letters was written to a church about sixty miles south of Smyrna, in the city of Magnesia on the Meander river.[8] Ignatius expressed his gratitude that the bishop of that church and some of the elders had visited him.[9] He counseled the church members in Magnesia to trust their leaders.[10] Then he offered the following warning:

> Do not be deceived by false opinions or old fables that are of no use. For if we are living according to Judaism presently, then we admit that we have not received God's gracious gift. . . . It is outlandish to proclaim Jesus Christ and practice Judaism.[11]

It is not clear what prompted Ignatius's invective against Christians believing or worshipping like Jews.[12] Perhaps the bishop of Magnesia had said something that concerned Ignatius. Perhaps Ignatius had recently encountered other Christians whose practices were too Jewish for his liking. Whatever the case, it is clear Ignatius thought that Christians ought to distinguish themselves from Jews. Yet he only provided a single hint regarding how a Christian might set herself or himself apart: by "no longer keeping the Sabbath [Saturday] but living according to the Lord's day [Sunday]."[13] It is difficult to say how many Christians in this period gathered with each other to worship the Lord on the Sabbath (Saturday), or how many Christians gathered in a synagogue with Jews to worship together on that day.[14] But these practices must have been common enough to warrant Ignatius's warning to the Magnesians: don't worship on the Sabbath (Saturday) like the Jews.

Even though Ignatius may have tried to distinguish Christianity from Judaism, in practice this was not so easily accomplished. In fact, Ignatius's only argument for why Christians should not observe the Sabbath *like Jews* was based on his reading of the Jewish Bible—the Christian Old Testament:

> For the most divine prophets lived according to Jesus Christ. . . . And so those who lived according to the old ways came to a new hope, no longer keeping the Sabbath but living according to the Lord's day.[15]

Ignatius did not defend this reading of the Old Testament. He provided no evidence to support his claim that the ancient prophets were actually Christians, meaning that they "lived according to Jesus Christ." But he was convinced—and assumed that his Christian readers would be too—that the ancient prophets not only were Christian, but also had already ceased observing the Sabbath and had begun worshipping on the Lord's day long ago.

Ignatius was not the only ancient Christian who believed that Christianity should distinguish itself from Judaism in practices of Sabbath observance, nor was he the only one to suggest that the Old Testament justified worship on the Lord's day rather than the Sabbath. Whereas Ignatius had only implied that the prophets of old did not keep the Sabbath, Justin Martyr provided evidence for this claim.

Justin Martyr

Justin Martyr was a convert to Christianity (died ca. AD 165).[16] In one of his writings, he provided a detailed account of his conversion.[17] He described how he sought for truth first among the philosophy of the Stoics and then among the Peripatetics and Pythagoreans before turning to the philosophy of Plato. One day, as he walked along the seashore pondering all he had learned, he happened upon an older gentleman who was a Christian. This man was kind and friendly. As they visited, the man listened to Justin's personal struggles with finding truth. At first, the old man only asked him questions. Then, when Justin was forced to acknowledge he did not have all the answers, the man began to teach him. He told Justin of prophets long ago that had foretold the coming of the Son of God who would redeem the world. He testified of God's purpose for humanity and of redemption in Jesus Christ. Justin's heart and mind were touched, and he became convinced that he had now discovered the only true philosophy: Christianity. Like Ignatius, Justin Martyr believed that Christianity needed to be distinguished from Judaism. Just as Justin believed that Christianity was the only true philosophy, he also believed that Christianity was the one and only true Israel—and he used the words of the ancient prophets of Israel to demonstrate his point.[18]

For Justin Martyr, true Israel observed not the Sabbath but the Lord's day. The Apostle Paul had once argued that circumcision was not necessary for Gentile-Christians to be redeemed by Christ because Abraham was justified by God for his faith prior to receiving circumcision (see Romans 4: 1–12; Galatians 3:1–18).[19] Justin now adopted that same logic and applied it to the Sabbath:

> And why did [God] not instruct those persons who lived before the time of Moses and Abraham to observe these same precepts; men who are called just and were pleasing to God, even though they were not circumcised in the flesh, and did not keep the Sabbaths?[20]

The implied answer is that God did not teach the people to observe the Sabbath until the time of Moses because the Sabbath itself is not necessary for salvation. And if the Sabbath was not necessary for those who lived before Moses, Justin thought, then it was not needed now.[21] Justin relied on this argument again and again.[22]

For Justin, the Jewish practice of resting on the Sabbath was nothing more than idleness: "You consider yourselves religious when you refrain from work on one day out of the week, and in doing so you don't understand the real meaning of that precept."[23] This was a common criticism lobbied against Jews; they were called "lazy" and "idle" for their refusal to work on the Sabbath.[24] For instance, the Roman poet Juvenal, writing around the same time as Ignatius, said of the Jews: "It's their fathers who are to blame, taking every seventh day as a day of laziness and separate from ordinary life."[25] Similarly, the Roman historian Tacitus, also writing in the early second century AD, connected the Jewish Sabbath and the Jubilee year prescribed in Leviticus 25 as equal opportunities for idleness: "They [the Jews] say that they first chose to rest on the seventh day because that day ended their toils; but after a time they were led by the charms of indolence to give over the seventh year as well to inactivity."[26] Justin adopted this common Roman criticism of the Jews, but he suggested that the reason for Jewish idleness was actually a misinterpretation of the Sabbath commandment. In one instance, Justin argued that the Sabbath was imposed on Jews for only one reason: so that they "would be forced to remember [God], as he himself said, *That you may know that I am God your Savior*."[27] In this paraphrase of Exodus 31:13 or Ezekiel 20:12, 20, Justin emphasized that knowledge of God—"that you may *know*"—is the primary purpose for the Sabbath and implied that the Jews misinterpreted this purpose. In another instance, Justin argued that the "true . . . Sabbath of God" is indeed to be a rest, but not from work as the Jews had assumed; instead, "the New Law demands that you observe a perpetual Sabbath"—that is, a rest from sinful deeds.[28] Whatever the purpose of the Sabbath command was intended to be, Justin was certain that it did not involve resting from work on the seventh day.

Even though Justin Martyr repeatedly discredited the idea of observing the seventh-day Sabbath, he was not against worshipping on a regular, set-apart day. At the end of Justin's *First Apology* (written ca. AD 155), a defense of Christianity that he wrote to the Roman emperor Hadrian, he explained Christian worship on Sunday in this way: "And it is on Sunday that we all make assembly in common, since it is the first day, on which God changed darkness and matter and made the world, and Jesus Christ our savior rose from the dead on the same day."[29] In Exodus, when the Sabbath commandment was given, the Lord explained the reason for resting on the seventh day by linking it to his work of creation: "For in six days the Lord made heaven and earth, the sea, and all that in them is, and rested the seventh day: wherefore the Lord blessed the sabbath day, and hallowed it" (Exodus 20:11). Justin, however, said that Christians worship on Sunday in order to remember not the conclusion of creation, but rather the first day of the creation of the world and the resurrection of Jesus—the *new* creation—because both occurred on the same day of the week.[30] In this way, Justin adapted the very logic used to explain the Sabbath commandment in Exodus in order to explain Christian worship on the Lord's day, Sunday.

Notice that Justin said nothing about resting from work on Sunday. Most Christians in this period did not have the luxury to neglect their work. Moreover, were Christians to abstain from work only one day after the Jews, it could reinforce the very assumption that people like Justin were laboring to avoid—that Christians were just a heretical sect of Judaism.[31]

The work of Ignatius and Justin Martyr was just the beginning. It would take many more centuries before Sunday was accepted as the most important day for Christian worship. And even in the fourth century AD, some Christians continued to worship with Jews on the Sabbath (Saturday).

John Chrysostom

The Christian bishop and orator John Chrysostom (AD 347–407) lived in a time very different from that of Ignatius and Justin Martyr. When John was born, Christianity had already been one of the official religions of the Roman Empire for more than thirty years. Under the Roman emperor Constantine the Great, persecution of Christians had ceased (due to the Edict of Milan, given AD 313) and the Lord's day, Sunday, was even declared an empire-wide day of rest (AD 321)—as was the Jewish Sabbath.[32] Constantine's Christian biographer celebrated these changes:

> [Constantine] decreed that all those under Roman government should rest on the days named after the Savior, and similarly that they should honor the days of the Sabbath. . . . The Day of Salvation then, which also bears the names of Light-Day and Sun-Day, he taught all the military to revere devoutly. To those who shared the divinely given faith [Christianity] he allowed free time to attend unhindered the church of God, on the assumption that with all impediments removed they would join in the prayers.[33]

Within a few years of John Chrysostom's thirtieth birthday, another major change occurred. The Roman emperor Theodosius I declared Christianity to be no longer *an* official religion but *the* official religion of the Roman Empire (February 27, 380).[34] Although certain protections were still extended to Jews and to pagans, Christians were now a preferred class of people. In a time such as this, one might assume that no Christian would be found celebrating Jewish festivals and other traditions, but many still did—even in Chrysostom's home city.

John Chrysostom grew up in the same city as Ignatius: Syrian Antioch. There he received the best education available. This training, combined with his innate talent for speaking, would eventually earn him the epithet "golden-mouthed" (*chrysostomos* in Greek). His family was wealthy, but as John grew and became increasingly devoted to the teachings of Jesus Christ, he felt the need to renounce his wealth and give it to the poor. So he became a monk, then later a deacon in Antioch who oversaw the distribution of aid to the poor. By AD 386, six years after Theodosius had declared Christianity the official religion of the Roman Empire, John Chrysostom was ordained to the priesthood and began preaching regularly to the Christian congregations in Antioch. He served in this capacity for the next decade, and word spread of his talent for preaching and leadership. In AD 398, he was invited to become the Bishop of Constantinople—one of the most important Christian leadership positions at that time. As the capital of the Eastern Empire, Constantinople was a wealthy city, and the church leaders there tended to be wealthy as well. True to his form, John Chrysostom ordered that their wealth be sold to feed the poor, and he regularly preached against the wealthy and powerful from the pulpit of the Great Church (*Magna Ecclesia*), which would later become Hagia Sophia.[35]

Most of Chrysostom's teachings about the Sabbath come from the early years after his ordination as he preached in Antioch (ca. AD 386–389).[36] One might think that the sharp rhetoric of people such as Ignatius of Antioch and Justin Martyr would have been sufficient to delineate between Christian and Jewish practices and to dissuade Christians from participating in any practices deemed too Jewish. Yet John Chrysostom lived more than two hundred and fifty years after those authors, and some Christians continued to observe Jewish festivals and worship with Jews on the Sabbath in addition to attending church on the Lord's day. John Chrysostom presented himself as a physician attempting to cure this "Judaizing disease" of his congregation:

> What is this disease? The festivals of the pitiful and miserable Jews are soon to march upon us one after the other and in quick succession: the feast of Trumpets, the feast of Tabernacles, the fasts. There are many in our ranks who say they think as we do. Yet some of these are going to watch the festivals, and others will join the Jews in keeping their

> feasts and observing their fasts. I wish to drive this perverse custom from the Church right now. . . . But now that the Jewish festivals are close by and at the very door, if I should fail to cure those who are sick with the Judaizing disease, I am afraid that, because of their ill-suited association and deep ignorance, some Christians may partake in the Jews' transgressions; once they have done so, I fear my discourses on these transgressions will be in vain. For if they hear no word from me today, they will then join the Jews in their fasts; once they have committed this sin, it will be useless for me to apply the remedy.[37]

Chrysostom concluded his sermon, declaring himself free from the blood and sins of any Christian who would dare to attend synagogue or worship with Jews, including on the Sabbath:

> If any of you, whether you are here present or not, shall go to the spectacle of the Trumpets, or rush off to the synagogue . . . or take part in the fasting, or share in the Sabbath, or observe any other Jewish ritual great or small, I call heaven and earth as my witnesses that I am guiltless of the blood of all of you.[38]

Chrysostom made it clear that Christians worshipping like Jews was a "perverse custom" which he hoped to drive from the church.[39]

Many Christian authors from the second century on had declared that Christians should no longer worship like Jews on the Sabbath. When the Christian "Lord's day," Sunday, had been decreed an official day of rest under Constantine, the Roman emperor's Christian biographer had declared that the Lord himself had transferred the weekly holy day from the Sabbath (Saturday) to the Lord's day (Sunday): "The Word [of God, Jesus Christ] conveyed and transferred the celebration of the Sabbath to the rising of the light, and he transmitted to us an image of true rest, the day of salvation, the day of the Lord, the first day of light."[40] The commandment issued in Exodus 20 was transferred from the last day of the week to the first, from the Sabbath day to the day of the Lord. Now, more than fifty years after this decree, Chrysostom was still trying to convince Christians to stop worshipping with Jews on the Sabbath.

Why would they not listen? How did those Christians who regularly celebrated the Jewish Sabbath and engaged in other Jewish activities justify their actions? Chrysostom's third sermon against Judaizing Christians contains a clue. A lengthy segment of this sermon is devoted to explaining why Jesus celebrated Jewish festivals, but Christians should not.[41] At the beginning of this section, Chrysostom argues:

> Christ did keep the Passover with them. Yet he did not do so with the idea that we should keep the Passover with them. He did so that he might bring the reality to what foreshadowed the reality. He also submitted to circumcision, kept the sabbath, observed the festival days, and ate the unleavened bread. But He did all these things in Jerusalem. However, we are subject to none of these things, and on this Paul spoke out loud and clear: "If you be circumcised, Christ shall be of no advantage to you."[42]

If Chrysostom had to spend so much time explaining why Jesus celebrated Jewish festivals, then it is likely at least some Christians were using accounts of Jesus's life from the Gospels to justify their own practices. Chrysostom continues:

> Why did Christ keep the Passover at that time? The old Passover was a type of the Passover to come, and the reality had to supplant the type. So Christ first showed the foreshadowing and then brought the reality to the banquet table. Once the reality has come, the type which foreshadowed it is henceforth lost in its own shadow and no longer fills the need.[43]

For Chrysostom, the Jewish celebration of the Passover was only a type and shadow of the "banquet table," that is, the sacrament of the Lord's Supper.[44] Chrysostom describes the true Passover as follows:

> [It is] the offering and sacrifice which is celebrated at each religious service. That you may know that this is true, listen to Paul when he says: "For Christ, our Passover, has been sacrificed" (1 Cor 5:7), and again: "As often as you shall eat this bread and drink the cup, you proclaim the death of the Lord" (1 Cor 11:26). So as often as you approach the sacrificial banquet with a clean conscience, you celebrate the Passover.[45]

John Chrysostom goes on to suggest that this logic applies to all Christian participation in what he has deemed Jewish practices. Certainly,

Chrysostom would agree with the synod in Laodicea (ca. AD 360), which tried to add authority to this type of anti-Sabbath polemic by decreeing, "Christians must not Judaize by resting on the Sabbath, but must work on that day, rather honoring the Lord's day; and, if they can, resting then as Christians."[46]

Chrysostom would probably also agree with a church order (that is, a church handbook of instruction) that originated in Antioch, likely during his life. This church order, the *Apostolic Constitutions*, declared, "If any clergy or laity enter a synagogue of Jews or of heretics to pray, let him be condemned and excommunicated."[47]

Christians such as Ignatius, Justin Martyr, and John Chrysostom held strong supersessionist views about Christianity's relationship to Judaism. We have seen how these views influenced their practices of Christian worship—particularly their beliefs about the day that Christians should gather to worship Jesus Christ. Some of these authors also held strong views about how proper Christian worship should be practiced on Sunday.

Christian Worship on the Lord's Day

Justin Martyr

When Justin Martyr wrote his defense of Christianity to the Roman emperor Hadrian, he not only explained that Christians worshipped on Sunday, but also shared a little about what that worship entailed. For Justin and many early Christians, Sunday worship was a time to gather as one, to listen to inspired messages, and to partake of the sacrament of the Lord's Supper (also known as the Eucharist or Communion):[48]

> And on the day called Sunday those who dwell in cities or the countryside gather together, and the memoirs of the apostles [the Gospels] or the writings of the prophets [from the Old Testament] are read for as long as there is time. Then, when the reader has stopped, the one presiding [gives] a sermon, admonishes [us] and invites [us] to imitate these good things [the words of scripture]. Then we all stand up together and pray. And . . . when we have stopped praying, bread and wine [mixed with] water are brought, and the one presiding prays and offers thanks in similar fashion, to the best of his ability, and the people give their ascent, saying "Amen." And the [bread and wine/water], over which thanks have been given, are distributed to each

> person and each partakes. And it is sent to those who are not present by means of the deacons.[49]

Christians did not yet have church buildings, so all the events Justin describes here would have taken place in small apartments, in the larger homes of wealthy Christians, or in a rented location such as a tavern or hotel.[50] The practices summarized here by Justin are not unique to the Christian gatherings he attended; many of these practices were already described in the first-century writings of the Apostle Paul (for example, see 1 Corinthians 11:23–26; 14:26–33).[51] And, by the beginning of the second century, when the Roman governor Pliny the Younger summarized his knowledge of Christian worship, it too sounds quite similar to Justin's description.

Pliny the Younger was governor of Pontus and Bithynia on the shore of the Black Sea, the northwest coast of modern-day Turkey. Around AD 112, Pliny wrote a letter to the Roman emperor Trajan to solicit advice regarding the decline in worship at the local pagan temples—a problem he attributed to a growing population of Christians. In this letter, Pliny explained to Trajan what he had come to learn about this new religious group. When we read the words of Pliny, we must remember that his description of Christian practices is based on secondhand knowledge, as Pliny himself never witnessed Christian worship. Pliny's report to Trajan is based on Pliny's own interpretation of what some Christians confessed when they had been arrested and accused of sedition. Some of these Christian confessions were even extracted under torture—"I [Pliny] judged it all the more necessary to find out what the truth was by torturing two female slaves who were called deaconesses."[52] Pliny was convinced that Christian practices must have been particularly pernicious, given that they were so stubborn in refusing to worship the image of the emperor. Ultimately, however, all that Pliny was able to ascertain about Christian practices was the following:

> [These Christians] asserted, however, that the sum and substance of their fault or error had been that they were accustomed to meet on a fixed day before dawn and sing responsively a hymn to Christ as to a god, and to bind themselves by oath, not to some crime, but not to commit fraud, theft, or adultery, not falsify their trust, nor to refuse to return a trust when called upon to do so. When this was over, it was

> their custom to depart and to assemble again to partake of food—but ordinary and innocent food.[53]

Despite the fact that this summary of Christian worship has been filtered through Pliny's own biases, we can still discern a pattern that corresponds with Justin Martyr's description. First, Christians regularly gathered on a fixed day, a day set apart for this purpose—most likely Saturday or Sunday.[54] Second, at this meeting they worshipped God together and celebrated their shared belief in Jesus Christ—Justin mentions scripture reading and prayer, whereas Pliny mentions hymn singing. Third, they used this time to recommit themselves to living a Christlike life of honesty and good works—Justin mentions a sermon or address admonishing members to live virtuous lives, and Pliny describes an oath Christians would affirm to live justly. Finally, both Justin and Pliny suggest that part of the regular Christian worship involved eating food. Whereas Christians who were confessing to Pliny only affirmed that this food was "ordinary and innocent," Justin described a sacred and symbolic meal in which ordinary bread and wine become sacred as they are blessed and then shared among all Christians (compare 1 Corinthians 11:23–26).[55]

Justin and Pliny do not provide us with any details about the content of the sermons, songs, or prayers that were part of early Christian worship. Fortunately, another Christian document, the Didache (written ca. AD 100), describes the prayers some Christians offered over the Eucharist.[56] First, it describes the blessing over the cup of wine: "We give you thanks, our Father, for the holy vine of David, your child, which you made known to us through Jesus your child. To you be the glory forever." This is followed by the blessing over the bread: "We give you thanks, our Father, for the life and knowledge that you made known to us through Jesus your child. To you be the glory forever."[57] After baptized Christians[58] finished partaking of the wine and bread, another prayer was offered:

> We give you thanks, holy Father, for your holy name which you have made reside in our hearts, and for the knowledge, faith, and immortality that you made known to us through Jesus your child. To you be the glory forever. You, O Master Almighty, created all things for the sake of your name, and gave both food and drink to humans for their refreshment, that they might give you thanks. And you graciously provided us with spiritual food and drink, and eternal life

> through your child. Above all we thank you because you are powerful. To you be the glory forever. Remember your church, O Lord; save it from all evil, and perfect it in your love. And gather it from the four winds into your kingdom, which you prepared for it. For yours is the power and the glory forever. May grace come and this world pass away. Hosanna to the God of David. If anyone is holy, let him come; if anyone is not, let him repent. Maranatha! Amen.[59]

It is not clear whether Ignatius, Justin Martyr, or the Christians interrogated by Pliny would have been familiar with these prayers, as worship varied somewhat from city to city. Nevertheless, with these few examples we see already at the beginning of the second century the development of a basic structure or pattern for Christian worship.

John Chrysostom and the Apostolic Constitutions

By the time of John Chrysostom, Christians had more time and space for worship. Since Constantine had declared Sunday a day for rest and worship, more Christians were now able to devote themselves to the Lord at least one day a week; and since Christians now belonged to a legal religion with government support, they could afford to erect buildings dedicated solely to Christian worship. Despite these changes, the basic structure of Christian worship remained quite similar to that outlined by Justin Martyr hundreds of years earlier. Details about worship in Chrysostom's church survive from the church order known as the *Apostolic Constitutions*.[60] Although church services throughout the Roman Empire and beyond its borders could vary, the *Apostolic Constitutions* provide one of the most detailed examples of how worship on the Lord's day might have been experienced.[61]

Several passages from the *Apostolic Constitutions* detail how the authors believed a church service should be organized. In one passage, the authors compare the church building to a ship, with the bishop serving as the captain, the deacons as mariners, and other church members as passengers.[62] The bishop was to sit on a seat in the front with elders (the "presbytery") on each side, while the deacons and deaconesses prepared places for the other church members to sit.[63] Everyone was invited to sit in silence before the meeting began.

When the meeting began, an appointed reader stood at the front to read from the Old Testament and then the New Testament. In antiquity, books were expensive, and reading was a luxury; only the wealthiest citizens in the

Roman Empire owned books. The overwhelming majority of Christians did not personally own any books, let alone scriptures.[64] Attending church was their one chance to hear the scriptures. So according to the *Apostolic Constitutions*, they sat together silently and listened as the assigned reader opened the Old Testament and read two selections of passages. Then another person stood and sang one of the Psalms, and the congregation "join[ed] at the conclusions of the verses."[65] Finally, a selection from Acts or Paul's letters was read aloud, followed by a selection from the Gospels.[66]

After the reading, the bishop, also called the high priest, stood and addressed the congregation, saying: "The grace of our Lord Jesus Christ, the love of God and the Father, and the fellowship of the Holy Ghost, be with you all." The congregation responded, "And with your spirit."[67] Some of the elders gave sermons, followed by a sermon from the bishop exhorting the congregation to live righteously.[68] Afterward, it was time for the sacrament of the Lord's Supper.

At this point, anyone in the congregation who had not been baptized or who was unworthy to partake of the sacrament was dismissed. The deacon who had dismissed that portion of the congregation would then address those who remained: "Let no one have anything against any one; let no one come in hypocrisy; let us stand upright before the Lord."[69] The men then greeted other men near them with a "holy kiss" (2 Corinthians 13:11–12), and the women did the same with other women.[70] While the congregation was engaged in this ritual kiss, the priests and deacons were preparing the sacrament.

They held such reverence and respect for the sacred rite of the sacrament that some deacons were assigned to stand near the bread and wine with "a fan, made up of thin membranes, or of the feathers of the peacock, or of fine cloth, and . . . silently drive away the small animals that fly about, that they may not come near to the cups."[71] As the sacrament portion of the service began, the bishop or high priest would "make the sign of the cross on his forehead with his hand" and address the congregation: "The grace of Almighty God, and the love of our Lord Jesus Christ, and the fellowship of the holy Ghost, be with you all," to which the congregation responded, "And with your spirit."[72] The bishop or high priest then said, "Let us give thanks to the Lord," and the people responded, "It is meet and right so to do." The *Apostolic Constitutions* explains that the high priest was then to bless the congregation with a prayer, "as Moses commanded the priests to bless the people."[73] The bishop could have offered a prayer similar to this one: "Save Your people, O Lord, and bless Your inheritance, which You have obtained with the precious blood of Your Christ, and have called a royal priesthood, and an holy nation."[74] Additional prayers were also offered for different groups of people and for the church as a whole.[75] All of this was meant to prepare the people to partake of the sacred elements of the Lord's Supper: the bread and wine. According to the *Apostolic Constitutions*, the final prayer spoken by the bishop was as follows:

> O God, who art great, and whose name is great, who art great in counsel and mighty in works, the God and Father of Your holy child Jesus, our Savior; look down upon us, and upon this Your flock, which You have chosen by Him to the glory of Your name; and sanctify our body and soul, and grant us the favor to be "made pure from all filthiness of flesh and spirit," (2 Corinthians 7:1) and to obtain the good things laid up for us, and do not account any of us unworthy; but be our comforter, helper, and protector, through Your Christ, with whom glory, honor, praise, doxology, and thanksgiving be to You and to the Holy Ghost forever. Amen.[76]

To this prayer, the people responded, "Amen." The bishop then said, "holy things for holy persons," and the congregation responded in unison:

> There is One that is holy; there is one Lord, one Jesus Christ, blessed forever, to the glory of God the Father. Amen. "Glory to God in the highest, and on earth peace, good-will among men. Hosanna to the son of David! Blessed be He that comes in the name of the Lord," being the Lord God who appeared to us, "Hosanna in the highest" (Luke 2:14 and Matthew 21:9).[77]

Afterward, the bishop was the first to partake of the bread and wine, followed by the male elders (presbyters/priests), deacons, readers, singers, and ascetics. Then the women officers, deaconesses, celibate-women, and widows, in that order, proceeded to partake with their heads covered. Finally, all the baptized children and the remainder of the congregation, baptized men and women, came forward to receive the bread and wine. As each person stepped forward, the bishop said, "The body of Christ," and the person who received the bread said, "Amen." Then the deacon offered the cup of wine, saying, "The blood of Christ, the cup of life," and the person who received it would say, "Amen."[78]

During this long process, as each individual had the opportunity to come forward one by one to encounter the body of the Lord, a singer chanted Psalm 33.[79] After the last person received the emblems of the body and blood of the Lord, some deacons removed any remaining bread and wine, while another deacon addressed the congregation:

> Now we have received the precious body and the precious blood of Christ, let us give thanks to Him who has thought us worthy to partake of these His holy mysteries; and let us beseech Him that it may not be to us for condemnation, but for salvation, to the advantage of soul and body, to the preservation of piety, to the remission of sins, and to the life of the world to come. Let us arise, and by the grace of Christ let us dedicate ourselves to God, to the only unbegotten God, and to His Christ.[80]

Additional prayers were offered by the bishop and a deacon, then the service concluded as a deacon spoke the words, "Depart in peace."[81]

In the time of John Chrysostom, the *Apostolic Constitutions* presents this liturgy as the ideal church service. There are hints in the text, however, that things did not always go according to plan. For instance, the document insists again and again that the congregation should be silent: "with all quietness and good order . . . they also keeping silence"; "stand up in great silence"; "keep them silent"; and "praying silently."[82] The *Apostolic Constitutions* even quotes a scripture to justify this emphasis on silence: "Be silent, and hear, O Israel" (see Deuteronomy 27:9).[83] The text emphasizes this point so strongly that it seems church services were probably not as silent as the bishop would have liked. Indeed, Chrysostom, along with other bishops and presbyters, occasionally felt the need to admonish their congregations to be quiet and pay attention.[84] On one occasion, Chrysostom complained that the local Christian women talked more during church services "than in the market, or at the [public] bath . . . as if they came here for recreation."[85] Elsewhere, Chrysostom complains that church members are too distracted during the sermon: "You are called to a kingdom, to the kingdom of the Son of God, and you sit there yawning, and scratching, and dozing?"[86]

Similarly, it seems that Christians in this time may not have attended church services with the frequency that church leadership would have liked. The *Apostolic Constitutions* instructs the local bishop to "command and exhort" his congregation that they should "come constantly to church morning and evening every day."[87] This daily church meeting was not a full service like the one previously described, but rather an opportunity to gather with other members of the church to sing psalms and pray. The bishop was also supposed to admonish his congregation as follows: "And on the day of our Lord's resurrection, which is the Lord's day, meet more diligently . . . Otherwise what apology will he make to God who does not assemble on that day to hear the saving word concerning the resurrection [and receive the sacrament], the gift of holy food?"[88] This admonishment was likely given because congregants were not coming to church.

In a sermon on the baptism of Christ, John Chrysostom took the opportunity to admonish those who were not regularly attending church. For Chrysostom, such people were stealing time from the Lord, "a holy day set apart for listening to spiritual words," by focusing on their own affairs on that day.[89] He begins by pointing out that the Lord could have chosen three or four days for himself, but instead allowed Christians six days to do whatever they want and only one day for himself. Then, using the story of the widow's mites from the Gospels, Chrysostom shows that the Lord does not even demand that Christians stay in church all day on Sunday. He encourages his congregants to be like the widow whom Jesus praised for her great sacrifice because she gave all she had: two small copper coins—two mites (Mark 12:41–44; Luke 21:1–4). Chrysostom says, "What the widow did in her almsgiving, so too you must do on the occasion of this day: just as she cast in two copper coins and gained much favor with God, so too you should lend two hours to God, and you will carry home the profit of countless days."[90] A century later, another church leader would complain: "When the herald gives the summons to church, everyone claims to be too tired. If there is flute and zither music [in the public square], they rush as though they had wings."[91]

John Chrysostom's primary desire was for Christians to attend church to worship on Sunday. Yet he also expressed some concern for how Christians spent their time on the Lord's day outside of church: "God teaches us in parables that one day in the weekly cycle should be wholly set apart and devoted to the service of spiritual things."[92] Statements such as this make it sound as though Chrysostom had begun to apply the biblical Sabbath day prohibitions to the Lord's day. Yet we cannot be certain, because elsewhere Chrysostom suggests that the biblical Sabbath regulations were "partial and temporary."[93] We do know, however, that even a century after Chrysostom, there was still no agreement on whether the prohibitions of the law of Moses against Sabbath-day work applied to Christians' celebration of the Lord's day.

In the late sixth century, Gregory of Tours (died ca. AD 594) wrote a series of anecdotes describing how certain Christians were punished for performing specific labors on the Lord's day. In one instance, a group of Christians near the town of Limoges (located today in France) was apparently consumed by fire from heaven for working on the Lord's day.[94] In another instance, Gregory describes how a Christian began to mill grain on the Lord's day, but as he turned the millstone his hand miraculously clenched shut and he could not open his fist.[95] Near the same time that Gregory of Tours related these accounts to affirm the Lord's day as the new biblical Sabbath, another Gregory proclaimed the opposite. Gregory the Great (died AD 604) allowed that one should "rest from worldly work and devote oneself entirely to prayer on the Lord's day," but also proclaimed that only the anti-Christ would "cause to abstain from all work on the Sabbath and the Lord's day."[96] It would be many more centuries before Sabbatarianism—that is, the belief that the prohibition on Sabbath-day work from Exodus 20 also applies to Christians' Sunday observance—became the norm in some Protestant traditions.

Conclusion

Today, throughout the world, many Christians are identifiable in part by their practices of worshipping together on Sunday. We have seen how these practices developed in the second through the sixth centuries. During this period, the preference for worshipping on Sunday instead of Saturday developed in an effort to distinguish Christianity from Judaism. Once Sunday was secured as the Christian holy day and Christians were seen as distinct from Jews, some Christians began to apply more freely the Sabbath prohibitions from the law of Moses to the Lord's day—including the prohibitions on work. Christians also developed their own distinctive practices of worship. While the basic framework for church services was already established by the beginning of the second century, greater Christian freedom in the fourth century and beyond allowed for further developments, including more time for sermons, the reading of scripture, and the celebration of the Eucharist. I have focused on only a handful of writings, from Ignatius of Antioch and Justin Martyr in the second century to John Chrysostom and the authors of the *Apostolic Constitutions* in the fourth and fifth centuries. Yet in this small sampling of texts, we have seen Christians striving to preserve their ancient traditions while simultaneously adapting their worship to the needs of new generations—even the shared Jewish and Christian practice of a weekly holy day.

Endnotes

1. Important studies on the history of the Sabbath and Sunday in early Christian literature include: Samuele Bacchiocchi, *From Sabbath to Sunday: A Historical Investigation of the Rise of Sunday Observance in Early Christianity* (Rome: Pontifical Gregorian University Press, 1977); Richard J. Bauckham, "Sabbath and Sunday in the Post-Apostolic Church," in *From Sabbath to Lord's Day: A Biblical, Historical, and Theological Investigation*, ed. D. A. Carson (Grand Rapids, MI: Zondervan, 1982), 251–98; Bauckham, "Sabbath and Sunday in the Medieval Church in the West," in Carson, *From Sabbath*, 299–309; Roger T. Beckwith and Wilfrid Stott, *This is the Day: The Biblical Doctrine of the Christian Sunday in its Jewish and Early Church Setting* (London: Marshall, Morgan & Scott, 1978); Jean Danielou, *The Bible and the Liturgy* (Notre Dame, IN: University of Notre Dame Press, 1956), 242–86; and Willy Rordorf, *Sunday: The History of the Day of Rest and Worship in the Earliest Centuries of the Christian Church*, trans. A. A. K. Graham (London: SCM Press, 1968). Rordorf also assembled an anthology of ancient Christian texts about the Sabbath and Sunday with German translation in *Sabbat und Sonntag in Alten Kirche* (Zürich: Theologischer Verlag Zürich, 1972).
2. For more on the function of anti-Jewish polemic in early Christian literature, see Daniel Boyarin, *Border Lines: The Partition of Judaeo-Christianity* (Philadelphia: University of Pennsylvania Press, 2004); Charlotte Fonrobert, "Jewish Christians, Judaizers, and Christian anti-Judaism," in *Late Ancient Christianity*, ed. Virginia Burrus, *A People's History of Christianity* 2 (Minneapolis, MN: Fortress Press, 2006), 234–54, 306–9; Paula Fredriksen and Oded Irshai, "Christian Anti-Judaism: Polemics and Policies from the Second to the Seventh Century," in *Cambridge History of Judaism*, vol. 4, *The Late Roman–Rabbinic Period*, ed. Steven T. Katz (Cambridge: Cambridge University Press, 2006), 977–1034; John G. Gager, *The Origins of Anti-Semitism: Attitudes Toward Judaism in Pagan and Christian Antiquity* (Oxford: Oxford University Press, 1983); Andrew S. Jacobs, *Christ Circumcised: A Study in Early Christian History and Difference* (Philadelphia: University of Pennsylvania Press, 2012); Judith M. Lieu, *Image and Reality: The Jews in the World of the Christians in the Second Century* (London: T&T Clark, 1996); Marcel Simon, *Verus Israel: A Study of the Relations between Christians and Jews in the Roman Empire AD 135–425*, trans. Henry McKeating (Portland, OR: Littman, 1986); and Miriam S. Taylor, *Anti-Judaism and Early Christian Identity: A Critique of the Scholarly Consensus*, Studia Post-Biblica 46 (Leiden: Brill, 1995). On the specific issue of Christian anti-Judaism and the Sabbath, see Bacchiocchi, *Anti-Judaism and the Origin of Sunday* (Rome: Pontifical Gregorian University

Press, 1975); Jason Robert Combs, "The Polemical Origin of Luke 6.5D: Dating Codex Bezae's Sabbath-Worker Agraphon," *Journal for the Study of the New Testament* 42, no. 2 (2019): 162–84; and Combs, "Christian Anti-Sabbath Polemic and the Textual Transmission of Luke 4:16 and 23:56," *TC: A Journal of Biblical Textual Criticism* 26 (2021): 1–18.

3. See Acts 20:7; 1 Corinthians 16:2; and Revelation 1:10. On the origin and significance of the "Lord's day," see Bauckham, "The Lord's Day," in Carson, *From Sabbath*, 221–50.
4. On Ignatius as bishop of Syria, see Ignatius, *Romans* (*Rom.*) 2. According to tradition, Ignatius was either the second bishop in Antioch, following Peter (Origen, *Homilies on Luke* 6.4), or the third, following Peter and Euodius (Eusebius, *Eccl. Hist.* 3.22, 36); see Bart D. Ehrman, *The Apostolic Fathers*, Loeb Classical Library (Cambridge, MA; Harvard University Press, 2003), 1:204; and William R. Schoedel, *Ignatius of Antioch: A Commentary on the Letters of Ignatius of Antioch*, Hermeneia (Minneapolis: Fortress Press, 1985), 10–15.
5. See Ignatius, *Ephesians* (*Eph.*) 1.2; 3.1; *Philadelphians* 5.1. On the date of Ignatius's letters, see Eusebius, *Ecclesiastical History* 3.36; and Schoedel, *Ignatius of Antioch*, 3–7.
6. On the ten-person guard, see Ignatius, *Rom.* 5.1; and on death by wild beasts, see Ignatius, *Eph.* 1.2; *Trallians* 10.1; *Rom.* 4.1–2; and 5.2–3.
7. I accept the scholarly consensus that the so-called middle recension best represents the earliest attainable text of Ignatius's letters; see Schoedel, *Ignatius of Antioch*, 4–5.
8. On the route of Ignatius's journey, see Schoedel, *Ignatius of Antioch*, 11.
9. Ignatius, *Magnesians* (*Magn.*) 2.1.
10. Ignatius, *Magn.* 2.1–7.2.
11. Ignatius, *Magn.* 8.1; 10.3; translation modified from Ehrman, *The Apostolic Fathers*, 1:249, 251. Unless otherwise indicated, all translations of Ignatius's letters are from Ehrman, *The Apostolic Fathers.*
12. "I am not writing these things, my beloved, because I have learned that some of you are behaving like this." Ignatius, *Magn.* 11.1.
13. Ignatius, *Magn.* 9.1. On the translation "Lord's day," see Schoedel, *Ignatius of Antioch*, 123n3. For more on Ignatius and the Sabbath, see Gager, *Origins of Anti-Semitism*, 127–28; Lieu, *Image and Reality*, 23–56; and Heather A. McKay, *Sabbath and Synagogue: The Question of Sabbath Worship in Ancient Judaism* (Leiden: Brill, 1994), 179–83.
14. "It would be consonant with Ignatius's concerns elsewhere," Lieu concludes, "if some [Christians] were meeting on the sabbath." *Image and Reality*, 46. It is possible that "observance" in Magnesia could have included synagogue attendance, but that is not explicit in Ignatius's letter. Moreover, "Sabbath observance" could refer to any number of alternative social practices; see Lieu, *Image and Reality,* 47; Schoedel, *Ignatius of Antioch*, 123; and Bacchiocchi, *From Sabbath to Sunday*, 213–18.
15. Ignatius, *Magn.* 8.2–9.1.
16. He came to be called Justin Martyr because, according to tradition, he died as a martyr in ca. AD 165. For more on the life of Justin Martyr, see Robert M. Grant,

Greek Apologists of the Second Century (Philadelphia: Westminster Press, 1988), 50–73; and David Rokeah, *Justin Martyr and the Jews* (Leiden: Brill, 2002).

17. Justin Martyr, *Dialogue with Trypho* (*Dial.*) 2–8.
18. Justin Martyr, *Dial.* 11.5; 123.5–8.
19. See Rokeah, *Justin Martyr and the Jews*, 43–44.
20. Justin Martyr, *Dial.* 27.5. Unless otherwise indicated, all translations of Justin's *Dialogue* are from Thomas B. Falls and Thomas P. Halton, *St. Justin Martyr: Dialogue with Trypho*, ed. Michael Slusser (Washington, DC: Catholic University of America Press, 2003).
21. Justin Martyr, *Dial.* 23.3.
22. See Justin Martyr, *Dial.* 19.5 (all the prophets); 23.1 (Enoch and others); and 92.2 (Enoch, Noah, Noah's children, and others).
23. Justin Martyr, *Dial.* 12.3.
24. See Louis H. Feldman, *Jew and Gentile in the Ancient World: Attitudes and Interactions from Alexander to Justinian* (Princeton, NJ: Princeton University Press, 1993), 166; McKay, *Sabbath and Synagogue*, 192; and Lieu, *Image and Reality*, 121.
25. Juvenal, *Satires* 14.105–6; translation from Susanna Morton Braund, ed., *Juvenal and Persius*, Loeb Classical Library 91 (Cambridge, MA: Harvard University Press, 2004).
26. Tacitus, *Histories* 5.4.3; translation from Clifford H. Moore and John Jackson, eds., *Tacitus, Histories: Books 4–5; Annals: Books 1–3*, Loeb Classical Library 249 (Cambridge, MA: Harvard University Press, 1931). The Roman philosopher Seneca is also remembered to have criticized the Jews for idleness based on their Sabbath practices; see Augustine, *The City of God* D-i 6.10–11.
27. Justin Martyr, *Dial.* 19.6; italics in original.
28. Justin Martyr, *Dial.* 12.3.
29. Justin Martyr, *First Apology* (*1 Apol.*) 67.8. Unless otherwise indicated, all translations of Justin's *First Apology* are from Denis Minns and Paul Parvis, eds., *Justin, Philosopher and Martyr: Apologies*, Oxford Early Christian Texts (Oxford: Oxford University Press, 2009).
30. Regarding Justin's logic, McKay has explained, "In this piece of apologetic, Justin turns on its head the Jewish view of creation as a sequential act with rest as its completion." *Sabbath and Synagogue*, 189.
31. In the wake of Marcion, who taught that Christians should have nothing to do with the Jewish Bible, Christians such as Irenaeus, Tertullian, and others sought to maintain a distinction from Judaism and simultaneously affirm a positive relation between the God of the Old Testament and Jesus. This resulted in affirmations of the Sabbath's end being accompanied by often contradictory reinterpretations of biblical Sabbath law intended to demonstrate Christian continuity with Judaism. For instance, Irenaeus maintains that the Sabbath was not "made void" but was "lawfully" observed by Jesus and others (*Against Heresies* [*Haer.*] 4.8.1–3); yet he then insists that Christians should not observe the Sabbath day but live a continual Sabbath (*Haer.* 4.16.1–2). Likewise, Tertullian claims that Jesus did not end but fulfilled Sabbath law (*Against Marcion* [*Marc.*] 4.12), while at the same time insisting (with his recent predecessors) that the Sabbath command had come to an end (*Marc.* 5.4). Kenneth Strand provides

a helpful summary of Tertullian's position that applies equally well to Irenaeus: "The unifying thread in [these discussions] is that the very same God was the God of both OT and NT dispensations and that the OT and NT do not contradict each other." "Tertullian and the Sabbath," *Andrews University Seminary Studies* 9, no. 2 (1971): 140. Strand shows that both Irenaeus and Tertullian argue this point fervently, even when it means that they contradict themselves. Strand provides a useful overview of Tertullian's thought on the Sabbath, but his conclusion that a shift in belief was caused by Tertullian's Montanist conversion is unconvincing. As Strand himself notes, the shift can be explained by the change from Tertullian's interpretation of passages in Luke to his interpretation of those in Paul. This note is adopted in part from Combs, "Christian Anti-Sabbath Polemic," 34n24.

32. See commentary in Averil Cameron and Stuart G. Hall, *Eusebius, Life of Constantine: Introduction, Translation, and Commentary* (Oxford: Clarendon, 1999), 317; and Christoph Markschies, *Between Two Worlds: Structures of Earliest Christianity*, trans. John Bowden (London: SCM Press, 1999), 34.
33. Translation modified from Cameron and Hall, *Eusebius: Life of Constantine*, 159.
34. For more on this edict, *Cunctos Populos* (*Theodosian Code* 16.1.2), see Clyde Pharr, *The Theodosian Code and Novels and the Sirmondian Constitutions: A Translation with Commentary, Glossary, and Bibliography* (Princeton University Press, 1952), 440. For a further discussion, see R. Malcolm Errington, "Christian Accounts of the Religious Legislation of Theodosius I," *Klio* 79, no. 2 (1997): 398–443.
35. For more on John Chrysostom's background, see Justo L. González, *The Story of Christianity*, vol. 1, *The Early Church to the Dawn of the Reformation*, rev. ed. (New York: HarperCollins, 2010), 227–28; and Robert L. Wilken, *John Chrysostom and the Jews: Rhetoric and Reality in the Late 4th Century* (Berkeley: University of California, 1983).
36. The sermons *Against Judaizing Christians* were most likely presented during John Chrysostom's first two years of preaching in Antioch; see Paul W. Harkins, ed., *Saint John Chrysostom: Discourses Against Judaizing Christians*, Fathers of the Church 68 (Catholic University of America Press, 1979), li–lx.
37. John Chrysostom, *Adv. Jud.* 1.1.5. Unless otherwise indicated, all translations of John Chrysostom's *Against Judaizing Christians* (*Adv. Jud.*) are from Harkins, ed., *Discourses Against Judaizing Christians.*
38. Chrysostom, *Adv. Jud.* 1.8.1.
39. Chrysostom, *Adv. Jud.* 1.1.5.
40. Eusebius, *Commentary on the Psalms* (*Comm. Ps.*), in Patrologia Graeca (PG) 23.1169c; my own translation. Bacchiocchi suggests that Eusebius was exaggerating in his statement that "the Logos" himself had transferred worship from Sabbath to Sunday because he (Eusebius) almost immediately contradicts that statement by saying "all that was prescribed for the Sabbath, we have transferred to the Lord's Day"; see *Origin of Sunday*, 117–118; Bacchiocchi is quoting Eusebius, *Comm. Ps.*, PG 23.1172. However, Eusebius's two statements are not necessarily contradictory. Eusebius could believe that the Logos had transferred the holy day from Sabbath to Sunday and that Christians, therefore, transferred "all that had been necessary to do on the Sabbath . . . to the Lord's

Day." Eusebius, *Comm. Ps.*, PG 23.1172a; my own translation. This note is adopted in part from Combs, "Christian Anti-Sabbath Polemic," 36n32.

41. Chrysostom, *Adv. Jud.* 3.3.9–3.4.1. For more on John Chrysostom's anti-Judaizing interpretation of Jesus's Jewish practices, see Joshua Garroway, "The Law-Observant Lord: John Chrysostom's Engagement with the Jewishness of Christ," *Journal of Early Christian Studies* 18 (2010): 591–615; Jacobs, *Christ Circumcised*, 116–17; and Fredriksen and Irshai, "Christian Anti-Judaism," 1005–7.
42. Chrysostom, *Adv. Jud.* 3.3.9; translation modified from Harkins, *Chrysostom: Discourses*, 58.
43. Chrysostom, *Adv. Jud.* 3.4.1; translation modified from Harkins, *Chrysostom: Discourses*, 59.
44. According to the Synoptic Gospels, Jesus instituted the sacrament (Eucharist) at a Passover meal; see Matthew 26:17–30; Mark 14:12–26; and Luke 22:7–39.
45. Chrysostom, *Adv. Jud.* 3.4.3–4; translation modified from Harkins, *Chrysostom: Discourses*, 60.
46. Canon 29, in *Nicene and Post-Nicene Fathers*, series 2, vol. 14, trans. Henry R. Percival (Oxford: Parker and Co.; New York: Charles Scribner's Sons, 1916), 148. For discussion on the minimal impact of this decree, see Bacchiocchi, *Origin of Sunday*, 118; and F. J. E. Boddens Hosang, *Establishing Boundaries: Christian–Jewish Relations in Early Council Texts and the Writings of Church Fathers* (Leiden: Brill, 2010), 93–99.
47. *Apostolic Constitutions* (*Const. Ap.*) 8.47.65; my own translation based on the Greek from Marcel Metzger, ed. and trans., *Les Constitutions Apostoliques*, III, SC 336 (Paris: Cerf, 1987), 298. See also Fredriksen and Irshai, "Christian Anti-Judaism," 1005.
48. On the history and development of ancient Christian worship, see Paul F. Bradshaw, *Reconstructing Early Christian Worship* (Collegeville, MN: Liturgical Press, 2009); Danielou, *Bible and Liturgy*; Robin M. Jensen and J. Patout Burns, "The Eucharistic Liturgy in Hippo's Basilica Major at the Time of Augustine," in *Augustine through the Ages: An Encyclopedia*, ed. Allan D. Fitzgerald (Grand Rapids, MI: Eerdmans, 1995), 335–38; and Andrew B. McGowan, *Ancient Christian Worship: Early Church Practices in Social, Historical, and Theological Perspective* (Grand Rapids, MI: Baker, 2014).
49. Justin Martyr, *1 Apol.* 67.3–5; translation modified from Minns and Parvis, *Justin, Philosopher and Martyr*, 259–261. On wine mixed with water, see Justin Martyr, *1 Apol.* 65.3.
50. Eventually, Christians would purchase such spaces and adapt them to function as churches—for instance, by adding a baptismal font into the basement; see Edward Adams, *The Earliest Christian Meeting Places: Almost Exclusively Houses?* (London: T&T Clark/Bloomsbury, 2013); and Michael Peppard, *The World's Oldest Church: Bible, Art, and Ritual at Dura-Europos, Syria* (New Haven, CT: Yale University Press, 2016).
51. For more on Christian worship practices in the first century, see Bradshaw, *The Search for the Origins of Christian Worship: Sources and Methods for the Study of Early Liturgy*, 2nd ed. (Oxford: Oxford University Press, 2002), 47–72; see

also Douglas R. de Lacey, "The Sabbath/Sunday Questions and the Law in the Pauline Corpus," in Carson, *From Sabbath*, 159–95.

52. Pliny the Younger, *Letters* 10.96, in Naphtali Lewis and Meyer Reinhold, eds. and trans., *Roman Civilization*, vol. 2, *The Empire* (New York: Columbia University Press, 1955), 583.
53. Pliny, *Letters* 10.96 (Lewis and Reinhold translation). See commentary in A. N. Sherwin-White, *The Letters of Pliny: A Historical and Social Commentary* (Oxford: Clarendon Press, 1966), 702–8.
54. While it is most likely that this occurred on a Saturday or Sunday based on the evidence reviewed in this chapter, there is evidence for Christians gathering regularly on other days of the week as well; see McGowan, *Ancient Christian Worship*, 217–60, especially 224–29.
55. It is possible that the meal described to Pliny was the Eucharist, but it also may have been quite literally a shared meal, such as a banquet or potluck. Additionally, some early Christians combined the practice of a shared meal with the practice of the Eucharist: see 1 Corinthians 11:17–34; and McGowan, *Ancient Christian Worship*, 19–64.
56. On the late first- or early second-century date of the Didache, see Ehrman, *Apostolic Fathers*, 1:411; and Kurt Niederwimmer, *The Didache: A Commentary*, trans. Linda M. Maloney; Hermeneia (Minneapolis: Fortress Press, 1998), 52–54.
57. Didache 9.1–3. All translations of the Didache are from Ehrman, *Apostolic Fathers*.
58. This document specifies that only the baptized were allowed to partake of the Eucharist; see Didache 9.5. It also specifies that even baptized Christians must first confess their sins and settle any quarrels prior to partaking of the Eucharist; see Didache 14.1–2.
59. Didache 10.2–6.
60. On connections between John Chrysostom and the *Apostolic Constitutions*, see Anders Ekenberg, "The Eucharist in Early Church Orders," in *The Eucharist—Its Origins and Contexts*, ed. David Hellholm and Dieter Sänger, vol. 2, *Patristic Traditions, Iconography* (Tübingen: Mohr Siebeck, 2017), 957–92, especially 970.
61. For more on early Christian worship in all its varieties, see note 48 above.
62. *Const. Ap.* 2.57.1–4.
63. *Const. Ap.* 2.57.1–4; 2.57.9–13.
64. See Harry Gamble, *Books and Readers in Early Christianity: A History of Early Christian Texts* (New Haven, CT: Yale University Press, 1995); and Larry W. Hurtado, *The Earliest Christian Artifacts: Manuscripts and Christian Origins* (Grand Rapids, MI: William B. Eerdmans, 2006).
65. *Const. Ap.* 2.57.5–6; 8.5.11, in Alexander Roberts and James Donaldson, eds. and trans., *Ante-Nicene Fathers* (hereafter *ANF*), American Edition (Buffalo: Christian Literature, 1886), 7:421.
66. *Const. Ap.* 2.57.7–8; 8.5.11.
67. *Const. Ap.* 8.5.11; trans. *ANF* 7:482–83.
68. *Const. Ap.* 2.57.9; 8.5.11–12.
69. *Const. Ap.* 2.57; trans. *ANF* 7.422.
70. *Const. Ap.* 2.57.15.
71. *Const. Ap.* 8.12; trans. *ANF* 7:486.

72. *Const. Ap.* 8.12.
73. *Const. Ap.* 2.57.21.
74. *Const. Ap.* 2.57.21. The *Apostolic Constitutions* provides an example of a much longer prayer as well; see *Const. Ap.* 8.12.4–51.
75. *Const. Ap.* 8.12.
76. *Const. Ap.* 8.13; trans. *ANF* 7:490. Compare *Const. Ap.* 2.57.21.
77. *Const. Ap.* 8.13; trans. *ANF* 7:490. Compare *Const. Ap.* 2.57.21.
78. *Const. Ap.* 8.13; trans. *ANF* 7:490–91.
79. *Const. Ap.* 8.13.
80. *Const. Ap.* 8.14; trans. *ANF* 7:491.
81. *Const. Ap.* 8.15.
82. *Const. Ap.* 2.57.4, 8, 15, and 21.
83. *Const. Ap.* 2.57.8.
84. See Neil Adkin, "A Problem in the Early Church: Noise during Sermon and Lesson," *Mnemosyne*, Fourth Series, 38, no. 1/2 (1985): 161–63.
85. Chrysostom, *Homily 9 on First Timothy*, in *Nicene and Post-Nicene Fathers*, series 1, vol. 13, trans. James Barmby (Oxford: Parker and Co.; New York: Christian Literature, 1898), 435.
86. Chrysostom, *Homily 2 on Colossians* 1.15; translation as found in James Daniel Cook, *Preaching and Popular Christianity: Reading the Sermons of John Chrysostom* (Oxford: Oxford University Press, 2019), 72.
87. *Const. Ap.* 2.59; trans. *ANF* 7:422.
88. *Const. Ap.* 2.59; trans. *ANF* 7:422–23.
89. Chrysostom, *Homily on the Baptism of Christ* (*Bapt.*; 387) PG 49; my own translation based on the original Greek and with consideration of German translation in Rordorf, *Sabbat und Sonntag* 198–99 (#124).
90. Chrysostom, *Bapt.* (387) PG 49; my own translation—see note 89.
91. Eusebius, *Sermon* XVI 1,4 and 8 (Pseudo-Eusebius of Alexandria); translation as found in Markschies, *Between Two Worlds*, 34–35, and 208nn69–70.
92. Chrysostom, *Homily on Genesis* 10.7; trans. as found in Bauckham, "Sunday in the Post-Apostolic Church," 287.
93. Based on the same evidence, Beckwith and Stott argue that John Chrysostom supported applying biblical Sabbath prohibitions to the Lord's day, while Bauckham argues that Chrysostom did not; see Beckwith and Stott, *This is the Day*, 134–36; and Bauckham, "Sunday in the Post-Apostolic Church," 286–87.
94. Gregory of Tours, *History of the Franks* 10.30; Rordorf, *Sabbat und Sonntag*, 232–33 (#146).
95. Gregory of Tours, *The Miracles of Bishop Martin* 3.3; Rordorf, *Sabbat und Sonntag*, 234–35 (#148).
96. Gregory the Great, *Letters* 13.3; trans. my own based on the original Latin and with consideration of German translation in Rordorf, *Sabbat und Sonntag*, 234–37 (#149). See Bauckham's discussion of Gregory of Tours and Gregory the Great on the Lord's day and the Sabbath in Bauckham, "Sunday in the Medieval Church," 303.

Chapter Seven

The Sabbath in Rabbinic Judaism: Exploring the How of Keeping the Commandments

Avram R. Shannon

Like other ancient believers in the Hebrew Bible (Old Testament), the ancient sages[1] of rabbinic literature were keenly interested in the Sabbath day. These ancient Jews, who lived from around 150 BC to AD 600,[2] composed numerous texts that explored and expanded on how to live the commandments. It is the Judaism that is expressed in these texts that I am speaking of in this study. These sages lived in Roman Palestine and in Persian Babylon. They were articulate readers of the scriptures who were keenly concerned with the process of living and keeping God's commandments, which were primarily contained in what is often called the law of Moses. Although the discussions and legal explorations of these ancient Jewish sages formed the basis for later Jewish discourse, I will focus primarily on the teachings on the Sabbath found in the Mishnah. This ancient compilation of law was collected and codified around AD 200 and serves as the foundation of rabbinic law.[3]

Within the Mishnah, the tractate on the Sabbath day called Shabbat (from the Hebrew word for Sabbath) is one of the largest, comprising twenty-four chapters. This mishnaic tractate also generated the largest amount of commentary in both the Babylonian and Jerusalem Talmuds, illustrating the importance of the Sabbath in rabbinic thinking.[4] Keeping the Sabbath day holy is also central to other tractates, such as Eruvin (concerned with travel on the Sabbath day) and Betzah (or Yom Tov, concerned with cases in which the commandments on keeping the Sabbath day holy are not clear). Discussion on how to live the Sabbath day was central to ancient Jewish thinking and discourse about their religion, forming a major part of their religious self-understanding. For example, Exodus Rabbah, a book of Jewish interpretation on the biblical book of Exodus that dates from the medieval period but contains earlier material, states: "R. [Rabbi] Levi said: If Israel kept the Sabbath properly even for one day, the son of David would come. Why? Because it is equivalent to all the commandments." For Rabbi Levi, keeping the Sabbath command is the example *par excellence* of people who are hearkening to the voice of the Lord.

The amount of material from the sages on keeping the Sabbath day holy means that a complete analysis of this material is outside the scope of this volume and this chapter since it would likely extend to several monographs. Therefore, I will concentrate on discussing the principles of rabbinic legal discourse to help readers see similarities and differences with approaches used by Latter-day Saints in their own attempts to keep the commandments.

A distinctive element of discussing rabbinic literature from its texts is that those texts focus on specific arguments about the living of the Sabbath. In many ways, reading rabbinic laws on the Sabbath is like listening in on the middle of a conversation: readers need to piece together details from contextual clues in the conversation. Indeed, many specific discussions of rabbinic living of the Sabbath day would be obscure to Latter-day Saints since their social and religious contexts are so different from those that drove the sages. Yet it is important to realize that these activities indicate the sages' strong desire to set apart the Sabbath as a special day. In considering some of their specific Sabbath interpretations, I will emphasize the principles behind them. The goal of this study is to help Latter-day Saint readers better understand and value the intent of the sages' discussions and interpretations. In so doing they may be led to likewise think deeply about the practical implications of keeping the Sabbath day holy in the modern world.

Many specific activities pertaining to Jewish Sabbath celebration today seem to have been already in place by the time of the sages. This is evident in the fact that they do not make laws about practices but rather assume those practices were being observed. Nevertheless, it is possible to piece together contextual clues about how the sages thought the Sabbath should be kept. For example, current Judaism calls for lighting candles on the Sabbath. Even though there is no specific law in either the Mishnah or the Talmud that mandates this practice, we know it had developed by the time of the sages because the Mishnah references it in a number of places (for example, m. Shabbat 2:1–7; m. Berakhot 7:5).

Numerous elements of Sabbath practice, like the lighting of candles, already appear by talmudic times. Drawing on numerous Sabbath passages in the Talmud, the *Encyclopaedia Judaica* provides a useful but nonetheless incomplete introduction to the Sabbath in Judaism:

> The Sabbath is a festive day and three meals should be eaten on it (Shab. 118a). It was considered meritorious for a man to make some preparations for the Sabbath himself, even if he had servants to do it for him (Kid. 41a). R. Safra used to singe the head of an animal, R. Huna used to light the lamp, R. Papa to plait the wicks, R. Ḥisda to cut up the beets, Rabbah and R. Joseph to chop the wood, R. Zera to kindle the fire (Shab. 119a). . . . Out of respect for the sacred day, it was forbidden to fast on the eve of the Sabbath (Ta'an. 27b). . . . At the beginning of the Sabbath, the special sanctification (*Kiddush*) is recited (Pes. 106a), and after the termination of the Sabbath the *Havdalah* ("distinction") benediction (which signifies the separation of the Sabbath from the weekday) is recited (Ber. 33a), both over a cup of wine. A man should wear special garments in honor of the Sabbath; he should walk differently from the way he does on a weekday, and even his speech should be different (Shab. 11a–b).[5]

In many ways, the thrust of keeping the Sabbath day holy in the Judaism described and lived by the rabbinic sages of the Mishnah and Talmud was to preserve its distinctive nature. For them the distinctiveness of the Sabbath mirrored the distinctiveness of Judaism itself.

First we will look at how the ancient Jewish sages applied scripture in determining how to keep the Sabbath commandment. (As mentioned, this discussion can provide ideas for Latter-day Saints as they consider their own application of scripture.)[6] Then we will turn to rabbinic legal discourse, called *halakah*, and consider specific examples in the tractate

Shabbat that illustrate how the ancient rabbis derived their understanding of how to live the Sabbath. In the final portion we will see how these ancient principles of discourse and understanding may fruitfully be applied to the Latter-day Saint practice of keeping the Sabbath day holy, as well as to other commandments.

Halakah

The rabbinic conception and discussion of the Sabbath comes under their larger treatment of how to live the Lord's commandments. Although the commandments are very clear on *what* one is supposed to do, understanding the *how* can be difficult.[7] As a result, there arose within Judaism a discourse practice focusing on how to live the various commandments in scripture. The Hebrew term for this reasoned commentary is *halakah*.[8] The term *halakah* comes from a word whose root meaning is "walk."[9] Thus this term refers to the godly walk of how one lives the commandments,[10] and halakah is therefore the discourse on how to live the commandments.

Exodus 20:8–11 contains the biblical law for keeping the Sabbath day holy: "Remember the sabbath day, to keep it holy. Six days shalt thou labour, and do all thy work: But the seventh day is the sabbath of the Lord thy God: in it thou shalt not do any work, thou, nor thy son, nor thy daughter, thy manservant, nor thy maidservant, nor thy cattle, nor thy stranger that is within thy gates: For in six days the Lord made heaven and earth, the sea, and all that in them is, and rested the seventh day: wherefore the Lord blessed the sabbath day, and hallowed it."[11] Like many of the commandments, this one tells a person what to do but does not indicate how to do it.[12] The Lord commands Israel not to "work" but does not define what constitutes work. Even the initial commandment to remember the Sabbath day and to keep it holy does not explain how that is to be done. In precise terms, then, what does it mean to keep a day "holy"?

As is very common with biblical laws, the specifics of this law are not worked out in the text of the Bible itself. To be sure, there are narrative hints, such as the provision of manna in Exodus 16.[13] The Israelites were commanded to collect a double portion of manna on the day before the Sabbath day (v. 22) because the Lord would not send manna on the seventh day (vv. 25–26). This suggests that collecting manna and preparing it for consumption were inappropriate Sabbath activities because the Lord expected that to be done on the sixth day (v. 23).[14] Stories such as this one give clues for interpretating the sabbath law. Such interpretive activity is at the center of halakic discourse.

That the law for keeping the Sabbath day holy needed further interpretation and exploration is made explicit with the story recorded in Numbers 15:32–36. Here an Israelite is caught gathering wood on the Sabbath day and is brought to Moses and Aaron for judgment. Numbers 15:34 is extraordinarily telling: "And they put him in ward [or "custody," Hebrew *mišmâh*], because it was not declared what should be done to him." This verse makes explicit what is implied elsewhere in scripture about keeping the Sabbath day holy: the laws are not sufficient on their own to enable one to completely live the law. Moreover, the punishment for breaking the Sabbath (or breaking it in that particular way) is not contained in the commandment on the Sabbath in Exodus. Thus, in order to keep this commandment properly, more inspiration and interpretation are necessary. In the example of this man gathering sticks, Moses inquires of Jehovah, who mandates that the man be put to death, underscoring the importance of the Sabbath day not only to the ancient Israelites but also to later readers of the scriptures.

This example emphasizes the importance of halakah in any discussion of keeping the Sabbath day holy. The question of *how* a person lives the commandment is at the heart of all rabbinic discussion about the keeping and living of the Sabbath. It also undergirds Jesus's interactions with the Pharisees in the Sabbath controversies in the New Testament and continues to inform Latter-day Saint discussions on how to live the Sabbath day.

Talking about Sabbath and Halakah: Jesus and the Pharisees

Jesus's discussions on the Sabbath with other Jews are also useful in understanding the halakah and the Sabbath day in Judaism and in Christianity.[15] They are especially helpful in light of the clear scriptural need to interpret the living of the Sabbath commandments. Jesus's engagement with the Sabbath commandments provides context for helping Christians, who are more familiar with the world of ancient Judaism from the New Testament rather than from Jewish sources, better understand some of the ideas behind the rabbinic understanding of the Sabbath. Christians, including Latter-day Saints, have sometimes interpreted Jesus's statements against the "scribes and the Pharisees"[16] to mean Jewish legal discourse, especially in Matthew 23:4.[17] This verse reads, "For they bind heavy burdens and grievous to be borne, and lay them on men's shoulders; but they themselves will not move them with one of their fingers." Under this interpretive strand, the "heavy burdens" are the interpretive regulations of the divine law from Mount Sinai.[18] This way of thinking interprets teachings like Jewish Sabbath regulations as onerous rules forced upon the people by a hypocritical ruling class. Yet the rabbinic texts under consideration here describe these regulations as a way of highlighting the joy and distinctiveness of the Sabbath day.[19]

This interpretation is problematized, however, by Jesus's opening statement: "The scribes and the Pharisees sit in Moses' seat: All therefore whatsoever they bid you observe, that observe and do; but do not ye after their works: for they say, and do not" (Matthew 23:2–3).[20] Some Christian interpreters have suggested that this statement from Jesus refers to the written law of Moses, while the grievous burdens are the halakic interpretations of that law.[21] In this view the Sabbath, as explained in Exodus, is to be kept, while any interpretations outside the immediate Exodus text are viewed as human interpolations of God's law. Contrarily, Jesus's reference to the Pharisees sitting "in Moses' seat" can be taken as suggesting they are authorized interpreters of the law of Moses. He cements this observation by telling the people, "Whatsoever they bid you observe, that observe and do." This would seem to endorse their interpretation of the law rather than condemn it.[22] Biblical scholar Mark Allan Powell acknowledges that this is the "apparent reading," although it is not the reading that he himself follows.[23]

The apparent meaning of Matthew 23:2 is actually the best reading here—namely, Jesus acknowledges the validity of the Pharisees' interpretations. Jesus could have urged the people to go and live the written law of Moses and not to listen to the interpretations of the scribes and Pharisees, since they were certainly not the only ancient Jews who taught and interpreted the law of Moses. The New Testament is full of stories of Jesus and his followers learning from the scriptures and interpreting them, including the living of the Sabbath. In Matthew, Jesus tells the people to listen to the Pharisees (v. 3). A reading that Jesus is condemning Pharisaic halakah is necessary only if one assumes that Jesus is opposed to the oral law and halakic discourse as a concept. This does not mean that Jesus even needs to agree with the specific halakah of the Pharisees (indeed, he often does not, especially when it concerns the Sabbath). It does mean, however, that Jesus approves of the process of discussing and interpreting the commandments, which he himself gave on Mount Sinai (see 3 Nephi 15:5).

Indeed, this difficulty may perhaps be explained most easily by suggesting that the "heavy burdens" in Matthew 23:4 do not refer to halakic discussion of the commandments, but instead are being presented as evidence for Jesus's actual condemnation of the scribes and the Pharisees: the fact that "they say, and do not" (v. 3).[24] In this reading the "heavy burdens" are actual physical burdens. The Pharisees make other people lift things for them but do not work themselves. The Pharisees' failing is grounded in the tendency of elites to have others do their physical labor for them.[25] Thus Jesus's problem with the Pharisees as religious leaders is not their interpretation of the commandments as such, but their unwillingness to follow even their own interpretations, just like they are unwilling to do their own work. This explains how Jesus can both tell the people to do whatever the Pharisees instruct them to do as well as warn them against the actions of the scribes and the Pharisees.

Jesus's teachings here in Matthew are not an inherent rejection of discussions of halakah. Indeed, as noted above, it would be impossible to keep the commandments without a corresponding knowledge of *how* to keep them. When Jesus and the Pharisees have discussions on Sabbath worship (for example, the plucking of grain in Matthew 12:1–8 and Mark 2:23–27), it is important to note that he is rejecting some of their specific interpretations, not their interpreting as such. In addition, at no point does Jesus reject the keeping of the Sabbath. That is not the disagreement. The disagreement is specifically in the *how*, or in other words, in the halakah.

As we apply some rabbinic notions of halakah, it is important to recognize that Jesus did not reject halakic discourse, even in regard to the Sabbath day.[26] In fact, thinking about and discussing the commandments can help the Lord's people become the kind of people he wants them to be.

The Joy of the Sabbath

The sages understood and kept their Sabbath as a joy. For them the Sabbath commandment was an ideal that represented their relationship with God. Although some non-Jewish authors in the ancient world remarked that Sabbath day observance indicated the Jewish people's laziness, the Jews viewed that special day as a chief joy of their religion.[27] For them it was like awaiting the coming of a queen or bride. B. Shabbat 119a says that "R. Hanina robed himself and stood at sunset of Sabbath eve [and] exclaimed, 'Come and let us go forth to welcome the queen Sabbath.' R. Jannai donned his robes, on Sabbath eve and exclaimed, 'Come, O bride, Come,

O bride!'" This passage shows how the sages welcomed the Sabbath. The various interpretations and discussions about how to keep the Sabbath day holy were never intended to bog down its practice in rules. Instead, they were understood as a way to adorn and set apart one of the key commandments given by the Lord to his covenant people.

Indeed, as a counternarrative to the claims that the Jews were lazy, the Babylonian Talmud records an interaction of R. Joshua b. Hananiah with the "Emperor." The emperor intended here is the Roman emperor Hadrian, who has numerous interactions with Joshua b. Hananiah in rabbinic literature.[28] This is the story in b. Shabbat 119a: "The emperor said to R. Joshua b. Hananiah, 'Why has the Sabbath dish such a fragrant odour?' 'We have a certain seasoning,' replied he, 'called the Sabbath, which we put into it, and that gives it a fragrant odour.' 'Give us some of it,' asked he. 'To him who keeps the Sabbath,' retorted he, 'it is efficacious; but to him who does not keep the Sabbath it is of no use.'"[29] Although this talmudic story is representative of similar legends in the Talmud, and so likely did not occur, it does say something about the importance of the Sabbath day in rabbinic thinking, as well as something about the sages' desire to present a counternarrative to their various detractors.

In this story the Roman emperor expresses a desire for a distinctive blessing of the Sabbath—its apparent ability to make food more savory. The story explains that this is a special blessing reserved for the Lord's covenant people; that is, only those who keep the Sabbath can appreciate the "seasoning" that is the Sabbath day. Because Hadrian is a non-Jew who does not keep the Jewish Sabbath, he cannot claim the blessings for himself. The Sabbath is a joy, but R. Joshua's interactions with the Roman emperor make it clear that that joy comes only to those who make the sacrifices to follow the directions of Jehovah and keep the Sabbath day holy.

Because Latter-day Saints do not follow the specific rabbinic regulations of the Sabbath day, it can be easy for us to view many of those regulations as needlessly minute and some kind of burden. We would do well to avoid that common error of using Jewish Sabbath practice as a rhetorical tool against Judaism, ancient or modern. Indeed, it is worth noting that this is not at all how Sabbath regulations are presented in the rabbinic texts. There they reflect one of the most joyful aspects of the religion. In his foreword to the Soncino edition of Tractate Shabbat in the Babylonian Talmud, J. H. Hertz, who was the Chief Rabbi of the United Kingdom from 1913 to 1946, notes the following:

> In all ages—from early Christian times to the present day—ignorant and unsympathetic critics have stigmatized these minutiae as an intolerable burden and asserted that they make the Sabbath not a day of rest but one of sorrow and anxiety. Such a view shows a complete misunderstanding of the spirit in which the Rabbis approached their task. It was their love for the Sabbath which led them to exert all their ingenuity in discovering ways of differentiating it from other days and making it more thoroughly a day of rest, a day in which man enjoys some foretaste of the pure bliss and happiness which are stored up for the righteous in the world to come.[30]

Thus, in the thought world of the rabbinic sages, the rules of the Sabbath do not make it into some kind of legalistic mire. Instead, the Sabbath is a chance to worship the Lord and to show love for his covenant and commandments.[31]

Laws in Mishnah Tractate Shabbat

At this point it is useful to explore specific laws in the mishnaic tractate of Shabbat since they illustrate the process of rabbinic thinking about the Sabbath. As noted above, the Mishnah is the earliest codification of the Jewish oral law.[32] It is divided into six orders that are arranged broadly by topic. These orders are then subdivided into individual tractates, which are further arranged by length, much like the letters of Paul in the New Testament, suggesting that this is a model of organization in ancient texts.[33] As one of the longest tractates in the Mishnah, Shabbat is the first tractate in the order of Moed, which is concerned with holidays and holy days.

Like most of the Mishnah, this tractate jumps right into the conversation without any preamble or introduction.[34] It begins, "There are two (which are, indeed, four) kinds of going out on the Sabbath for him that is inside, and two (which are, indeed, four) for him that is outside" (m. Shabbat 1:1).[35] The first point that the sages discuss in this tractate is the concept of "going out." This refers to the kinds of admissible leaving and travel while carrying objects that a Jew would be able to do on the Sabbath, a concept that is actually rooted in the Bible.

This first law illustrates a key idea in rabbinic discourse on the Sabbath, one related to the broader idea of halakah. The sages are not simply arbitrarily deciding that it is not possible to "go out" on the Sabbath. Rather, the rabbinic commandment derives from the Lord's injunctions to

Moses for the Israelites to abide in their place on the seventh day.[36] In the story of gathering the manna, the Lord commands Israel through Moses: "Abide ye every man in his place, let no man *go out* of his place on the seventh day" (Exodus 16:29; emphasis added). Thus the rabbinic sages are not making up new material here but rather attempting to live the law they have received.

This first law in Mishnah Shabbat also connects "going out" with a prohibition on carrying items during the Sabbath. The sages derived this from Jeremiah 17:22, where the Lord commands through the prophet Jeremiah, "Neither carry forth a burden out of your houses on the sabbath day, neither do ye any work, but hallow ye the sabbath day, as I commanded your fathers."[37] The sages connect this commandment to the commandment in Exodus 16 through the verb for "going out," which is used in both Exodus and Jeremiah.[38] This is why m. Shabbat can begin with a discussion of "going out"; the combination of these commandments specifies what is part of the command to keep the Sabbath day holy. As with the original commandment in Exodus 20, it leaves much unspecified, giving place for discussion, interpretation, and the exercise of agency.

The next question the sages address is what qualifies as a "carrying a burden."[39] The sages of the Mishnah understand, at least on some level, "carrying a burden" to be carrying something for work or practicing a trade. Seeing the biblical basis for this logic helps explain prohibitions like that found in m. Shabbat 1:3, which states, "The tailor does not go out with his needle [on Friday] near nightfall, in case he forgets and 'goes out.' Neither should the copyist with his pen."[40] The logic here is clear. The needle is the primary tool of the tailor's trade, just as a pen is the primary tool of the copyist or professional scribe.[41] The Mishnah calls these items out specifically here because they are so small and easy to forget. It is unlikely that a farmer would forget that he is carrying a plow and so inadvertently break the biblical injunction of carrying a burden. The idea here is that it is not the size of the burden that matters for keeping the commandment found in Jeremiah but rather the purpose of the item being carried. Since needles and pens are clearly tools of trade for tailors and scribes, those tradesmen need to be extra careful since it is much more likely those small instruments will be carried. Again, without context these rules could seem arbitrary, but instead they represent a logical derivation from biblical law. The context in which the discussion is happening is important in matters of discovering halakah.

Deriving Rules from Principles

The fact is that the sages are attempting to articulate the *how* of keeping the Sabbath day holy, and although their rulings contain more lists than Latter-day Saints generally generate, the whole halakic enterprise is still primarily about working through the principles in order to be able to more effectively preserve the holiness of the Sabbath day. As part of this process, the sages are interested in thinking deeply about the definition of work as it pertains to keeping the Sabbath day holy. They identify thirty-nine primary categories of work or labor, the performance of any of which qualifies as breaking the Sabbath day. These are as follows:

> Sowing, plowing, reaping, binding sheaves, threshing, winnowing, cleansing crops, grinding, sifting, kneading, baking, shearing wool, washing or beating or dyeing it, spinning, weaving, making two loops, weaving two threads, separating two threads, tying [a knot], untying [a knot], sewing two stitches, tearing in order to sew two stitches, hunting a gazelle, slaughtering or flaying or salting it or curing its skin, scraping it or cutting it up, writing two letters, erasing in order to write two letters, building, putting down, putting out a fire, lighting a fire, striking with a hammer, [or] moving from [one] domain to [another] domain. (m. Shabbat 7:2)[42]

What I describe as "primary categories" are from a Hebrew collocation, "fathers of work."[43] This means that these are the categories from which other categories of potential Sabbath breaking can be derived. The Mishnah is primarily a legal document, so its core purpose is identifying those activities that form the foundational tools for thinking about how to keep the Sabbath day holy. Shaye J. D. Cohen points out that the process of listing out these principles is distinctive to the mishnaic process of halakic thinking. This list of thirty-nine categories is unknown in the written law of Moses or in earlier Jewish legal thinkers such as Philo.[44] The concept here is that these "fathers of work" can be used to extrapolate other activities and even to adapt the law to changing cultural and technological circumstances.[45] For example, the prohibition against lighting a fire (which as we saw in Exodus 16 has strong biblical roots) serves as the basis in Judaism for discussions about the use of electricity on the Sabbath day.[46]

The list of primary categories can appear to modern eyes, especially Christian eyes unused to halakic discourse, as simply a laundry list of disapproved activities. This is not the case, as this list is actually the basis for a reasoned, thoughtful discussion on the important topic of *how* to keep the Sabbath day holy. It is a great example of a principle-based approach to keeping the commandments. Instead of spelling out every single example of how the Sabbath is to be lived, the sages identify those activities from which other activities can be extrapolated. This reasoning process involving the considered application of scriptural principles is one that Latter-day Saints too can appreciate as they consider how to keep the Sabbath day holy.

Discussion and Discourse

Indeed, the discussion of keeping the Sabbath day holy in the Mishnah and the Talmud often preserves the conversation as much as it does the solutions. There is a compelling example of this in m. Shabbat 1:4–8, where the Mishnah preserves different rulings between the house of Shammai and the house of Hillel.[47] Although both houses agree on the importance of keeping the Sabbath day holy, the Mishnah preserves places where they disagree on the proper way to do that. In other words, there is a disagreement on the *how* of living the Sabbath day. A brief examination of a few of these disagreements can give insight into the halakic process and so give Latter-day Saints models for their own discourse on keeping the commandments.

The general context of these discussions has to do with making sure to give enough time for activities to be completed before the start of the Sabbath in order to prevent the Sabbath from being inadvertently broken.

> The Mishnah begins: "The School of Shammai say: Ink, dyestuffs, or vetches[48] may not be soaked [on a Friday] unless there is time for them to be [wholly] soaked in the same day. And the School of Hillel permit it. The School of Shammai say: Bundles of flax may not be put in an oven[49] unless there is time for them to steam off the same day; nor may wool be put into a [dyer's] cauldron unless there is time for it to absorb the color the same day. And the School of Hillel permit it" (m. Shabbat 1:5–6).[50]

In general in this passage, the house of Shammai has the more restrictive position on how to live the Sabbath day, but the specific legal matters are not what I am focusing on here. My interest is in the fact that the Mishnah preserves the discussion. While not stating specifically whose reading of how to keep the commandments is the more correct,[51] the Mishnah preserves a number of activities that the house of Shammai forbids but the house of Hillel permits. The dividing line is their different understanding of what counts as work on the Sabbath day. Halakic discourse is not necessarily about coming to the one right answer, but instead about learning how to apply the commandments as individuals and communities in the often-messy world of everyday life.

Halakic Discourse and Agency

As we have seen, halakic discourse requires thinking about the commandments. This was true for the ancient Jews, but it is also true for us today. In Deuteronomy 6:7, Israel is commanded not only to keep the commandments but also to talk about them in the morning and at night. In other words, Israel is to think about and discuss the commandments at all times. This conversation about commandments fits into the Book of Mormon reminder that religious practice and experience are not limited to one day or one part of a person's life (see Alma 32:9–11).

Another strength of halakic discourse from a Latter-day Saint perspective is that it allows the exercise of human agency. In Doctrine and Covenants 58:26–27, the Lord tells the newly arrived Saints in Missouri: "It is not meet that I should command in all things; for he that is compelled in all things, the same is a slothful and not a wise servant; wherefore he receiveth no reward. Verily I say, men should be anxiously engaged in a good cause, and do many things of their own free will, and bring to pass much righteousness." In allowing his covenant people, ancient and modern, to learn for themselves how to keep the commandments, the Lord is giving them opportunities to be "anxiously engaged."

This is not to say that halakah is about deciding that one can do whatever one wants in connection with the commandments. Halakic decisions need to be grounded in both the text and the community. The Word of Wisdom in Doctrine and Covenants 89 provides a key example of this. Section 89:9 states, "Hot drinks are not for the body or belly." The revelation does not specify what those hot drinks are. From the perspective of the text, this could be read as simply forbidding drinks above a certain temperature. Within the interpretive world of The Church of Jesus Christ of Latter-day Saints, however, latter-day prophets and apostles have taught that the phrase "hot drinks" refers to tea and coffee. Because of this, any halakic discussion of the proper way to live the Word of Wisdom and the proper interpretation of "hot drinks" must be understood in connection with this directive.[52] Latter-day Saint discourse on this topic follows similar contours to rabbinic discussions on keeping the Sabbath day that we have seen—it is not about justifying bad behavior but about exploring and explaining the proper ways to live and follow Jehovah's covenant law.

As Latter-day Saints think about keeping the Sabbath day holy, this focus on figuring out the principles is a useful beginning point. In class, when discussing the Sabbath controversies between Jesus and some of the Pharisees in the New Testament, I ask my students to make their own halakic arguments, especially in regard to places where the interpretation of the commandments is not immediately clear. I ask them whether buying from a vending machine on Sunday counts as breaking the Sabbath. I try to make it very clear that I do not think this is a question that has one clear-cut right answer and that I am interested in the students' perspectives. I also make it clear that I want them to explain the arguments behind their halakic positions.

I receive a wide variety of responses from students. Some students argue that it is permissible on the grounds that although purchasing from a vending machine is spending money, it is not making anyone work. Others argue that it is not permissible because keeping the Sabbath day holy is something that requires planning ahead, so purchasing from a vending machine on Sunday would be contrary to the spirit of keeping the Sabbath day holy. Some students take this question to its next logical conclusion and discuss purchasing items from the internet on the Sabbath. I like doing this exercise with students because it illustrates that halakic discussions have a place in Latter-day Saint discourse. It also shows the value in being able to articulate the thinking behind one's practices while respecting those who see things differently.

This extends well beyond keeping the Sabbath day holy, as can be seen in the above example of the Word of Wisdom. There are many practices in the Church of Jesus Christ, such as clothing and grooming, where there can be a wide variety of ways to live the commandments. Being able to accept this variety yet also disagree in a way that builds unity promotes the cause of Zion. The way that the ancient rabbinic sages reflect a variety of approaches to honoring the Sabbath and show respectful, reasoned disagreement can be a very useful model for Latter-day Saints and others who seek to keep the Lord's commandments.

"The Ox in the Mire"

Dealing with the sometimes-messy world in which we live is part and parcel with trying to live the Sabbath day the way the scriptures indicate, both in rabbinic literature and in Latter-day Saint experience. In the New Testament, after healing a man on the Sabbath day, Jesus asks, "Which of you shall have an ass or an ox fallen into a pit, and will not straightway pull him out on the sabbath day?" (Luke 14:5). This statement, used by Jesus to explain his willingness to heal on the Sabbath day, provides a scriptural backdrop for the Latter-day Saint notion of "the ox in the mire," which in our discourse essentially means acceptable reasons to break, or at least bend, the fourth commandment.[53] Although Jesus's point here is not about when and where it is acceptable to break the Sabbath day, sometimes Latter-day Saint discourse may push in that direction.[54] In recognition of this trend, Jeffrey R. Holland of the Quorum of the Twelve Apostles humorously but pointedly noted, "If the ox is in the mire *every* Sunday, then we strongly recommend that you sell the ox or fill the mire."[55]

Although rabbinic discourse on the Sabbath as it has come down to us tends to focus on those difficult places where the *how* of living the commandments is not immediately clear, the ancient sages do allow for something like "the ox in the mire" in their discourse on the keeping of the Sabbath day. First and foremost of these is the concept known as *piquaḥ nefesh*, a phrase that according to the standard dictionary on Hebrew in the rabbinic period means "removing a person from under debris."[56] This collocation refers to the fact that it is okay to remove a living person from a fallen building or debris on the Sabbath, and it has come to refer to the idea that saving life can abrogate other commandments. This idea is based on Leviticus 18:5: "Ye shall therefore keep my statutes, and my judgments: which if a man do, he shall live in them: I am the Lord." Since the commandment is to "live in" the law, this cannot be done if someone is dead.[57] Therefore, this legal principle suggests that there are circumstances in which the law may be abrogated in order to save life.

The rabbinic sages have noted principles governing the use of *piquaḥ nefesh*. It is not to be used as a blanket justification for breaking the Sabbath commandments. In fact, the mishnaic tractate Yoma 8:4–7 describes a variety of specific circumstances in which the saving of life supersedes the fasting on or the keeping of the Sabbath. As regards the Sabbath day, m. Yoma 8:7 states, "If a building fell down upon a man and there is doubt whether he is there or not, or whether he is alive or dead, or whether he is a non-Jew or an Israelite, they may clear away the ruin from above him. If they find him alive they may clear it away [still more] from above him; but if he is dead, they leave him."[58] This is the law that gives the principle of *piquaḥ nefesh* its name, and essentially it means that the preservation of life is the most important principle in keeping the law and covenant.[59] The only laws that could not be broken as part of *piquaḥ nefesh* were the commandments against sexual sin, the worshipping of a god besides the God of Israel, and murder (*murder* is defined here as deliberate killing, as rabbinic literature allows for killing in times of war or in self-defense).[60]

Latter-day Saints do not insist that Sabbath worship happen on a specific day throughout the world. For example, Latter-day Saints living in the state of Israel, whether as part of BYU's Jerusalem Center or otherwise, rest on Saturday, as this is the Sabbath practiced by Judaism. In Arab countries, the Saints hold their worship services on Friday, corresponding to the day of prayer in Islam. For Latter-day Saints, the specific day is not as important as the concept of the Sabbath.[61]

For Rabbinic Judaism, this particular flexibility was not an option since the Lord made it clear from Mount Sinai that the Sabbath was to be the seventh day of the week (Exodus 20:10).[62] This means that there is no discussion about when to celebrate the Sabbath in Judaism—it was a foregone conclusion. Thus it is no surprise that the sages who explored the halakic keeping of the Sabbath did not discuss which day should be designated as the Sabbath. There was simply no reason to have that conversation. (It should be noted that the Christian idea of worshipping on the first day of the week is a result of the resurrection of Jesus Christ on that day.)

Conclusion

The Sabbath day has been part of the Lord's covenant path for a very long time—as a formal commandment at least since the time of Moses and the Sinai Covenant, with its significance enshrined in Creation itself.[63] The directive in the Ten Commandments to remember the Sabbath day and keep it holy is a vital part of what it means to be part of the covenant people of the God of Israel. As with most of the commandments, however, the scriptures do not explain specifically which activities are and are not allowed in keeping the Sabbath holy. Sorting out such specifics is a privilege that the Lord has extended to his people to help them learn to be agents who do not need to be commanded in all things.[64]

The book of Deuteronomy makes it very clear that the Lord wants his people to be discussing and thinking about his commandments and how to live them. As some of those who have tried to live and understand the commandments and covenants of the God of Israel, the ancient rabbinic sages of the Mishnah and the Talmud left a rich and complex literature on their experience in learning and living the law of Moses. Living the Sabbath day was a key part of this literature, comprising the largest single portion of Talmudic commentary. The sages provided a great example of how to discuss the keeping of the commandments.

The idea of halakah and halakic discourse is useful for considering our own experiences with keeping the commandments. A kind of halakic discourse happens in our own religious experience every day. Exploring the experience of the rabbinic sages enables us to be more explicit in thinking about how we keep the Sabbath day holy. We can recognize that there are more ways than one to live and keep the commandments. We can articulate the logic behind why we interpret the commandments the way we do. We can also exercise our agency to become the kind of people the Lord wants us to be without needing to be commanded in all things.

Endnotes

1. *Sage* is the preferred term of reference for the authors and tradents of Jewish oral law.
2. Rabbinic literature can be roughly divided into three periods: the Tannaitic period, which is the earliest period, spanning the schools of Hillel and Shammai and up until the early third century AD; the Amoraic period, which goes from there through about AD 550; and the Saboraic period, covering the period immediately following the compilation of the Babylonian Talmud. See H. L. Strack and Günter Stemberger, *Introduction to the Talmud and Midrash*, trans. Markus Bockmuehl (Minneapolis: Fortress, 1996), 7. Some authors start the rabbinic period with Rabbi Yoḥanan b. Zakkai around AD 70. For example, see the time line in Charlotte Elisheva Fonrobert and Martin S. Jafee, eds., *The Cambridge Companion to the Talmud and Rabbinic Literature* (Cambridge: Cambridge University Press, 2007), xiv.
3. For a discussion of the oral law and the texts of rabbinic Judaism, including the Mishnah, from a Latter-day Saint perspective, see Avram R. Shannon, "Torah in the Mouth: An Introduction to the Jewish Oral Law," *Religious Educator* 19 (January/February 2018): 138–59. For further discussion in a more specialist vein, see Strack and Stemberger, *Introduction to the Talmud and Midrash*, 108–48; Jacob Neusner, *Introduction to Rabbinic Literature* (New York: Doubleday, 1994); and Abraham Goldberg, "Mishna—A Study Book of Halakha," in *The Literature of the Sages, Part 1: Oral Tora, Halakha, Mishna, Tosefta, Talmud, External*

Tractates, ed. Shmuel Safrai (Assen/Masstricht: Van Gorcum and Philadelphia: Fortress, 1987), 211–43.

4. There are 157 pages of commentary in the Babylonian Talmud and 92 in the Jerusalem Talmud. The next largest tractate (Yevamot) has 122 pages of commentary in the Babylonian Talmud and 85 in the Jerusalem Talmud.
5. Michael J. Graetz, Louis Jacobs, Efraim Gottlieb, and Susan Nashman Fraiman, "Sabbath," in *Encyclopaedia Judaica*, ed. Michael Berenbaum and Fred Skolnik, 2nd ed. (Detroit: Macmillan Reference USA, 2007), 17:616–22, quotation on 618–19.
6. As a Latter-day Saint, although I am trained in Hebrew language and rabbinic literature, I am still an outsider to Judaism and thus can provide only an outsider's perspective. Readers who desire in-depth discussion of the Sabbath in Judaism are encouraged to consult the following more specialized works on Jewish belief and practice: Jacob Neusner, *The Way of the Torah: An Introduction to Judaism* (Belmont, CA: Wadsworth, 1993), 106–11; Pinchas Peli, *The Jewish Sabbath: A Renewed Encounter* (New York: Schocken, 1991); Louis Jacobs, *The Book of Jewish Belief* (West Orange, NJ: Behrman House, 1984), 96–104; Jacobs, *The Book of Jewish Practice* (West Orange, NJ: Behrman House, 1987), 74–80; and Abraham Joshua Heschel, *The Sabbath: Its Meaning for Modern Man* (New York: Farrar, Strauss, and Giroux, 1951).
7. Philip Sigal, *The Halakhah of Jesus of Nazareth according to the Gospel of Matthew* (Atlanta: Society of Biblical Literature, 2007), 146.
8. Marcus Jastrow, *Dictionary of the Targumim, the Talmud Bavli and Yerushalmi, and the Midrashic Literature* (New York: Judaica Treasury, 1971), 353; and Shmuel Safrai, "Halakha," in Safrai, *Literature of the Sages*, 121–208, discussion and definition on 121–28.
9. Jastrow, *Dictionary of the Targumim*, 352–3; Shaye D. Cohen, "The Judean Legal Tradition and the *Halakhah* of the Mishnah," in *The Cambridge Companion to the Talmud and Rabbinic Literature*, ed. Charlotte Elisheva Fonrobert and Martin S. Jaffee (Cambridge: Cambridge University Press, 2007), 121–43; and Strack and Stemberger, *Introduction to the Talmud and Midrash*, 15–16.
10. Some scholars have suggested a similar conceptual derivation from Latin *regula*, which referred to a fixed land tax and then came to mean "fixed rule." Safrai, "Halakha," 121. For a discussion on the various derivations of this term, see Saul Lieberman, *Hellenism in Jewish Palestine*, originally published in 1950, republished with *Greek in Jewish Palestine* (1942) as *Greek in Jewish Palestine/Hellenism in Jewish Palestine* (New York: Jewish Theological Seminary of America, 1994), 83n3.
11. The parallel version of this commandment in Deuteronomy 5:12–15 is largely the same as the version recorded in Exodus. The primary difference is the reason given for the commandment. In Exodus the reason is the Lord's creation and his resting on the seventh day. In Deuteronomy it is a memorial to the bondage and forced labor in Egypt. All translations of biblical verses herein are from the King James Version.
12. All the following scriptural passages are discussed in Dana M. Pike's chapter in this volume. The purpose of introducing these scriptures here is to illustrate that the starting point for all rabbinic lawmaking, including on the Sabbath, is the biblical text.

13. Nahum M. Sarna, *The JPS Torah Commentary: Exodus* (Philadelphia: Jewish Publication Society, 1991), 112. Ze'ev Falk discusses legislating from precedent in the Hebrew law corpus; see his *Hebrew Law in Biblical Times: An Introduction*, ed. John W. Welch (Provo, UT: Neal A. Maxwell Institute for Religious Scholarship, Brigham Young University), 12.
14. This story is placed before the giving of the law in Exodus 20 and following. This suggests that the law of Moses was a continuation of a previous law and covenant rather than something wholly new. See Kerry Muhlestein, Joshua M. Sears, and Avram R. Shannon, "New and Everlasting: The Relationship of Gospel Covenants in History," *The Religious Educator* 21, no. 2 (2020): 21–40.
15. For the premishnaic nature of Jewish law and halakic discourse, see Shaye J. D. Cohen, "The Judean Legal Tradition and the *Halakhah* of the Mishnah," in *The Cambridge Companion to the Talmud and Rabbinic Literature*, ed. Charlotte Elisheva Fonrobert and Martin S. Jaffee (Cambridge: Cambridge University Press, 2007), 121–43.
16. The Pharisees are not the same as the rabbinic sages of the Mishnah and the Talmud, but there is enough continuity that they are occasionally tarred with the same brush. See Shannon, "Torah in the Mouth," 144.
17. Note, for example, the interpretation of James E. Talmage in *Jesus the Christ*, 6th ed. (Salt Lake City: Deseret Book, 1922), 552. Matthew Grey has shown that Talmage derived much of his discussion on this point from late Victorian Protestant scholarship. See Matthew J. Grey, "Latter-day Saint Perceptions of Jewish Apostasy in the Time of Christ," in *Standing Apart: Mormon Historical Consciousness and the Concept of Apostasy*, ed. Miranda Wilcox and John D. Young (Oxford: Oxford University Press, 2014), 147–73. Indeed, Grey's observation that the goal of these scholars was to portray Jesus in a manner similar to European Protestants of the late nineteenth and early twentieth centuries can help explain much of the difficulty that Latter-day Saints and other Christians sometimes have in connecting Jesus to ancient Judaism.
18. Craig A. Evans, *Matthew*, New Cambridge Bible Commentary (New York: Cambridge University Press, 2012), 389.
19. For a very positive reading of Jesus's relationship with the Pharisees written by a Latter-day Saint author but without a specific Latter-day Saint argument, see Trevan G. Hatch, *A Stranger in Jerusalem* (Eugene, OR: Wipf and Stock, 2019), 154–84. The Babylonian Talmud, tractate Shabbat 119a contains numerous stories about the joys of the Sabbath. I explore a few of these below.
20. For an in-depth discussion of the difficulty presented to Christian interpreters by this statement from Matthew and the various solutions suggested by scholars, see Mark Allan Powell, "Do and Keep What Moses Says (Matthew 23:2–7)," *Journal of Biblical Literature* 114, no. 3 (1995): 419–35.
21. This is in many ways the inherited reading. See David Nirenberg, *Anti-Judaism: The Western Tradition* (New York: W. W. Norton, 2013), 73–77. For examples, see Evans, *Matthew*, 389; and Ben Witherington III, *Matthew* (Macon, GA: Smyth and Helwys, 2006), 423–24.
22. Sigal, *Halakhah of Jesus*, 167; and Günther Bornkamm, "End Expectation and the Church in Matthew," in *Tradition and Interpretation in Matthew*, ed. Günther

Bornkamm, Gerhard Barth, and H. J. Held, trans. Percy Scott (Philadelphia: Westminster, 1963), 24.

23. Powell, "What Moses Says," 420–21. Powell rejects this meaning because he does not have Jesus agreeing with the Pharisees and suggests that Jesus is simply acknowledging that in a largely illiterate populace the scribes and Pharisees control access to the law of Moses.
24. Hatch, *Stranger in Jerusalem*, 207.
25. This is something that we see throughout the scriptures, including the Book of Mormon. See, for example, the oppression of Alma's people by Amulon and the other wicked priests of Noah (Mosiah 24:8–9).
26. This does not mean that everything in rabbinic literature corresponds with the New Testament, either in general or in specific. Indeed, it is important to be very cautious with comparisons. On this point, see Avram R. Shannon, "Rabbinic Judaism and the New Testament," in *New Testament History Culture and Society*, ed. Lincoln H. Blumell (Provo, UT: Religious Studies Center, Brigham Young University; Salt Lake City: Deseret Book, 2019), 122–38.
27. Juvenal, *Satires* 14:102–6. For ancient anti-Semitism generally, see Peter Schäfer, *Judeophobia: Attitudes towards the Jews in the Ancient World* (Cambridge, MA: Harvard University Press, 1997). Schäfer discusses the Sabbath starting on page 82.
28. On the construction of Rome vis-à-vis Israel by the Babylonian sages, see Ron Naiweld, "The Use of Rabbinic Traditions about Rome in the Babylonian Talmud," *Revue l'histoire des Religions* 233, no. 2 (2016): 255–85. On the interaction between the sages and other Romans in rabbinic storytelling and teaching, see Moshe D. Herr, "The Historical Significance of the Dialogues between Jewish Sages and Roman Dignitaries," *Scripta Hierosolymitana* 22 (1971): 123–50. Herr points out that the stories probably did not happen but plausibly could have. See also Sarit Kattan Gribetz and Moulie Vidas, "Rabbis and Others in Conversation," *Jewish Studies Quarterly* 19, no. 2 (2012): 91–103.
29. Translation from the Soncino Talmud. I have changed some punctuation for clarity and have occasionally updated spelling.
30. Joseph H. Hertz, "Sabbath, Festival and Fast in Judaism," in *The Hebrew English Edition of the Babylonian Talmud: Shabbath*, ed. Isidore Epstein (London: Soncino, 1987), vii–ix, quotation on vii.
31. Jacobs, *Book of Jewish Belief*, 100.
32. See further Shannon, "Torah in the Mouth," 145–47.
33. Mishnaic passages are cited by Mishnah (abbreviated m.), tractate, chapter number, and paragraph number. So the first paragraph in tractate Shabbat would be cited m. Shabbat 1:1. For convenience of readers without knowledge of Hebrew, translations come from the English translation in Herbert Danby, *The Mishnah: Translated from the Hebrew with Introduction and Brief Explanatory Notes* (Oxford: Oxford University Press, 1933, reprinted many times).
34. The Mishnah is very much a text that consists of insiders to Judaism addressing other insiders. See Shannon, "Torah in the Mouth," 151–52.
35. Danby, *Mishnah*, 100.
36. This is not to say that the sages were unaware of their interpretive activities. In m. Hagigah 1:8, the sages acknowledge, "The *halakhah* about the Sabbath, Festal-offerings, and Sacrilege are like mountains suspended by a hair, [because

there is] little scripture and much *halakhah*." Danby, *Mishnah*, 212. The sages go on to note that their halakah on the sacrificial laws is on the solidest scriptural ground and therefore is the "body of the Law." See the discussion in Michal Bar-Asher Siegal, "Mountains Hanging by a Strand? Re-reading Mishnah Hagiga 1:8," *Journal of Ancient Judaism* 4 (2013): 235–56. Siegal suggests that instead of "mountains" (Hebrew *hararim*), this passage should be read as "desert plants" (Hebrew *ḥararim*) that are desiccated and barely hanging on by their roots. Siegal's suggestion is useful on a philological level but does not change the essential point that the sages were aware that different halakic arguments had different rootedness in scripture.

37. See Cohen, "Judean Legal Tradition," 135.
38. This interpretive process, called "verbal analogy," is based on the idea that the omnisignificance of scripture makes it possible to interpret a word in light of its use in different passages. For a Latter-day Saint perspective on this, see Matthew L. Bowen, "Jewish Hermeneutics in the New Testament Period," in Blumell, *New Testament History, Culture, and Society*, 86–108, discussion on 90–94. See further Lieberman, *Hellenism in Jewish Palestine*, 53–62, discussion on 57–62; and Strack and Stemberger, *Introduction to Talmud and Midrash*, 16–20.
39. See the discussion in Cohen, "Judean Legal Tradition," 136–37.
40. Danby, *Mishnah*, 100.
41. The Hebrew word used for a scribe or copyist here is *liblar*, which is a loanword from Latin *librarius*. This differentiates from scribes as a class of scriptural expert, such as Christian readers often see the term used in the New Testament. The Hebrew word for this type of scribe is *soferim*. For more discussion on scribes, see Lieberman, *Hellenism in Jewish Palestine*, 47–48.
42. Danby, *Mishnah*, 106.
43. Shaye Cohen translates this very nicely as "archetypal category of labor." "Judean Legal Tradition," 135.
44. "It is not just the Torah that knows nothing of these mishnaic ideas; this list of thirty-nine labors and this system of classification of archetypal labors and subordinate labors is unknown to Philo and all other pre-mishnaic documents." Cohen, "Judean Legal Tradition," 135.
45. Louis Jacobs describes these categories, including the process of adapting the law, in *Book of Jewish Belief*, 98–99.
46. Michael Broyde and Howard Jachter, "The Use of Electricity on Shabbat and Yom Tov," *Journal of Halacha and Contemporary Society* 21 (Spring 1991): 4–47.
47. These were the two main halakic schools in early rabbinic Judaism. See Jacob Neusner, *Invitation to the Talmud: A Teaching Book* (Atlanta, GA: Scholars Press, 1998; repr., Eugene, OR: Wipf and Stock, 2003), 39–40.
48. Used here to mean lampwicks.
49. In order to dry them out.
50. Danby, *Mishnah*, 100–101.
51. The Babylonian Talmud *Eruvin* 13b records that a voice from heaven came down and stated that the words of both houses were "the words of the living God, but the halakah is in agreement with the rulings of Beit Hillel."
52. There is an excellent discussion on the ongoing halakic debate around the Word of Wisdom in Steven C. Harper, *Making Sense of the Doctrine and Covenants: A*

Guided Tour through Modern Revelations (Salt Lake City, UT: Deseret, 2008), 328–330.

53. On this point, see Tiffany Gee Lewis, "The Ever-Expanding Ox in the Mire," *Deseret News*, July 13, 2017.
54. See Franklyn W. Dunford and Phillip R. Kunz, "Will the Real Ox in the Mire Please Stand Up," *Ensign*, June 1972, 18–21.
55. Jeffrey R. Holland, "Behold the Lamb of God," *Ensign*, May 2019, 44–46, quotation on 45.
56. Jastrow, *Dictionary*, 1169. This collocation derives from the verbal root *P/Q/Ḥ*, which in the *Piel* means to "break through, to open." Jastrow, *Dictionary*, 1209. *Nefesh* is a Hebrew word that is often translated as "soul" in the King James Version of the Bible but has a meaning of "self," "person," or "life." Ludwig Koehler and Walter Baumgartner, *The Hebrew and Aramaic Lexicon of the Old Testament* (Leiden: Brill 2001), 711–3; and Jastrow, *Dictionary*, 926–27.
57. See b. Sanhedrin 74a.
58. Danby, *Mishnah*, 172.
59. In Jesus's own halakic discussions in the New Testament, this principle governs much of his teaching on keeping the Sabbath day holy. It can be seen as underscoring his statement "the sabbath was made for man, and not man for the sabbath" (Mark 2:27). Even his healing on the Sabbath seems to be rooted in the sense that preservation of humanity and life is the greatest good.
60. The Babylonian Talmud Sanhedrin 74a states, "R. Joḥanan said in the R. Simeon b. Jehozadak: By a majority vote it was resolved . . . that in every [other] law of the Torah, if a man is commanded: 'Transgress and suffer not death' he may transgress and not suffer death, excepting idolatry, incest, [which includes adultery] and murder." The discussion here is about martyrdom, but it is applied to the principle of *piquaḥ nefesh* because it also relates to times when it is appropriate to abrogate the commandments in order to save life.
61. The Church of Jesus Christ of Latter-day Saints primarily celebrates the Sabbath day on Sunday, in conformity with much of the rest of Christianity. Some other Restoration groups, such as The Church of Jesus Christ of Latter Day Saints (Strangite) practice a Saturday Sabbath. See Russel J. Thomsen, "The History of the Sabbath in Mormonism" (master's thesis, Loma Linda University, 1968), 23–42.
62. The earliest Christians seem to have honored both the seventh day and the first day, but for much of the history of Christianity, starting in the fourth century AD, the Sabbath was understood as Sunday. There have always been Christians who preferred to celebrate the Sabbath on the seventh day. See the history in the anthology by D. A. Carson, ed., *From Sabbath to the Lord's Day: A Biblical, Historical, and Theological Investigation* (Eugene, OR: Wipf and Stock, 1999).
63. Louis Jacobs suggests that this is part of why the "fathers of work" in Mishnah Shabbat 7:2, discussed above, are *creative* work—because the Sabbath is kept in honor of the Creator. Jacobs, *Book of Jewish Belief*, 99.
64. Harper, *Making Sense of the Doctrine and Covenants,* 330–32.

Chapter Eight

"A Visible Figure of an Invisible Grace": Sixteenth-Century Evangelical Religious Reformers and the Sabbath Day

Jan J. Martin

In the April 2015 General Conference, President Russell M. Nelson, who was then serving as a member of the Quorum of the Twelve Apostles, explained that he did not need a list of dos and don'ts to tell him how to behave on the Sabbath, a day that is traditionally honored on Sunday by Latter-day Saints and many other Christians.[1] He had learned from his study of the scriptures that his conduct and attitude on the Sabbath "constituted a *sign*" between him and his Heavenly Father. President Nelson explained that whenever he needed to decide whether an activity was appropriate for the Sabbath, he simply asked himself, "What *sign* do I want to give to God?" That question made his "choices about the Sabbath day crystal clear."[2]

President Nelson's remarks are a good reminder that questions about the Sabbath day are asked by believers in every generation. As the previous chapters in this volume have shown, a variety of questions about the Sabbath day have been asked and discussed for centuries.[3] In this chapter, I will explore sixteenth-century protestant, or evangelical, Sabbatarian[4] teachings in Europe and England during the sixteenth century.[5] To make a complicated subject within a religiously tumultuous century easier to portray, I will frame my discussion around five common theological questions:

1. How should believers feel about the Sabbath day?
2. What are the benefits of Sabbath-day worship?
3. Why is the Sabbath day theologically significant?
4. What activities are appropriate for the Sabbath?
5. How do believers make the Sabbath day holy?

I will then examine theological teachings published between 1520 and 1600 to show that even though sixteenth-century religious reformers and theologians largely agreed that the fourth commandment should be obeyed by the Christians of their day, they disagreed on how the Sabbath day should be observed. Most early evangelical reformers strongly rejected strict obedience to formulated behavioral rules or legalistic interpretations of Sabbath observance in favor of maintaining what they called Christian liberty. However, later reformers began to support legalistic interpretations in reaction to what they saw as neglect or abuse of the Sabbath day, though they often differed in the degree of legalism they thought was appropriate.[6]

How Should Christians Feel about the Sabbath Day?

Robert Mannyng of Brunne[7] (ca. 1275–ca. 1338), a medieval English chronicler, poet, and Gilbertine monk, fervently desired to help English laypeople avoid sin.[8] In 1303 he wrote *Handlyng Synne,* a long Middle English poem composed to provide spiritually edifying and wholesome entertainment for those who could not read and who loved to hear stories and rhymes. In *Handlyng Synne,* Mannyng reviewed the Ten Commandments, the seven deadly sins, and confession.[9] As he taught about each commandment in the Decalogue, he explained that "Holy Sunday men ought to spare, Holy Sunday is before all free." Mannyng advised believers that they could keep the Sabbath "well" by praying, by performing God's errands, and by seeking to be forgiven of their misdeeds. He also felt that believers should avoid going to the tavern, a place he expressively described as the "devil's knife," and should not engage in wrestling, field sports, carols, or plays on Sunday.[10] Mannyng was not alone in wanting believers to respect the Sabbath. A contemporary Dominican friar and preacher, John Bromyard (d. 1352), dispiritedly observed how little the Christians of his day were doing for their souls on Sundays and how burdensome they seemed to find it. He wrote,

> They get up late, and come late to church, and wish to be so little there, that they will urge the priest to be quick because they have a friend coming to dinner. If there should be a sermon about their salvation, they excuse themselves from hearing it, by saying that it is getting too late for them to remain. . . . Even the short time that they cannot help remaining in the church they spend in unnecessary talk, forgetting that the house of God is the house of prayer. Then they go away to dinner or to the tavern, and there they are in no hurry for some spend the whole rest of the day and even till late at night, like the Amalecites "eating and drinking and as it were keeping a festival day." (1 Kings xxv. 16)[11]

For Christians in the Middle Ages, resting on Sunday was a general law of the Catholic church and had been since the Decretals of Gregory IX were issued in AD 1234.[12] The law was designed to grant believers leisure time for worship in an economically hard-pressed society that easily distracted people's minds away from God.[13] However, over time and in response to complaints that Sunday leisure was being abused, ecclesiastical and civic leaders became more insistent that Christians were morally bound to observe Sunday as a day dedicated to God[14] and that believers were supposed to follow "the spiritual exercises prescribed and enforced by ecclesiastical authorities on Sundays,"[15] including attending morning and afternoon church services, ceasing all servile work for twenty-four hours, and avoiding inappropriate recreational activities.[16]

Thomas Arundel (1353–1414), the Archbishop of Canterbury in England, was one religious leader who was very displeased with violations of the Catholic church's Sabbath expectations. In 1414, he became so upset that the barbers around him were violating Sabbath rest that he complained to the mayor and aldermen of London. He claimed that because the barbers had no "zeal for the law of God," they were pursuing their craft on the Lord's Day "just as busily and in the same way as on any day in the week." He threatened excommunication and wanted the city to levy heavy fines against these Sabbath breakers.[17] Arundel's reactions show how easily deviation from the Catholic church's expectations for Sabbath behavior could result in ecclesiastical and civic discipline. However, a growing number of Christians were becoming more and more frustrated with these penalties because they made the Sabbath feel like a heavy encumbrance rather than a day of rest.[18] A century later, the theological dissatisfactions of one Christian would lead to significant and widespread religious upheaval, generating heated debates about many doctrines, including the Sabbath day and how it should be observed.

Between 1518 and 1525, the German Augustinian monk Martin Luther (1483–1546) successfully persuaded large lay audiences across Europe that the Catholic church had strayed from primitive Christianity and needed reform. Through a flood of printed materials primarily written in German,[19] Luther argued that scripture was "a source of authority independent of the church," that the individual Christian was "an independent authority in the interpretation of scripture,"[20] and that believers had a right to "pronounce on doctrine."[21] And pronounce he did. Luther's theological teachings, including the supremacy of scripture over religious tradition and justification by faith rather than works, effectively shattered the Christian unity of Europe that had existed since AD 1054, paving the way for the rise of religious pluralism. Because of Luther's emphasis on *sola scriptura* (scripture alone), a phrase which essentially means that God's word is sufficient for understanding all Christian truth,[22] interest in Old Testament laws and how those laws applied to contemporary Christians significantly increased.[23] Two of the many doctrines under discussion during the 1520s were (1) whether Christians were morally bound to observe Sunday as a day dedicated to God and (2) what believers were supposed to do or not do on Sunday.

As the central figure in the formative years of the evangelical reformation, Luther and his theological approach to Sabbath-day observance were extremely influential.[24] In his catechisms and other writings, Luther stated that the "commandment concerning the Sabbath" was still in effect and applied "to the whole world," but he condemned the Catholic church's decision to declare Sunday as the Christian Sabbath, and he rejected legalistic understandings that imposed burdensome rules such as fasting, praying, sexual abstinence, collecting on loans, or resting from daily labor.[25] He passionately declared that if anyone established Sabbath observance on a legalistic foundation, he wanted Christians to revolt. He ordered believers burdened with a legalistic Sabbath "to work on it, to ride on it, to dance on it, to feast on it, to do anything" that would remove what he felt to be an "encroachment on Christian liberty."[26]

However, as much as Luther wanted Christians to be free of heavy Sabbath regulations, he also boldly denounced neglectful behavior on the Sabbath day, including failing to attend church "to hear God's word"; failing to improve one's understanding of God's word; or wasting the day in greedy frivolities, idleness, or drunkenness.[27] In Luther's mind, there was a middle way between punitive legalism and thoughtless neglect. The middle way involved devoting oneself to "the [w]ord of God . . . at home and especially in church."[28] Luther believed that the word of God was "the sanctuary above all sanctuaries" and that it was "the treasure which sanctifies everything." For Luther the Sabbath became delightful when one heard and studied the word of God because God's word awakened "new understanding, pleasure, and devotion," constantly created "clean hearts and minds," and made Christians holy.[29] Thus Luther declared that at whatever hour "God's Word is taught, preached, heard, read or meditated upon, there the person, day, and work are sanctified" because the word "makes saints of us all."[30] This perspective, along with his rejection of the Catholic church's authority to declare Sunday as the Christian Sabbath, caused Luther to avoid designating one day of the week as *the* Sabbath, since one could "rest, celebrate, and keep the Sabbath on whatever day or at whatever hour God's word [was] preached." However, he willingly acknowledged that appointing a specific day, like Sunday, for Christians to gather for worship was an orderly, practical necessity that protected against unnecessary innovation. But more importantly for Luther, gathering in church on Sundays provided an essential learning environment because he knew that "God's word cannot be heard or taught when one is preoccupied with something else or when one is not quiet."[31]

As persuasive and vociferous as Luther was, he wasn't the only Christian successfully advocating for religious reform in the early 1500s. In Switzerland, Huldrych Zwingli (1484–1531), a well-educated Catholic priest who taught himself Greek so that he could study and preach from the Greek New Testament, also revolutionized religious thought. In 1523, Zwingli wrote *Sixty-Seven Articles*, a document defending specific theological reforms that he felt should be made in the church in Zürich. Among other changes, Zwingli wanted Christ to be the sole remitter of sins and the center of salvation; he wanted the word of God to be the supreme authority; and he wanted priests to be able to marry.[32] Though many of his ideas closely resembled Luther's, Zwingli claimed that he obtained his teachings from the holy scriptures and not from Luther's writings, which had been circulating around him.[33] One of Zwingli's earliest biographers wrote that even though the name of Luther "became more celebrated as his books were more and more sedulously thumbed by all," Zwingli "himself kept away from them" because he wanted people to "perceive the parity in spirit between himself and Luther" that came because both of them drew their ideas "out of the Divine Scriptures."[34] Zwingli's theological teachings were popular throughout Europe, spreading across Switzerland and southern Germany, into France and Holland, and across to England and Scotland.[35]

Regarding Sabbath-day observance, Zwingli believed the fourth commandment was a divine law that still applied to the Christians of his day.[36] From the teachings of Christ in the New Testament, Zwingli learned that "the Sabbath is made for man and not man for the Sabbath." He interpreted this to mean that "the Sabbath is in the power of man, not man in the power of the Sabbath." In other words, if Christians wanted to take delight in the Sabbath, they needed to first comprehend that the day was "for the service of men, not for their oppression."[37] In Zwingli's eyes, the Sabbath was supposed to be a wonderful blessing because it freed Christians from day-to-day drudgery and allowed them time to "consider God's kind deeds with thankfulness." For him, the Sabbath became a holy day when Christians desired that which was holy and participated in holy behaviors, such as caring for their neighbors, hearing God's word, praising him, and serving him.[38] Zwingli accepted Sunday as both a traditional and convenient day of worship for Christians, but he wanted flexibility in its observation. He was quite happy for individuals or entire congregations to "transfer the solemnity and rest of the Lord's Day . . . to some other day" when necessity required.[39] Though Zwingli believed that it was lawful for a Christian to pursue his or her daily labors on Sunday, he felt that attending worship services was a priority that should be attended to first and that doing so enabled and facilitated delight in the Sabbath.[40]

What Benefits Come from Sabbath Day Observance?

In 1524, Andreas Karlstadt (1486–1541) published the first evangelical treatise about the Sabbath day, entitled *Regarding the Sabbath and Statutory Holy Days*. Karlstadt was another early German religious reformer who began his career as one of Luther's allies, but the two parted ways in the mid-1520s due to theological and liturgical differences.[41] Like Luther and Zwingli, Karlstadt argued that the fourth commandment was applicable in a literal sense to the Christians of his time. However, he differed from the other two by envisioning the Sabbath as a day of rest that followed any six consecutive days of labor. Karlstadt felt that God hadn't dictated a specific day of the week in order to give believers the freedom to "select and set the seventh day" as they pleased.[42]

Despite his desire for weekly flexibility, Karlstadt was much more attentive to behavioral regulations than either Luther or Zwingli, and he placed a greater doctrinal emphasis on the physical and spiritual rest associated with keeping the Sabbath day holy. While Luther accepted that "menservants and maidservants who have gone about their work or trade all week long should also retire for a day to rest and be refreshed," his main Sabbath focus was assembling to hear the word of God.[43] Karlstadt, however, fervently insisted that no one should work on the Sabbath, including servants and beasts of burden, because he felt that people and animals needed to revive and fortify themselves "to refresh their bones and restore [their] strength." He also took a unique position in believing that Christians "ought to be idle" during the Sabbath day, "do[ing] nothing, and endur[ing] the long time." In his mind the Sabbath had been instituted for a person's "spirit to reach a point of boredom" so that the Christian could "learn something during the idle time."[44] Additionally, Karlstadt begged Christians to "never forget that the Sabbath included forgiveness of sins" because they could not "be sanctified and enter into God's forgiveness" without it. He vividly described how "it would be good if on a Sabbath we were to put our head in our hands, bow down, and acknowledge our misfortune and weakness with great sorrow" so that Christians would "rush more quickly to the One (who alone cleanses and sanctifies.)" For Karlstadt, Sabbath observance provided essential physical renewal and the opportunity for a spiritual cleansing and sanctifying, an inward change involving a willing rejection of everything that "[was] unholy."[45] It wasn't long before another early reformer began elaborating on the importance of physical and spiritual rest on the Sabbath.

Towards the end of 1531, Heinrich Bullinger (1504–1575) replaced Huldrych Zwingli as the main pastor in Zürich. While acting as chaplain, Zwingli had been tragically killed in a battle between evangelical and Catholic forces at Kappel on October 11, 1531. One scholar has described Bullinger as a "wise and patient man and a great preacher" who steered Zurich's reformation back into stability by refusing to use violence against those who did not share his beliefs.[46] Bullinger exerted considerable theological influence through his preaching and Bible commentaries. He taught that the "Sabbath signifies rest" and explained that "we rest from servile work, in abstaining from sin, and doing our best not to have our own will found in ourselves, nor to work our own works."[47] Like Karlstadt, Bullinger wasn't shy about teaching that "outward rest" from physical labors was commanded on the Sabbath "so that spiritual work [would] not be hindered by bodily business." He candidly wrote,

> The Lord allows you sufficient time for your labour, in which to get a living for yourself and your household. For six days you may work, but the Lord claims the seventh day, and requires it to be consecrated to him and his holy rest. Every week has seven days: and of those seven the Lord requires but one for himself. Who then can rightly complain, I beseech you, or say that injury has been done to him? More time is allowed to work in, than to keep the sabbath holy: and the one who requires to have this sabbath kept is God: the maker, the father, and the Lord of all mankind.[48]

In addition to physical rest, Bullinger believed that "the spiritual sabbath is charged especially and above all things." He argued that Christians should assemble and occupy themselves with four spiritual activities on the Sabbath: (1) hearing the word of God, (2) praising, thanking, and praying to God, (3) administering the sacraments, and (4) relieving the poor. For Bullinger, "these are the duties in which the Lord's sabbath is kept holy even in the church of Christians. And it is kept holy so much the greater, if an earnest good will to do no evil all the day long is added to these."[49]

Why Is the Sabbath Day Significant?

An exiled English priest and evangelical reformer named William Tyndale (ca. 1494–1536) thought he knew why the Sabbath day had significance. As one of the many people who were inspired by Luther, Tyndale courageously began his own systematic vernacular religious printing campaign from the Low Countries.[50] As the prime spokesman of the first generation of English religious reformers, Tyndale provided the most serious threat to Catholic Christianity and political stability in England in the 1520s and 1530s.[51] Hoping to induce English laypeople to reform the Christian church in England, Tyndale published an English translation of the New Testament (1526), the first to be rendered into English from Greek source texts, followed by an English translation of the first five books of Moses (1530), the first to be rendered into English from Hebrew source texts. With help from friends and supporters, Tyndale had both volumes ingeniously smuggled into England aboard merchant ships.[52] These illicit translations, along with many expository books written by Tyndale, helped extend European religious debates into England. Vernacular scriptures were particularly important to Tyndale because he believed that the Bible was the touchstone of all truth, and he wanted English laypeople to use it to judge the veracity of all other doctrines and ideas, including his own.[53]

In 1530, Tyndale explained in a marginal note for Exodus 31 that the Sabbath day had two essential purposes: hearing the word of God and spiritually reconciling with God's will. Tyndale believed that the Sabbath was "a sign" unto Christians to "put them in remembrance that it was the Lord that sanctified them with his holy spirit and not they themselves with their holy works."[54] In Tyndale's understanding, signs were given to help Christians remember and understand the covenant of salvation, which was a promise between the Father, the Son, and the Holy Ghost "to restore creation to its original state so man could once again have fellowship with God."[55] Tyndale believed that Christians who obediently kept the Sabbath day holy demonstrated their belief and trust in God's covenant promise. As the faithful attended Sabbath worship services and heard the word of God preached to them, God sanctified them through "his holy spirit and word," making them new creatures, or children of God.[56] Much like Luther, Tyndale felt that the Catholic church's legalistic behavioral restrictions made Christians superstitious servants of the Sabbath who believed that they were spiritually purified as long as they abstained from bodily labor on Sundays even while neglecting legitimate sanctifying activities like prayer, hearing the word of God, visiting the sick and needy, giving alms, or helping a neighbor.[57] Like other early reformers, Tyndale also rejected a rigid day of the week for the Sabbath, declaring that "we be lords over the sabbath and may yet change it" to a Monday, hold it every tenth day, or have it twice in a week if that were needed to teach Christians properly. Because the covenant was of paramount importance to Tyndale, he went a bit further theologically than other reformers by arguing that Christians didn't need a specific holy day at all "if the people might be taught without it."[58] As long as Christians were clearly and effectively instructed to believe that faith "in God the Father, through our Lord Jesus Christ, according to the covenants and appointment made between God and us, is our salvation," Tyndale was satisfied and wasn't overly concerned about when or where the instruction occurred.[59]

Tyndale was not alone in believing that the Sabbath was a sign of a perpetual covenant of sanctification. An associate, John Frith (1503–1533), who had a reputation in England and on the Continent for his outstanding learning and scholarly abilities, also advocated for religious reform and published an interpretation of the fourth commandment. Writing from the Tower of London in 1533 while imprisoned on charges of religious heresy, Frith explained that the Sabbath was "instituted and commanded of God to be kept of the children of Israel" as a sign "that it was God which sanctified them with his spirit, and not themselves with their holy works." He believed that ceremonies like the Sabbath ceased after Christ came, explaining that the primitive church abrogated Sabbath observance to give Christians an example of Christian liberty: "that they might know that neither the keeping of the Sabbath, nor of any other day, is necessary." Along with the continental reformers, Frith willingly accepted the practical realities of reserving a day "in the which the people might come together" to "hear God's word, receive the sacraments, and give God thanks," but once those things had been accomplished, he felt that Christians could "return unto their houses and do their business as well as any other day."[60] In fact, Frith argued that anyone who taught that "a man sinneth which worketh on the holy day" was either weak, ignorant, or of the devil because such a person made "sin in such as God leaveth free."[61]

Across the English Channel, an early French evangelical reformer named John Calvin (1509–1564) also valued the Sabbath as a perpetual covenant of sanctification. In 1536, Calvin unexpectedly set up shop in Geneva. Having just published the landmark and instantly bestselling text *Institutes of the Christian Religion*, Calvin was a wanted man by reformers and Catholics alike. The *Institutes* was Calvin's early attempt to standardize the theories of reformed Christianity for those who wanted to know more about the faith. In the volume, he explained his views on such things as justification, the church, the sacraments, original sin, free will, and political governments. Calvin expanded and revised the *Institutes* many times before publishing the definitive edition in 1559. Calvin initially intended to pass through Geneva, but since the Catholic church and its bishop had been repudiated and no new church had yet been organized, the active reformers in residence quickly pressured Calvin to stay and help them. Calvin's relationship with the city was long and ultimately fruitful, but it was also marred by theological conflict and his own three-year absence from 1538 to 1541.[62] When he returned to Geneva, Calvin introduced new forms of church government and liturgy and preached over two thousand sermons, many of which touched on the Sabbath day and its observance.[63]

Like Tyndale and Frith, Calvin argued that "the Sabbath was the symbol of sanctification" and that God "commanded the Israelites to rest on the seventh day" so that they would "acknowledge themselves separated by God . . . from the profane nations to be God's peculiar inheritance." He believed that God wanted the Israelites "to experience him for their Father in all things" so they would "know that he was their sanctifier."[64] For these reasons, Calvin believed that the fourth commandment was applicable to the Christians of his day. He taught that Sabbath observance allowed Christians to put aside their own works so that God could perform "his own works" within them. Calvin explained that "God was not satisfied by the people's resting from their occupations" because their "inward sanctification was always the chief end in view." Thus he eloquently described the Sabbath as "an outward symbol" that "contained a spiritual mystery" and as "a sacrament" or "a visible figure of an invisible grace."[65] Like Frith, Calvin felt that the Jewish Saturday Sabbath had been abolished by Jesus Christ at his Resurrection and that "the early Christians had substituted" Sunday, or "what we call the Lord's day," for the Saturday Sabbath. The substitution was made "to warn Christians against adhering to a shadowy ceremony." However, like other reformers, Calvin understood the practical value of a designated day of worship. He declared, "Religious meetings are enjoined us by the word of God; their necessity, experience itself sufficiently demonstrates. But unless these meetings are stated, and have fixed days allotted to them, how can they be held? We must . . . do all things decently and in order."[66]

What Activities are Appropriate for the Sabbath Day?

As the second generation of evangelical religious reformers slowly began to replace the first, and as the second generation continued to grapple with how to organize church practice, a "widespread practical concern for Sunday observance" with more attention to specific behaviors began to emerge, especially in England.[67] In 1547, for example, the young evangelical king of England, Edward VI (1537–1553), issued a series of injunctions that were intended to advance "the true honour of Almighty God," suppress "idolatry and superstition," and "plant true religion" throughout his realms. The twenty-fourth injunction stated that because there was too much "idleness, pride, drunkenness, quarrelling, and brawling" upon "the holy-day" the king wanted his "faithful and loving subjects" to keep the Sabbath "according to God's holy will and pleasure," not their own. Consequently, he ordered them to spend their Sabbaths "in hearing the word of God read and taught; in private and public prayer; in [ac]knowledging their offences to God . . . in reconciling themselves charitably to their neighbours . . . in visiting the poor and sick; in using all soberness and godly conversation." However, the new king wanted all "parsons, vicars, and curates" to be sure to declare to their parishioners "that they may with a safe and quiet conscience, in the time of harvest, labour" upon Sunday so they could "save" their harvests. He did not want any Christian in his realm to "superstitiously abstain from working" on the Sabbath because that approach was inappropriately legalistic and would "grievously offend and displease God."[68]

A year after Edward VI's injunctions went into effect, John Hooper (ca. 1500–1555), an English reformer, published *A Declaration of the Ten Holy Commandments* (1548). Because of doctrinal disagreements that got him into trouble with conservative members of the English clergy, Hooper moved to Zürich in the late 1540s, where he developed a close friendship with Bullinger. Hooper eventually returned to England and became the Bishop of Gloucester and then of Worcester. Bullinger's influence on Hooper's Sabbatarian thought is evident in Hooper's prescriptions of what constituted holy works on the Sabbath; however, Hooper went further than Bullinger by also prescribing what *shouldn't* be done on the Sabbath. Ironically, Hooper's prohibitions resemble medieval Catholic restrictions and show how the theological pendulum was swinging back towards previously rejected elements of Catholic legalism.

In *A Declaration,* Hooper explained that even though the Sabbath day was not holier than any other day of the week, "God sanctified" it and "appointed it" to be separated from other days so it could be used for holy purposes, such as "study of the scripture, hearing of the word of God, [calling] upon God with ardent prayer, [using] and exercis[ing] the sacraments of God, confer[ring] and . . . giv[ing] . . . alms to the comforting of the poor."[69] For him, "That day is always most holy in the which we most apply and give ourselves unto holy works." Therefore, on Sunday, a Christian should "call his [intentions] & thoughts from the lusts, pleasures, vanities, and concupiscence of the world." Hooper strongly objected to those who abused "the rest, and ease of the Sabbath with sports, games, and pastimes, keeping of markets & fairs . . . and unlawful plays." He even went so far as to discuss the development of self-discipline, what he called mortification, by discoursing on the need to be patient in adversity and temperate in felicity, including with "meat, drink, and all other things." In his mind, gluttony and drunkenness, especially on the Sabbath, could only be overcome by fasting and prayer. Hooper closed his discussion of the fourth commandment with a plea: "Would to God people would follow the scripture in this mortification, then the world would amend doubtless, but there is now nothing but a carnal liberty of the gospel which hindereth much the glory of God."[70] Because Hooper was very popular as a preacher and lecturer, his published writings were widely read and thus influenced later Sabbatarian developments in Elizabethan England.[71]

How do Christians make the Sabbath Day holy?

Thomas Becon (ca. 1512–1567), a theologian, clergyman, and one of England's leading evangelical writers between the 1540s and 1560s, believed that setting one day aside each week for God was a spiritually vital act of consecration. Once Queen Elizabeth I acceded to the English throne and made reformed religion acceptable in England again, Becon returned from continental exile where he had been living to escape Catholic queen Mary I's persecution of evangelicals. In 1564, Becon published a massive three-volume edition of his collected writings, which included the first printed edition of *A new catechism*, a dialogue between a fictional father and son that presented "Christ and his doctrine" so plainly that Becon felt "no man living" could be deceived.[72] Becon's fictional characters discussed many subjects, including education, the Decalogue, and the study of both the scriptures and classical works.

While addressing the fourth commandment, the fictional father asks his fictional son, "What is it to sanctify the Sabbath day?" Echoing both Bullinger and Hooper, who were early influences on Becon's theology, the son answers, "Not to pass over that day idly in lewd pastimes," which included feasting, throwing dice, playing cards, dancing, bear baiting, bowling, shooting, laughing, prostitution, bargaining, buying, selling, or going to fairs or markets. In Becon's eyes, these activities profaned and defiled a day that was supposed to be holy. To make the day holy, Becon wanted "the mind utterly sequestered from all worldly things," and he wanted the body "free from all servile works" so that Christians could apply their whole selves to "godly and spiritual exercises." Becon believed that a deliberate and careful consecration of the Sabbath would lead to an individual consecration, which meant "the whole giving over of ourselves unto the good will of God, to work in us by his Holy Spirit, whatsoever his blessed pleasure shall be, that he alone may live, rule, reign and triumph in us."[73] Becon utilized an Augustinian theological element by arguing that consecrated Christians who honored the day could experience "godly and everlasting quietness and rest," which through Christ they "shall have after this life in the kingdom of God the father."[74] This was because Christians who were "quiet with God" in their consciences after ceasing from evil works and submitting themselves fully to the will of God carried heaven in their breasts. In other words, consecration made "the Sabbath of Christians . . . spiritual and everlasting."[75]

Thirty years later, another Church of England clergyman and religious writer, Nicholas Bownd (d. 1613), published *Doctrine of the Sabbath* (1595), a work that one scholar describes as "the most influential and important treatise on the Sabbath among English Puritans."[76] Bownd's book made the Sabbath a potentially explosive issue because he argued that Christ himself appointed the first day of the week to be the "new Sabbath,"[77] a unique theological position, and because he adopted a legalistic interpretation by advocating for stringent behavioral rules and swift civic punishment for Sabbath breakers.[78] Bownd's Sabbatarian theology was centered on a Sabbath that was consecrated by Christ himself after he completed the redemption of mankind and experienced a "new creation" through his Resurrection on Sunday morning. Quoting from Jerome Zanchius (1516–1590), an Italian evangelical reformer and one of the most learned theologians of the later sixteenth century, Bownd explained that the words *sanctified* and *consecrated* meant the same thing: "to be put apart from other things unto a holy use." In Bownd's mind, the Bible repeatedly commended the truth that God had sanctified, or consecrated, "unto himself the Sabbath day" when he originally selected Saturday as his day of rest after the creation of the world. Bownd insisted that the New Testament showed how Christ changed the Sabbath to Sunday, consecrating it as a new day of rest after completing the work of redemption with the Resurrection. Christ's Resurrection was a second creation because it made all things new.[79] Such a consecration altered the very nature of Sunday, making it a completely different kind of day than the rest of the days in the week. Its sacred nature required Christians to "use it only to that holy end for which it was ordained, and so by the right use of it, to maintain . . . that holiness, which at the first was put upon it." He explained that it was a divine law that consecrated things "may not otherwise be employed then [sic] to [God's] use."[80] Thus the consecrated Sabbath should "not be partly his" and "partly ours by doing our own work," but the day should be "altogether [God's]."[81]

Like many of his evangelical predecessors, Bownd wanted Christians to spend their Sundays in dedicated service to God. Appropriate service included attending "holy meetings of the Church" where they could hear God's voice, "learn his most holy will," and "make provision" for their souls that they "might be the fitter to serve him the whole week following."[82] Bownd insisted that Christians cast away all "vain pretences (as that the weather is too hot, or too cold, the ways are too foul, the journey too long, and a thousand more)" that prevented them from attending church to engage with God's word and participate in prayer, both of which were the "head and the foot" of keeping the Sabbath day holy. But he also wanted Christians to partake of the sacraments and participate in "all other parts of [God's] holy discipline and government," which included looking after the poor, a "work most acceptable unto God, profitable to our brethren," and appropriate for the Sabbath.[83] Bownd recognized that there were instances of necessity that might require bodily labor to be performed on Sunday, such as seeing a physician, dealing with unexpected floods or fires, or attending to the needs of animals, though he also knew that "the wise men of this world make many things necessary, which indeed are not." His rule of thumb was to determine if the work could be deferred to another day of the week. If it could be deferred, the work was not necessary and should not be performed on the Sabbath.[84]

However, unlike many of his evangelical predecessors, especially those who were writing about the Sabbath in the early sixteenth century, Bownd wanted "princes and [m]agistrates" to enact laws that would preserve the sanctity of the Sabbath, such as prohibiting public fairs, travel to fairs, shipment of goods from town to town, horse riding, and working in the fields at harvest. He also wanted magistrates to forbid people from visiting taverns, alehouses, inns, shoemakers, and tailors on Sunday; to end all buying and selling of food, along with the making of marriage dinners and other needless feasts on the Sabbath; and to provide stern and swift civic punishments for Sabbath breakers.[85] Bownd declared his strong belief that these laws would preserve the Commonwealth "from many grievous punishments and common plagues which either have already come upon it, or do most justly hang over the head of it" because people were neglecting the fourth commandment. He recognized that there were "many and mighty enemies" to his teachings about the Sabbath, even among other evangelical reformers, and remarked that he did not think "that there is any one point of our religion that is so in controversy among the learned of all sorts . . . wherein many friends do disagree." However, he confidently supported his position by quoting Bullinger: "He that despiseth the Sabbath makes no great account of the true religion."[86]

Bownd's treatise was enormously influential, but because it was perceived by some as dangerously advocating for Puritan Sabbatarianism, it was recalled in 1599 by Archbishop John Whitgift (1530–1604), Queen Elizabeth I's last and favorite Archbishop of Canterbury, and was then officially banned by the Lord Chief Justice in 1600.[87] However, an expanded version of Bownd's book was reissued in 1606 when Sabbatarian controversy was once again flowing thick and fast thanks to a proclamation issued on May 7, 1603 by the newly crowned King James VI and I (1566–1625).[88] James declared, "We are informed that there hath been heretofore great neglect in the kingdom of keeping the Sabbath day." To avoid "all impious profanation," the king commanded "that no bear-baiting, bull-baiting, in their lewd common plays, or other like disordered and unlawful exercises and pastimes, be frequented, kept, or used at any time hereafter upon the sabbath-day."[89] As the seventeenth century proceeded, one advocate remarked that "the Sabbath itself had no rest" because of the many and continuing debates about it.[90] In fact, the Sabbath became such an important issue in England that some seventeenth-century Dutch divines called it "*Figmentum Anglicanum*," or "the invention of the Anglicans," because English Puritans developed a Sabbatarianism that was unlike that of their European evangelical counterparts.[91] Puritan Sabbatarianism was distinguished by its belief in the morality of the fourth commandment, by its insistence that Sunday was a consecrated day of rest following Christ's second creation, and by its rigorous behavioral expectations.[92] During the eighteenth century, Sabbatarian practice in England declined; however, by the nineteenth century, it again became such an important and controversial subject that one English theologian, though unsupportive of Puritan interpretations, proudly declared that England had "the best idea of the Sabbath-day which is to be found anywhere."[93]

Conclusion

In this study, I have explored Sabbatarian teachings as expounded by evangelical reformers in Europe and in England primarily during the sixteenth century. Framing my discussion around five common theological questions, I have shown that while sixteenth-century religious reformers and theologians consistently believed that the fourth commandment in the Decalogue should be obeyed by the Christians of their day, they differed in their judgment of how the Sabbath day should be observed. In the early 1500s, reformers largely rejected legalistic interpretations of Sabbath-day observance in favor of maintaining Christian liberty. However, as the sixteenth century progressed and reformers worked to establish and refine reformed church practice, they became more concerned with behavioral violations of the Sabbath. As a result, many later reformers became advocates of legalistic interpretations, though they disagreed on the amount of legalism that was acceptable and continued to debate the matter into subsequent centuries, where the Sabbath day remained an important theological subject.

Endnotes

1. See Jason R. Combs's chapter in this volume.
2. Russell M. Nelson, "The Sabbath Is a Delight," *Ensign* or *Liahona*, May 2015, 129–30.
3. For a good overview of Sabbath day teachings over the centuries, see D. A. Carson, ed., *From Sabbath to Lord's Day: A Biblical, Historical, and Theological Investigation* (Grand Rapids, MI: Zondervan 1982).
4. *Sabbatarianism* is defined as "the doctrine of those Christians who believe that the Sabbath (usually on Sundays) should be observed in accordance with the Fourth Commandment, which forbids work on the Sabbath because it is a holy day." *Encyclopedia Britannica*, s.v. "Sabbatarianism," updated May 15, 2020, https://www.britannica.com/topic/Sabbatarianism.
5. Rather than using the word *protestant* to describe the reformers, I will use *evangelical.* Diarmaid MacCulloch astutely recommended *evangelical* in place of the often-anachronistic *protestant* because *evangelical* "was widely used and recognized at the time" and because "it also encapsulates what was most important to this collection of activists: the good news of the Gospel, in Latinized Greek, the *evangelium.*" *Reformation: Europe's House Divided, 1490–1700* (London: Penguin Books, 2003), xx.
6. The *Oxford English Dictionary Online* (*OED*) defines *legalism* as "attribution of great importance to law or formulated rule; strict adherence to the letter rather than the spirit of law." S.v. "legalism," last modified June 2022, https://www.oed.com/view/Entry/107010.

7. Today Brunne is known as Bourne, Lincolnshire. The Gilbertine Order of Canons Regular was a religious order for men and women. It was founded in England by Gilbert of Sempringham in the 1130s.
8. Raymond G. Biggar, "Robert Mannyng," in *Oxford Dictionary of National Biography* (hereafter *ODNB*; Oxford: Oxford University Press, 2004), published online September 23, 2004, https://doi.org/10.1093/ref:odnb/17986.
9. *Handlyng Synne* is a Middle English "translation, adaptation, and expansion of the Anglo-Norman *Manuel des péchés* [Manuel of Sin]" by William of Waddington written between 1250 and 1270. Because of the Fourth Lateran Council's (1215) desire to reform the Catholic church, preaching and missionary work revived across Europe and England, influencing the production of literature that influenced individual religious improvement. See Biggar, "Robert Mannyng."
10. Robert Mannyng, *Handlyng Synne*, ed. Idelle Sullens (Binghamton, NY: Medieval & Renaissance Texts & Studies, 1983), 23–29.
11. Quoted in T. E. Bridgett, *History of the Holy Eucharist in Great Britain* (London: C. Kegan Paul, 1881), 2:264.
12. R. J. Bauckham, "The Lord's Day," in *From Sabbath*, 303.
13. For an anecdotal description of the difficulties medieval peasants had in balancing Sabbath laws and necessary agricultural labor, see Craig Harline, "Sunday Middle-Aged: An English Village in 1300," in *Sunday: A History of the First Day from Babylonia to the Super Bowl* (New Haven & London: Yale University Press, 2007), 26–32.
14. R. N. Swanson, *Religion and Devotion in Europe, c. 1215–c. 1515* (New York: Cambridge University Press, 1995), 93; and Kenneth L. Parker, *The English Sabbath: A Study of Doctrine and Discipline from the Reformation to the Civil War* (Cambridge: Cambridge University Press, 1988), 9–16.
15. Parker, *English Sabbath*, 23.
16. Bauckham, "Lord's Day," 303; and Harline, "Sunday Middle-Aged," 60–65.
17. James Hamilton Wylie and W. T. Waugh, *The Reign of Henry the Fifth, 1413–1415* (Cambridge: Cambridge University Press, 1914), 1:243.
18. P. Gerard Damsteegt, "The Sabbath and the Most Prominent Magisterial Reformers," Andrews University, August 2011, https://works.bepress.com/p_gerard_damsteegt/33.
19. Scholars estimate that approximately 10,000 pamphlets were printed in the German-speaking lands between 1500 and 1530 on a variety of topics, and that Martin Luther was responsible for roughly 20 percent of these. See Mark U. Edwards, *Printing, Propaganda, and Martin Luther* (Berkeley: University of California Press, 1994), 17.
20. Brian Cummings, *The Literary Culture of the Reformation: Grammar and Grace* (Oxford: Oxford University Press, 2002), 16, 30. Edwards argues that despite low levels of literacy in early sixteenth-century Germany, many people learned about Luther's message by word of mouth; see *Printing*, 2–5, 21, 37–38.
21. MacCulloch, *Reformation*, 132.
22. Ralph S. Werrell, *The Theology of William Tyndale* (Cambridge: James Clarke, 2006), 24.
23. Parker, *English Sabbath*, 24.

24. For example, Thomas Aquinas (d. 1274) transformed earlier medieval theological thought by arguing that the moral obligations of the Ten Commandments were binding upon Christians but that the ceremonial aspects had been fulfilled in Christ; see Brian Davies, *Thomas Aquinas's* Summa Theologiae*: A Guide and Commentary* (New York: Oxford University Press, 2014), 218; and Bauckham, "Sabbath and Sunday in the Medieval Church in the West," in *From Sabbath*, 304–6.
25. John W. Doberstein and Helmut T. Lehmann, eds., *Luther's Works*, vol. 51, *Sermons*, American ed. (Philadelphia: Fortress and Concordia, 1955), 143; and Hans Wiersma, "On Keeping the Sabbath Holy in Martin Luther's Catechisms and Other Writings," *Word & World* 36, no. 3 (Summer 2016): 242.
26. Martin Luther, quoted in James Augustus Hessey, *Sunday: Its Origin, History, and Present Obligation, Considered in Eight Lectures Preached Before the University of Oxford in the Year MDCCCLX*, 2nd ed. (London: John Murray, 1861), 222. Luther was particularly against an extreme form of Sabbatarianism that developed in Silesia and Moravia under the direction of Oswald Glaidt (d. 1546) and Andreas Fischer. These men called for a return to a Saturday Sabbath and many other Jewish practices; see Martin Rothkegel, "Anabaptist Sabbatarianism in Sixteenth-Century Moravia," trans. James M. Stayer, *Mennonite Quarterly Review* 87 (October 2013): 519–94.
27. Martin Luther, "The Large Catechism," in *The Book of Concord: The Confessions of the Evangelical Lutheran Church*, ed. Robert Kolb and Timothy J. Wengert (Minneapolis: Fortress, 2000), 399; and Doberstein and Lehmann, *Luther's Works*, 51:144.
28. Doberstein and Lehmann, 51:143.
29. Luther, "Large Catechism," 398–99.
30. Luther, 399.
31. Doberstein and Lehmann, *Luther's Works*, 47:91–92.
32. Carl S. Meyer, trans., *Luther's and Zwingli's Propositions for Debate: The Ninety-Five Theses of 31 October 1517 and the Sixty-Seven Articles of 19 January 1523* (Leiden, Netherlands: Brill, 1963), 36–51.
33. Huldrych Zwingli, *Writings*, trans. H. W. Pipkin, vol. 2, *In Search of the True Religion: Reformation, Pastoral, and Eucharistic Writings* (Eugene, OR: Pickwick Publications, 1984), 116–17.
34. Oswald Myconius, "The Original Life of Zwingli," in *The Latin Works and the Correspondence of Huldreich Zwingli*, ed. Samuel Macauley Jackson, trans. Henry Preble, Walter Lichtenstein, and Lawrence A. McLouth, vol. 1, *Together with Selections from His German Works; 1510–1522* (New York: Knickerbocker, 1912), 9.
35. John B. Payne, "Zwingli and Luther: The Giant vs. Hercules," *Christianity Today* 2, no. 4 (1984): 2.
36. Huldrych Zwingli, "Liberty Respecting Food in Lent," in *Latin Works*, 81–82.
37. Zwingli, "Liberty," 81–82.
38. Zwingli, *Sämtliche Werke*, Corpus Reformatorum 88–101, ed. Emil Egli et al. (Berlin: C. A. Schwetchke and Son; Zurich: Theologischer Verlag, 1905–1956), 13:16.
39. Zwingli, quoted in Hessey, *Sunday*, 446.

40. Robert Cox, *Sabbath Laws and Sabbath Duties: Considered in Relation to Their Natural and Scriptural Grounds, and to the Principles of Religious Liberty* (Edinburgh: Maclachlan & Stewart, 1853), 287.
41. Gordon Rupp, "Andrew Karlstadt and Reformation Puritanism," *Journal of Theological Studies* 10, no. 2 (October 1959): 311–17.
42. Andreas von Karlstadt, "On the Sabbath," in *The Essential Carlstadt: Fifteen Tracts*, trans. and ed. E. J. Furcha (Scottdale, PA: Herald Press, 1995), 319, 334.
43. Luther, "Large Catechism," 397.
44. Karlstadt, "On the Sabbath," 324, 332–33.
45. Karlstadt, 333, 335, 338.
46. MacCulloch, *Reformation*, 176.
47. Heinrich Bullinger, *Fiftie godly and learned sermons, divided into five decades, containing the chiefe and principall points of Christian religion, written in three severall tomes or sections,* trans. H.I. (London: H. Middleton & J. Wolfe, 1584), 137, https://babel.hathitrust.org/cgi/pt?id=dul1.ark:/13960/t6f19z869; grammar and spelling modernized in all quotations from this source.
48. Bullinger, *Fiftie*, 138.
49. Bullinger, 141.
50. For historical purposes, the Low Countries region is generally understood to refer to areas currently occupied by Belgium, the Netherlands, and Luxembourg.
51. Andrew Hope, "Plagiarizing the Word of God: Tyndale between More and Joye" in *Plagiarism in Early Modern England*, ed. Paulina Kewes (Basingstoke: Palgrave Macmillan, 2003), 103.
52. Mary Jane Barnett, "Tyndale's Heretical Translation: Lollards, Lutherans, and an Economy of Circulation," *Renaissance Papers* (1996): 7.
53. William Tyndale, *The obedie[n]ce of a Christen man* (Antwerp: J. Hoochstraten, 1528), fols. xvi^{r}, xxviii^{v}; and Tyndale, *The exposition of the fyrst epistle of seynt Jhon* (Antwerp: Martin de Keyser, 1533), sig. Fii^{v}.
54. Tyndale, *The Pentateuch* (Antwerp: Johan Hoochstraten, 1530), fol. lix^{r}, spelling modernized.
55. Werrell, *Theology of William Tyndale*, 41, 46.
56. Tyndale, *An Answer unto Sir Thomas More's Dialogue: The Independent Works of William Tyndale*, ed. Anne M. O'Donnell and Jared Wicks (Washington DC: The Catholic University of America Press, 2000), 66, 96, spelling modernized; and Werrell, *Theology of William Tyndale*, 44–45.
57. Werrell acknowledges Tyndale's theological debt to Luther but argues that Tyndale developed a unique reformed theology that differed from him in "most doctrines." *Theology of William Tyndale*, 15–16.
58. Tyndale, *Answer to Sir Thomas*, 66, 96, spelling modernized.
59. Tyndale, *The newe Testament, dylygently corrected and compared with the Greke* (Antwerp: Martin Emperowr, 1534), sig. *iii^{v}, spelling modernized.
60. John Frith, *A myrroure or lookynge glasse wherin you may beholde the Sacramente of baptisme described* (London: John Daye, 1548), sigs. Ciiii^{r-v}, Cv^{v}, Cvi^{r}, spelling modernized.
61. Frith, *Myrroure or lookynge glasse*, sigs. Ciiii^{r-v}, Cv^{v}, Cvi^{r}, spelling modernized.
62. MacCulloch, *Reformation*, 194–97.

63. Dawn DeVries, "Calvin's Preaching," in *The Cambridge Companion to John Calvin*, ed. Donald K. McKim (Cambridge: Cambridge University Press, 2004), 106.
64. John Calvin, *The Whole Doctrine of Calvin about the Sabbath and the Lord's Day: Extracted from His Commentaries, Catechism, and Institutes of the Christian Religion*, ed. Robert Cox (Edinburgh: Maclachlan & Stewart, 1860), 24–25.
65. Calvin, *Whole Doctrine*, 26–27, 77.
66. Calvin, 82–83.
67. Parker, *English Sabbath*, 37; Bauckham, "Sabbath and Sunday," 322.
68. Edward Cardwell, *Documentary Annals of the Reformed Church of England: Being a Collection of Injunctions, Declarations, Orders, Articles of Inquiry, &c. from the Year 1546 to the Year 1716; with Notes Historical and Explanatory* (Oxford: Oxford University Press, 1844), 1:4, 15–16.
69. John Hooper, *A Declaration of the ten holy commandments of allmygthye God, wroten Exo. 20. Deu. 5. Collectyd out of the scripture Canonicall, by Joanne Hopper* (London: Richard Jugge, 1548), fol. xliii^{r}.
70. Hooper, *Declaration*, fols. xlii^{v}, xliii^{r}, xlviii^{r-v}, xlix^{v}.
71. D. G. Newcombe, "John Hooper," in *ODNB*, published online September 23, 2016, https://doi.org/10.1093/ref:odnb/13706; and Parker, *English Sabbath*, 40.
72. Thomas Becon, *The worckes of Thomas Becon: whiche he hath hitherto made and published, with diverse other newe bookes added to the same, heretofore neuer set forth in print, divided into thre tomes or parts and amended this present [six] of our Lord 1564; perused and allowed, according to thorder appointed in the Quenes maiesties iniunctions. Works of Thomas Becon* (London: John Day, 1564), fol. cclxxxviii^{r}.
73. Becon, *Worckes*, fol. cccxli^{v}.
74. Becon, fol. ccxliii^{r}. Augustine (354–430) was a theologian and philosopher during the patristic age. Bauckham has described him as "the fountainhead of medieval theology in the West" whose "treatment of the ten commandments as the norm for Christian morality was to remain unquestioned in most subsequent theology." "Sabbath and Sunday," 300.
75. Becon, *Worckes*, fol. ccxliii^{r}; and Bauckham, "Sabbath and Sunday," 300–301.
76. Jon English Lee, "An Examination of the Origins of English Puritan Sabbatarianism," *Puritan Reformed Journal* 7, no. 1 (2015): 118. English evangelicals who wanted more reformation within the Church of England were often called "precise" by those who disagreed with them, a term that was eventually replaced by "Puritan"; see MacCulloch, *Reformation*, 383.
77. As we have seen, most evangelical reformers rejected the Catholic church's designation of Sunday as the Christian Sabbath and argued that Sunday was merely a convenient day to gather for worship. By claiming that Christ designated Sunday as the new Sabbath, Nicholas Bownd could then insist that Sunday "must continue in his first honor of sanctification unto the end of all things." *The Doctrine of the Sabbath* (London: John Porter & Thomas Man, 1595), 44–47; spelling and grammar modernized in all quotations from this source.
78. Richard L. Greaves, "The Origins of English Sabbatarian Thought," *Sixteenth Century Journal* 12, no. 3 (Autumn 1981): 30–31.
79. Bownd, *Doctrine of the Sabbath*, 45–47.
80. Bownd, 150–52.
81. Bownd, 158.

82. Bownd, 164.
83. Bownd, 171, 191.
84. Bownd, 59, 113, 129.
85. Bownd, 94.
86. Bullinger, *Jeremias fidelissimus et laboriosissimus dei propheta* (Tiguri: Christophorum Froschouerum, 1575), 121, quoted in Bownd, *Doctrine of the Sabbath*, 284.
87. Patrick Collinson, "The Beginnings of English Sabbatarianism," *Studies in Church History* 1 (1964): 220. For a good discussion of the issues surrounding the suppression of Bownd's treatise, see Kenneth L. Parker, "Thomas Rogers and the English Sabbath: The Case for a Reappraisal," *Church History* 53, no. 3 (September 1984): 332–47.
88. James acceded to the throne in Scotland as James VI beginning on July 24, 1567. He also became king of England and Ireland on March 24, 1603, ruling there as James I until his death.
89. John Strype, *Annals of the Reformation and Establishment of Religion, and Other Various Occurrences in the Church of England, during Queen Elizabeth's Happy Reign: Together with an Appendix of Original Papers of State, Records, and Letters*, vol. 4 (Oxford: Clarendon Press, 1824), 531, https://archive.org/details/annalsofreformat04stryuoft/page/531.
90. Thomas Fuller, *The Church History of Britain, from the Birth of Jesus Christ until the Year 1648*, ed. J. S. Brewer (Oxford: Oxford University Press, 1865), 5:219.
91. John Eliot, quoted in Cotton Mather, *The Life and Death of the Reverend Mr. John Eliot, Who was the First Preacher of the Gospel to the Indians in America* [. . .] (London: John Dunton, 1694), 29.
92. Bauckham, "Sabbath and Sunday," 324–26.
93. F. D. Maurice, *Sermons on the Sabbath-day, on the Character of the Warrior, and on the Interpretation of History* (London: John W. Parker and Son, 1853), 49.

Chapter Nine

"Not Man for the Sabbath": Sabbath Day Observance among the Early Latter-day Saints, 1830–1837

Richard E. Bennett

The famous Congregationalist clergyman Henry Ward Beecher once wrote: "A world without a Sabbath would be like a man without a smile, like a summer without flowers, and like a homestead without a garden. It is the joyous day of the whole week."[1] On the other hand, Mark Twain recalled how he kept the Sabbath Day as a boy: "But we were good boys . . . we didn't break the Sabbath often enough to signify—once a week perhaps. . . . Anyway, we were good Presbyterian boys when the weather was doubtful; when it was fair, we did wander a little from the fold."[2] Emily Dickinson added: "Some keep the Sabbath going to church, I keep it staying at home, with a bobolink for a chorister, and an orchard for a dome."[3]

The history of Sabbath day observance in America is a complex subject. From the Puritans to the Second Great Awakening, observing the Sabbath received many a thunderous sermon of devotion. Jonathan Edwards, whose remarkable sermonizing helped spark the First Great Awakening a century before Joseph Smith, was as influential as any other cleric in extolling the virtues of strictly observing the Sabbath day. In his sermon "The Perpetuity and Change of the Sabbath," he referred to the Christian Sabbath as the "grace and blessing" of Christ, "one of the most precious enjoyments of the visible church," the one day in seven especially marked for joy, and the one day of the week to remember the resurrection and redemption of the Son of God. And to reverence it he called for a particular effort toward avoidance of sin, abstinence from worldly concerns, and attendance to spiritual exercises with the greatest diligence "as the rest and refreshment of the soul." It was the day to remember Christ's redemption through partaking of the Lord's Supper, and to practice works of "mercy and charity" since "it is a day kept in commemoration of the greatest work of mercy and love towards us that ever was wrought."[4]

With the passage of time, however, strict Sabbath day observance declined, as did religious devotions generally. With the ascent of rationalism, the growing Deism of the Enlightenment and of the French Revolution, and the migration of so many Americans from New England westward to make a new living on the ever-expanding frontier, the years immediately following the American Revolution were, in historian Gordon S. Wood's words, "the most irreligious period in American history," the "period of the lowest ebb-tide of vitality in the history of American Christianity."[5] As Perry Miller famously phrased it, Americans' "errand into the wilderness"[6] often meant trading Sunday devotions for newfound business opportunities and other more secular pursuits. Joseph Smith Jr., born in Vermont in 1805, joined with his parents and siblings in moving from New England to the western reaches of upstate New York in 1816 and shared in this time of uprooting with many others. "Mormonism" must therefore be seen as one of many efforts at the time of the Second Great Awakening to reclaim religious devotion among an ever increasingly unchurched and disconnected population.[7]

The purpose of this chapter is to discuss the nature of Sabbath day worship among the early Latter-day Saints and how they kept this day holy in the formative early history of the Church from its inception in April 1830 until 1837, the so-called Kirtland, Ohio period. This topic has received surprisingly little attention among scholars. The task of pursuing it has been made much more doable today, thanks to the recent publication of the Joseph Smith Papers, the digitization of several early Latter-day Saint journals, and the availability of several other contemporary sources.[8]

The Latter-day Saints found scriptural injunction to keep the Sabbath day holy not only from reading the Holy Bible but also from their study of the Book of Commandments (or as it was later renamed, the Doctrine and Covenants), as well as the Book of Mormon. In the Doctrine and Covenants especially, one sees a very early commitment to observing this holy day. For example, a revelation to the Church dated August 1831 states: "And that thou mayest more fully keep thyself unspotted from the world, thou shalt go to the house of prayer and offer up thy sacraments upon my holy day; for verily this is a day appointed unto you to rest from your labors, and to pay thy devotions unto the Most High . . . , confessing thy sins unto thy brethren, and before the Lord. And on this day thou shalt do none other thing, only let thy food be prepared with singleness of heart that thy fasting may be perfect, or, in other words, that thy joy may be full" (59:9–10, 12–13). And this from a second revelation received three months later: "And they shall also teach their children to pray, and to walk uprightly before the Lord. And the inhabitants of Zion shall also observe the Sabbath day to keep it holy" (68:28–29). Likewise, the Book of Mormon repeatedly speaks directly of the centrality of the Sabbath (Jarom 1:5, Mosiah 13:16–19), stating that the Church in previous times "did meet together oft, to fast and to pray, and to speak one with another concerning the welfare of their souls," and also to partake of the "bread and wine, in remembrance of the Lord Jesus" (Moroni 6:5–6). Alma, one of the better-known prophets of the Book of Mormon, commanded his people "that they should observe the sabbath day, and keep it holy, and also every day they should give thanks to the Lord their God" (Mosiah 18:23).

The Saints, therefore, felt enjoined to keep the Ten Commandments, including the fourth command to keep the Sabbath day holy; however, they viewed this injunction with a good deal of latitude or "wiggle room" in how to keep that commandment, preferring a distinctly practical, less rigid interpretation. The Saints always registered a distaste for, if not an opposition to, the traditional formalities of preaching and worshipping then common in many other established Christian religions of the day.

As for the choice of day for the Sabbath, little, if anything, in Latter-day Saint scripture speaks directly to which day of the week this should be. Nor did Joseph Smith Jr. give much commentary on the topic. While the Church propounded a great many new and distinctive doctrines and practices, the assumption that Sunday was the appropriate day to honor the Sabbath was a product of a host American rural frontier culture, and it applied local custom, tradition, and interpretation to the topic. It was never a point of debate or serious discussion. More to the point, the specific day was less important than the spirit of the occasion.[9]

"In the Remembrance of the Lord Jesus"

From the beginning the sacrament lay at the heart of Sabbath day devotions in the early restored Church. A revelation given on April 6, 1830, the day the Church was organized, specified that the Sabbath day—which the Saints took to mean Sunday—was to be reserved for partaking of the sacrament (or Communion) in grateful remembrance of the atoning sacrifice of Jesus Christ. "It is expedient that the church meet together often to partake of bread and wine in the remembrance of the Lord Jesus" (Doctrine and Covenants 20:75).

Nevertheless, the sacrament was not restricted just to Sundays. For instance, the sacrament was administered on the day the Church was organized in Fayette, New York, on a Tuesday—April 6, 1830. It was again administered on the day of the first Church conference two months later—also a Tuesday, June 1, 1830.[10] From time to time the sacrament was blessed and passed at weekday missionary conferences.[11] A very special presentation of the sacrament occurred at the postdedication services of the Kirtland Temple, on March 30, 1836—a Friday.[12]

If the day of the week was less important to the Saints than the spirit of worship, so too were the tokens or emblems of the sacrament of less importance than the covenants of the sacrament. "It mattereth not what ye shall eat or what ye shall drink when ye partake of the sacrament, if it so be that ye do it with an eye single to my glory," read another early revelation (Doctrine and Covenants 27:2). The Saints viewed the sacrament as an essential renewal of their faith and a cleansing of the soul rather than a literal, mysterious reenactment of the crucifixion of Christ, well known in the Roman Catholic doctrine of transubstantiation, which held that the bread and wine literally turned into the body and blood of Christ.

Nevertheless, the sacrament was often a spiritual highlight in the Sabbath day observance of these early congregants, a time of renewing sacred covenants in a spirit of joy and thanksgiving. "In the afternoon, administered the Lords Supper, as we are wont to do on every Sabath," one early member recalled, "and the Lord blessed our souls with the out pouring of his spirit, and we were made to rejoice in his goodness."[13] And again from Joseph Smith's own records: "Having opened by singing and prayer, we partook together of the emblems of the body and blood of our Lord Jesus Christ, we then proceeded to confirm several who had lately been baptized; after which we called out and ordained severals to the various offices of the Priesthood. Much exhortation and instruction was given; and the Holy Ghost was poured out upon us in a miraculous manner."[14]

"The People Collected"

While Sunday meeting times remained fluid, by 1836 the Saints had settled on meeting twice on Sundays as well as at other times throughout the week. A typical Sabbath day, at least in Kirtland in the mid-1830s, looked as follows:

10:00 a.m. – Noon	Preaching service (often held outdoors)
Noon – 2:00 p.m.	"Intermission"—lunch or dinner—also baptisms, confirmations, interviews, and visits
2:00 p.m. – 4:00 p.m.	Preaching service/sacrament
4:00 p.m. – 7:00 p.m.	Supper and family time
Evenings	Marriages, visiting family and friends, administering to the sick, choir singing, prayer meetings, disciplinary councils, scripture study, reading, and writing letters

A typical service included hymn singing, prayers, observance of the sacrament, and sermonizing, and it was sometimes referred to as "a refreshing time."[15] Among the favorite songs were "O God the Eternal Father" and "Gently Raise the Sacred Strain," both included in the Church's earliest hymnbooks.[16] During their intermissions, the Saints often performed outdoor baptisms in nearby rivers, lakes, or streams followed by confirmations and priesthood ordinations. Early missionaries often baptized and confirmed their followers on the Sabbath. "I opened the meeting by prayer and exhortation," one missionary recalled. "I then opened a door for the reception of new members. Bro. Reuben Field's wife came forward. We then repaired to the water about two miles distant. I baptized them though it was a cold day and considerable snow on the ground. We then appointed a confirmation meeting at Bro. Field's that evening."[17] On Sabbath evenings, they would often reconvene for choir singing, candlelight prayer meetings, and even weddings and funerals. There was no requirement at the time that all branches of the Church follow a prescribed worship or meeting format or schedule. Rather, there was a wonderful localization, freedom, and spontaneity in their worship services that was designed to fit local needs and priorities. For instance, while some held worship services in the afternoon, others did so in the evening.[18]

The blessing of children was a particular delight for Sunday worship. "On some occasions we assembled fifty or sixty little children in one circle," remembered Parley P. Pratt, "in the midst of the assembly of the saints, and laid our hands upon them all, and prayed for them, and blessed them in the name of Jesus."[19]

Their "house of prayer" in those early days before any temple or chapel had been constructed was a private home, a small schoolhouse, a nearby barn, or, more often than not, an open-air clearing or grove. A day after meeting Joseph Smith for the first time, Parley P. Pratt spoke of a Sunday meeting in the Smith home in Manchester, New York, in the autumn of 1830. "On Sunday we held a meeting at his house. The two large rooms were filled with attentive listeners, and he invited me to preach. I did so, and afterwards listened with interest to a discourse from his own mouth, filled with intelligence and wisdom. We repaired from the meeting to the water's edge, and, at his request, I baptized several persons."[20]

Some of these meetings were sparely attended; others counted as many as five hundred congregants. Some preachers, like John E. Page, who was nicknamed "son of thunder" for his loud, booming voice, could be heard almost a mile away preaching from an outdoor, wooden pulpit. As George A. Smith later phrased it, early "Mormonism flourished best out of doors."[21]

"Like Apples of Gold"—A Day of Instruction and Spiritual Uplift

Some of Joseph Smith's sermons and those of his counselors in the early First Presidency, most noticeably Sidney Rigdon, sometimes lasted up to three hours. Among the most dominant themes of discourse and singing were the imminent expectation of Christ's Second Coming, the agency of the will or soul to choose, and the need for restored priesthood authority (with references to Daniel and the "stone cut out of the mountain without hands" as their favorite passage of scripture). Indeed, their sermons contained as many references to the Old Testament (Isaiah, Ezekiel, Daniel, etc.) as they did to the New Testament, and the content was based far more on the Bible than on their own Book of Mormon.[22]

Sundays were not, however, the only day for gospel instruction. The School of the Prophets and School of the Elders were held during weekdays, usually in an upstairs room of the Newel K. Whitney Store. Such gatherings often featured highly instructive sermons, as evidenced by the following from Joseph Smith's journal: "went to meeting . . . Elder [Isaac] morley preach[ed] and Bishop [Edward] Partridge in the afternoon; their discourses were well adapted to the times in which we live, and the circumstances under which we are placed, their words were words of wisdom, like apples of gold in picture's of silver [Proverbs 25:11], spoken in the simple accents of a child, yet sublime as the voice of an angels."[23] Wilford Woodruff, referencing his first Sabbath day in Kirtland as a new member of the Church, wrote as follows: "on the 27th of Aprail [1834] being the Lords day I attended meeting and herd several of the Brethren preach. Brother Sidney Rigdon. Orson Hide. Orson Pratt and others spoke Joseph Smith Closing during the meeting It appeared to me there was more light mad[e] manifest at that meeting respecting the gospel and Kingdom of God than I had ever receieved from the whole Sectarian world."[24]

The tone of preaching among the Latter-day Saints reflected the fact that the Church never employed a paid or highly trained clergy. Speakers, almost all of whom were men, changed from week to week as the Saints took responsibility for their meetings and what should be said therein. Lacking formality and erudite sermonizing, Latter-day Saint Sabbath meetings were more democratic and less aristocratic in nature than those typical of the times and were characterized by enthusiastic but untrained missionaries eager to spontaneously share recent soul-stirring experiences and testimonials, as evidenced in the following description by William E. McLellin: "I had some desire to address the people, and with prayer in my heart, I arose. And it seemed to me that the whole volume of Truth was opened before me. My heart was animated and burning; and my tongue seemed to be untied. I spoke about an hour and a half. Many hearts were affected and many eyes filled with tears. I ceased to proclaim and seated myself. [I was] Filled with astonishment to behold the wonderful works of the Mighty God while wrapped in his 'Eternal Spirit.'"[25]

On the very first Sabbath after having been baptized a member of the Church in 1830, Parley P. Pratt preached a sermon on his conversion. "The Holy Ghost came upon me mightily," he said. "I spoke the word of God with power, reasoning out of the scriptures and the Book of Mormon. The people were convinced, overwhelmed with tears, and four heads of families came forward, expressing their faith, and were baptized."[26]

Outdoor Methodist-style camp meetings were not, however, a characteristic of Latter-day Saint worship, and neither were excessive manifestations of the various gifts of the Spirit such as speaking in tongues or the interpretation of such. McLellin verified that fact in the following entry. Speaking of one Sabbath evening prayer meeting in 1831, he recorded the following: "[I]nstead of shouting, screaming, jumping or shaking of hands in confusion[,] Peace, order, harmony and the spirit of God seemed to cheer every heart, warm every bosom and animate every Tongue. I really felt happy that I had seen the day that I could meet with such a people and worship God in the beauty of Holiness, For I saw more beauty in Christianity now than I ever had seen before."[27] Nevertheless, the manifestations of such gifts of the Spirit as speaking in tongues were quite common, as shown later in this chapter.

"The Social Fireside"—A Day of Family Strengthening

As important as Sundays were to the early Saints, church attendance was not the only way to keep the Sabbath holy. Attending church was more an expectation than it was a commandment—a healthy, spiritual expectation but not the only measure of Christian devotion. Joseph Smith himself occasionally chose to stay home on Sunday with his family, not on account of sickness but perhaps to make up for times away. "At home all day. took solid comfort with my family," he wrote on Sunday a few days before Christmas in 1835.[28] And again, "Spent the day at home in the enjoyment of the Society of my family, around the social fireside."[29] There were, in other words, other ways to keep the day holy besides always attending church services.

"A Prophecy Was Put into Our Hearts"—A Day of Reflection, Meditation, and Revelation

The Sabbath was also a day for receiving answers to prayer, inspiration, and even revelation, in and out of church. For instance, while deeply troubled over the cost of building the Kirtland Temple, Joseph Smith spent one particular Sabbath in prayer: "Sabbath evening. . . . While reflecting upon the goodness and mercy of the Lord, this evening, a prophecy was put into our hearts, that in a short time the Lord would arrange his providences in a merciful manner and send us assistance to deliver us from debt and bondage."[30] Homes were also considered as much a place for inspiration as a church service. Likewise, Sabbath time could be spent in studying and learning, such as when Joseph Smith was a student in Joshua Seixas's Hebrew School near the time the temple was dedicated: "Spent the day at home in reading, meditation and prayer. I reviewed my lesson in Hebrew."[31] Once again we see an emphasis not on rigid conformity to rules or traditions but on making the day pay spiritual dividends in whatever way the Saints deemed most appropriate.

"I Visited on Him All Day"—A Day of Prayer, Visiting, and Healing the Sick

The Saints also looked upon praying for, blessing, and visiting one another as appropriate Sabbath observances. With services often held outdoors, it was but a natural extension to go around from house to house doing good. Part of that effort included manifesting the gifts of the Spirit. Whether it was the gift of tongues, interpretation of tongues, discernment, or most commonly healing of the sick, Sundays often included a veritable parade of such gifts of the Holy Spirit. Wrote Joseph Smith on Sunday, October 11, 1835: "visited my Father again who was verry sick in secret prayer in the morning the Lord said my servant thy father shall live I waited on him all this day with my heart raised to god in the name of Jesus Christ that he would restore him to health again . . . to the great joy and satisfaction of our souls, our aged Father arose and . . . praised the Lord."[32]

On another Sunday in late 1835, after blessing a newly married couple, Joseph Smith attended a prayer meeting in the evening and exhorted the Brethren and sisters for about one hour. "The Lord poured out his spirit and some glorious things, were spoken in the gift of toung[e]s, and interpreted concerning the redemption of Zion."[33]

Nor was such home visiting just for the healing of the body. The Saints would often visit one another to strengthen each other's wavering faith and testimony, so it was a church of the hearth and home and not only of the formal congregation. Wrote William E. McLellin: "This [Sabbath] evening I visited old Sister Simmons and spent a very interesting evening and morning with her, she had been very sorely tempted the week past but now her faith seemed to be increased and her confidence established and her mind at ease."[34]

As time went on, Joseph Smith began to associate one's being healed to his or her keeping the ordinances of the Church, particularly the partaking of the sacrament. "I spoke and admonished the church . . . to make clean the inside of the platter, and to meet on the next sabbath to partake of the

Sacrament in order that by our obedience to the ordinances, we might be enabled to prevail with God against the destroyer, and that the sick might be healed."[35] Joseph Smith seems increasingly to have associated healings and other spiritual gifts with attendance at church, signifying a gradual shift from the spontaneous, less formal observances of the Sabbath in the early 1830s to greater expectations of church attendance and to more clearly defined forms of Sabbath worship.

The Sabbath—A Day of Reconciliation, Repentance, and Forgiveness

One other highly important characteristic of the early Saints' Sabbath day observance pertained to reconciliation, repentance, and the forgiveness of sins. It was a day of wiping the slate clean, of putting past sins and grievances behind them, of confessing openly and in private the wrongs they had committed or perpetuated. Such a bearing of the soul was an unscripted, often unplanned event, but one that was still enjoined and from time to time expected of members. In November 1835, during a Sabbath afternoon meeting, Isaac Hills made a public confession "after which the ordinance of the Lord Supper was administered."[36] On a later occasion, after the First Presidency and Twelve had each spoken in turn, "the Lord poured out his Spirit upon us," Joseph Smith recorded in 1836, "and the brethren began to confess their faults one to the other, and the congregation were soon overwhelmed in tears, and some of our hearts were too big for utterance. The gift of tongues came on us also like the rushing of a mighty wind, and my soul was filled with the Glory of God."[37]

To conclude, the history of Sabbath day observance in the early days of the Church shows a strong commitment to Sunday worship without either strict expectation of attendance or rigid adherence to formal rites of worship. While it was assumed that the Saints would attend church primarily to partake of the sacrament, receive spiritual instruction, and enjoy fine preaching, exceptions could be made, and the sacrament and other devotions could be held on other days of the week. One might occasionally observe the fourth commandment as much by visiting and healing the sick and otherwise afflicted as by attending Sunday meetings. In so many ways, the early Church of Jesus Christ of Latter-day Saints was a church in progress, developing and defining new ways of belief and worship, including what it meant to keep the Sabbath. And in their characteristic way of applying pragmatic overtures to spiritual convictions, the Saints believed "the Sabbath was made for man, and not man for the Sabbath" (Mark 2:27).

Endnotes

1. Henry Ward Beecher, *Royal Truths* (Edinburgh: Alexander Strahan and Co., 1862), 245.
2. "Sixty-Seventh Birthday at the Metropolitan Club, New York, November 28, 1902," in *Mark Twain's Speeches* (New York: Harper & Brothers, 1910), 371.
3. *Emily Dickinson's Poems: As She Preserved Them*, ed. Cristanne Miller (Cambridge, MA: Harvard University Press, 2016), 115.
4. Rev. Jonathan Edwards, "The Perpetuity and Change of the Sabbath," in *The Works of Jonathan Edwards, A.M.: With an Essay on His Genius and Writings, by Henry Rogers*, 2 vols. (London: F. Westley and A. H. Davis, 1840), 2:103.
5. Gordon S. Wood, "Evangelical America and Early Mormonism," *New York History* 61, no. 4 (October 1980): 364. Wood cites John W. Chandler, "The Communitarian Quest for Perfection," in *A Miscellany of American Christianity: Essays in Honor of H. Shelton Smith*, ed. Stuart C. Henry (Durham, NC: Duke University Press, 1963), 58; William Warren Sweet, *The Story of Religions in America* (New York: Harper & Brothers, 1930), 322; and Franklin Hamlin Littell, *From State Church to Pluralism: A Protestant Interpretation of Religion in American History* (London: Routledge, 1962), 29.
6. Perry Miller, *Errand into the Wilderness* (Cambridge, MA: Harvard University Press, 1956).
7. The term *Mormonism* is here used in the sense of the early history, doctrines, culture, and teachings of Joseph Smith and the Latter-day Saints. Though the extended name, The Church of Jesus Christ of Latter-day Saints, is the title much preferred by the Church today, this appellation did not come into use until 1838.
8. There is a dearth of scholarship on the topic of early Latter-day Saint Sabbath day observance. Of the few works on the topic, a worthy though short study is William G. Hartley, "Mormon Sundays," *Ensign*, January 1978, 19–25. See also Russel J. Thomsen, "History of the Sabbath in Mormonism" (master's thesis, Loma Linda University, 1968), published as *Latter-day Saints and the Sabbath* (Mountain View, CA: Pacific Press, 1971).
9. Little has been written in early Latter-day Saint literature about the day of the week on which the Sabbath was to be honored. In more recent times, Joseph Fielding Smith, a great-nephew of Joseph Smith and eleventh President of the Church, wrote: "It is universally conceded that our Savior was in the tomb during the Jewish Sabbath, and that he came forth on the early morning of the first day of the week. All four of the evangelists have written that it was early on the morning of the first day when Jesus appeared to some of his disciples. . . . This would indicate that the Lord himself had changed the date of the Sabbath, and from that time forth it should be the first day of the week." Joseph Fielding Smith, *Answers to Gospel Questions*, 5 vols. (Salt Lake City: Deseret Book, 1966), 2:61.
10. "History, 1838–1856, volume A-1 [23 December 1805–30 August 1834] [addenda]," 41 (June 1830), josephsmithpapers.org.
11. "History, 1838–1856, volume A-1," 41 (June 1830).

12. "Journal, 1835–1836," 187 (March 30, 1836), josephsmithpapers.org. Although the journal entries capture in detail the words and actions of Joseph Smith Jr., it must be understood that he neither wrote nor dictated them. They are actually the work of several companions who acted as his scribes or private secretaries, among them Willard Richards and William Clayton.
13. "Journal, 1835–1836," 171 (March 20, 1836). See also "History, 1838–1856, volume B-1 [1 September 1834–2 November 1838]," 712 (March 20, 1836), josephsmithpapers.org.
14. "History, 1838–1856, volume A-1," 41 (June 1830).
15. *The Journals of William E. McLellin, 1831–1836*, ed. Jan Shipps and John W. Welch (Provo, UT: BYU Studies; Urbana, IL: University of Illinois Press, 1994), 98 (March 3, 1833).
16. "Collection of Sacred Hymns, 1835," 30, 75, josephsmithpapers.org.
17. *Journals of William E. McLellin*, 63 (November 29, 1831).
18. *Journals of William E. McLellin*, 69 (January 8, 1832).
19. *Autobiography of Parley P. Pratt* (Salt Lake City: Deseret Book, 1985), 51.
20. *Autobiography of Parley P. Pratt*, 31.
21. From an address by George A. Smith, "Preaching the Gospel," August 12, 1855, *Deseret News*, August 29, 1855, 194.
22. Grant Underwood, "Book of Mormon Usage in Early LDS Theology," *Dialogue: A Journal of Mormon Thought* 17 (Autumn 1984): 35–74. See also Grant Underwood, "Joseph Smith's Use of the Old Testament," in *The Old Testament and the Latter-day Saints: The 14th Annual Sidney B. Sperry Symposium* (Salt Lake City: Randall Book, 1986), 381–413.
23. "Journal, 1835–1836," 52 (November 29, 1835); see also "History, 1834–1836," 138 (November 29, 1835), josephsmithpapers.org.
24. "Journal (December 29, 1833–January 3, 1838)," 17 (under April 25, 1834, heading), www.wilfordwoodruffpapers.org.
25. *Journals of William E. McLellin*, 36 (August 28, 1831). On other occasions, McLellin experienced exactly opposite feelings. One Sunday, while he and Hyrum Smith were preaching to an audience of disbelievers, he arose and attempted to preach but could not. "I had no animation in it," he confessed, "no memory, and in truth I had lost the spirit of God. Hence I was confounded, I set down and told bro. H. to preach for I could not." *Journals of William E. McLellin*, 41 (September 18, 1831).
26. *Autobiography of Parley P. Pratt*, 27.
27. *Journals of William E. McLellin*, 34 (August 21, 1832).
28. "History, 1838–1856, volume B-1," 672 (December 20, 1835).
29. "History, 1838–1856, volume B-1," 710–11 (March 6, 1836).
30. "Journal, 1832–1834," 92 (November 30, 1834), josephsmithpapers.org.
31. "History 1838–1856, volume B-1," 706 (February 21, 1836). See also "Journal, 1835–1836," 159 (February 21, 1836).
32. "Journal, 1835–1836," 7 (October 11, 1835).
33. "Journal, 1835–1836," 9 (October 25, 1835).
34. *Journals of William E. McLellin*, 121 (May 2, 1833).
35. "History, 1838–1856, volume C-1," 964 (July 28, 1839); see also "Journal, 1839," 9 (28 July 1839).

36. "Journal, 1835–1836," 37 (November 15, 1835); see also "History, 1838–1856, volume B-1," 643 (November 15, 1835).
37. "History, 1838–1856, volume B-1," 693 (January 17, 1836); see also "Journal, 1835–1836," 126 (January 17, 1836).

Chapter Ten

The Sabbath, the Sacrament, and the Latter-day Saints

Justin Bray

For members of The Church of Jesus Christ of Latter-day Saints in the twenty-first century, the sacrament of the Lord's Supper is an essential part of Sabbath-day worship. This ritual meal has come to serve as both a memorial to Jesus Christ and a renewal of Church members' commitment to keep his commandments. It is a familiar scene for churchgoers: priesthood holders (often teenage boys) in white shirts and neckties prepare, bless, and pass morsels of white bread and thimble-sized cups of tap water to the congregation in a solemn, reverential manner. Part of the beauty of the service is in its simplicity, as it is often performed against a backdrop of scratchy wall coverings, hanging basketball hoops, and folding metal chairs. The sound of clinking plastic cups echoes throughout the chapel, and the musty smell of wood benches and crumb-covered pew cushions fills the air. This is what Sabbath worship looks like for many Latter-day Saints. With some regional variations, one can find similar services nearly every Sunday in meetinghouses from Salt Lake City to São Paulo and from Auckland to Accra.

The administration of the Latter-day Saint sacrament, however, did not always look, smell, sound, feel, and taste the same as it does today. This chapter traces the history of this sacred ordinance from the Church's organization in 1830 to the present. Beginning in the early Restoration period, the Prophet Joseph Smith and other Church leaders adopted both theological and procedural elements of the Lord's Supper from their previous religious backgrounds, adapted them with new scriptures and modern-day revelations, and folded them into the ritual life of their new faith. The preparing, blessing, and passing of the sacrament was then shaped by time and place, as Latter-day Saints migrated to the Salt Lake Valley and scattered throughout the Great Basin region. Without handbooks and centralized policies governing sacramental procedures in the nineteenth century, the administration of the bread and water/wine varied between congregations, often depending on the preference of local Church leaders. In the twentieth century, as the Church began to expand outside the pioneer corridor, Latter-day Saint leaders harmonized the various sacramental procedures, codified them into handbooks, and standardized the ordinance into the look and feel that Latter-day Saints have come to expect today.

* * *

The sacrament has been a main feature of Latter-day Saint worship since the earliest days of the Restoration. According to some accounts, the Prophet Joseph Smith introduced the ritual of bread and wine at the inaugural meeting of the faith on April 6, 1830. On that occasion, Smith and Oliver Cowdery followed God's command to "bless bread and break it with them, and to take wine, bless it, and drink it with them."[1] Beyond brief references such as this, there is little information about how the bread and wine were prepared, distributed, and cleaned up, let alone what the ritual meant to communicants.

To better understand Latter-day Saint conceptions of the Lord's Supper, it is important to note that their views are based not only on Last Supper narratives in the New Testament but also on a narrative in the Book of Mormon. Latter-day Saints believe that the Book of Mormon contains an account of Jesus Christ appearing to the ancient inhabitants of the Americas soon after his death and resurrection. During this climactic visit to the New World, the Savior instituted a Last Supper–like meal of bread and wine, but with important differences. As he distributed bread to the Nephite multitude, Jesus explained, "And this shall ye do in remembrance of my body, which I have shown unto you" (3 Nephi 18:7). This reference to the resurrected body of Christ was a marked difference from the accounts in the New Testament that focused on the impending suffering and death of Jesus. For most Christians, the Lord's Supper served as a memorial of the Crucifixion—a final meal before betrayal and arrest. For Latter-day Saints, the sacrament might remind communicants of life after death through resurrection—that is, of the risen rather than soon-to-be-crucified Savior. To what extent early Latter-day Saints interpreted the sacrament through this new scriptural lens is unclear. But this unique account of a second ceremonial meal of bread and wine had the potential to separate the Church from the rest of Christendom, reframing the Lord's Supper in profound ways.[2]

There is evidence that Latter-day Saints did not always strictly follow these new scriptural narratives. This was the case with the sacramental prayers. Both the Book of Mormon and the revelations received by Joseph Smith provide specific blessings for the bread and wine (see Moroni 4–5; Doctrine and Covenants 20:75–79). Over time, Church leaders ensured that these prayers were carefully followed and recited with exactness, word for word, and repeated if necessary. But during the early Restoration period, priesthood-holding men who blessed the bread and wine sometimes offered extemporaneous prayers over the emblems. The free-flowing, unscripted prayers might have resembled the formal blessings in the Book of Mormon and Doctrine and Covenants with slight variations, but Latter-day Saints did not seem to feel strictly tied to these scriptural blessings. This allowance for some variation in sacramental prayers was similar to the practices of some Protestant ministers at the time who, looking to avoid formal prayers and set liturgies, believed ad-libbing allowed for more sincere expression as guided by the Holy Spirit.[3]

Because prayers rarely appear in early Latter-day Saint records, it is difficult to determine how often and to what degree officiators deviated from those prescribed for the bread and wine. In 1845, however, George D. Watt transcribed sacramental prayers given by Brigham Young and Heber C. Kimball in Nauvoo, Illinois, providing a glimpse into their improvised nature at the time. Both apostles followed a basic outline of invoking the name of God and asking him in the name of Jesus Christ to "bless and sanctify" the bread and wine. But there was also room for variation. Young began his prayer with, "Our Father in Heaven, in the name of Jesus we pray that thou would bless and sanctify this bread to the use of and benefit of all that take of it." He further asked that the bread become "the bread of life" to all who partake, "realizing what thou hast done for us." He added, "Our Lord[,] help us to repent of all our sins[,] to return from all our evils[,] to do thy will and work righteousness that we may be accepted of thee." Heber C. Kimball is said to have given a similar extemporaneous prayer over the water.[4] Even the slightest alteration to a word or two would be noticeable to a modern Latter-day Saint, let alone full sentences like those employed by Young and Kimball. Yet it appears that, at the time, this was common practice.

Those administering the sacrament continued to improvise at the table until Church leaders took corrective action decades later. When Brigham Young visited Payson, Utah, in 1865, for example, he "called attention to the administering the sacrament, noticing how few in blessing the bread and water followed the form laid down in the Doctrine and Covenants."[5] He made similar observations in Paris, Idaho, in 1873 and offered a stern rebuke against the practice. "When you administer the sacrament," he taught, "take this book [the Doctrine and Covenants] and read this prayer. Take the opportunity to read this prayer until you can remember it. You cannot get up anything that is better, and not even equal to it. . . . The people have various ideas with regard to this prayer. They sometimes cannot hear six feet from the one who is praying, and in whose prayer, perhaps, there are not three words of the prayer that is in this book, that the Lord tells us that we should use."[6] Latter-day Saint leaders continued to correct extemporaneous sacramental prayers into the 1880s and 1890s.[7] A verbatim reading of the written forms became the standard over time, but this practice required continued admonishments from Church leaders and eventually led to the printing of sacramental prayer cards at the turn of the twentieth century.[8]

The extemporaneous nature of the sacramental prayers highlights one of the defining features of the early Latter-day Saint movement: the constant evolution and growth of procedures. There was a looseness to policies and sermonizing in the early Church that modern Latter-day Saints in the current era of handbooks and global correlation might not recognize. The Church and its practices evolved little by little as Joseph Smith received, printed, and distributed additional revelations. He and other early Latter-day Saint leaders were in a constant process of "figuring things out." The intricacies of the sacrament and its administration were very much part of the gradual development of the Church and its policies and procedures.

Even the name of the ordinance varied. Although the Church's founding documents in 1830 called it "the sacrament," Latter-day Saints referred to the ordinance by a number of monikers, including but not limited to "the bread and wine," "the Lord's Supper," "the Communion," "the Passover," "the Eucharist," "the flesh and blood," and "the feast." In fact, one of the most common ways to refer to the ordinance in the 1830s was "breaking bread."[9] These names carried over from other Christian traditions and reflected the varying meanings of the Lord's Supper that converts brought with them into the new faith.

When, where, and how often the sacrament should be administered were likewise unsettled questions during the lifetime of Joseph Smith. The Lord's table was spread for the first time on April 6, 1830—a Tuesday. Further, Sunday was not designated as the day to meet and administer the sacrament each week until a revelation was received in August of 1831, a year and four months after the organization of the Church (see Doctrine and Covenants 59:9). In the meantime, members were counseled to "meet together often" to administer the ordinance (Doctrine and Covenants 20:75). However, early Church records suggest that the sacrament continued to be performed sporadically until the completion of the Kirtland Temple in 1836. At that point, the temple provided adequate space and shelter for large congregational worship services.[10] Yet even then, members and missionaries away from Church headquarters continued to administer the Lord's Supper only when occasion permitted. For example, Latter-day Saints in 1840s Iowa performed the ordinance "every second Sabbath."[11] This pattern of performing the sacrament more frequently among the main body of Saints than in the outlying settlements continued after the migration to Utah, when "country wards" outside of Salt Lake City distributed the emblems in regional meetings, sometimes just once a month.[12]

In terms of who administered the Lord's Supper in the early Latter-day Saint movement, Joseph Smith's revelations called on elders in the Melchizedek Priesthood and priests in the Aaronic Priesthood to be responsible for officiating at the sacrament table and blessing the bread and wine/water. Yet early records reveal other Church leaders, such as apostles, bishops, and missionaries, breaking bread and filling cups. The scriptures did not mention the passing of the emblems to the congregation, though the role was similarly filled by various priesthood-holding men—not primarily by deacons in the Aaronic Priesthood, as would become the case later in the Church's history.[13]

The practice of preparing the sacrament (as modern Latter-day Saints have come to understand it) would not become a responsibility of teachers in the Aaronic Priesthood until the 1930s, a period we will examine later in this chapter. Joseph Smith's revelations did not specify who should procure the bread and wine, nor who should set up and take down the sacrament table. As was the case in other aspects of the Church, Latter-day Saint women filled in where the scriptures were silent. Indeed, women seemed to have a strong sense of stewardship over sacramental objects for much of the Church's history. While records from the 1830s and 1840s are sparse on this topic, later accounts from Utah reveal a network of women baking and bringing the sacrament bread; washing and caring for the sacrament dishes; and making and laundering linens for the sacrament table. It appears their contributions began during the earliest days of the Church.[14]

Women's contributions were not limited to baking bread. Latter-day Saint women also became the primary vintners in Zion, following an August 1830 revelation that Church members "not purchase wine . . . of your enemies" (Doctrine and Covenants 27:2–4). Elizabeth Ann Whitney was one such contributor. She explained that her family had "a very great quantity of red currants, from which we had ourselves manufactured wine." Emphasizing that the wine they produced was "purely domestic, or homemade," and thus in compliance with the revelation that Joseph Smith had received, they were able to partake of "this wine [they] had appropriated for the sacrament."[15] Similarly, when John Murdock served as a missionary in Delaware County, New York, he used wine made by Latter-day Saint women. Murdock had not been able to administer the sacrament for over six months before baptizing Benjamin and Deidamia Turner and their twenty-three-year-old daughter Amoranda on July 21, 1833. Just weeks later, on August 11, Murdock administered the sacrament for the first time in the region. "By my advice," he noted in his diary, "the [Turner] sisters gathered currants and made wine for our communion." The wine was likely made sometime during the three-week period following the Turners' baptisms, as Murdock noted how he personally witnessed the women strain the berries through a white cloth. Three weeks would have been enough time to harvest, press, and bottle the juice and allow it to ferment.[16]

It is difficult to assess how Latter-day Saint women may have viewed their role in preparing the sacrament. The sources tying women to the ritual in the early Latter-day Saint movement are scarce and vague. It is clear that women participated in the ordinance but not necessarily what that participation meant to them. The preparation was not always the most glamorous work. In fact, it was likely a thankless job, performed behind the scenes and outside of meetings. Some women may have found these seemingly simple tasks empowering, allowing them to contribute to their new faith. Perhaps the acts of baking bread, of picking, pressing, and bottling grapes, and of caring for the dishes and linens served as their unique form of consecrated labor—their sacrifice for God. Or perhaps for some women it was all mere drudgery, a messy process that required time and effort and stained hands and clothes. Most likely, the work meant different things to different women in ways that scholars may never fully understand. What is clear is that women contributed to the sacrament in important ways from the early Restoration period into the twentieth century.

* * *

As Latter-day Saints migrated westward and colonized the Great Basin region in the nineteenth century, there were still no centralized Church handbooks governing all aspects of sacramental administration, and the Lord's Supper continued to look different depending on time and place. Of course, Latter-day Saints had the Doctrine and Covenants and letters from headquarters, but priesthood and Church government was in many ways an oral tradition in nineteenth-century frontier settlements. Local leaders—often immigrant converts with little experience in the Church—used a mix of scriptures, personal observations from sacrament services in Salt Lake City, and good judgment to manage the Church in their far-flung communities.

Depending on when and where one looked, one might find a number of variations in the sacrament. At different times, Latter-day Saints met indoors or outdoors, every week or once a month.[17] Older and more mature men passed the emblems in most Latter-day Saint congregations, but after 1877 one might see young men begin to participate in small numbers. The officiator blessing the emblems might do so standing, sitting, or kneeling, perhaps with both arms raised or with the right arm to the square. The metal flagons at the table used to refill the cups might or might not have their lids opened during the prayer—and the prayers, as mentioned above, might vary widely between wards. Some congregations were strict about the bread being used, preferring white over wheat, possibly with the crusts removed.[18] Some stakes practiced a more closed communion than others, restricting those who were not members of the Church from partaking of the emblems.[19] Indeed, members did not always know what to expect in sacrament services across units.

That was certainly the case for Latter-day Saints traveling through southern Utah, who might get an unexpected gulp of wine from the sacrament cup. After the migration to Utah, most congregations used only water in the Lord's Supper. However, in order to bolster their efforts as a self-sufficient community and to produce wine "of [their] own make" (Doctrine and Covenants 89:6), the Saints turned to growing vineyards in the warmer climates around St. George, Utah, beginning in 1861. At its peak, Latter-day Saint winemaking projects manufactured thousands of gallons of wine a year. Despite potential markets and an established infrastructure to sell or trade wine throughout the pioneer corridor, sacramental wine was not used much outside of St. George beyond private sacrament meetings among members of the First Presidency and the Quorum of the Twelve in Salt Lake City.[20] Wine was unique to southern Utah sacrament services until the manufacturing plants were closed in the 1880s and the use of sacramental wine was discouraged in the 1890s.[21]

While one might find wine being used in sacrament services in southern Utah, in other parts of the territory one might come across a kneeling congregation during the sacramental prayers. Indeed, the Doctrine and Covenants revealed that the person blessing the bread and water or wine should "kneel with the church" (Doctrine and Covenants 20:76). There was much debate about the interpretation of this scripture in the nineteenth century, and wards and stakes adopted different practices. When President L. John Nuttall of the Kanab Stake noticed Latter-day Saints sitting during the prayers in 1879, he "desired the Saints to kneel at the prayer on the sacrament."[22] Other Latter-day Saints similarly reported entire congregations kneeling together during the prayers.[23] Yet this was far from a universal practice. In 1893, for example, Franklin Marsh Ogden of Richfield, Utah, visited his grandmother in Salt Lake City and attended Church services with her in the Nineteenth Ward. He was surprised when "all knelt down as a congregation when the blessing on the bread and water was given for the sacrament," because in his central Utah town, the Saints always remained seated during the sacrament.[24]

The practice of congregational kneeling during the sacramental prayers was disputed even among the apostles. George Q. Cannon, a member of the Quorum of the Twelve Apostles in 1888, believed "where circumstances permit" that "the elder and the whole congregation should kneel together."

However, he witnessed congregations sit during the sacramental prayers in meetings where Joseph Smith and Brigham Young presided. Thus, "he did not feel disposed to say that it was wrong" if Latter-day Saints remained seated in the pews. Another apostle in the same meeting, John Henry Smith, counseled Church members to "conform as strictly as possible to the written word" and encouraged congregational kneeling.[25] Yet in 1893, Joseph F. Smith, a counselor in the First Presidency, explained that having the whole congregation kneel was "quite difficult and probably inappropriate." There was just too much "confusion and noise." The small size of Latter-day Saint meetinghouses and the limited space between the pews "[made] that practice rather impracticable."[26] From these examples, we can see that even the most senior Church leaders had differing opinions on the matter.

The dispute over congregational kneeling was officially settled in a meeting of the First Presidency and Quorum of the Twelve Apostles in June 1901. Elder Rudger Clawson of the Twelve attended the meeting and reported that "in order to establish uniform procedure through the church," the General Authorities had decided "that one, and only one—the party officiating—should kneel."[27] Besides seeking consistency between the wards, Elder Marriner W. Merrill of the Twelve suggested that group kneeling was indeed a space issue. "In our circumstances," he wrote after the meeting, "the whole congregation cannot kneel."[28] These different performative elements in the sacrament across congregations reveal the loose and free-flowing nature of Church policies that carried over from the early Restoration era of the 1830s and 1840s. But the discourse around the Lord's Supper also reflected some of the communitarian impulses unique to the Latter-day Saints in the early Utah period. In the twenty-first century, the sacrament has come to serve largely as a measuring stick for individual commitment to the Church and personal communion with God; in the nineteenth century, however, the ritual meal also served as a sign of fellowship among churchgoers. The administration of the sacrament, for example, was often preceded by public confessions and group forgiveness.[29] Additionally, Church leaders during the early Utah period cautioned Church members against participating in the sacrament if they harbored ill will toward other members of the congregation, echoing the language of Latter-day Saint prayer circles at the time.[30] "What are we partaking of these emblems for?" Joseph F. Smith of the First Presidency asked in 1892. "If I have aught against my brother, it is my duty to go to him alone and talk it over in prayer and settle that difficulty before partaking of the sacrament."[31] Elizabeth A. Howard gave similar counsel to members of the Nineteenth Ward Relief Society in 1888: "I ask myself when I partake of the sacrament, is there a person that walks the earth I would not speak to?"[32] Harmony between communicants was essential for the Saints of the time to unlock the full potential of the Lord's Supper. If contention existed, the bread and water might be withheld from the entire congregation until restitution was made. A dispute between even two people could spoil the ordinance for all. This practice was meant to build unity, and the absence of the sacrament could be a sign of fractured community.

Perhaps the best example of Church leaders withholding the sacrament on a large scale was the so-called reformation period beginning in the 1850s. Perceiving low morale and a lack of adherence to Church teachings among members, leaders called the Saints to repentance, rebaptism, and recommitment to the faith. At the peak of this campaign, the sacrament was being prepared in a November 1856 worship service in Salt Lake City. However, before the members could partake, President Jedediah M. Grant, the second counselor in the First Presidency, commanded "every person to leave the bread in the salvers and the water in the cups and not partake of the sacrament."[33] The emblems were then "removed from the table" and "withheld from the Saints for some months."[34] The ban on the sacrament spread throughout the Church, reaching as far as the mission fields in Great Britain.[35] It was a startling action. The Saints had grown accustomed to the administration of the Lord's Supper each week. Wilford Woodruff called it "a loud sermon to the people."[36] Indeed, the churchgoers felt its absence and celebrated its return. "The sacrament was restored this afternoon to the Saints," Thomas E. Jeremy wrote about the end of the ban in April 1857. "Thank God for His kindness to His people, and I pray in the name of Jesus Christ to my Heavenly Father that He may bless me and my family that we may ever be worthy of partaking of this most holy ordinance acceptably."[37]

Not every Latter-day Saint at the time deserved suspension from the sacrament; no doubt some lived their religion. But the moratorium on the Lord's Supper had an intentional communal purpose. According to Heber C. Kimball, the first counselor in the First Presidency, "There are a great many people in this congregation and in this valley who could justly and beneficially partake of the sacrament, but they are prohibited for the present in consequence of the wickedness of some who would also partake and thus eat and drink to their condemnation."[38] The collective nature of the ban put the responsibility on Church members to encourage one another to repent and resolve conflicts. Inasmuch as the sacrament was an expression of union and fellowship among the Saints, its loss was a shared burden, and its reconciliation required group effort. When the Saints in Kanab, Utah, could "no longer feel the spirit of brotherhood," the sacrament was withdrawn from the congregation for several months in 1875.[39] Similar communal bans took place in Saint David, Arizona, in 1886, and in Honeyville, Utah, in 1894, again reflecting the close-knit Latter-day Saint communities of the nineteenth century.[40] Even the faithful were excluded for the behavior of others.

* * *

Inasmuch as the sacrament reflected the Latter-day Saint communitarian project in the nineteenth century with group bans, shared cups, and congregational kneeling, the ordinance was shaped by an age of national reform at the turn of the twentieth century, a period often referred to as the Progressive era. Some of these changes have already been noted, but this period in Church history saw the end of the following practices: the use of wine as an emblem (1892), extemporaneous prayers (1890s), multiple-ward sacrament meetings (1894), right arms to the square (1898), and congregational kneeling (1901). This was also a time defined in part by national movements in and innovations toward health and hygiene, juvenile rehabilitation, and scientific management, among other economic and social reforms. A younger generation of Latter-day Saints who had studied at universities outside the Book of Mormon Belt were returning to Zion in greater numbers with progressive-minded ideas. Their new understanding of the modern world would have a major influence on the Church and its sacramental policies. Indeed, some of the most recognizable features in the administration of the Latter-day Saint sacrament today were introduced at the turn of the twentieth century.

Like their Protestant counterparts in Progressive-era America, Latter-day Saints harbored a growing concern for the wellbeing of their young men and women. Church leaders believed their youth might fall prey to the perceived evils of an increasingly urban and secular society.[41] This fear was rooted in major demographic and social changes in Salt Lake City in the closing decades of the nineteenth century. Between 1880 and 1890, the city's population more than doubled from 20,700 to 44,800, and many of the newcomers were not members of the Church. The proportion of Latter-day Saints in Salt Lake City declined during this period from nearly four-fifths to about two-thirds. Utah also rapidly urbanized around this time with the establishment of lumber yards, smelting refineries, and railroad depots as well as sugar, dairy, and meat processing plants. In 1890, Utah was considered 65 percent rural and 35 percent urban, but by 1910 it had become nearly an equal mix. Many Church members also moved away from the Intermountain West in search of jobs in bigger cities—part of a growing outmigration from Zion at the time. The Church was indeed coming out of obscurity and entering a new era of assimilation and accommodation. Some parents and leaders worried the youth would get lost in the fray.[42]

To thwart the threat of "juvenile delinquency," Latter-day Saint leaders began looking for ways to encourage young men to stay true to the Church and its teachings. In 1908, a committee tasked with studying the matter recommended that young men be ordained to different offices in the Aaronic Priesthood at fixed ages: deacons at age twelve, teachers at fifteen, and priests at eighteen. Each quorum of teenage boys would also receive a set of pastoral responsibilities. As part of their duties, priests would bless the sacramental bread and water each Sunday, while deacons would pass the emblems to the congregation. Beginning in the late 1930s, teachers in the Aaronic Priesthood would set the sacrament table.[43] These changes represented what one historian aptly referred to as a shift "from men to boys,"[44] and teenagers have played a critical role in the administration of the sacrament ever since.

As juvenile reform took hold in Progressive-era America, a national hygiene and sanitation movement swept the nation as well. Germ theory, or the idea that microscopic pathogens could invade the body and cause disease, had been promoted by scientists for decades, but it gained more acceptance with the general population in the 1890s.[45] At this time, public health advocates across the country mounted a campaign to warn the masses about these "invisible enemies" and "silent travelers."[46] They increasingly blamed the shared cup chained to public drinking fountains as a main culprit for spreading germs. Soon, churches began to question common vessels in communion services. However, switching to individual cups was not an easy change for some faiths. There were potential theological ramifications. Some pointed out that Jesus used "the cup" in the Last Supper (Luke 22:17), suggesting that only one cup should be used in the ordinance. Debates among ecclesiastical higher-ups ensued, but many Protestant churches began to adopt individual cups as well. In

1891, the Scovill Avenue Methodist Episcopal Church in Cleveland, Ohio, introduced individual cups into the Lord's Supper—believed to be the first church in the United States to do so.[47]

Despite this trend, Latter-day Saint sacrament services did not adopt the practice of individual sacrament cups as quickly as some other churches, though many members of the Church were aware of the debates over individual cups in the East. The newspapers in Utah occasionally made references to this point of controversy.[48] These reports captured the attention of Selden Irwin Clawson, a member of the Eighteenth Ward in Salt Lake City. Clawson, a mechanical engineer with several patents to his name, saw the potential of using individual cups in Latter-day Saint sacrament services and pitched the idea in December 1900 to George Q. Cannon, the first counselor in the First Presidency. Clawson later wrote that Cannon seemed favorable to the idea and that he would consider the proposal after a trip to California. When Cannon died in April 1901 before returning, Clawson interpreted his death as "an omen from the other world" warning him not to meddle with the sacred ordinance. He shelved the idea of individual sacrament cups for the next ten years.[49]

In the meantime, the national health and hygiene movement gained traction in Salt Lake City. In 1902, James Charles Elliott King, the Salt Lake City health commissioner, condemned the use of shared vessels in communion services. He called the cups "filthy" and "exceedingly dangerous" and wondered "why the churches do not change their custom."[50] Some did over the next several years, including the First Congregational Church in 1904 and the Westminster Presbyterian Church in 1906.[51] Two years later, Andrew J. Stewart, a Latter-day Saint physician from Mount Pleasant, Utah, "strenuously condemned the common usage of the communion cup as it now exists in a great many churches."[52] Yet Latter-day Saints continued employing the common cup in sacrament services. The calls for change were followed by the installation of hygienic drinking fountains along Main Street in Salt Lake City in 1909. Around this same time, a statewide increase in tuberculosis cases and deaths forced some Latter-day Saint Sunday Schools to close.[53] There was much momentum swinging toward change in sacrament cups.

Against this backdrop of disease, death, and mounting public pressure, Selden Clawson once again proposed that Latter-day Saints adopt individual cups for the sacrament. In September 1910, he made his case in the Eighteenth Ward Sunday School. Enlisting the help of David L. McDonald, a neighbor and physician, Clawson brought a microscope and petri dishes to the meetinghouse "to have the members see the germs of diphtheria and of tuberculosis." McDonald instructed the class that "persons may have the diphtheria germ in the mouth and not know it at the time they partake of the sacrament. These germs and many others are left on the rim of the cup and passed along the row to others."[54] Indeed, McDonald went so far as to blame the shared sacrament cup for an outbreak of diphtheria in Gunnison, Utah, wherein "thirty or more" people contracted the disease and several people died. The demonstration by McDonald and Clawson made their stance on the matter clear: the use of individual cups rather than a communal cup was a matter of life and death.[55]

The idea of germs on the chalice was not a surprise to many Latter-day Saints. Those who lived through the change in sacrament cups later reminisced that the common cup often contained more than just water. They remembered a host of tastes and smells attached to the sacrament cup that made their stomachs turn.[56] Because infants could partake, some churchgoers reported slobber and food particles floating atop the chalice.[57] The sight of runny noses, drooping mustaches, and long beards of other members discouraged some from participating altogether. Some considered faking a sip, while others searched for the cleanest-looking spot on the rim, often wiping the cup with a handkerchief before pressing their lips to it. It was a bit of a cat-and-mouse game to find the safest place from which to drink. The place where churchgoers sat was also a gamble, as members were likely to find out if the "previous drinker had recently been chewing peppermint or had eaten onions or fish."[58] Church members in the common cup era often arrived at the meetinghouse early and chose their seats carefully. Indeed, the front row was the most desirable spot in the room, where they would be among the first to drink.

Individual cups were a welcome change for many but not all Latter-day Saints. Despite the evidence for its safety, some resisted the idea of switching to more hygienic cups. Clawson spoke of how a "strong conservative group opposed the change" to individual sacrament cups in his Sunday School class. He later wrote, "Those opposing the change agreed that Joseph Smith the Prophet approved and used the goblet. The duly appointed servants of the Lord blessed and consecrated the sacrament. For any of the Saints to question it showed their weakness in the faith."[59] There was a "Jesus is my protection" mentality among Church members at the time. One woman in the class remarked, "I am not afraid to drink or to have my children drink from the same cup as my brothers and sisters. My fear is that my children and I may not live worthy to partake of the sacrament."[60] For this woman, the risk of disease was the price to pay to participate in the sacrament. If her family fell ill on the Lord's errand, so be it. The debate over sacrament cups in the Eighteenth Ward thus reflected broader tensions emerging between liberal and fundamentalist Christians in America at the time. Latter-day Saints, like their Protestant counterparts, blended reason, rationality, and faith in uneven ways.[61]

But Clawson was not alone in his pleas. He convinced some of his Sunday School class of the danger of germs. "The progressive members," he wrote, "argued that in the beginning wine was used [in the sacrament]. Wine contained alcohol which was therapeutic to germs. Therefore, people using water are exposed to contagious diseases. If the individual sets could be used, we will avoid contagion that precedes disease."[62] The debate was brought before the Eighteenth Ward bishop and the Salt Lake Stake president before finally reaching the highest councils of the Church. President Joseph F. Smith sympathized with Clawson but questioned whether Latter-day Saints would accept a change to the traditional method of administering the Lord's Supper. He assumed Church members would "prefer to use the old system." Clawson ultimately received approval to test individual sacrament cups in the Eighteenth Ward, which began to take place on June 11, 1911.[63] Despite their positive reception and a strong endorsement from the First Presidency, individual cups spread slowly to other Latter-day Saint congregations over the next several years due to cost and germ theory denialism.[64] It was not until the influenza pandemic of 1918 that they spread more rapidly throughout the Church.[65]

Although seemingly small and insignificant, the shift to individual sacrament cups represents some of the generational tensions of a church in transition. It was not easy for some aging Latter-day Saints to abandon time-honored traditions. Indeed, some members felt like casualties in the Church's quest for assimilation. This is a constant theme throughout Church history that continues today. The uniqueness of the Church is continually questioned as the next generation balances its peculiarity with public acceptance. Some Latter-day Saints found changes in something as simple as sacrament cups as a step toward being "just another church," rather than God's chosen people who are set apart from the world. Looking at the shift in sacramental cups highlights these enduring anxieties.

Individual sacrament cups also represented a transition away from the Latter-day Saint communal identity of the nineteenth century. Before it was seen as a transmitter of contagion and a site of contention, the common cup was the great equalizer. Everyone drank from it regardless of race, class, gender, age, or position in the Church. No one was above it.[66] But the shift to individual cups marked an end to the group mentality in sacrament participation. It was no longer seen as the communal meal that required peace between churchgoers. Rather, the sacrament had become a demonstration of personal commitment and a time of individual self-inspection. Communicants were encouraged to think about Jesus, not their neighbor. Elder David O. McKay of the Twelve recognized the difference over time. "I remember when I was a boy," he explained in 1929, "that there was emphasized even more than we hear emphasized now the necessity of no one's partaking of the sacrament who had ill feelings toward another." He remembered men approaching one another on Sunday mornings in a spirit of apology and forgiveness in order to partake of the sacrament with a clean conscience. He lamented the loss of some of those practices as the Church evolved.[67]

* * *

At about the same time that Latter-day Saints abandoned common cups in the 1910s, Church leaders began to place increased emphasis on Sabbath-day observance and sacrament meeting attendance as more essential parts of discipleship. In the nineteenth century, one could be considered a fully active Latter-day Saint and only occasionally attend Sunday worship services. A person's commitment to the faith was often manifested through their participation in establishing settlements, communal living, and public works projects, not necessarily gathering at the meetinghouse. Indeed, as late as 1920, the Church's average sacrament meeting attendance was just above 15 percent.[68] But with Latter-day Saints no longer establishing new colonies in the American West, Church leaders began to reemphasize the holiness of the Sabbath, with the sacrament ordinance at the center of Sunday worship. With this renewed focus, Church leaders looked to make the ordinance a more consistent, reverent, and sacred experience.

One of the lasting additions from this era was the wearing of white shirts and conservative neckties among boys passing the sacrament. The tradition can be traced to the 1920s. Prior to that time, there had long been complaints that deacons failed to take the sacrament seriously. As far back as the 1870s, when Brigham Young encouraged teenage boys to participate more in Aaronic Priesthood work, local leaders refused to assign them the administration of the sacrament because of the lack of respect they showed toward the sacred ordinance. Bishops often chose more mature Melchizedek Priesthood–holding men to act as priests, teachers, and deacons in performing these sacramental duties.[69] Even after Aaronic Priesthood reforms in the early 1900s gave young men more of a role in the Lord's Supper, adult Latter-day Saints registered complaints about the behavior they witnessed at the table. Deacons were often heard talking, snickering, and making "other unnecessary noises" prior to and during the administration of the sacrament. Other deacons would point fingers, chew gum, doze off, or "hitch at [their] trousers every half minute" throughout the meeting. Their dress and grooming habits also failed to meet the expectations of some members of the congregation, with deacons wearing an array of tattered and wrinkled shirts, sweaters, and coats. Some felt that there was no dignity in the deacons' appearance and behavior, and that the Lord's Supper deserved the best.[70]

Earl J. Glade Jr. decided to do something about it. Glade, a Young Men Mutual Improvement Association supervisor in the Highland Park Ward in Salt Lake City and an emerging young professional in the broadcast radio industry, tapped into a national dress-code trend in the workplace at the time. In the 1920s, looking to replace the lampooned image of the ragtag traveling salesman with one of professionalism and respectability, business leaders throughout the United States increasingly required workers (particularly salesmen representing their companies) to wear starched white shirts and neckties. The uniforms, it was believed, inspired compliance, created a team-first mentality, and enhanced pride in one's work.[71] Uniforms had already been employed by Latter-day Saints in schools, sports, and Boy Scout programs. Glade saw an opportunity to fold these ideas about men's workwear into the deacons' quorums of the Church.[72]

Glade proposed a "uniform apparel for passing the sacrament" for boys in the Highland Park Ward in September 1928. The dress code consisted of "a clean, white shirt with a neat bow tie and dark trousers." The uniforms were met with instant success. The adult members of the ward were said to be "greatly impressed" with the demeanor and solemnity shown by those passing the sacrament. The twelve- and thirteen-year-old deacons themselves "adopted the plan unanimously," and the matching outfits energized the boys, even helping to bring some that had been wavering back to the faith. Additionally, younger boys—the deacons-in-waiting—

looked forward to the day they too could don the white shirt and black bow tie.[73] Glade stated that the uniform "peps up the group appearance, and we all like to belong to a snappy-looking group." He added, "Boys in their early teens are starting to think about how they look! We capitalize that instinct, and the quorum gets the benefit." Beyond the apparent social benefits, the deacon uniforms prepared the young men for Latter-day Saint manhood. The ensemble, Glade believed, disciplined mind and body and trained boys in "proper grooming," "gentility," "the art of personal control and the fundamentals of order," "dependability," "promptness," "loyalty," and "reverence."[74] The uniforms inspired more than just respect for the sacrament. They readied the boys for life.

The deacon uniforms in the Highland Park Ward soon "attracted widespread attention and approval," and nearby wards and stakes adopted similar plans for their boys passing the sacrament.[75] Some dress codes varied between congregations and might include white trousers and long neckties rather than bow ties. Deacons' uniforms spread into more remote corners of the Church after Glade presented about them at an Aaronic Priesthood general convention in April 1933. The white-shirt-and-bow-tie uniform earned the endorsement of "prominent church leaders," according to Glade, likely referring to Elder Joseph Fielding Smith and Elder Joseph F. Merrill, of the Quorum of the Twelve, and Presiding Bishop Sylvester Q. Cannon, who presided at the convention. Following his speech, Glade published an article on the value of deacon uniforms in the Church's *Improvement Era* magazine. Within a few years, there were reports of deacon uniforms in Arizona, California, and Oregon.[76]

What began as the innocent adoption of deacon uniforms grew into an elaborate performance in passing the bread and water. Some local Latter-day Saint leaders included "additional features" in their instructions to the deacons, such as lining up the boys according to height, having them march with their left arms behind their backs, and teaching them to never lower the sacrament trays below their waists. In their efforts to encourage reverence, these well-meaning ward leaders enforced strict requirements on those administering the sacrament.[77] Others dramatized the administration. Robert L. Simpson later remembered passing the bread and wine as a twelve-year-old deacon in the Hollywood Ward in the 1930s and recalled how the young men employed "a system of musical chimes" to signal the opening of red velvet drapes, revealing a painting of the Last Supper just before the sacramental prayers. He referred to it as the

"'Hollywood' version of the sacrament."[78] Latter-day Saint leaders at the general level increasingly discouraged such practices, hoping to avoid what they termed "formalism" in the sacrament.[79] But while some of these new elements were discontinued, many have survived and continue to be seen in the Church today.

One practice that gained popularity at the midcentury period is the use of the right hand in partaking of the sacrament—a practice that is still being discussed today. Latter-day Saints had long been encouraged by individual Church leaders to take the sacrament with the right hand, but it was never a universally accepted rule.[80] As far as can be concluded, communicants throughout Church history have not been denied the bread and water when reaching with left hands. However, there have been varying opinions on the matter. In 1946, President Joseph Fielding Smith, a member of the Quorum of the Twelve Apostles at the time, downplayed the need to take the sacrament with just the right hand. He grouped the practice with other "changes and innovations" that "are innocently adopted, but in course of time there is the danger that they will become fixed customs and considered as necessary to the welfare of the Church."[81] In 1952, the First Presidency discussed whether taking the sacrament with the left hand constituted "a breach in proper procedure," but they concluded that it did not. "The Brethren felt we should keep away from formalities," President David O. McKay noted after the meeting. "They felt that while the partaking of the sacrament is a covenant [and] that it is the custom to use the right hand in making covenants, failure so to do would not vitiate the covenant."[82] An *Improvement Era* article in 1955 mentioned that taking the sacrament with the right hand was "deemed advisable" but that "certain people do not have right hands" because of injury or disability, thus rendering its universal practice unfeasible.[83]

Yet around this time, President Joseph Fielding Smith took a stronger stance against reaching for the sacrament with the left hand. In a seeming reversal from his earlier statements, President Smith published a short article on the right hand as "a symbol of righteousness." He cited scriptures mentioning the use of the right hand, although they were not in reference to the sacrament. "The right hand or side is called the dexter and the left the sinister," he concluded. "Dexter connotes something favorable; sinister, something unfavorable or unfortunate. It is a well-established practice in the Church to partake of the sacrament with the right hand and also to anoint with the right hand, according to the custom which the scriptures indicate is, and always was, approved by divine injunction."[84] As Smith pointed to somewhat ambiguous scriptural references and modern American cultural norms as the basis for not using left hands, taking the sacrament with only right hands continued to be customary but not required—that is, the practice was taught but was not strictly enforced.[85]

As Church leaders sought answers to the right-hand-only question, they also codified the passing of the bread and water to the presiding authority first. This was another practice that had long been taught by individual Latter-day Saint leaders but had not been universally followed. In fact, some earlier Church leaders seem to have even discouraged the practice. John E. Booth, bishop of the Provo 4th Ward in 1894, remembered attending a Sunday service in which Brigham Young presided, likely in the 1860s. President Young sat on the opposite side of the room from the sacrament table, and when one of the priesthood holders carrying the bread skipped a row of people to deliver it first to the prophet, Young "censured that conduct quite severely." According to Booth, Young "stated that when it came to partaking of the sacrament all were equal, and the Latter-day Saints should partake of it as their turn came. None should be passed in order that a superior officer might be served first."[86] Another Latter-day Saint remembered similar sentiments coming from President Heber J. Grant in the 1920s after a deacon skipped others to serve him first. "We all come here as children of God, equals, and there's no deference being shown to anyone," he allegedly said.[87]

After President Grant's death, however, Church leaders clarified that the practice of passing the sacrament first to the presiding authority should be strictly followed. With the Church expanding both nationally and internationally, the era of lifetime bishops and stake presidents—when everyone knew who presided in a meeting, because that person served for decades—was gone. Latter-day Saints were more mobile than ever, and wards and stakes experienced turnover in membership and leadership like never before. Against this backdrop, Church leaders believed passing the sacrament to the presiding authority would serve as "a lesson in Church government" to the younger boys in the Aaronic Priesthood, teaching them to recognize the order of priesthood offices. Anticipating that some Latter-day Saints might interpret the new rule as overly deferential to leaders, President David O. McKay, a counselor in the First Presidency, explained in his April 1946 General Conference talk that it was meant "not to honor [the individual] but the office."[88] Less than a month later, the First

Presidency sent a letter to bishops and stake presidents outlining the policy. It was added to the next version of the Church's general handbook in 1960 and has been a staple in sacrament meetings ever since.[89]

The same First Presidency letter that taught boys to pass the bread and water to the presiding authority first also ended the practice of playing instrumental music or congregational hymns during the passing of the sacrament. Prior to this policy change, it was almost never silent during the sacrament. During the early years of the Church, leaders often delivered sermons as the emblems were distributed. They would abruptly pause for the sacrament prayers and then resume their talks.[90] Over time, it became more common to have music playing during the passing of the sacrament, and the songs were not limited to official hymnbooks. Latter-day Saints often chose classical selections, like Bach or Brahms, while employing a range of instruments, from woodwinds to brass. By the 1940s, however, Latter-day Saint leaders looked to redefine the sound of worship. Led in large part by President David O. McKay, Church officials had come to believe that the absence of sound was the essence of worship.[91] For some, background music was distracting and disruptive; a period of meditative silence was preferable. Church leaders began to teach more widely that a quiet room provided the best medium to commune with God.[92]

Latter-day Saints had mixed reactions to the 1946 announcement. Aurelia Shimer, the music director in the Murray 1st Ward, lamented the new policy, and she was not alone. "Many people were unhappy," she later wrote. "It seemed odd to have it so quiet." The reverential music was replaced with what she believed to be awkward silence. The babble from newborn babies in the congregation was suddenly augmented, whereas the music had once muffled the sound. Shimer also missed the messages about Jesus that were reflected through the "sweet refrains."[93] Melda Hacking of the Timpanogos 1st Ward had a similar reaction to the First Presidency announcement. As a ward organist, she had played the devotional music during the passing of the sacrament for twenty-eight years, from 1918 to 1946. The sacramental music had become an integral part of her Sabbath worship and Church service. "I loved that assignment," she wrote. But the new rules meant fewer ward organists were needed, leaving Hacking without a calling. "It was a sad day for me when word came from Salt Lake that the playing of music during the sacrament was to be discontinued," she wrote. "Music has always been a very important part of my life."[94]

Even with the absence of music and the addition of meetinghouse foyers to which parents could retreat with crying babies, silence during the sacrament remained elusive. In the 1940s, Latter-day Saints used individual glass cups for the Lord's Supper, which were fragile and often broke during the meeting. Mayre Naisbitt Nielsen of the Hooper Ward remembered cringing at the sound of shattered glass. "These accidents not only made unpleasant noises," she later wrote, "but caused worry, frustration, and at times even anger" among those trying to renew their covenants in peace.[95] Jeane Erickson Burton of the Tenth Ward remembered dropping a glass cup and wishing for "the floor to open up and swallow me" out of embarrassment for not only breaking the cup but also breaking the silence.[96]

As the Church transitioned to disposable paper and plastic cups around the mid-twentieth century, a new sacrament meeting soundscape emerged—again with mixed reactions. For some, the pinging of plastic cups in the metal trays was a distracting noise. Diane Brown said that her father "was outraged at the way these noisy new cups disrupted the essential reverence of the sacrament." However, Brown herself found the noise to be soothing. "I would be lost without the soft symphony of those cups dropping into metal trays," she wrote. "When concentration is impossible, and the atonement—at best—a mystery, I close my eyes and welcome the hypnosis that comes from focusing on the sound of cups."[97] Although some local leaders looked to muffle the sound with damp paper towels at the bottom of the trays, the clinking of plastic cups could be heard—for better or worse—in Latter-day Saint sacrament meetings for decades.

* * *

As Latter-day Saints moved toward the twenty-first century, the sacrament and its procedures continued to evolve. In 1980, a consolidated three-hour block of Sunday meetings was instituted, followed decades later by a two-hour schedule in 2019.[98] Other minor changes have also seen kneelers, finger bowls, and hand sanitizer come and go from the sacrament table. In 2013, the Church announced that members who suffer from celiac disease or other food intolerance may use a "bread-like substitute" as an alternative for the bread, such as crackers, chips, rice cakes, or cereal.[99] Two years later, Church leaders began a major initiative to encourage Latter-day Saints to "keep the Sabbath day holy," including a renewed focus on the sacrament. Before the initiative, the sacrament meeting could fall in any order in the consolidated Sunday schedule. But to highlight its importance, the sacrament was made the first meeting in all Church units throughout the world.[100]

The COVID-19 pandemic also reaffirmed the centrality of the sacrament in Sabbath day worship. When Church leaders temporarily suspended Sunday meetings worldwide on March 12, 2020, Latter-day Saints were expected to worship from their couches rather than the pews. But "home church" affected members in uneven ways. For many, the sacrament provided stability during a period of heightened emotion, material hardship, disease, and death. But according to Church policies, women and children were not able to participate in the sacrament without an authorized male priesthood holder in the home to perform the ordinance. Writer Jana Riess lauded the Church for postponing in-person meetings to limit the spread of COVID-19 but lamented "the two-tiered way we are addressing the sacrament." She estimated that as many as 60 percent of Latter-day Saint women in America were unable to participate in the ordinance at home, either because they did not have a priesthood holder in their home or because of their husband's inactivity in the Church. Riess predicted a much larger proportion of Latter-day Saint women in the same situation outside the United States, where the Church was less established.[101] Those "doing without" commented on blogs, social media posts, and internet message boards that their Sabbath day observance felt incomplete without the bread and water.[102] Indeed, the limitations caused by COVID-19 reminded both those who could and could not participate in the ordinance at home of its importance and power, which may have been taken for granted before. The Sabbath day, whether at home or in the meetinghouse, is not the same without the sacrament, and many have felt its loss during the pandemic.

As Latter-day Saints returned to in-person worship services amid the ongoing pandemic, sacrament meeting became a site of contention between COVID deniers and COVID compliers. Some questioned the use of face masks, physical distancing, and the heightened sanitary measures around the administration of the sacred ordinance. Others hoped for even more protections. Writer McKay Coppins suggested that the division among Latter-day Saints in the chapel may have been "a factor of not meeting for sacrament meetings for so long or not spending the same time together in church."[103] As COVID-19 forced Latter-day Saints to spend their Sabbath days at home rather than at church, many found community in virtual spaces, often with anonymous users who only reaffirmed their own worldviews. The COVID-19 shutdown facilitated this silo effect that cut Church members off from one another.

As these differences have intensified, the sacrament continues to carry the potential to unify. Nothing brings people together like food. Indeed, food brings out the best in Latter-day Saints. When it comes to delivering dinners to those in need, Church members are often quick to grab the clipboard. Plates of cookies often accompany moving trucks along the Book of Mormon Belt. Some Church members may have loathed the former three-hour block of Sunday meetings, but they would happily "linger longer" to "munch and mingle" at the meetinghouse. Indeed, food is a cornerstone of Latter-day Saint culture, and sharing meals is a common act of fellowship, celebration, and welcome in Zion. It may be that Church members need to see the sacrament as the meal it is. Despite its small portions, the Lord's Supper, by its very name, is a holy meal. Perhaps it can unite the Saints in a post-COVID world.

Endnotes

1. "Joseph Smith History, 1838–1856, vol. A-1, 23 December 1805–30 August 1834," 26, The Joseph Smith Papers, https://www.josephsmithpapers.org/paper-summary/history-1838-1856-volume-a-1-23-december-1805-30-august-1834/33.
2. Kathleen Flake, "Supping with the Lord: A Liturgical Theology of the LDS Sacrament," *Sunstone*, July 1993, 18–27.
3. Karen B. Westerfield Tucker, *American Methodist Worship* (New York: Oxford University Press, 2011), 126, 227.
4. As cited in David W. Grua, "'Strictly Adhering to the Inspired Form': Early Latter-day Saint Sacramental Worship and the Canonical Prayers" (unpublished paper presented at "Joseph Smith Papers Conference: Joseph Smith and Sacred Text in Nineteenth-Century America," Salt Lake City, September 10, 2021). Extemporaneous sacrament prayers continued to be given as Latter-day Saints migrated to the Great Basin region. In 1852 Heber C. Kimball said, "We have dedicated this sacrament to the Father and to the Son, that the saving principles of life may be in it and that, in partaking of it, we may become sanctified. We bless the water as well as the bread and ask God to sanctify it and fill it with life and the principles of salvation." "Discourse," *Deseret News*, February 3, 1852, 2. In 1863, Kimball explained, "We are now partaking of the sacrament of the Lord's Supper; when we partake of the bread, let us pray the Father that strength may be given to our bodies that they may not wither, but be strengthened to reach a good old age; when we partage of the wine—or water—which is emblematic of his blood, let us ask the Father that our blood may never be spilled unless it is necessary for the advancement of his kingdom and the glory of God." "Remarks," *Deseret News*, March 11, 1863, 1.

5. "President Young's Trip to Utah County Continued," *Deseret News*, June 21, 1865, 5.
6. Brigham Young, "Discourse," *Deseret News*, vol. 22, no. 33, September 17, 1873, 16.
7. Donald F. Godfrey and Kenneth W. Godfrey, *The Diaries of Charles Ora Card: The Utah Years, 1871–1886* (Provo, UT: Religious Studies Center, 2006), 273, 303, 307; "Sunday Services," *Utah Enquirer*, January 15, 1889, 1; and "The Sacrament," *Daily Enquirer*, May 11, 1891, 5.
8. See Charles W. Penrose, "The Sacrament of the Lord's Supper," *Millennial Star*, December 3, 1908, 778. For sacrament prayer cards, see Francis Marion Lyman, "The Administration of the Sacrament in the Sunday School," in *Proceedings of the First Sunday School Convention*, 1898, 77, CHL.
9. See, for example, Jan Shipps and John W. Welch, eds., *The Journals of William E. McLellin, 1831–1836* (Provo, UT: BYU Studies), 1994, 117–146.
10. "Conference Minutes," *Times and Seasons* 5, no. 14 (August 1, 1844): 596.
11. "Conference Minutes," *Times and Seasons* 5, no. 22 (December 1, 1844): 725.
12. William G. Hartley, *My Fellow Servants: Essays on the History of the Priesthood* (Provo, UT: BYU Studies, 2010), 346–47.
13. In 1898, Elder Francis M. Lyman of the Twelve was asked whether "members not holding the priesthood" could pass the sacrament. He responded: "You pass it to one another, do you not, all the time, all you sisters and all you brethren? Then why ask the question? The administering of the sacrament is not passing it to the people. The administering of the sacrament is when the brethren offer the prayer in blessing the bread or water. That is the administration of the sacrament." "The Administration of the Sacrament in the Sunday School," 74–77. In 1928, President Heber J. Grant explained that there was "no rule in the Church" that only priesthood holders could distribute the emblems among the pews. It had become only "custom" for them to perform this duty, which practice developed during Joseph Smith's lifetime. Apparently, Grant had "no objection" to allowing "brethren lacking priesthood" to participate in the ordinance if there were no ordained men available. Heber J. Grant to Henry H. Rolapp, June 28, 1928; quoted in William G. Hartley, "From Men to Boys: LDS Aaronic Priesthood Offices, 1829–1996," *Journal of Mormon History* 22, no. 1 (Spring 1996): 130.
14. Kristine Wright, "'We Baked a Lot of Bread': Re-conceptualizing Mormon Women and Ritual Objects," in *Women and Mormonism: Historical and Contemporary Perspectives*, ed. Kate Holbrook and Matthew Bowman (Salt Lake City: University of Utah, 2016), 86–87.
15. Elizabeth Anne Whitney, "A Leaf from an Autobiography," *Woman's Exponent*, October 1, 1878, 71.
16. John Murdock, journal and autobiography, August 11, 1833, MS 1194, folder 3, page 21, image 47, CHL.
17. The first Latter-day Saint sacrament meeting in the Salt Lake Valley took place in a wagon encampment circle the day after the official arrival of the Saints into the valley on Sunday, July 25, 1847. Wilford Woodruff wrote that they met in the morning for prayer and sermons from Church leaders and then again at 2:00 p.m. when the "bishops broke bread to the congregation." By the next week, the Saints had erected a makeshift "bowery" made of wood poles and a thatched

roof of boughs, shrubs, and sagebrush. The bowery provided churchgoers shade and shelter for worship services, but it was not always conducive to providing protection against high winds and cold temperatures. More permanent structures followed over the years, including the Old Tabernacle in 1852, the Salt Lake Tabernacle in 1867, and the Salt Lake Assembly Hall in 1882. Until these buildings were dedicated, the Saints met in varied ways, including outdoor community-wide sacrament services in the summer and smaller cottage meetings in private homes in the winter. Journal entry, July 25, 1847, in *Wilford Woodruff's Journal*, ed. Scott G. Kenney (Salt Lake City: Signature Books, 1983), 3:235. See also Ronald W. Walker, "The Salt Lake Tabernacle in the Nineteenth Century: A Glimpse of Early Mormonism," *Journal of Mormon History* 31, no. 2 (Fall 2005): 198–240; and Walker, "'Going to Meeting' in Salt Lake City's Thirteenth Ward, 1849–1881: A Microanalysis," in *New Views of Mormon History: Essays in Honor of Leonard J. Arrington*, ed. Davis Bitton and Maureen Ursenbach Beecher (Salt Lake City: University of Utah Press, 1987), 138–61.

18. William A. Hyde, "Sacrament of the Lord's Supper," *Improvement Era* 14, no. 7 (May 1911): 577.
19. Hyde, "Sacrament of the Lord's Supper," 580.
20. Church leaders used wine for the sacrament in their meetings until 1906. See Thomas G. Alexander, *Mormonism in Transition: A History of the Latter-day Saints, 1890–1930* (Urbana: University of Illinois Press, 1986), 261.
21. Saint George Utah Stake manuscript history and historical reports, July 9, 1892, LR 7836 2, box 3, vol. 4, folder 2, CHL. See also Saint George Utah Stake general minutes, July 5–17, 1892, LR 7836 11, vol. 19, 226–228, CHL. The use of wine in Latter-day Saint sacrament meetings did not end all at once. Instead, it diminished over time. For example, wine was used for the sacrament at the Salt Lake Temple dedication in 1893. See Brian H. Stuy, "'Come, Let Us Go Up to the Mountain of the Lord': The Salt Lake Temple Dedication," *Dialogue: A Journal of Mormon Thought* 31, no. 3 (1998): 120. Additionally, reports exist of wine being used in the "vineyard districts" of southern Utah as late as 1900. See James E. Talmage, *The Articles of Faith: A Series of Lectures on the Principal Doctrines of The Church of Jesus Christ of Latter-day Saints* (Salt Lake City: Deseret News, 1899), 180; and "Word of Wisdom," *Young Woman's Journal* 11, no. 4 (April 1900): 187. When ten-year-old Olive Woolley of Salt Lake City visited her grandparents in Toquerville in 1904, she remembered being "delightfully shocked to get a mouthful of sweet wine instead of the tasteless water I was accustomed to in the Salt Lake City religious services." As cited in Dennis R. Lancaster, "Dixie Wine" (master's thesis, Brigham Young University, 1972), 130.
22. L. John Nuttall, diary, April 6, 1879, MSS 790, L. Tom Perry Special Collections, Harold B. Lee Library, Brigham Young University, Provo, UT (hereafter Perry Special Collections).
23. Joseph Bond Harris remembered how in the Henefer Ward in northeastern Utah "we all knelt down to attend the sacrament service." "Autobiography of Joseph Bond Harris, Son of Micah Francis Harris and Mary Jane Bond Harris," (1963), 8–9, *Family History Books*, FamilySearch Library. John E. Booth of the Provo 4th Ward explained, "As to the mode of administering the sacrament, it matters not so much if the one who administers the same has but authority.

Whether he kneels alone, or whether comrades kneel with, or whether the whole congregation kneels with the one administering the sacrament, cannot affect the law itself. It is a mere matter of form and the several forms above mentioned have all been practiced in Provo." "About Administering the Sacrament," *Daily Enquirer*, February 5, 1894, 1.

24. "Ann Horrocks: 1829–1917" (2013), 1, FamilySearch.org.
25. "Priesthood Meeting," *Deseret Evening News*, September 3, 1881, 3.
26. Joseph F. Smith, discourse, July 16, 1893, in *Collected Discourses Delivered by President Wilford Woodruff, His Two Counselors, the Twelve Apostles, and Others*, ed. Brian H. Stuy (Burbank, CA: B.H.S. Publishing, 1987), 3:308. See also Joseph E. Taylor, November 18, 1894, in Stuy, *Collected Discourses*, 5:21.
27. Rudger Clawson, diary, June 13, 1901, in *A Ministry of Meetings: The Apostolic Diaries of Rudger Clawson*, ed. Stan Larson (Salt Lake City: Signature Books, 1993), 284.
28. Marriner W. Merrill, diary, June 13, 1901, in *New Mormon Studies: A Comprehensive Resource Library* (San Francisco: Smith Research Associates, 1998), CD-ROM. See also James B. Allen, "I Have a Question," *Ensign*, March 1978, 23.
29. Edward L. Kimball, "Confession in LDS Doctrine and Practice," *BYU Studies Quarterly* 36, no. 2 (1996–1997): 45–46.
30. According to an entry in the *Encyclopedia of Mormonism*, "The formation of the prayer circle suggests wholeness and eternity, and the participants, having affirmed that they bear no negative feelings toward other members of the circle (cf. Matthew 5:23–24), evoke communal harmony in collective prayer." George S. Tate, "Prayer Circle," in *Encyclopedia of Mormonism*, ed. Daniel H. Ludlow (New York: Macmillan, 1992), 3:1120–21. See also D. Michael Quinn, "Latter-day Saint Prayer Circles," *BYU Studies Quarterly* 19, no. 1 (1979): 102–103.
31. Joseph F. Smith, February 21, 1892, in Stuy, *Collected Discourses*, 2:366. This language of harmony and communion in the sacrament was prominent in Latter-day Saint discourse in the nineteenth century. Among the many examples, Elder George A. Smith of the Quorum of the Twelve Apostles taught in 1867, "The occasion of the administration of the sacrament gives rise to reflections peculiar in themselves, such as, Am I what I profess to be? Am I united with my brethren and sisters in heart, while I stretch out my hand with them and partake of the consecrated bread? We are united in relation to our mode of worship." "President B. Young's Trip North," *Deseret News*, September 18, 1867, 4. In 1887, George G. Bywater said, "None should partake who had malice or hatred in his heart, as it was an emblem of love and forgiveness." "The Sacrament," *Salt Lake Herald*, June 7, 1887, 6. In 1890, John Morgan explained, "We have come together to partake of the sacrament as an evidence that we remember Him and testify that we will live according to the laws He has given us, and also to testify to each other that we entertain feelings of fraternity and are at peace with one another." "Sunday Services," *Deseret News*, December 2, 1890, 3. In 1892, Elder Francis M. Lyman of the Twelve taught, "We should partake of the sacrament worthily and have no hard feelings to our neighbors." Sanpete Stake Historical Record, May 14, 1892, LR 8046 11, CHL.
32. Nineteenth Ward Relief Society Minute Book, May 4, 1888, LR 6092 14, vol. 3, 241–42, CHL.

33. Jedediah M. Grant, "Discourse," *Deseret News*, vol. 6, no. 37, November 19, 1856, 291.
34. Brigham Young to George A. Smith, January 26, 1857, in Journal History of the Church, CR 100 137, vol. 43, 117, CHL.
35. For sacrament withdrawal in Great Britain, see Lorenzo Hill Hatch, diary, May 28 and July 5, 1857, MS 1480, vol. 2, CHL. For St. Louis, MO, see Erastus Snow to Brigham Young, April 25, 1857, CR 1234 1, box 42, folder 16, 3, CHL. For Farmington, UT, see Joseph L. Robinson, diary, October 24, 1856, in *The Journal of Joseph Lee Robinson, Mormon Pioneer,* ed. Kevin Merrell et al. (2003), 147. For Manti, UT, see Samuel K. Gifford, reminiscences, MS 8167, 16, CHL.
36. Wilford Woodruff, "Remarks," *Deseret News*, vol. 4, no. 43, December 31, 1856, 340.
37. Thomas E. Jeremy, diary, April 5, 1857, MS 1248, vol. 3, 241–42, CHL.
38. Heber C. Kimball, "Discourse," *Deseret News*, vol. 4, no. 46, January 21, 1857, 364.
39. John R. Young to Brigham Young, March 1, 1875, as cited in P. T. Reilly, "Kanab United Order: The President's Nephew and the Bishop," *Utah Historical Quarterly* 42, no. 2 (Spring 1974): 157–58. See also Kanab Ward general minutes, February 7, 1875, LR 4303 11, CHL.
40. The Saint David Ward example is more ambiguous. On June 27, 1886, the ward sacrament meeting minutes make an ominous reference to the sacrament being "omitted" without explanation. The sacrament was administered the next week, but there is evidence that there was division among members of the ward at the time. At least two people were "cut off from the church" in the following weeks. Saint David Ward general minutes, June 27–August 17, 1886, LR 7745 23, vol. 2, CHL. The Honeyville Ward example is much better documented. Following a very publicized ecclesiastical court case in town, about two-thirds of the ward protested the ruling and signed a petition for a retrial. There was such "disunion and strife" among them that Rudger Clawson, president of the Box Elder Stake, directed Benjamin H. Tolman, bishop of the Honeyville Ward, to withdraw the sacrament from the entire ward. The ban lasted seven months. Eventually, Elders John Henry Smith and Heber J. Grant of the Twelve visited the ward "to bring the people into a condition to partake of the sacrament." It took several meetings "to harmonize the feeling of the brethren," but the sacrament was ultimately restored. David S. Hoopes and Roy Hoopes, *The Making of a Mormon Apostle: The Story of Rudger Clawson* (New York: Madison Book, 1990), 165; Rudger Clawson diary, June 17, 1894, MS 481, box 5, vol. 5, Special Collections, J. Willard Marriott Library, University of Utah, Salt Lake City (hereafter Marriott Special Collections); and D. Michael Quinn, *Same-Sex Dynamics Among Nineteenth-Century Americans: A Mormon Example* (Urbana, IL: University of Illinois Press, 1996), 286–87.
41. See, for example, Clifford Putney, *Muscular Christianity: Manhood and Sports in Protestant America, 1880–1920* (Cambridge: Harvard University Press, 2003), 45–72; and Richard Ian Kimball, "Muscular Mormonism," *International Journal of the History of Sport* 25, no. 5 (April 2008): 549–78.

42. Ethan R. Yorgason, *Transformation of the Mormon Culture Region* (Urbana, IL: University of Illinois Press, 2003), 80–84; and Dean L. May, *Utah: A People's History* (Salt Lake City: University of Utah Press, 1987), 164–65.
43. Preparing the sacrament began to be a responsibility for teachers in the Aaronic Priesthood in the 1930s. The proceedings of an Aaronic Priesthood convention in 1932, for example, suggested that teachers could prepare the bread and water as part of their duties, but it was more of a passing reference than a general church policy. In 1939, however, the practice began to formalize. The Aaronic Priesthood section of the *Improvement Era* that year listed "four major objectives stressed for 1939," including "having ordained teachers supervise the preparation of sacrament tables." The article continued: "Comments are frequently made that priests who are designated to administer the sacrament and deacons who are usually appointed to pass the sacrament are provided for in the Church program, but that the teachers are neglected." If local church leaders assigned teachers to set the table, it "[would] eliminate any impression that teachers' quorum members [were] not provided for in the sacrament service." Over the next several years, these suggestions became policy and were codified in handbooks. "The Importance of Activity in Aaronic Priesthood Quorums," *Improvement Era* 36, no. 2 (December 1932): 104. See also "Four Major Objectives Stressed for 1939," *Improvement Era* 32, no. 3 (March 1939): 170; "Teachers to Prepare the Sacrament Table," *Church News*, April 2, 1950, 11; and "Suggestions for Aaronic Priesthood Bearers Officiating in the Sacrament Service," *Improvement Era* 58, no. 6 (June 1955): 466. The 1940 *Aaronic Priesthood Handbook* (which was likely written in 1939) makes no mention of sacrament preparation. In the section outlining the duties of teachers, the handbook only mentions that they can help pass the sacrament. The next edition of the *Aaronic Priesthood Handbook* in 1943, however, has "prepare the sacrament table" under the "Assignments for Teachers" section. Instructions for teachers in the Aaronic Priesthood to prepare the sacrament did not appear in general Church handbooks until 1976. *Aaronic Priesthood Handbook* (Salt Lake City: The Presiding Bishopric, 1940), 77–78; *Aaronic Priesthood Handbook* (Salt Lake City: The Presiding Bishopric, 1943), 57; and *General Handbook: Serving in The Church of Jesus Christ of Latter-day Saints* (Salt Lake City: The Church of Jesus Christ of Latter-day Saints, 1976), 47–48.
44. Hartley, "From Men to Boys."
45. Nancy Tomes, "American Attitudes Toward the Germ Theory of Disease: Phyllis Allen Richmond Revisited," *Journal of the History of Medicine* 52, no. 1 (January 1997): 17–50.
46. Nancy Tomes, *The Gospel of Germs: Men, Women, and the Microbe in American Life* (Cambridge: Harvard University Press, 1999), 91–156.
47. Richard A. Burridge, *Holy Communion in Contagious Times: Celebrating the Eucharist in the Everyday and Online Worlds* (Eugene, OR: Cascade Books, 2022), 63.
48. See, for example, "A Lively Session," *Salt Lake Herald-Republican*, March 13, 1895, 1; "Local News," *Salt Lake Herald-Republican*, December 6, 1896, 4; "For Public Health," *Salt Lake Herald-Republican*, October 29, 1897, 2; and "The Common Drinking Cup," *Deseret News*, December 10, 1898, 11.

49. Selden Clawson, reminiscences, in Helen Clawson Wells papers, MS 257, box 18, folder 6, Marriott Special Collections.
50. "Germs Lurk in Communion Cup," *Salt Lake Herald-Republican*, May 6, 1902, 5.
51. "Innovation in Communion," *Salt Lake Telegram*, March 28, 1904, 10; "City and Neighborhood," *Salt Lake Tribune*, March 27, 1904, 10; and "Individual Cups Used for Communion," *Salt Lake Telegram*, April 9, 1906, 4.
52. "Physician Attacks Use of Communion Cup," *Salt Lake Tribune*, April 5, 1908, 24.
53. "Wide Prevalence of Disease Shown by State Bulletin," *Salt Lake Herald-Republican*, January 18, 1908, 12; "Fighting the Great White Plague in Utah," *Inter-Mountain Republican*, September 27, 1908, 17; "Tuberculosis Day Observed Sunday," *Salt Lake Herald-Republican*, April 22, 1910, 5; "The Fight Against Tuberculosis," *Carbon County News*, February 18, 2010, 7; "Strict Measures to Fight Tuberculosis," *Salt Lake Telegram*, February 21, 1910, 2; and "Fighting the White Plague," *Millard County Progress Review*, December 23, 1910, 8.
54. David L. McDonald, "The Individual Sacrament Cup," *Young Woman's Journal* 23, no. 4 (April 1912): 216.
55. After Clawson received permission to test individual sacrament cups in the Eighteenth Ward, public pressure increased to make a change. On January 30, 1911, the Association of Health Officers of Utah met in Salt Lake City and deliberated over measures to reduce the spread of disease in the state, including a possible ban on shared communion cups in local churches. That same day, a committee was appointed to study the matter and make recommendations to state leaders. At first, the committee consisted of three Latter-day Saint physicians: Parley Pratt Nelson of Manti, Walter T. Hasler of Lehi, and Herbet A. Adamson of Richmond. However, Hasler and Adamson believed even a hypothetical ban on shared sacramental cups "was going too far," and both asked to be removed from the committee. Theodore B. Beatty, the state health commissioner, who was not a Latter-day Saint, commented that "it was unusual that so much objection to such a resolution should be raised." The debate over communion vessels likely had less to do with questions over science and religion and more to do with government influence over religious activity. Indeed, Hasler had earlier voiced support for eliminating shared cups in worship services. "It would not be sacrilegious," he explained months before, "to devise some other means of partaking of the sacrament to avoid disease germs." The state medical leaders ultimately compromised and drafted a resolution condemning the practice of sharing cups, but they did not call for a legislative ban on shared cups in churches, schools, and other public venues. Hasler and Adamson agreed to the terms, and the resolution passed with unanimous consent. "Individual Communion Cups Asked," *Salt Lake Telegram,* January 30, 1911, 10; "Doctors Discuss Health Measures," *Salt Lake Herald*, January 10, 1910, 5; and "Doctors Urge Sanitary Cups," *Salt Lake Tribune*, January 31, 1911, 14.
56. Because the Word of Wisdom was not as strictly enforced during this time, many tobacco users would drink from the common cup—to the dismay of many Latter-day Saints. In 1892 Elder Abraham H. Cannon of the Twelve said, "The man who has been using tobacco comes here and partakes of the sacrament and passes it to some delicate lady, who is nauseated by the smell of tobacco."

"Sunday Services," *Utah Journal*, August 10, 1891, 5. In 1897, President George Q. Cannon of the First Presidency agreed with some Latter-day Saints who believed tobacco users should "sit together in partaking of the sacrament, as many of them leave the fumes of tobacco in the water after they have drunk from the cup." "Editorial Thoughts," *Juvenile Instructor* 32, no. 6 (March 15, 1897): 188.

57. William A. Hyde, the president of the Pocatello Stake in Idaho, wrote that Latter-day Saints had complained to him about partaking of the sacramental water after infants that had "been eating cake" beforehand, because the infants often left "particles" in the common cup. He suggested local leaders have a decoy cup "that is different from the sacrament goblets" and have children drink from it as practice for the real thing when they were older. "The Sacrament of the Lord's Supper," 579.
58. Irwin Clawson to Richard L. Evans, March 22, 1954, in Helen Clawson Wells papers, MS 257, box 18, folder 6, Marriott Special Collections. James L. Jacobs of Sanpete County, Utah, later remembered, "It was interesting to watch people as the water goblets were passed to them. Some would carefully turn the goblets so they could drink right over the handle. Others placed their hands on each side of the goblet and tipped it up but did not actually touch their lips to it. Still others sipped obediently, then wiped their lips vigorously with handkerchiefs to remove any trace that might have been picked up from previous drinkers." "Sacrament at Conference," *Saga of the Sanpitch* 15 (1983): 8. A young Spencer W. Kimball similarly remembered how the deacons were often amused at members who rotated the cup for a spot to drink and how the "supposedly untouched spot quickly became the most used part of the cup's rim." Quoted in Edward L. Kimball, *Spencer W. Kimball: Twelfth President of the Church of Jesus Christ of Latter-day Saints* (Salt Lake City: Bookcraft, 1979), 55–56.
59. Selden Clawson, reminiscences, n.d., MS 257, box 3, folder 3, Marriott Special Collections.
60. McDonald, "Individual Sacrament Cup," 216.
61. Like Clawson, Frederick J. Pack faced resistance from members of the Thirty-Third Ward in Salt Lake City. Pack, a scientist at the University of Utah and a counselor in the bishopric, raised the issue of sacrament cups in his own Sunday School class in the fall of 1911. "We are going to ask the people to assist in preventing [the] spread of tuberculosis," he told a gathering of Latter-day Saints. "We want an individual sacrament service. Let us not be last in adopting new ideas. Don't go home now and think Bro. Pack was cranky as usual tonight." But Pack anticipated opposition. When he asked how many would support the bishopric in purchasing a set of individual sacrament cups, he was met with defiance from "the older members of the ward." The clerk of the meeting noted in the minutes: "Not a unanimous vote. But no negative." The older group was clearly at odds with those supporting reform. Their refusal to vote was silent protest. Thirty-Third Ward general minutes, September 17, 1911, LR 9120 11, CHL. Joseph E. Greaves received similar pushback to individual sacrament cups in 1919. Greaves, a bacteriologist at Utah State Agricultural College, had lost his wife to influenza the year before. In an instant, he became a widower and single father of five children. The tragedy tested his faith. When he saw the common cup still being passed in his Logan 9th Ward in February 1919, he approached

the bishop about the danger in continuing to use a shared cup for the sacrament. Their exchange highlights the hostility between old- and new-guard Latter-day Saints at the time. "Brother Greaves," the bishop insisted, "do you really think that God would allow his sacred water, which has been blessed by the priesthood, to cause disease, to make people sick?" Greaves responded, "Bishop, do you really think that God would have given us brains if he didn't expect us to use them?" The bishop rebuked Greaves and told him to repent of his sharp comments, to which Greaves replied, "Horse feathers!" As cited in Frances Lee Menlove, "A Listening Heart: Reflections on 1 Kings 3:5–9," *Sunstone*, October 2002, 20.

62. Selden Clawson, reminiscences, in Helen Clawson Wells papers, MS 257, box 3, folder 3, Marriott Special Collections.
63. Selden Clawson, diary, June 11, 1911, in Helen Clawson Wells papers, MS 257, box 3, folder 3, Marriott Special Collections; and Thomas A. Clawson, diary, June 11, 1911, MSS B 106, box 2, folder 3, Utah State Historical Society, Salt Lake City. According to an April 1911 *Deseret News* article, the American Fork 1st Ward had "taken the lead in ordering sacrament sets with individual cups" and "other wards will no doubt adopt this sanitary method of service." "Lehi," *Deseret News*, April 8, 1911, 12. It is unclear when the American Fork 1st Ward introduced individual cups into its sacrament services, but it is possible they did so before the Eighteenth Ward in June. "Lehi," 12.
64. One of the most common defenses of shared sacrament cups was a literal interpretation of the sacramental blessings. Many believed that the prayer on the water "killed" any germs. Members of the Groveland Ward in eastern Idaho, for example, used a common cup throughout the 1918 influenza pandemic and beyond. In 1921, they had their own debates over the sacrament cup issue. Daniel Foss Olsen, a member of the ward, later wrote about the deliberation between ward members. "Some people were very reluctant to make the change [to individual cups]," Olsen related. "When others pointed out that this was being done as a sanitary measure to keep people from drinking other people's germs, those favoring the old way responded that the sacramental prayer would kill the germs away." Janice Elaine Olsen Williams, "Daniel Foss Olsen: Always a Teacher," 2006, 79–80, FamilySearch.org. Lola Newbold of Cambridge, Idaho, later wrote, "Mother said the water was blessed so we wouldn't get any germs." Linda Hamilton Clark and Larry G. Hamilton, "Lola Pearl Newbold Hamilton: The Early Years, 1911–1932," 2009, 6, FamilySearch.org. Max Francis Jensen of the Independence Ward in eastern Idaho similarly remembered, "Mother would always say it had been blessed if we got a little squeamish about it." "Life History of Max Francis Jensen," 1982, 29–30, FamilySearch.org.
65. Selden Clawson, reminiscences. For additional information regarding the story of Selden Clawson and individual sacrament cups, see Justin R. Bray, "The Lord's Supper during the Progressive Era, 1890–1930," *Journal of Mormon History* 38, no. 4 (Fall 2012): 88–104; and Bray, "The Sacrament of the Lord's Supper and the Influenza Epidemic of 1918," *Church History Library Blog*, January 14, 2019, https://history.churchofjesuschrist.org/blog/sacrament-cup-influenza-epidemic-1918.
66. There is evidence that some Latter-day Saints fell short of this ideal. Annie Clara Tanner Fotland remembered segregated seating in the Indianola Ward

in Sanpete County, Utah, in the late 1880s. "I went to school with the Indian children," she wrote, "and we all went to church together and took the sacrament from the same cup. But the Indians would sit in the back of the room, and the white people were given the sacrament first." "Annie Clara Tanner Fotland," FamilySearch.org. David L. McDonald, the physician who helped petition for individual sacrament cups, expressed similar resentment at drinking from the same cup as people of African descent—although in a nonchurch setting. See "Individual Sacrament Cup," 216.

67. David O. McKay, in Conference Report, October 1929, 12.
68. Jan Shipps, *Mormonism: The Story of a New Religious Tradition* (Urbana, IL: University of Illinois Press, 1985), 125; and Richard O. Cowan, *The Living Church: The Unfolding of the Programs and Organization of the Church of Jesus Christ during the Twentieth Century* (Provo, UT: Brigham Young University Printing Service, 1974), 190.
69. Hartley, "From Men to Boys," 104.
70. Minutes of the Aaronic Priesthood convention, April 8, 1933, M257.44 M266 1933, CHL.
71. Dean Brough, "The Story of the Men's White Shirt," *Conversation*, May 13, 2014; James W. Cortada, *IBM: The Rise and Fall and Reinvention of a Global Icon* (Cambridge, MA: MIT Press, 2019), 236–237; and Jane Tynan, "Utility Chic: Where Fashion and Uniform Meet," in *Uniform: Clothing and Discipline in the Modern World*, ed. Jane Tynan and Lisa Godson (New York: Bloomberg Publishing, 2019), 227.
72. Earl J. Glade, "Highland Park Ward Sacrament Service," *Improvement Era* 36, no. 4 (April 1933): 361.
73. "The 1937 Highland Parker: Twenty-First Birthday Issue," M277.9225 H638h, CHL.
74. Minutes of the Aaronic Priesthood convention, April 8, 1933, M257.44 M266 1933, CHL.
75. "The 1937 Highland Parker." For Hawthorne Ward, see Fred J. Curtis, "The Importance of Activity in Aaronic Priesthood Quorums," *Improvement Era* 36, no. 2 (December 1932): 104; and "Hawthorne Ward Makes Outstanding Record," *Improvement Era* 41, no. 6 (June 1938): 366. For Fourteenth Ward, see Fourteenth Ward photographs, PH 2842, CHL. For Cottonwood Ward, see Deacons of Cottonwood Ward, PH 271, CHL. For Sugar House Ward, see Paul and Sandra Crookston, "Carlton Crookston and Annie Ruth Griffin," (2005), 48–49, FamilySearch.org. For Provo 1st Ward, see "Provo First Ward Deacons Have Good Record," *Improvement Era* 38, no. 6 (June 1935): 373. For Fourth Ward, see "Pioneer Fourth Ward Priesthood Active," *Improvement Era* 41, no. 4 (April 1938), 236. For Wasatch Ward and Millcreek Ward, see "Two Wards Report on Boy Awards," *Church News*, February 21, 1942, 3.
76. For Arizona, see Lela J. Dalton, "The Life Story of Oscar Fernando Jesperson," 1998, 48, FamilySearch.org; and Virgil Lehi Harris, "A Personal History of Virgil Lehi Harris," n.d., 15, FamilySearch.org. For California, see Mark Skousen, "Thunder Broke the Heavens: The Life of LeRoy B. Skousen," (1984), 17, FamilySearch.org; and Robert L. Simpson, "We Thank Thee, O God, for

a Prophet," *BYU Speeches*, June 24, 1986, 4. For Oregon, see "Uniforms in Sacrament Service," *Improvement Era* 36, no. 9 (September 1933): 687.

77. "Item Number Two: Regulations Regarding Passing the Sacrament," *Improvement Era* 58, no. 2 (February 1955): 113, 120.
78. Robert L. Simpson, "We Thank Thee, O God, for a Prophet," *BYU Speeches*, June 24, 1986, 4.
79. "Suggestions for Increasing Sacrament Meeting Attendance," *Progress of the Church* 6, no. 2 (February 1943): 7.
80. In 1867, Daniel H. Wells taught, "You should always put forth the right hand when taking either the bread or the cup." "Remarks," August 18, 1867, *Deseret News*, vol. 17, no. 7, March 25, 1868, 50. In 1908, Elder George Albert Smith of the Twelve explained, "Our people have been taught to take the sacrament with the right hand; we believe that is appropriate, and proper, and acceptable to our Father." In Conference Report, April 1908, 36. In 1916, leaders in the First Ward discussed the issue: "Bro Albert Schoenfeld reported that some sisters take the sacrament with their left hand, and with glove on same, suggesting to have this corrected. Bp Duncan pronounced this improper and promised to have it corrected." First Ward general minutes, March 27, 1916, LR 6581 11, vol. 3, 55, CHL.
81. Joseph Fielding Smith, *Church History and Modern Revelation* (Salt Lake City: Deseret Book, 1946), 1:103–104.
82. David O. McKay, diary, February 20, 1952, in Harvard S. Heath, *Confidence Amid Change: The Presidential Diaries of David O. McKay, 1951–1970* (Salt Lake City: Signature Books, 2019), 43.
83. "Regulations Regarding Passing the Sacrament," *Improvement Era* 58, no. 2 (February 1955), 113.
84. Joseph Fielding Smith, "The Right Hand," *Improvement Era* 59, no. 1 (January 1956): 14–15.
85. "What is Your Problem?," *Millennial Star* 128, no. 12 (December 1966): 76. See also J. Stapley, "2020 Handbook: The Lord's Supper and the Right Hand," *By Common Consent*, February 23, 2020. The issue of right hands has resurfaced in recent years. In 1983, President Russell M. Nelson, who was serving at the time as a Regional Representative of the Twelve and was a former Sunday School General President, wrote about the symbolism of using right hands and referenced Joseph Fielding Smith's article from 1956. However, President Nelson also recognized some flexibility in the practice. "The hand used in partaking of the sacrament would logically be the same hand used in making any other sacred oath," he wrote. "For most of us, that would be the right hand. However, sacramental covenants—and other eternal covenants as well—can be and are made by those who have lost the use of the right hand, or who have no hands at all. Much more important than concern over which hand is used in partaking of the sacrament is that the sacrament be partaken with a deep realization of the atoning sacrifice that the sacrament represents." "Is It Necessary to Take the Sacrament with One's Right Hand?," *Ensign*, March 1983, 68–69. In 2020, President Dallin H. Oaks taught a group of young men, "When we partake of the sacrament, we partake with our right hand, not our left hand. And today, I saw quite a few of the deacons take the sacrament with their left hand. Don't do that, because

you set the wrong example for the congregation if you do that." As cited in Jana Riess, "A left-handed Latter-day Saints' dilemma," *Religion News Service*, February 27, 2020. Shortly after President Oaks's message, the Church's handbook was updated to reflect the practice of using right hands—again, with some flexibility. It reads: "Members partake with their right hand when possible." *General Handbook: Serving in the Church of Jesus Christ of Latter-day Saints*, 18.9.4, https://www.churchofjesuschrist.org/study/manual/general-handbook/18-priesthood-ordinances-and-blessings.

86. "About Administering the Sacrament," *Daily Enquirer*, February 5, 1894, 1.
87. T. Edgar Lyon, oral history, in T. Edgar Lyon Sr. Collection, MSS 2341, box 2, folder 1, 33, Perry Special Collections. See also Gary James Bergera, *Confessions of a Mormon Historian: The Diaries of Leonard J. Arrington, 1971–1997* (Salt Lake City: Signature Books, 2018), 2:108.
88. David O. McKay, in Conference Report, April 1946, 116.
89. *General Handbook of Instructions*, 18 (Salt Lake City: The Church of Jesus Christ of Latter-day Saints, 1960), 45.
90. Ronald Walker, "The Salt Lake Tabernacle in the Nineteenth Century: A Glimpse of Early Mormonism," *Journal of Mormon History* 31, no. 2 (Fall 2005): 237.
91. See David O. McKay, "Meditation, Communion, Reverence," *The Instructor* 101 (October 1966): 369–371.
92. Matthew Bowman, *The Mormon People: The Making of an American Faith* (New York: Random House, 2012), 187–88.
93. Merle Casper, *Murray First's First Century: A Commemorative History of the First One Hundred Years of Murray/Murray First Ward* (2000), 6, CHL.
94. "Melda Severina Farley Hacking" (2014), http://dianestokoe.com/jennieandcarl/jennieandcarl_chapter_1.pdf. Elma B. Whitesides Dickson of the Layton Ward later remembered, "It was also the custom to play beautiful music while the sacrament was being passed. Some of my most enjoyable memories are of the melodious music played during this time in meetings. In fact, it was a sacred period devoted to listening to the lovely strains of the organ." David D. Dickson, "The Life Story of Elma B. Whitesides Dickson" (1987), 6, FamilySearch.org.
95. *A Bicentennial History: Hooper–Kanesville* (1976), 64, FamilySearch.org.
96. Jeane Erickson Burton, "Eldred Hilmar Erickson, 1919–1989" (2000), 15, FamilySearch.org.
97. Diane Brown, "The Sacrament of the Lord's Supper: Reflections in Fifteen Fragments," *Exponent II* 19, no. 1 (1995): 4–5.
98. "Church Consolidates Meeting Schedules," *Ensign*, March 1980, 73–78; "Changes Help Balance Gospel Instruction at Home and at Church," *Church News*, October 6, 2018.
99. *General Handbook*, 18.9.3. See also "Sacrament Bread Tray," General Discussions forum, The Church of Jesus Christ of Latter-day Saints, October 9, 2017, https://tech.churchofjesuschrist.org/forum/viewtopic.php?t=29872; and "Celiac disease," General Discussions forum, The Church of Jesus Christ of Latter-day Saints, March 6, 2011, https://tech.churchofjesuschrist.org/forum/viewtopic.php?t=7193.

100. "Church Leaders Call for Better Observance of Sabbath Day," *Church News*, July 15, 2015; "Leaders Hope Emphasis on Sabbath Observance Increases Faith in God," *Church News*, December 30, 2015.
101. Jana Riess, "When Mormon women can't have the sacrament," *Religion News Service* (blog), March 12, 2020, https://religionnews.com/2020/05/12/when-mormon-women-cant-have-the-sacrament.
102. See comments on Riess, "When Mormon women can't have the sacrament." See also Jared Cook, "Blessing the Sacrament Remotely: Contagion, Technology, and Liturgical Adaptation," *By Common Consent* (blog), March 12, 2020, https://bycommonconsent.com/2020/03/12/blessing-the-sacrament-remotely-contagion-technology-and-liturgical-adaptation; Sam Brunson, "Excluding Our Fellow Saints from the Sacrament," *By Common Consent* (blog), April 29, 2020, https://bycommonconsent.com/2020/04/29/excluding-our-fellow-saints-from-the-sacrament; ElleK, "Sacrament at Home: Allowances That Could Be Made for Women," *Exponent II* (blog), April 21, 2020, https://www.the-exponent.com/sacrament-at-home-allowances-that-could-be-made-for-women-copingwithcovid19; Brunson, "Coronavirus and the Sacrament," *By Common Consent* (blog), February 25, 2020, https://bycommonconsent.com/2020/02/25/coronavirus-and-the-sacrament; Brunson, "Shelter-in-Place and the Sacrament," *By Common Consent* (blog), March 20, 2020, https://bycommonconsent.com/2020/03/20/shelter-in-place-and-the-sacrament; Violadiva, "The (Male) Privilege of Partaking," *Exponent II* (blog), April 5, 2020, https://www.the-exponent.com/the-male-privilege-of-partaking; Maren C., "A Few Questions about the Sacrament and Single Sisters," *Exponent II* (blog), June 16, 2020, https://www.the-exponent.com/guest-post-a-few-questions-about-the-sacrament-and-single-sisters-copingwithcovid19; and Cheryl B. Preston, "Women in The Church of Jesus Christ of Latter-day Saints and the COVID-19 Freeze," *SquareTwo* 15, no. 3 (Fall 2020).
103. "The Atlantic's McKay Coppins on the LDS Church's quest for approval and its future," interview by David Noyce and Peggy Fletcher Stack, Mormon Land, podcast, December 16, 2020, https://www.sltrib.com/religion/2020/12/16/mormon-land-atlantics.

Chapter Eleven

Commandment, Covenant, and Joy: The Development of Sabbath Day Counsel from Leaders of The Church of Jesus Christ of Latter-day Saints

Mary Jane Woodger

The commandment to keep the Sabbath day holy is as ancient as the earth itself, dating back to the creation of the world, when after six days of labor the Lord rested from his work (Genesis 2:2–3). God then commanded Moses on Mount Sinai, "Remember the Sabbath day, to keep it holy" (Exodus 20:8). Then in 2015, for the first time a Church-wide "local and regional leadership training" was conducted where leaders received "instruction on the topic of strengthening faith in God by observing the Sabbath day with greater purpose."[1] This emphasis on keeping the Sabbath day holy was initiated in a general conference address given by President Russell M. Nelson in April of that same year, while he was still serving as a member of the Quorum of the Twelve. President Nelson explained, "The Sabbath was given as a perpetual covenant, a constant reminder that the Lord may sanctify His people." With the restoration of all things, this covenant was made between the Lord and his people once again. As President Nelson said, "it has been renewed in these latter days as part of a new covenant with a promise" (see Doctrine and Covenants 59:9–16).[2] It is interesting that even before Russell M. Nelson became the president of the

Church, he consistently spoke about the Sabbath day and would eventually institute new programs that would greatly change the way that Latter-day Saints hallow the Sabbath.

The Need for a Consolidated Meeting Block

Throughout the history of The Church of Jesus Christ of Latter-day Saints, the ways in which members of the Church have organized their worship services have changed periodically. In the early years before the Church was organized, the Saints did not have chapels, so they met whenever and wherever they could. They did not partake of the sacrament every week, but rather only on certain occasions such as quarterly conferences when the members met together as a whole.

In August 1831, the Saints began meeting every Sunday, and in 1836 when the Kirtland Temple was completed, they began offering the sacrament weekly as well. Large groups of Saints held two separate meetings on Sunday and met out-of-doors. Smaller branches also held weekly meetings, though they sometimes occurred on days other than Sunday.

As the Church grew, it was not always possible to accommodate all members at once, and because of this, multiple meetings were often held; adults would partake of the sacrament on Sunday, and children on a weekday. As more meetinghouses were built, all members were able to partake of the sacrament on Sundays,[3] but other meetings, such as Relief Society, Priesthood meeting, Primary, and Sunday School, were spread out throughout the week.[4] Often a family would travel multiple times a week or even multiple times a day to attend various meetings.[5]

In 1980, the First Presidency announced that organized Church meetings would be consolidated into a single three-hour block on Sunday each week. They made this change "(1) to reemphasize personal and family responsibility for learning, living, and teaching the gospel and (2) to allow Church members more time for personal gospel study, for service to others, and for meaningful activities." They further clarified several purposes for the new schedule:

1. Help every Latter-day Saint home become a place where family members love to be, where they can enrich their lives and find mutual love, support, appreciation, and encouragement.
2. Emphasize home-centered Sabbath activities.
3. Make more flexible a weekday activity program for all members.

4. Reduce the amount of travel by Church members and provide opportunities for family members to travel together and participate in Church activities.
5. Conserve energy resources and reduce the nonessential costs required for members to participate in Church activities.[6]

The three-hour block would remain the standard until 2018, when President Russell M. Nelson announced a change to the Sunday worship services to place even more emphasis on the importance of gospel learning in the home.[7] These changes will be discussed in greater depth in this article.

Part of the New and Everlasting Covenant Restored by Joseph Smith

President Brigham Young made the following observation that the Sabbath day was indeed part of the new covenant: "As to keeping the Sabbath according to the Mosaic Law, indeed, I do not; for it would be almost beyond my power. Still, under the new covenant, we should remember to preserve holy one day in the week as a day of rest—as a memorial of the rest of the Lord and the rest of the Saints; also for our temporal advantage, for it is instituted for the express purpose of benefiting man."[8]

Brigham Young saw the commandment to hallow the Sabbath day as a part of the new and everlasting covenant revealed by our Father in Heaven in this dispensation, and other apostles and prophets agreed. For instance, Elder John W. Taylor of the Quorum of the Twelve declared that Sabbath-day observance was "part and parcel of the new covenant God has made with his people in the latter day."[9]

Prominence of the Sabbath Day in General Conference Addresses

The repetition of this commandment has become commonplace among Latter-day Saints since August 7, 1831, when section 59 of the Doctrine and Covenants was revealed. The word "Sabbath" has been used 2,866 times in general conferences from 1850 to October 2020. As shown in figure 1, there have been times when there has been an increase in counsel about Sabbath-day observance. Though General Authorities seldom give justification for emphasizing the Sabbath day in their general conference addresses, some reasons may be deduced for a heavier emphasis on this topic at certain times. One explanation is that cultural trends often preclude General Authority inclusion. For instance, stressing Sabbath-day observance between 1880 and 1900 coincided with a move away from agrarian life to urban living. With this shift came more opportunity for Latter-day Saints to be gainfully employed on Sundays; therefore, this new way to break the commandment was addressed. Another increase in General Authority attention to this subject took place from 1920 to 1940. This intensification is in parallel with the trend of Latter-day Saints participating in more sports and attending more movies on Sunday. It can also be observed that during the Great Depression and World War II, the topic of keeping the Sabbath day holy was advanced often, although it was never linked to these events in leaders' talks.

Some General Authorities have included this subject in their addresses more than others. President Joseph Fielding Smith spoke more frequently about keeping the Sabbath day holy than any other General Authority has. During his service in the Quorum of the Twelve Apostles, a period spanning from 1910 to 1970, the amount of times the Sabbath day was mentioned in general conference was frequent, especially when compared with the decades immediately before and after his apostleship (see figure 1). Joseph Fielding Smith explained his reasons for constantly speaking on this topic:

> We have been taught to observe the Sabbath day from the beginning, and to keep it holy. And many other commandments, which we hear reiterated from the stand . . . God has given unto us, that we might grow nearer unto him and be built up in the faith and strengthened. No commandment, at any time, has He given us, that was not for our comfort and blessing. They are not given merely to please the Lord, but to make us better men and women, and worthy of salvation and exaltation in His kingdom. We know our duty; we know what is required of us, and that the Lord will not hold him guiltless who, understanding these things, will go contrary to that which he has been commanded.[10]

Though past General Authorities have had much to say on the topic, the recent emphasis on the Sabbath day is incomparable to that of any other era. From 2010 to 2020, there were 294 instances where the term "Sabbath day" was mentioned in general conference (see figure 1), meaning that in the last decade we have had more mentions of the Sabbath day in general conference than in any previous decade. With the current emphasis on Sabbath-day observance, one is hard-pressed to find a cultural parallel for this constant inclusion or a prominence of any particular leader speaking on the subject, as could be seen in decades past. Elder M. Russell Ballard gave this brief explanation for the current priority given to keeping the Sabbath day holy: "We felt that it was urgent that we strengthen the faith of our people. The world seems to be getting a little . . . more difficult. . . . We're hoping that home activities will be more centered on learning and knowing more about the life and ministry of the Savior and the great plan of happiness that our Heavenly Father has given us to live by."[11]

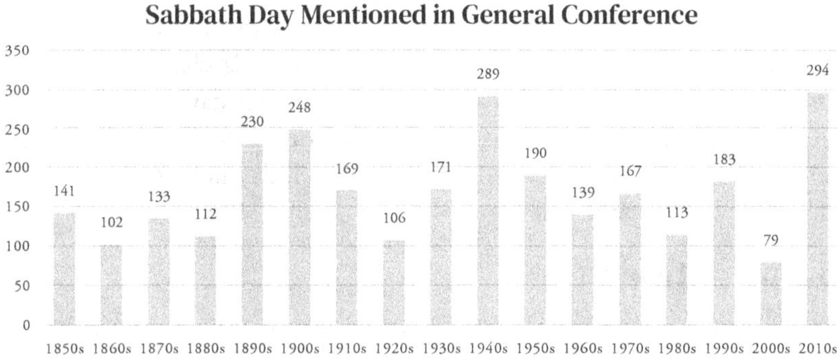

Figure 1. Bar graph depicting mentions of the phrase "Sabbath day" in general conference in various decades.

From Rules and Regulation to a Sign of Devotion

An underlining message in all general conference addresses about keeping the Sabbath day holy is consistent: we are counseled to act in a way that shows our love, respect, and honor for God. Despite this consistency, interpretation and instruction concerning the Sabbath day has not been constant throughout the history of the Church. A pattern can be observed in various modern counsels about Sabbath-day observance that replicates ancient patterns of counsel, which went from providing specific regulations and rules to inviting the inward adoption of gospel principles. Though each generation can be seen as having unique circumstances that make counsel vary to some degree throughout the years, the pattern still exists. From the beginning of the Church to the present day, the phrase "keeping the Sabbath day holy" has evolved in its role, prevalence, and usage by prophets.

This evolution of the Sabbath-day principle in the latter days closely follows the progress that took place from the institution of Mosaic law to

Christian practice. President James E. Faust said, "The Mosaic injunctions of Sabbath day observance contained many detailed do's and don'ts. This may have been necessary to teach obedience to those who had been in captivity and had long been denied individual freedom of choice. Thereafter, these Mosaic instructions were carried to many unwarranted extremes which the Savior condemned." President Faust reiterated that in our generation, "God has recognized our intelligence by not requiring endless restrictions. Perhaps this was done with a hope that we would catch more of the spirit of Sabbath worship rather than the letter thereof."[12]

Just as the Savior tried to turn people's hearts to the Sabbath instead of restricting them to Mosaic rules, so too can this change be seen in the history of The Church of Jesus Christ of Latter-day Saints. Counsel given in general conference has progressed from detailed dos and don'ts to a broader view in which keeping the Sabbath day holy is a sign of our devotion written upon our hearts.

Scriptural Foundation

During the nineteenth and early twentieth centuries, General Authorities consistently used two Sabbath-day scriptural passages to link Mosaic law to the new and everlasting covenant. Most often, they would first cite the Sabbath-day passage from the Ten Commandments given to Moses on Mount Sinai:

> Remember the sabbath day, to keep it holy.
>
> Six days shalt thou labor, and do all thy work:
>
> But the seventh day is the sabbath of the Lord thy God: in it thou shalt not do any work, thou, nor thy son, nor thy daughter, thy manservant, nor thy maidservant, nor thy cattle, nor thy stranger that is within thy gates:
>
> For in six days the Lord made heaven and earth, the sea, and all that in them is, and rested the seventh day: wherefore the Lord blessed the sabbath day, and hallowed it. (Exodus 20:8–11)

General Authorities reiterated that this fourth commandment was a perpetual covenant that had never been rescinded. Most especially, the first three prophets of the twentieth century, Joseph F. Smith, Heber J. Grant, and George Albert Smith, repeated the commandment given on Mount Sinai. George Albert Smith was adamant that the commandment was still binding for latter-day Israel. He also declared, "If the people of the world had observed the Ten Commandments from that time until now, we would have a different world. There would be millions of people who would live longer than they have lived and be happier."[13] The proceeding generation of General Authorities also spoke authoritatively about the fourth commandment. For instance, President Joseph Fielding Smith was very clear that the Saints should not believe that the commandment to keep the Sabbath day had been done away with in Christ. He proclaimed, "the Decalogue was older than Moses, it continued after Moses passed away. The Lord has reiterated these commandments, he has renewed them and commanded us in our day to observe them and keep them sacredly and holy."[14] Mid- and latter-twentieth-century General Authorities, including Sylvester Q. Cannon, Spencer W. Kimball, N. Eldon Tanner, L. Tom Perry, James E. Faust, and Russell M. Nelson, also referred to the Decalogue.[15] Moreover, President James E. Faust observed that "the divine law of the Sabbath has been emphasized repeatedly over the centuries more than any other commandment."[16] Elder L. Tom Perry said that our treatment of the Sabbath day could be compared to those of former generations. He suggested, "One way to measure ourselves and compare us to previous generations is by one of the oldest standards known to man—the Ten Commandments."[17]

In 1949, President J. Reuben Clark Jr. explained that the reason this Mosaic law became so rule- and regulation-oriented was because it was one of the hardest commandments for the children of Israel to keep. He explained:

> Ancient Israel found that one of its most difficult commandments to observe was that of remembering the Sabbath day. After they were led into captivity, they were among a people who knew not the Sabbath which they knew, and very soon they began to partake, as we are partaking (and let me say it is amazing how we follow round the clock of earlier peoples in our wanderings, or beginning of wanderings from the early tenets as they were taught to us) of the sins of those among whom they lived. It came to be, as it is with us, that not alone was the matter one of laboring on the Sabbath, but it was also one of recreation on the Sabbath. So rather trivial regulations (as they seem to us) were made by captive Israel in order to prevent ancient Israel from breaking the Sabbath.[18]

President Clark's observation also explains why in the early days of the modern Church there was much more specificity in the counsel given on hallowing the Sabbath day.

The other scriptural passage that General Authorities most often use in counsel to keep the Sabbath day holy comes from section 59 of the Doctrine and Covenants. In almost every case, when a modern apostle has spoken of the Sabbath day, passages or at least wording from this scripture block have been included in his address:

> For verily this is a day appointed unto you to rest from your labors, and to pay thy devotions unto the Most High; Nevertheless thy vows shall be offered up in righteousness on all days and at all times; But remember that on this, the Lord's day, thou shalt offer thine oblations and thy sacraments unto the Most High, confessing thy sins unto thy brethren, and before the Lord. And on this day thou shalt do none other thing, only let thy food be prepared with singleness of heart that thy fasting may be perfect, or, in other words, that thy joy may be full. (vv. 10–13)

This passage of scripture became the basis of counsel given over the history of the Church. Section 59 has been referred to in general conference addresses regarding the Sabbath day more in the twentieth century than even in the nineteenth century when it was first received.

Working on the Sabbath

It is noteworthy that the Sabbath day is one of the first things that President Brigham Young spoke of upon entering the Salt Lake Valley. This incident has been brought up by Joseph Fielding Smith, LeGrand Richards, George Albert Smith, and Gordon B. Hinckley in general conference.[19] President Hinckley described what happened:

> On July 24, 1847, the pioneer company of our people came into this valley. . . . The next day, Sabbath services were held both in the morning and in the afternoon. There was no hall of any kind in which to meet. I suppose that in the blistering heat of that July Sunday they sat on the tongues of their wagons and leaned against the wheels while the Brethren spoke. The season was late, and they were faced with a gargantuan and immediate task if they were to grow seed for the next

> season. But President Young pleaded with them not to violate the Sabbath then or in the future.[20]

On that first Sabbath in the Salt Lake Valley, President Brigham Young told the brethren that they must not work on Sunday and that they would lose five times as much as they would gain by it.[21] He was adamant from the very outset that the Latter-day Saints of his generation keep the covenant of hallowing the Sabbath day.

Pioneers did not have to worry about specific counsel regarding shopping, attending sports, or going to the theatre on Sunday, but they did have a lot of work to do in order to survive in a new land, especially with regard to the planting of crops. Brigham Young, in trying to teach the Saints about keeping the Sabbath day holy, encouraged them not to work on the hallowed day. At one point, he even criticized one Latter-day Saint "because he planted some potatoes on the Sabbath day before he came to church."[22] President Wilford Woodruff also warned about farming on the Sabbath: "I do not believe that any man, who has ever belonged to this Church and kingdom, since its organization, has made anything by attending to his farm on the Sabbath. . . . The Spirit of God does not like it, it withdraws itself from us, and we make no money by it."[23] Not working on the Sabbath has been consistently addressed throughout all generations of The Church of Jesus Christ of Latter-day Saints.

The idea that working on the Sabbath would not prove to be beneficial was mentioned repeatedly over the years. For instance, President George Albert Smith said, "I want to say that you lose every time you violate the Sabbath day, you lose more than you can gain, no matter what you may think you are going to gain."[24] Likewise, President David O. McKay declared, "The farmer who makes his boys go out and haul hay, even when a storm is coming, is doing his boys an injustice. It would be much better to let that hay be destroyed than to deprive those boys of a sense of coming nearer to the Eternal Spirit, and partake of the sacrament."[25]

As Latter-day Saints progressed from an agrarian society to an urban one, counsel changed in relationship to working on the Sabbath day. In 1953, President Spencer W. Kimball was pleased to report that in his extensive travels he found "many faithful people who forgo the Sabbath day profits."[26] Then, in a new addition of counsel more than twenty years later, he cautioned Latter-day Saints to not make others work either. He taught, "Businesses will not be open on the Sabbath if they are not patronized on that holy day. The same is true of resorts, sporting events, and recreation areas of all kinds. Pursuit of the almighty dollar is winning, it seems, over the Lord's commandment, 'Keep my Sabbaths, and reverence my sanctuary' (Leviticus 19:30)." President Kimball continued, clarifying that keeping the Sabbath requires more than sacrificing worldly pleasures. He said, "It is not enough to refrain from moviegoing, hunting, fishing, sports, and unnecessary labor on the Sabbath."[27] Elder Mark E. Petersen of the Quorum of the Twelve taught, "If we are to do none other thing on Sunday but to devote the day to holy purposes, what is our situation if we willfully choose to operate our businesses on the Sabbath, or if we patronize such Sunday businesses, or if we go to places of recreation on Sunday?"[28]

Inappropriate Activities on the Sabbath

The quote above brings up another repeated Sabbath-day counsel: many recreational activities are not Sabbath-day worthy. The concern for young people and their activities on the Sabbath day was a constant in the addresses of General Authorities. For example, President Joseph F. Smith spoke of "gangs about the streets, using obscene language, throwing rocks at and scuffling with each other, going riding, walking, fishing, hunting, &c., on the Sabbath day."[29] He warned, "One of these evils is a growing tendency, especially on the part of our youth, to pay but little attention to, if not to ignore, the observance of the Sabbath day. The Sabbath is a day of rest and of worship, designated and set apart by special commandment of the Lord to the Church of Jesus Christ of Latter-day Saints, and we should honor and keep it holy. We should also teach our children this principle."[30]

Some Latter-day Saints began to think that if they attended their religious meetings on Sunday, then they could do anything else they wanted to do and still be honoring the Sabbath. General Authorities clearly stated that this was not the case, and members of the Church would pay a price for such actions. President George Albert Smith cautioned that with such behavior, "the Spirit of our heavenly Father will withdraw from them."[31] As sports and media became more prominent in the lives of Latter-day Saints, General Authorities also spoke of these aspects of life being incongruent with Sabbath day worship. In the 1970s, shopping on Sunday became a topic of concern. President Spencer W. Kimball said, "We call attention also to the habit in which many buy their commodities on the Sabbath. Many employed people would be released for rest and worship on the Sabbath if we did not shop on that day. Numerous excuses and rationalizations are presented to justify the Sunday buying. We call upon all of you to keep the Sabbath holy and make no Sunday purchases."[32]

Regulation- and Rule-Bound Counsel

In going from Mosaic regulation to heartfelt devotion, there have been many steps along the way in counsel from General Authorities. One sees in early Church history the listing of many dos and don'ts of what Latter-day Saints could and could not do on the Sabbath day. One interesting incident from Elder George A. Smith shows the extreme strictness that was going on in Sabbath observance. On one occasion when he was visiting a stake, he found local leaders debating about whether Latter-day Saints could even discuss the subject of temporal welfare on the Sabbath. Local leaders were telling their congregations that they should not speak of such things as "donations, emigration, teams, building meetinghouses, or of Tithing," on the Sabbath. After learning of this particular stake's eccentric restrictions, Elders George A. Smith and Ezra T. Benson spent the whole Sabbath day "telling how to make bread, build cities, make farms, fences, and in fact [they] told them how to do every useful thing that [they] could think of." They "asserted that a certain amount of temporal preparation was necessary in order that a man might enjoy his religion."[33]

Specific rules such as the one discussed above were often given late into the nineteenth and early twentieth centuries. For instance, President Joseph F. Smith discouraged listening to secular music on the Sabbath.[34] In 1908, Elder Francis M. Lyman gave a list of appropriate Sunday activities, saying, "The Sabbath day should be occupied in our home temples, in home study, in home reading, in home prayer." He also suggested that "the fathers and mothers will, perhaps, find themselves pretty well 'stumped' at times to know just exactly how to handle the little ones; but they must not be wearied."[35]

Elder John Henry Smith of the Quorum of the Twelve Apostles was very decisive in his list of dos and don'ts. He counseled that the Sabbath day "should not be spent in visiting neighbors, in mingling with one another upon the streets, or in going to pleasure resorts." Instead, the Saints "should seek to study the Scriptures at home, and equip [them]selves by communion with the Spirit."[36] Even as late as September 1, 1928, the First Presidency published an editorial in the *Deseret News*, which commanded specifically that "Latter-day Saints may not go on Sunday to movies, to baseball, football, or basketball games, or to any other kind of commercial entertainments, or engage in avoidable commercial activities, or go hunting, fishing, golfing, or skiing on this day."[37]

In 1949, the subject of Sunday music was broached once again, but the regulation was tempered when President J. Reuben Clark Jr. of the First Presidency suggested that Latter-day Saints could "listen to good music in the home," but they were not to "go joy riding, nor to beach parties, nor on picnics!"[38] On the subject of watching movies, he instructed, "There is a great difference between looking at a good movie in your home and going to a movie house, a very great difference. But the home movies we look at should be of a kind that teach things specified in the revelations as in order in the house of prayer."[39]

Twenty years later in 1969, President Spencer W. Kimball published *The Miracle of Forgiveness*. Within this volume, he gave lists of what to do on the Sabbath, unlike his predecessors, who had listed what not to do. He wrote:

> Abstinence from work and recreation is important but insufficient. The Sabbath calls for constructive thoughts and acts, and if one merely lounges about doing nothing on the Sabbath, he is breaking it. To observe it, one will be on his knees in prayer, preparing lessons, studying the gospel, meditating, visiting the ill and distressed, sleeping, reading wholesome material, and attending all the meetings of that day to which he is expected. To fail to do these proper things is a transgression on the omission side.[40]

As the Prophet, President Spencer W. Kimball continued giving lists of appropriate Sabbath activities to the Saints. In 1978, President Kimball's list of appropriate Sabbath activities also included "studying the scriptures, attending church meetings to learn and to worship, writing letters to absent loved ones, comforting the sorrowing, visiting the sick, and, in general, doing what the Lord would have us do on this, his holy day."[41] President Kimball's administration instituted the consolidated meeting schedule. As the Prophet, he made it clear that the extra hours on the Sabbath day no longer spent in Church meetings should be spent with families: "Therefore, take time to be together as families to converse with one another, to study the scriptures, to visit friends, relatives, and the sick and lonely. This is also an excellent time to work on your journals and genealogy. Do not neglect those among us who do not now have the blessings of living in traditional families. These are special souls who often have special needs. Do not let them become isolated from you or the activities of your ward or your branch."[42]

Counsel to Attend Church Meetings

One teaching that has not changed over the span of generations is that Latter-day Saints are instructed to attend Church meetings on the Sabbath. Especially in the first two decades of the twentieth century, this counsel was renewed repeatedly. In October 1906 Elder Hyrum M. Smith of the Quorum of the Twelve Apostles reported that some "sacrament meetings and Sabbath meetings [were] not as well attended as they should be."[43] Elder George Albert Smith also spoke in general conference about low attendance and cautioned, "Men and women who go from year to year without partaking of the Lord's Supper, gradually lose the Spirit of our Heavenly Father; they forfeit its companionship where they have had opportunity to participate in that blessing, but have failed to take advantage of it. The sacrament is of great importance. The Lord Himself ordained that we partake of these emblems."[44]

In 1907, President Anthon H. Lund of the First Presidency talked about the great expense the Church was incurring in erecting meeting houses and tied it to the importance of Sabbath worship: "We hope that the people who are so willing to build meeting houses will also be willing to use them . . . on the Sabbath day." He then warned, "Unless the Saints attend their meetings it will be hard for them to keep alive in the Gospel."[45] Nine years later, he spoke of ways to make the meetings more attractive through music[46] and defined that it was "[the Saints'] duty in attending their meetings" to listen to what was said; then, quoting section 59 of the Doctrine and Covenants, he admonished Latter-day Saints to "go to the house of prayer" and renew their covenants so they could keep "unspotted from the world."[47]

In October 1916, Elder Rudger J. Clawson also encouraged Saints to go to church. He warned that it was not enough to "remain at home upon the Sabbath day, even to read, or to read good books, or to read the scriptures, when they ought to be in the house of prayer, in the house of worship, in the house of the Lord, where they are commanded to go."[48]

In 1936, Elder Richard R. Lyman of the Quorum of the Twelve Apostles outlined the purpose of Sunday meetings as follows:

> We do not go to our places of worship for the purpose of acquiring scholarship; we do not go there to learn history or mathematics or science. The purpose of our going to our sacrament meetings is to worship. We cannot get faith by logic any more than we can get learning by simply longing for it. Partaking worthily of the Sacrament of the Lord's Supper is an important and fundamental part of that worship, and it is this intense and genuine worship, this prayerful spirit that will bring . . . light and inspiration.[49]

Attending Church meetings was the most important thing to do on the Sabbath, and according to President Kimball, resting did not mean "indolent lounging about the home all day or puttering around in the garden, but a consistent attendance at meetings for the worship of the Lord." President Kimball told the Saints they should not expect to go to Sabbath meetings to be entertained or amused but should go to worship. He was clear that worshipping during the sacrament meeting was the responsibility of the individual member: "If the Sacrament meeting is a failure to you, you are the one that has failed. No one can worship for you, you must do your own serving of the Lord."[50]

In the April general conference of 1946, Elder Marion G. Romney said that it was of overwhelming importance to have regular attendance of sacrament meetings and also gave a promise to the Saints if they would go to church: "If we will increase our attendance from about twenty percent to forty percent, we shall double our spiritual power for righteousness in the world."[51]

Individual Internalization

As time went on, counsel from General Authorities in relationship to Sabbath-day observance became more internal, less rigid, and less explicit. This type of instruction appeared first sporadically and then with more and more frequency. In April 1915, President Joseph F. Smith began to give this type of counsel: "God made or designated the Sabbath day for a day of rest, day of worship, a day for goodly deeds, and for humility and penitence, and the worship of the Almighty in spirit and in truth."[52] Here specific rules were not mentioned. Latter-day Saints were not told exactly what goodly deeds to do, only that they were to do them. President Francis M. Lyman of the Quorum of the Twelve also gave some very general counsel when he instructed that on the Sabbath, Latter-day Saints should "refrain from all labor, from all secular and improper pleasures, and spend the day in the service and worship of the Lord."[53] Again, the Saints were told to spend the day in service and worship but were not told what that entailed. Listeners in general conference had to internalize what such instruction meant for each one of them in their individual lives.

A few years later in 1923, Elder James E. Talmage simply told the Saints that they were not obeying the law if they were idle, and he instructed, "We should be active and in service, but Sabbath-day work should be directly the service of God and not the secular and wage-earning service of man."[54] This vague counsel left it up to the individual to decide what "the service of God" entailed. Presiding Bishop Sylvester Cannon was aware that many Latter-day Saints did not want this new type of counsel; instead, they wanted a list so that they could justify doing something if it was not declared unacceptable by the leaders of the Church. In April 1926 General Conference, Bishop Cannon gave a broad definition of what was appropriate without defining specific activities that would break the Sabbath:

> Many people question at times how we should observe it, or what it is that might be considered as breaking the Sabbath. Surely anything that interferes with the spirit of peace conformable to the Sabbath is breaking the Sabbath. There should be nothing that interferes with our worship or that causes our minds to be diverted, nor any act of ours that causes our minds to be detracted from the spirit of that day; but in all of our acts upon that day we should exercise and devote our minds and thoughts to those things that shall help us to grow in faith, in righteousness and in good works.[55]

Except for these sparse examples cited above, most other counsel for Sabbath-day observance was very explicit. It was not until the 1980s that most of the General Authorities gave counsel that was broad and self-determined. For instance, in 1991 Elder Marvin J. Ashton of the Quorum of the Twelve Apostles gave direction about each Latter-day Saint's personal involvement with the Sabbath. He instructed, "Sometimes the freedoms and blessings of the Sabbath can be lost by attitudes that allow selfishness and lack of personal involvement in tried-and-true patterns. Sabbath days can be lost an hour at a time. Sabbath days can be lost an outing at a time."[56]

Sacrament Spirituality

Though counsel during the last two decades of the twentieth century took on a more general, less detailed tone, one constant was always present in teachings about hallowing the Sabbath: the sacrament was to be the preeminent activity for Latter-day Saints on Sunday. Whereas earlier, attending all Church meetings had been of great importance, what was done during the sacrament became the focus in the twenty-first century. The sacrament service became even more internalized as the years went by. By way of illustration, in 2006 Elder L. Tom Perry of the Quorum of the Twelve Apostles shared his memory of how when he was a little child, beautiful music was played during the passing of the sacrament. He then explained that this practice was stopped because General Authorities wanted the minds of the Latter-day Saints to focus on the atoning sacrifice of their Lord and Savior, Jesus Christ. Elder Perry also gave some individually prescribed counsel, suggesting that during the administration of the sacrament, Latter-day Saints set aside the world. As he put it, the sacrament should be a "period of spiritual renewal as we recognize the deep spiritual significance of the ordinance offered to each of us personally. If we were to become casual in partaking of the sacrament, we would lose the opportunity for spiritual growth."[57]

Elder L. Tom Perry spoke on the importance of the sacrament in 1984 as well as in 2006. In 1984 he explained, "Partaking of the sacrament [is] basic for our observance of the Lord's day."[58] He spoke of the power of the sacrament for each individual by telling the story of a poor woman who faithfully went to church every week. Her husband, however, did not. Week after week, she urged him, but he wouldn't go. "Finally, tiring of her pestering, he said, 'Give me one good reason why I should go to church.' Her reply was, 'I can't explain to you why I go. All I can tell you is that I go in empty and come out full.'"[59] As illustrated in this story, counsel about the sacrament was now about thoughts, feelings, and attitudes rather than behaviors and actions.

This type of counsel was very pronounced in the general conference held directly after the Sabbath-day leadership training mentioned at the beginning of this chapter. In October 2015, three General Authorities all gave the same kind of counsel that concentrated on emotions and spirituality. Elder Claudio R. M. Costa of the First Quorum of the Seventy disclosed:

> While pondering on the Sabbath day, I felt a deep gratitude for the blessing and privilege of being able to partake of the sacrament. For me that is a very solemn, sacred, and spiritual moment. . . . The sacrament is . . . a time for Heavenly Father to teach us about the Atonement of His Beloved Son—Our Savior, Jesus Christ—and for us to receive revelation about it. . . . It is a time for us to reverently ask God for this knowledge. And if we do, I have no doubt that we will receive this knowledge, which will bless our lives beyond measure. I love the Sabbath, the sacrament, and what they mean.[60]

Elder D. Todd Christofferson concurred when he pointed out, "The wards and branches of the Church offer a weekly gathering of respite and renewal, a time and place to leave the world behind—the Sabbath. It is a day to 'delight thyself in the Lord,' to experience the spiritual healing that comes with the sacrament, and to receive the renewed promise of His Spirit to be with us."[61] In addition, President Henry B. Eyring said, "You know from the words of the sacrament prayer how that promise is fulfilled . . . 'that they may *always* have his Spirit to be with them.' . . . For that reason alone, it is easy to see why the Lord's servants have tried to increase our desire to worship God in our sacrament meetings. If we partake of the sacrament in faith, the Holy Ghost will then be able to protect us and those we love from the temptations that come with increasing intensity and frequency."[62]

Devotion and Personal Application

In 1991, Elder James E. Faust made a very clear demarcation that Sabbath-day doings were no longer going to be defined by official counsel from General Authorities. That responsibility was now clearly under the jurisdiction of each Latter-day Saint. He acknowledged:

> Where is the line as to what is acceptable and unacceptable on the Sabbath? Within the guidelines, each of us must answer this question for ourselves. While these guidelines are contained in the scriptures and in the words of the modern prophets, they must also be written in our hearts and governed by our conscience. . . . It is quite unlikely that there will be any serious violation of Sabbath worship if we come humbly before the Lord and offer him all our heart, our soul, and our mind. (See Matt. 22:37.) . . . What is worthy or unworthy on

> the Sabbath day will have to be judged by each of us by trying to be honest with the Lord. On the Sabbath day we should do what we have to do and what we ought to do in an attitude of worshipfulness and then limit our other activities.[63]

Here Elder Faust was clearly placing keeping the covenant of hallowing the Sabbath Day in the realm of personal accountability. Though some Latter-day Saints were clamoring for another list of "acceptable" and "unacceptable" activities, Elder Faust placed Sabbath-day decisions squarely on the shoulders of each individual.

In 1999, then-Elder Dallin H. Oaks of the Quorum of the Twelve Apostles made it clear that specific rules about the Sabbath were a thing of the past. He stated, "Teachers who are commanded to teach 'the principles of [the] gospel' and 'the doctrine of the kingdom' (D&C 88:77) should generally forgo teaching specific rules or applications. For example, . . . they would not provide a list of *dos* and *don'ts* for keeping the Sabbath day holy." Elder Oaks was clear that once teachers have "taught the doctrine and the associated principles from the scriptures and the living prophets, such specific applications or rules are generally the responsibility of individuals and families."[64] Sabbath-day instruction had covered the same path that the children of Israel had trod; it had gone from rules and regulations to devotion and personal application.

Elder Quentin L. Cook described the result of this new form of Sabbath counsel in October 2015 General Conference: "For members of The Church of Jesus Christ of Latter-day Saints, honoring the Sabbath is a form of righteousness that will bless and strengthen families, connect us with our Creator, and increase happiness. The Sabbath can help separate us from that which is frivolous, inappropriate, or immoral. It allows us to be in the world but not of the world."[65]

Additionally, in 2015 President Russell M. Nelson used his own life experience as a pattern for what had happened Church-wide in Sabbath-day counsel. He disclosed that as a youth he had participated in the Mosaic approach to the Sabbath, in which he had studied others who had a compiled list of things to do and things not to do. He then explained how the Sabbath day later became internalized in his life:

> It wasn't until later that I learned from the scriptures that my conduct and my attitude on the Sabbath constituted a sign between me and

my Heavenly Father. With that understanding, I no longer needed lists of dos and don'ts. When I had to make a decision whether or not an activity was appropriate for the Sabbath, I simply asked myself, "What *sign* do I want to give to God?" That question made my choices about the Sabbath day crystal clear. Though the doctrine pertaining to the Sabbath day is of ancient origin, it has been renewed in these latter days as part of a new covenant with a promise.[66]

Home-Centered Gospel Learning

In 2018, as Russell M. Nelson became the prophet, he declared that it was "time for a *home-centered Church,* supported by what takes place inside our branch, ward, and stake buildings."[67] Elder David A. Bednar, acting as the voice to introduce this new program, declared that members of the Church "should not expect the Church as an organization to teach or tell us everything we need to know and do to become devoted disciples and endure valiantly to the end."[68] Instead there would now be a more personal responsibility for each member to learn the gospel and choose to live it. Elder M. Russell Ballard related this new program to the joy that President Nelson talked about experiencing on the Sabbath Day. He declared that home-centered gospel learning is "an important way to find joy and happiness in our lives." Speaking of the new way to worship on the Sabbath, he said, "The Sabbath-day adjustments that emphasize home-centered, Church-supported gospel learning and studying are an opportunity to renew our spirit and our devotion to God within the walls of our homes. What could possibly be more simple, basic, and profound?"[69]

In order to help members of the Church bring the Gospel more fully into their homes, starting in January 2019, organized church services were reduced from a three-hour block to a two-hour block.[70] This change allowed members to have more time on Sundays to teach and learn the gospel together in their homes as families, which is the "ultimate setting for learning, living, and becoming" more like the Savior.[71] With this new two-hour block, the *Come, Follow Me* program was also instituted to subsidize gospel learning in the home.

The Sabbath as a Delight and Sign of Our Devotion

With the current emphasis on Sabbath-day observance by the First Presidency and Quorum of the Twelve, a new way of looking at our part in the covenant of hallowing the Sabbath has taken place. Recent apostles have talked about how living the commandment to keep the Sabbath day holy is an individual commitment that signifies our love for the Lord. Detailed lists of dos and don'ts for keeping the Sabbath day holy are no longer taught. Moreover, President Russell M. Nelson challenged Latter-day Saints to write this perpetual covenant in their hearts.[72]

As General Authority counsel has evolved from Mosaic rules to personal devotion, President Nelson described the difference that following such counsel has made in the lives of Latter-day Saints: "A sacred Sabbath truly is a delight."[73] Likewise, Elder Quentin L. Cook also pronounced the improvement that had come about with the direction members had been given about hallowing the Sabbath day. In the October 2015 General Conference he disclosed:

> In the last six months, a most remarkable change has occurred in the Church. This has been in the response of the members to renewed emphasis on the Sabbath by the First Presidency and Quorum of the Twelve and to President Russell M. Nelson's challenge to make the Sabbath a delight. Many members understand that truly keeping the Sabbath day holy is a refuge from the storms of this life. It is also a sign of our devotion to our Father in Heaven and an increased understanding of the sacredness of sacrament meeting. Still, we have a long way to go, but we have a wonderful beginning. I challenge all of us to continue to embrace this counsel and improve our Sabbath worship.[74]

The reason that General Authority counsel has changed from a list of dos and don'ts to suggestions in recent trainings is unclear. Many reasons can be postulated for this transformation. Recently it was pointed out that General Authorities did not want to prescribe what to do and not to do on the Sabbath.[75] One reason might be that Latter-day Saints are now living in a time when they use agency more wisely to make decisions on their own. Another cause for this lack of specifics might be that Latter-day Saints will qualify for even more blessings as they individually receive their own revelation about appropriate Sabbath-day activities. Whatever the reason, one thing is clear as we study the evolution of counsel on this subject. Unlike the previous generations, the responsibility has now shifted from leaders to individual members and home-centered gospel learning to find out what the Lord would have Latter-day Saints do.

Promises and blessings have expanded as this new responsibility has been given. As Elder L. Whitney Clayton of the Presidency of the Seventy described, "The day would become sweeter for them individually, sweeter for them as families, sweeter for all the members of the Church. Their faith would be deepened, their ability to move ahead in life with confidence and optimism and happiness at home and at church and in every situation would be amplified by their having turned to the Lord more fully on the Sabbath Day."[76] As Latter-day Saints embrace Sabbath-day counsel that emphasizes inner strength, spirituality, and faith rather than temporal rules, Sabbath worship will become a delight and a sign of each Latter-day Saint's devotion.

Endnotes

1. The Church of Jesus Christ of Latter-day Saints, "Church Leaders Call for Better Observance of Sabbath Day," news release, June 30, 2015, https://newsroom.churchofjesuschrist.org/article/church-leaders-call-for-better-observance-of-sabbath-day.
2. Russell M. Nelson, "The Sabbath is a Delight," *Ensign* or *Liahona*, May 2015, 129–130.
3. Church History Topics, "Sacrament Meetings," https://www.churchofjesuschrist.org/study/history/topics/sacrament-meetings.
4. Trent Toone, "Church Meeting Schedules Will Change in 2019. Here's a Short History of Past Schedules," *Deseret News*, October 6, 2018, https://www.deseret.com/2018/10/6/20655341/church-meeting-schedules-will-change-in-2019-here-s-a-short-history-of-past-schedules.
5. Toone, "Church Meeting Schedules."
6. "Church Consolidates Meeting Schedules," *Ensign*, March 1980, 73, https://www.churchofjesuschrist.org/study/ensign/1980/03/news-of-the-church/church-consolidates-meeting-schedules.
7. Russell M. Nelson, "Opening Remarks," *Ensign* or *Liahona*, November 2018, 7–8.
8. Brigham Young, at a Special Conference held in the Tabernacle, Salt Lake City, August 29, 1852. Reported by G. D. Watt in *Journal of Discourses* (London: Latter-day Saints' Book Depot, 1854–86), 6:277–78.
9. John W. Taylor, in *Journal of Discourses* (London: Latter-day Saints' Book Depot, 1854–86), 10:113.
10. Joseph Fielding Smith, in Conference Report, April 1911, 86.
11. "Church Leaders Call for Better Observance of Sabbath Day."
12. James E. Faust, "The Lord's Day," *Ensign*, November 1991, 35.
13. George Albert Smith, in Conference Report, October 1950, 7; see also George Albert Smith, in Conference Report, October 1935, 119–20.
14. Joseph Fielding Smith, in Conference Report, October 1935, 14.
15. Sylvester Q. Cannon, in Conference Report, October 1928, 48–49; Spencer W. Kimball, "Why Call Me Lord, Lord, and Do Not the Things Which I Say?," *Ensign*, May 1975, 7; N. Eldon Tanner, in Conference Report, April 1970, 64–65;

L. Tom Perry, "Obedience to Law is Liberty," *Ensign* or *Liahona*, May 2013, 87; James E. Faust, "Lord's Day," 33–35; and Russell M. Nelson, "Self-Mastery," *Ensign*, November 1985, 30.

16. James E. Faust, "Lord's Day," 33.
17. L. Tom Perry, "Obedience to Law is Liberty," *Ensign* or *Liahona*, May 2013, 87.
18. J. Reuben Clark Jr., in Conference Report, October 1949, 107–108.
19. Joseph Fielding Smith, in Conference Report, October 1938, 38; LeGrand Richards, in Conference Report, October 1947, 73; George Albert Smith, in Conference Report, April 1947, 161; and Gordon B. Hinckley, "An Ensign to the Nations," *Ensign*, November 1989, 51.
20. Gordon B. Hinckley, "Ensign to the Nations," 51.
21. *Wilford Woodruff's Journal*, ed. Scott G. Kenney, vol. 3 (Midvale, UT: Signature Books, 1983), 235. See also Joseph Fielding Smith, in Conference Report, October 1938, 38.
22. George Albert Smith, in Conference Report, April 1947, 161.
23. Wilford Woodruff, in *Journal of Discourses*, 21:191.
24. George Albert Smith, in Conference Report, October 1948, 188.
25. David O. McKay, in Conference Report, October 1956, 90.
26. Spencer W. Kimball, Conference Report, October 1953, 55.
27. Spencer W. Kimball, "Hold Fast to the Iron Rod," *Ensign*, November 1978, 6.
28. Mark E. Peterson, "Remember the Sabbath Day," *Ensign*, May 1975, 49.
29. Joseph F. Smith, in Conference Report, September 1871.
30. Joseph F. Smith, in Conference Report, October 1901, 1–2.
31. George Albert Smith, in Conference Report, April 1923, 78.
32. Spencer W. Kimball, "God Will Not Be Mocked," *Ensign*, November 1974, 6.
33. George A. Smith, in *Journal of Discourses*, 10:60.
34. Francis M. Lyman, in Conference Report, October 1900, 77.
35. Francis M. Lyman, in Conference Report, October 1908, 58.
36. John Henry Smith, in Conference Report, April 1906, 83–84.
37. Joseph F. Merrill, in Conference Report, April 1949, 29.
38. J. Reuben Clark Jr., in Conference Report, October 1949, 110.
39. J. Reuben Clark Jr., in Conference Report, October 1949, 110.
40. Spencer W. Kimball, *The Miracle of Forgiveness* (Salt Lake City: Bookcraft, 1969), 96–97.
41. Spencer W. Kimball, "Hold Fast to the Iron Rod," 6.
42. Spencer W. Kimball, "Rendering Service to Others," *Ensign*, May 1981, 45.
43. Hyrum M. Smith, in Conference Report, October 1906, 43.
44. George Albert Smith, in Conference Report, April 1908, 34–35.
45. Anthon H. Lund, in Conference Report, October 1907, 9.
46. Lund, in Conference Report, October 1916, 11.
47. Lund, in Conference Report, October 1916, 10.
48. Rudger J. Clawson, in Conference Report, October 1916, 36–37.
49. Richard R. Lyman, in Conference Report, April 1936, 99.
50. Spencer W. Kimball, in Conference Report, April 1944, 145.
51. Marion G. Romney, in Conference Report, April 1946, 40.
52. Joseph F. Smith, in Conference Report, April 1915, 10.
53. Francis M. Lyman, in Conference Report, October 1908, 57.

54. James E. Talmage, in Conference Report, April 1923, 141.
55. Sylvester Q. Cannon, in Conference Report, April 1926, 93.
56. Marvin J. Ashton, "Strengthen the Feeble Knees," *Ensign*, November 1991, 71.
57. L. Tom Perry, "As Now We Take the Sacrament," *Ensign*, May 2006, 41.
58. L. Tom Perry, "And Why Call Ye Me, Lord, Lord, and Do Not the Things Which I Say?," *Ensign*, November 1984, 19.
59. Rick Walton and Fern Oviatt, eds., *Stories for Mormons* (Salt Lake City: Bookcraft, 1983), 112, quoted in Perry, "Why Call Ye Me," 19.
60. Claudio R. M. Costa, "That They Do Always Remember Him," *Ensign* or *Liahona*, November 2015, 101–103.
61. D. Todd Christofferson, "Why the Church," *Ensign* or *Liahona*, November 2015, 109.
62. Henry B. Eyring, "The Holy Ghost as Your Companion," *Ensign* or *Liahona*, November 2015, 104.
63. James E. Faust, "Lord's Day," 35.
64. Dallin H. Oaks, "Gospel Teaching," *Ensign*, November 1999, 79.
65. Quentin L. Cook, "Shipshape and Bristol Fashion: Be Temple Worthy—in Good Times and Bad Times," *Ensign* or *Liahona*, November 2015, 41–42.
66. Russell M. Nelson, "Sabbath Is a Delight," 130.
67. Russell M. Nelson, "Opening Remarks," *Ensign* or *Liahona*, November 2018, 7.
68. David A. Bednar, "Prepared to Obtain Every Needful Thing," *Ensign* or *Liahona*, May 2019, 102.
69. M. Russell Ballard, "The True, Pure, and Simple Gospel of Jesus Christ," *Ensign* or *Liahona*, May 2019, 29.
70. Quentin L. Cook, "Deep and Lasting Conversion to Heavenly Father and the Lord Jesus Christ," *Ensign* or *Liahona*, November 2018, 8–11.
71. David A. Bednar, "Prepared to Obtain Every Needful Thing," *Ensign* or *Liahona*, May 2019, 102.
72. Russell M. Nelson, "Sabbath Is a Delight," 129–132.
73. Russell M. Nelson, "Sabbath Is a Delight," 132.
74. Quentin L. Cook, "Shipshape and Bristol Fashion," 42.
75. "Church Leaders Call for Better Observance of Sabbath Day."
76. "Sabbath Day Observance: an interview with M. Russell Ballard, L. Whitney Clayton, and Rosemary M. Wixom," Church Newsroom, June 2015, video, 14:05, available for download at the following link: https://web.archive.org/web/20150702224722/http://www.mormonnewsroom.org/article/church-leaders-call-for-better-observance-of-sabbath-day.

Chapter Twelve

"The Erosion of Sabbath Worship is Now Extensive": The Imperative to Learn Holiness from Other Religious Traditions

Andrew C. Reed

For Latter-day Saints, the Sabbath occupies a vital link to lived religious ritual and tradition. It is a day of community association and communal education, a day of sacrality through sacramental participation, and often a dedicated time for family gathering. The Sabbath day has been at the center of recent Latter-day Saint reforms and institutional adjustments geared toward improving Sabbath observance. As the explicit intent of this chapter (and the volume of which it is a part) is to aid interested readers in expanding appreciation for Sabbath observance, the approach here will attempt to provide a wide set of evidence for the holy day's place among other religious traditions. The hope in this chapter is that readers will find this approach to the Sabbath useful in developing a deeper understanding of why the biblical command remains relevant and essential for lived religious experience today. Additionally, by expanding the examples and insights to include other religious traditions, a more creative approach to Sabbath observance may be identified that allows readers to situate their Sabbath day observance to their specific needs and experiences.

Such an effort to identify and bring into conversation different views of "Sabbath" among religious traditions faces a few challenges. First, there is the problem of scope; there are essentially two world religions (with billions of members and numerous denominational branches within them) that maintain Sabbath observance as part of their lived devotional life today—namely, Christianity and Judaism.[1] With such a large population and so many denominations, there will naturally be a myriad of differing opinions about Sabbath purpose and practices. Second, but not untethered from the first concern, is the question of whether it is a legitimate scholarly endeavor to draw parallels between these two diverse traditions of Christianity and Judaism that the communities themselves might not naturally draw. In approaching the study of a religious tradition that is not our own, it is wise practice to allow the practitioners of that religion to speak for themselves whenever possible. To accommodate this desire to hear the voices of religious adherents throughout this chapter, scriptural and community sources are used to provide evidence for the claims made herein. It is important to keep in mind that even when a canonized text is used to explain a particular concept or idea, these texts are never to be fully understood outside of the hermeneutical tradition and individual or collective ways of reading the text.

A third point of caution is that speaking of too many traditions too broadly usually misrepresents some aspect of a religious community and its practices. In order to limit this kind of overgeneralization I will, where possible, attempt to clarify to which denomination a text or interpretive voice belongs.

To illustrate the blessings of understanding the place of the Sabbath in more rich and inspiring ways, this chapter will proceed in the following way. First, I will analyze why this effort by religious communities to reengage believers with the Sabbath, including efforts by leaders of The Church of Jesus Christ of Latter-day Saints, has necessarily involved thinking about the secular. I will use this information to lay out what is truly at stake in this Sabbath conversation. Next, the discussion will move to ways that Jews and Christians think about sacred time, including the Sabbath. Finally, we will look at potential applications for Latter-day Saints in their effort to keep holy this sacred day.

Being in the World with Religious Identities

The modern world poses significant challenges to those who hold faith and ritual as central elements of their identity and whose lived experience leads them to frame their worldview through a particular religious vantage point. The modern worldview, shaped through a post-Enlightenment lens, pushes away from the mysterious and numinous toward the rational, reproducible safety of a secular stance. Because of this, capturing deeply mysterious, spirit-infused moments of revelation and inspiration can, for many of us, seem near impossible at times. The difficulty of obtaining revelatory moments forces seekers into one of at least two possible stances: either there is no hope of receiving revelatory insight, or such revelation is entirely dependent upon external forces. The pursuit of divine inspiration, with its incumbent motivational impetus and requisite demand of action, is often described as too distant or too difficult to access in the harried minutes of the everyday. One might suppose, given this frame, that the modern world is, above all else, antithetical to spirituality. However, this resigned perspective reflects too easily the subtractive thesis of secularization that has been challenged in recent years. In his collected meditations, Latter-day Saint author Samuel Brown described the modern world in this way:

> One area where I sense a substantial and growing blindness is in how we in this current age—with its glistening technology and accompanying ecological crisis, of individual self-fashioning and ruptured communities, of public secularism and private spiritual distress—tend to think about God and life in God. Entire categories of belief and life have been classified as outside the scope of polite society.[2]

Brown drew much of his thinking about the modern world from the writing of Charles Taylor, a Christian philosopher whose work on the secular has become standard reading for those studying the roles of belief and faith in today's world. Taylor described this gradual removal of the theocentric involvement in the world as the result of the rise of "alternative construals of fulness."[3] According to some perspectives, God, as an explanatory force in the natural world, has been supplanted with more naturalistic interpretations of phenomena, the consequences of which are manifest in many forms. The modern retraction from God's will as explanation for earthquakes, floods, and illness has put new interpretive models in play. However, as Taylor made clear, this was not the subtractive removal of God, but rather the emergence of new alternatives to give reason and purpose to observable occurrences. Given this "disenchantment" of the world since the European Enlightenment period, many religious adherents feel under attack because their willingness to allow God to continually serve as explanation for some phenomena runs afoul at times of the more dominant secular explanatory models. According to one hardline set of atheistic writers known collectively as the "Four Horsemen," faithful explanations of God's work without empirical evidence have become the peddled wares of the irrational, the uneducated, or the duped.[4]

This direct dismissal of religion's validity has been challenged by another atheist, Tim Crane, who argued that the Four Horsemen have missed a critical piece of the religious puzzle today:

> Contemporary atheist accounts tend to present religion as a kind of primitive cosmology—a primitive or proto-scientific theory of the universe as a whole—or as simply a moral code, or as some combination of these two things. While I think there are both cosmological and moral elements in religious belief, I reject the reduction in religious belief, I reject the reduction of religious belief to either of them, or even to their combination. Religious belief is not simply a cosmology or simply a morality, and it is not simply a cosmology-plus-morality.[5]

For Crane, what is missing from the New Atheists'[6] stance toward religion is an appreciative capacity to see belief as a purposeful effort toward discovering the "meaning of life."[7] The episteme of belief requires a willingness toward suspension of disbelief when there is no evidentiary certitude. Therefore, within the modern world, we see two epistemological frames. Where New Atheism has decried anything other than scientific explanation, religious people continue to allow for divine presence here and now to provide a sense of purpose.[8] The will to believe remains in the world and in religious communities. In fact, it is ironic that atheists often push religious believers to abandon core beliefs because when atheists do so, they sometimes actually shore up believers' desire to enliven their religious activity.

Latter-day Saints have faced these issues head-on in past decades and continue to do so today. In 1934, Latter-day Saint writer Elsie Talmage Brandley laid bare the challenge that religious believers face by operating within a scaffolding of knowledge that is both religious and secular. In a critical speech to youth leaders in The Church of Jesus Christ of Latter-day Saints, Brandley reiterated the necessity of questions as pathways to answers and discovery. With clear recognition of the apparent challenge of science to religion, Brandley suggested that it was the knowledge of the "fundamental truths of the gospel" that "leave one free to go far and wide, anchored by that knowledge, in search of all else that earth and sea and skies have to teach."[9]

The tensions between our deeply held religious beliefs and the epistemology that shapes how we act in the world were not new in 1934, and they remain ever present in modern society. In the foreword to Steven Peck's *Evolving Faith*, scholar George Handley suggests that "seeking to understand life, the universe, and everything . . . is an infinite, impossible, and yet indispensable human task that seems to mimic the divine mind."[10] The complexity of this task forces us to negotiate the sometimes all-too-tangible tension between the world we hope for and the one we actually live in.

Part of the frustration for those who value and employ the divine as a causational element of life is the seeming lack of spiritual elements in the lives of friends, neighbors, and colleagues. More frustrating still to some religious believers is the fact that their neighbors seem so unaware of this gaping hole in their personal lives. James K. A. Smith described this difficulty in encountering people who disavow religious affiliation:

> You're a pastor or a church planter who has moved to Brooklyn or Berkeley or Boulder. Maybe you received a call to transplant yourself from Georgia or Grand Rapids or some other "religious" region of the country, sensing a burden to proclaim the gospel in one of the many so-called "godless" urban regions of North America. You've left your Jerusalem on a mission to Babylon. You came with what you thought were all the answers to the unanswered questions these "secular" people had. But it didn't take long for you to realize that the questions weren't just unanswered; they were unasked. And they weren't questions. That is, your "secular" neighbors aren't looking for "answers"—for some bit of information that is missing from their mental maps. You've realized that instead of nagging questions about God or the afterlife, your neighbors are oriented by all sorts of longings and "projects" and quests for significance. There doesn't seem to be anything "missing" from their lives—so you can't just come proclaiming the good news of a Jesus who fills their "God-shaped hole." They don't have any sense that the "secular" lives they've constructed are missing a second floor. In many ways, they have constructed webs of meaning that provide

> almost all the significance they need in their lives (though a lot hinges on that "almost").[11]

For Brown, Taylor, and Smith, the challenge that confronts modern religious individuals is one of displacement, not replacement. Taylor argues that disenchantment in society eroded human beings' dependency on religion as an explanatory source, and thus it became one among many options for explaining the world around us. The place of religion in society has shifted, but it most definitely has not been replaced by some other institution. In the modern world, as religion has become identified as a distinctive element of society in parallel with an emergent secular element, religious identity is at the core of many human understandings of the self.[12] The frame has always been malleable, but recently religion has become one among many variables that people use to determine self-understanding.[13] Within the changed context of the modern period and a broader set of categories for the formation of self-conception, religious people often negotiate a competitive relationship with secular versions of identity. Many people are entirely comfortable being in the world without dependence upon the divine to explain or to act within modern society. This reality, while foreign to many religious people, forces those who preserve room for God to hold those views publicly, though they often do so timidly.

Connected to this notion of a disenchanted world—that is, the long-term societal decentralization of religious affiliation from collective and individual identity construction—the modern religious person faces challenges in their efforts to find a place and context for religious belonging. In our effort to build the familiar frames of reference that provide a sense of unity with the surrounding environment, we as religious individuals often face a discomforting realization: we do not belong here. Elder Marvin J. Ashton once noted, "When we have a yearning and don't know what it is for, perhaps it's our soul longing for its heartland, longing to be no longer alienated from the Lord and the pursuit of something higher, better, and more fulfilling than anything this earth has to offer."[14] As remarkable as this sentiment of longing for a spiritual heartland is, there are competing factors at play in our search for belonging. James K. A. Smith suggested the following difficulties:

> Ours is a pilgrimage without a destination—which is to say, it's not a pilgrimage at all but rather a pilgrimage deferred, not because we

> stay home but because we revel in the roaming, or at least try to talk ourselves into that. Our ancestors sang psalms of ascent as they marched to Zion or made the arduous hajj to Mecca or wended their way to Canterbury. We've inherited their pilgrim penchant, but it's morphed into unsettledness, a baseline antsy feeling that leaves us never feeling at home (which brings to mind the Freudian notion of the "uncanny," the *Unheimlich*, not-at-home-ness). We're always on the move, restless, vaguely chasing something rather than oriented to a destination.[15]

Roth suggested that in our search for the divine, we act on the Sabbath in a way to see ourselves "among the work of his hands"—a work that pushed God to rest after the sixth creative period.[16] So intense is daily human existence that God insisted upon rest, realignment, and renewal as central elements of our individual and collective refinement through Sabbath observance. God modeled this for us on the seventh day—a day to be reminded of eternity rather than that which is most proximate. Therefore, in our efforts as religious beings and as religious communities to find God, we often strive to emulate God's act of rest.

The Institution of the Sabbath and Sacred Time

Observance of a Sabbath day is a practice limited to Judaism and Christianity. Thus, other authors in this volume have drawn upon a long-held set of practices and teachings that are housed within the Torah, Talmud, New Testament, and elsewhere to explain the history of the Sabbath day. This territory is well trodden and will not be dealt with extensively here; instead it will be used to shape the discussion about some of the contemporary Sabbath-day concerns felt by practitioners within these two religious traditions. While only Judaism and Christianity have a concrete Sabbath set aside, many other religious practitioners hold similar concerns about the loss of sacred ritual and time. Islam, as we will examine later, is instructive for thinking about the ways that sacred time is maintained in a secular age where people of opposing faiths engage productively or destructively with one another. After a review of how other religious practitioners view the Sabbath and aspects of sacred or holy time, some reflection from a Latter-day Saint vantage point suggests possible applications of these varying ideas.

The Sabbath, as an institution, was biblically instated and thereby fits within Jewish and Christian liturgical and ritual cycles. The Sabbath historically occupied a central organizing function for much of religious life within these two traditions, and the emergence of a distinctive Christian community separate from its Jewish roots led to the gradual move away from the close connection of Jewish Shabbat practices among Christians.

Readers will remember how Jewish scripture has repeatedly recalled and reminded Jews from all time periods about their obligation to observe the Sabbath properly and the attached blessings attained through doing so. The author(s) of the *Sefer Ha-Zohar* (Book of Radiance), a thirteenth-century Jewish mystical text closely associated with the thought of Moses de Leon of Guadalajara, argued in tractate 1:14a that there are two commandments associated with the Sabbath day: first, to "observe the Sabbath," and second, to accomplish the work of "endowing that day with holiness."[17] There are surely countless interpretations of what these two aspects of practice entail, but the act of "observing" the Sabbath seems to fall within the Decalogue's encouragement to "not do any work." Historically, it was the rabbis who sought to invest the Sabbath with special meaning through the articulation of 39 categories of "work" (*melachot*).[18] Even then, God and the rabbis knew that work is intrusive; there is always more of it, and there will always be our sense of needing to do something better. Thus the first commandment is to remember the Sabbath by setting aside a day without work. The secondary aspect, that of "remembering the sabbath day, to keep it holy" (Exodus 20:9–10), must bear more in mind than mere temporary reduction of labor. The dual commandment is one that many Christian and Jewish community leaders are now hoping to recover as a means to reenliven their sense of the Sabbath.

When religious people attempt to reform, recall, or adjust lived religious practice, the experience of other religious practitioners within and outside their own religions can be very helpful because these experiences can help practitioners to see new ways of thinking or even to recapture ideas that may have been a part of their tradition in the past but have slipped away. Just as Jewish observance of the Sabbath throughout history has served as an example of close adherence to the command to keep the day holy for Christians, it might be time for both communities to now look to each other for guidance in the promotion of a more dedicated religious practice.[19]

The "Erosion" of Sabbath Observance

Within Judaism and Christianity, the footprint of Sabbath observance and sacredness continues to bear influence on the modern world. However, the gradual move away from religious institutions generally as central organizing bodies in the public sphere has led to a reduced emphasis on the sacrality of time and space with regard to Sabbath observance. Increasingly, the Sabbath has become a remainder of ancient practices that people might dip into if or when they desired to connect with their religious community—and individual preference determines how and to what degree that observance might be manifested. In North America and Europe, the Sabbath as a day of rest for Christians has faced incursions from shopping centers and other sites of consumerism that choose to remain open on the Sabbath. Where once these were closed shops and silent malls, today there is competition for our attention on the Sabbath. While this may be a more recent development within Christianity, these challenges have been present for Jews for a much longer period, as the majority Christians have maintained Friday evening and Saturday as common days for work and other activities. In this way, it is important to recognize the community differences between these two religious groups, as well as the denominational experiences that allow for a much more nuanced context. This sense of loss of holiness on the day of rest for both traditions is not a new sentiment, but its rapid expansion is cause for concern and deep reflection on what is lost when the Sabbath (and the emphasis on sacred time more generally) exits the world. The disappearance of traditional Sabbath practices is lamented in many circles, including in this popular country music line: "Sunday was a day of rest / Now, it's one more day for progress / And we can't slow down / 'Cause more is less / It's all an endless process."[20] Gradual marginalization of observance through practice is eroding more than just the sense of being grounded in the tradition. Whole institutional strongholds are shaken if not continually renewed and reinvented by religious people.

The collected chapters of this volume speak to the enormity of the worldwide project to better understand the Sabbath's history, sacrality, and ritual importance for Latter-day Saints. Throughout history, not just a little ink has found its way onto page after page where writers have articulated the significance of the Sabbath for observant Jews and Christians. For millions of people, the Sabbath continues to mark the traditional day of rest and recommitment to God. However, as *The Oxford Dictionary of World Religions* suggested in the late 1990s, "the erosion of 'sabbath observance' is now extensive."[21] With such hopelessness about the Sabbath and its future, it comes as little surprise that the erosion of these key institutions in modern society seems to prelude the loss of more than just a set of rituals.

Anne McCue's folk-rock song "Stupid" summarizes this sense of potential loss well in its opening stanza: "Lennon said there are no institutions / There's nothing to believe anymore."[22] McCue's lyrics have several layers of wisdom. The sense that loss of institutions and frameworks preludes loss of belief motivates within many people the desire to reinstitute Sabbath practice in their own lives and in the world. Doing so, they seem to believe, will push belief in God and his covenant back into the world.

The challenge for the modern world is to reengage with millennia of deeply religious acts that refocus the sacred at the heart of society. President Russell M. Nelson stated, "God gave us this special day, not for amusement or daily labor but for a rest from duty, with physical and spiritual relief."[23] In recent years, both Jews and Christians (including Latter-day Saints) have found maintaining the Sabbath to be difficult for countless reasons, not the least of which is a compelling cultural shift away from religious adherence among growing numbers of the world's population. The distractions that pull people away from Sabbath worship are plentiful, and while as a society we have sought to maintain the injunction to "not do any work," the essential effort to maintain holiness seems to have slipped into a negotiation with our surrounding cultural environment.

It will be useful here to talk about the context of institutions and about the Sabbath as an institution. Institutions frame human social engagements and are built upon the existence of definable and repeatable rituals or actions that fill those spaces with meaning. In recent years, talk of the Sabbath as an institution has recirculated among religious communities as they try to capture both the physicality (ritual) of the weekly event and the meaning of the rituals and practices associated with it.[24] Jewish historian Cecil Roth has reflected on the common root of Judaism that Christianity splintered away from and identified the unique concerns that both traditions have emphasized in their own way. Roth makes clear that even with significant differences in the way the Sabbath was observed, Christians and Jews shared a central concern for human capacity to improve and realize a world made holy through their efforts to mend the broken (or fallen) world (*tikkun olam*):

> Men need a vision which gives meaning to moral striving. This can take the form of one or two ideals in which present inequalities are redressed, the one that of a perfected social order, the other that of a perfected individual life-cycle. Both these ideals took shape in the

> Hebraic tradition, the former receiving more stress in Judaism, the latter in Christianity. Although obviously compatible with one another they have appealed separately to different persons and different ages, and both have stimulated reflection, the one on the practical problem of social justice, the other on the religious problem of immortality. If one adds the institution of the Sabbath, which is nothing other than the voluntary limitation of the hours of labour which raises man above the beasts and asserts man's moral dignity as a human being, we have a trio of Hebraic ideals directly derived from the Old Testament which yet have a role to play in our civilisation.[25]

The Sabbath, which Roth apparently views as "nothing other than the voluntary limitation . . . of labour," is at the same time elevated as the mechanism for "asserting moral dignity." If the choice to restrict human work bears the power to elevate respect for human capacity to do good in the world, then our stewardship of the physical world, whether in agriculture or husbandry, signifies a sincere effort to put the created world, human existence, and God into proper relationship.

For Christians and Jews, Isaiah paints a similar call for first ushering in the Sabbath "Queen" (Talmud 119a) in holiness, and second, having done so, "seek[ing] the favor of the Lord" (Isaiah 58:13–14, Tanakh). Such readings of this text locate the Sabbath at the heart of each tradition, rather than as a negotiable aspect of ritual life. Exodus 20 provides clear evidence for acting differently on the Sabbath, as it is "the sabbath of the Lord thy God" and he "blessed" it and "hallowed it" (vv. 10–11). For Christians, the proper maintenance of the Sabbath ensures blessings, protections, and the extension of God's grace. The Christian tradition draws heavily upon the Jewish understanding of the Sabbath as a moment of ritual observance coupled with distinctive forms of hospitality, reverence, and study of sacred texts. The New Testament writers' frequency of mentioning the Jewish Sabbath as a setting for Jesus performing some noteworthy action, such as reading (see Luke 4:16), teaching (see Matthew 13), healing (see Luke 14:1–6), or even his resurrecting after the Sabbath (see Matthew 28:1 and parallels), locates the Sabbath as a central point of intersection between Jesus and the Jewish community in which he was a participant. Given this centrality, early Christians needed to work with the concept of Sabbath even as they sought to redefine the term and its practice for themselves in the early centuries after Christ.[26]

In the modern world, those who seek to understand the how and why of Sabbath observance are reinvesting in their sacred texts as a means of ensuring the blessings that are promised through the holy day. The Talmud shapes a similar sentiment for observing the Sabbath and maintaining proper ritual as a means of receiving divine blessings. In the Talmud the story of Joseph the Sabbath lover is instructive for all of us. After a Gentile miraculously recovers his jewel from a fish who had swallowed it, the Talmud reminds readers that "he who lends to the Sabbath—the Sabbath pays him back."[27] So important was the proper keeping of the Sabbath that Talmudic sages suggested that if the people could keep two full Sabbaths properly, the messiah would come. Israel would have been saved and not ruled over because keeping the Sabbath is the fulfillment of all *mitzvot* (commandments).[28] So while the Sabbath may be perceived as a prohibitive day where pleasures and self-willed enjoyment have no place, a deeper study of the ways in which the Sabbath can be celebrated should offer hope that the day becomes a day of rest that does more than while away time.

Latter-day Saints have a close connection to the concept of self-mastery as a method to exert control on the world around us. We believe that as we attain a higher moral relationship, we gain enlightenment and mastery of the physical world. Latter-day Saints have always emphasized a particular set of rituals that occur only in certain places or at certain times, not because they are inaccessible at other times, but because of Saints' efforts to place such rituals in proper relationship with other events in life and to invite God's power into the lives of those who partake of these ordinances (see Doctrine and Covenants 84:20–22; 88:66–68). Elsewhere in the Doctrine and Covenants, Joseph Smith was reminded of this need to seek moral purity; God told him, "go to the house of prayer and offer up thy sacraments upon my holy day; . . . inasmuch as ye do this, the fulness of the earth is yours" (Doctrine and Covenants 59:9, 16). Many who in the past have participated in Sunday School lessons about the Sabbath day have likely found themselves focused on the permissible and restricted activities involved in proper Sabbath observance. Perhaps the most common method for examining how to best live the Sabbath rituals and requirements is to turn to a list of dos and don'ts. Anyone who has undertaken such an effort must have concluded that this is also a surefire way to raise ire and discontent among religious adherents. One of the reasons people tend to get upset or uncomfortable in the prescriptive modes often employed when speaking of such "lists" is that teachers and preachers often attempt to encourage or enforce religious standards that might not have current application in the twenty-first century. Additionally, too often Christians juxtapose proper "spirit-filled" Sabbath observance against legalistic readings of the New Testament context between Jesus and his Jewish interlocutors. Doing so eliminates the space where Saints might learn from Jewish practices as sources of inspiration rather than degradation. Unfortunately for Christians, the default mode of reading scripture through a supersessionist lens causes Christian readers of the Bible to gloss over and misunderstand the purpose of Jewish Sabbath regulation. As a possible corrective, students of the Bible might venture on occasion into an informed reading of Jewish literature to look for aspects of deep respect for and observance of Sabbath. One might look to Mishnaic debates about whether a tailor with a needle or a scrivener with a pen ought to leave the house on Friday afternoon and, as a result, question the sanctity (or even relevancy) of the command as interpreted by the early rabbis.[29] But there is an alternative option: viewing such teachings as evidence of a strong desire to see a protection of the Sabbath through carefully constructed ritual practices. Christians in general and Latter-day Saints in particular can be inspired to take stock of where their rituals are in need of shoring up to better sanctify the day with holiness. With proper respect for another religion's sacred texts, we may thereby locate lessons that aid us in our effort to find truth and enlightenment about this central command to keep the Sabbath day holy.

Religious texts become sacred texts over time, and their transcendent value exponentially increases with longevity. Religious communities and their practitioners bring texts to life by fulfilling the rituals these texts inspire. Jewish efforts to "remember" and sanctify the Sabbath accomplish this every week even as they reinvent anew each week the forms of those rituals. Many modern readers of scripture too often look to sacred texts as a compendium of exact stipulations rather than as contextualized hypothetical examples to evoke the conversation about what a person should or should not do on the Sabbath. Perhaps with a more open set of expectations about what sacred texts could say to a modern world, and with a radically generous insistence on a hermeneutic of possibility, a new way of thinking on the subject can increase Sabbath "productivity" in the ways God seemed to intend. While the religious believer of any tradition has to deal with the reality that our sacred texts were written within a particular context with relation to specific people, the transcendence of the text across time can also inspire religious practitioners toward universal lessons and maxims.[30] Using as an example the *I Ching* (a ninth-century-BC Chinese text that bore influence for Confucianism, Taoism, and Buddhism), Hellmut Wilhelm suggested that while the book has its roots in the Zhou period of Chinese history, its lessons cross millennia: "The situations are always raised above temporal manifestations into a realm where they bear an archetypal character; historical recollections are used to illustrate the archetype but never to tie it to a particular manifestation. Thus the system of the text appears timeless, or above time."[31] Wilhelm's sentiment about the transcendent nature of religious text should be a good reminder that we read these inspired texts not because they were written in our day, but because their concerns speak to the human condition, the longings of human hearts, and the religious experiences with the divine had by others who lived long before us. When we can see a common desire to encounter the divine through our sacred texts, much can be revealed that is both pertinent and expansive in scope.

In very different ways, Christians have emphasized the aspect of remembrance as central to the work we do on the Sabbath day. Christians have longed for Sabbath observance to signal both a present belief in the need to recall creation and also as a means of enacting the very elements of ritual that connect them to the divine sacrifice of Jesus Christ. It is not insignificant that for Latter-day Saints the Sabbath is the day we are enjoined to "remember" as a means of receiving sanctification and blessings at the sacramental table (Moroni 4–5). Our desire to remember the crowning achievements of God in the past (that is, the Creation, the Atonement, the Resurrection) has led Christians to locate ritual around a particular day. The result for Christians then is to protect the day from incursions of the mundane activities of life. Failure to do so would inevitably shake the roots of Christian religious life—so the stakes are quite high.

Saving Sabbath—Isn't it about Time?

In its modern form, the Sabbath is characterized by rituals, space, and time. Each of these elements works variously across the Sabbath-observance traditions to highlight the sacrality of the period. The purpose of the Sabbath, both from its biblical origins and in its more recent Latter-day Saint emphasis, builds upon the need for a reflective engagement with sacred time. Sacred time, ensconced within creation, lends itself to a sense of imagination and renewal through the participants' temporal withdrawal from the mundane or profane. For practitioners, the effort to order the Sabbath begins with the process of demarcating the day differently than other days. This can happen through the employment of space or time. The demarcation through ritual often signals a change in space or time even if only through symbolic change. And, even then, the physical sensibilities of a day dedicated away from the mundane draws us nearer to a clarity of understanding and purpose. Dan Bellm's poem "Sabbath" excellently evokes this feeling of nearness and distance:

> Then will I carry
> you within me for as long
> as I can: not a
>
> consolation but
> a promise, and not because
> I must: not as you
>
> carried me but to
> be your keeper, a place where
> you remain the one
>
> bearing life: not as
> a god or idol that I
> have made too small, but
>
> only blessing you
> do I keep the blessing safe:
> infant image of
>
> the created one
> I long to be, Sabbath-self
> concealed in the guise
>
> of ordinary
> time, my life the covering
> that protects the vow.[32]

It is this longing for connection that seems to resonate with those who strive to keep the Sabbath day holy. The Sabbath was designed to become an event, or a site where an interconnected web of separation, concealment, and reparation make one whole again after a week of toil.

When we look at other religions and their protection of sacred time, there are some instructive points that might be drawn upon to shore up a Latter-day Saint effort toward holiness on the Sabbath. While there are only two world religions (in many different denominational stripes) that observe the Sabbath by divine command, other religious traditions can help us in identifying other ways of demarcating efforts to become holy through sanctification of a period of time. Such an exploration in its fullest form is far too large an undertaking for this chapter, but Islam might serve as a good case study on the ways that time and sanctification work in tandem. Islam teaches that there are five "pillars," or practices, that should become part of daily spiritual practice. These include *shahada* (declaration of faith), *salat* (prayer), *zakat* (alms), *sawm* (fasting), and *hajj* (pilgrimage). The most important moment when Muslims participate in prayer is *al-Juma*, which takes place on Friday afternoon. Muslims look to the Qur'an and the *sahih hadith* (authentic sayings of the Prophet Muhammad) for instruction as to why the Friday (*Yawm al-Jum'ah,* "day of gathering") afternoon prayers are considered vital to their well-being. While Islam does not maintain the Sabbath as practiced in the other Abrahamic traditions, there are historical references in central texts that do make an effort to identify a similarity across all three religions. According to Al-Bukhari's hadith, Muslims should think of their fulfillment of Friday prayers (*al-Juma*) as the most complete (updated) version of Jewish and Christian observances: "This was their day (Friday) on which the celebration was made compulsory for them but they differed about it. So Allah gave us the guidance for it (Friday) and all the other people are behind us in this respect: the Jews' (holy day) is tomorrow (Saturday) and the Christians' is the day after tomorrow (Sunday)."[33] From this we see that even very early on in the history of Islam, there were leading figures who focused on and thought about the Sabbath as a specific form of ritual activity that was meant to be protected from mundane violations of the everyday.

Time, regardless of duration, signals a requisite remembering of something outside of the profane world. It serves as a gathering point, bringing unity and strength to those who seek it. Collin Turner, a scholar of Islam, makes clear that Muslims do not maintain a day on which they withdraw from other daily activities in the way that Jews and Christians do, but the need to justify a complete (albeit temporary) abstention from work is clearly pointed out in the Qur'an.[34] God instructed Muhammad that "when the call to prayer is made on the day of assembly, hurry to the remembrance of God, and leave business aside. That is better for you, if (only) you knew. Then, when the prayer is finished, disperse on the earth and seek some favor from God. And remember God often, so that you may prosper. But when they see (the chance of) some (business) transaction or diversion, they rush off to it, and leave you standing. Say: 'What is with God is better than any diversion or transaction. God is the best of providers'" (Qur'an 62:9–11).[35] Muslims demarcate their sacred time by participating in the afternoon prayers, by abstaining from other mundane activities, and by gathering together in mosques in an effort to solidify the community's commitment to and the individual's participation in holy ritual. In this sense, there is a common Abrahamic concern among these three great religions to find locations and space for the preservation of a transcendent time.

In all of these traditions, prayer is deeply ingrained in the ritualization of the Sabbath. The engagement with God via prayer signals to oneself a reprioritization of the divine act of worshipping with community as well as a remembrance of the divine creation. The parallels from the Qur'anic passage above map easily onto Jewish and Christian approaches to the Sabbath. In Islam, the act of recalling a rest period as a culmination of the creative period is based in hadith literature, where Adam and Eve's creation is seen as a pinnacle of Godly creation (the sixth day). Given the holiness of the act of prayer, Muslims are told to bathe (perform ablutions) in preparation for the communal prayer.[36] This kind of preparation for holy engagement is likewise seen in Judaism, where ritual handwashing is accompanied by prayer before the Sabbath meal.

This necessary aspect of reconnection through withdrawal is a familiar framework for many religious rituals. While we build ways of distinguishing purpose through architectural means, the architecture of human life is less easily parceled apart. The demarcation of time provides the participant with a framework that encourages suspension of other activities in an otherwise distractable world. The Jewish philosopher Emmanuel Levinas suggested that we should think of "time not as a degradation of eternity, but as the relationship to *that* which—of itself unassimilable, absolutely other—would not allow itself to be assimilated by experience; or to that which—of itself infinite—would not allow itself to be comprehended."[37] The Sabbath alludes to the eternal without placing it only in the physical, earthly realm. It is the very pursuit of a relationship that remains only distantly viable that makes this demarcated time sacred. Levinas again insists that "time signifies

. . . this always of the relationship, an aspiration and an awaiting."[38] N. T. Wright, a Christian theologian, echoed a Jewish reading of the Psalms to remind Christians of this sense of anticipation: "God in his wisdom knows that we shall want and need to express the pain of being caught in the crack of time. . . . Our confidence in the future restorative justice of God may even give us confidence to do justice ourselves in the present."[39] Craig Harline, a scholar of Reformation Europe, suggested that "with their temple destroyed and their people scattered across Babylon, exiled Jews developed sacred *time* (the Sabbath) to compensate for the loss of sacred *space* (the temple)."[40] The destruction of the temple forced Judaism into a new mode of religious observance, one that reemphasized the divine creation narrative, demarcated by time rather than human construction of sacred places. At the same time, the mandate to make new that which was shattered led Judaism into a reshaping of Sabbath adherence, one that demanded the most creative and sincere efforts by human beings to capture the sense of what it means to be holy. Just as the tangible sense of loss during the first century AD made this sense of awaiting much more present in the religious imagination of Jews who had just lost the temple in Jerusalem, Christian hopes mirror this desire for a world repaired by God. The Sabbath also works to remind us of our shared interest in that project.

The great rabbi, civil rights activist, and writer Abraham Joshua Heschel sought to capture this sense of space and time in pursuit of holiness. Heschel recognized that what defined the sacred nature of the Sabbath was not space, but time. Human work perpetuates the monument of accomplishment, of mastery, of domination over the physical world. Within Heschel's mind, the Sabbath remained the one place where human architecture and manipulation could not supplant or replace holiness. Rather, what was properly needed was the construction of a "palace in time."[41] Heschel noted that "to gain control of the world of space is certainly one of our tasks. The danger begins when in gaining power in the realm of space we forfeit all aspirations in the realm of time. There is a realm of time where the goal is not to have but to be, not to own but to give, not to control but to share, not to subdue but to be in accord."[42]

Similarly, Wright showed that our current state is entirely dependent upon God's work with us in time and space. "We are called to live," Wright argued, "joyfully and painfully, in the story that is both his and ours. Our times are in his hands."[43] The challenges are many, but a broad investigation of how various religious traditions are recapturing sacred time through ritual, cultural liturgy, and reappropriation of past thought highlights how the Sabbath can reoccupy its place of divinely commanded prominence for the modern world. The traditional modes with which people attempt to dominate their physical space are wholly insufficient to align the intended use of the Sabbath with modern contexts. The problem is simply that "labor is a craft, but perfect rest is an art."[44] Our understanding of what work entails and how it is done has changed—when work was largely manual effort and toil, we were closer to its immediacy.[45] In our work, we are largely distant from the actual product through technology and computers. It is for this reason that we have to reinstitute barriers of time that allow us to turn off the instruments of work that are so easily blurred with the instruments of entertainment and allow rest to be central to our existence rather than a peripheral element.

Rest has been at the core of Sabbath observance since the very beginning of Judaism and Christianity, even if our thinking about rest has changed over time. Even the early Christian church father Saint Augustine called upon God at the close of his *Confessions* to pull us forward toward a more perfected form of rest. Early on, he asked God for "rest."[46] The reader of *Confessions* will recall the tumultuous self-realization process that Augustine experienced and emerged from at the end with this beautiful meditation on the Sabbath. Recalling the creative act, Augustine suggested that "the seventh day has no evening and no sunset, because you have sanctified it to abide eternally. As a result, the voice of your book would tell us that after your works of creation that were "very good" (even though you did them in a state of repose) you do not see in time, act in time, rest in time; but yet you create our seeing in time, and time itself, and rest in time."[47] It is this hope for eternal rest that is best recalled to memory through a commitment to locating the purpose of such rest, both physically and spiritually, through renewal of Sabbath observances.

Appreciative Examples Within the Christian Tradition

So then, how do Christians obtain this rest and holiness to which we are called through scripture, through human longing for peace, and through our desire to seek communion with the divine? What do other Christians foster in terms of practice and ritual that binds them to the Sabbath and the pursuit of the divine will? For Latter-day Saints, the challenge is readily apparent, even as a way out may not be so clear. One of the clear paths forward is the way of liturgical celebration and communal worship, but this is a path to which Latter-day Saints are less accustomed. It is true that Latter-day Saints do gather together, though worship services may feel overly fluid and lack the characteristic high liturgy of many other traditions. A much-sung hymn in the current Latter-day Saint hymnal speaks to an element of Christian worship that is noticeably absent from the typical sacrament meeting. The joyful anthem "Praise to the Lord, the Almighty" calls the congregation to "Join the great throng / Psaltery, organ and song / Sounding in glad adoration!" Should a survey of those in the congregation be taken, the results might reveal a lack of awareness of the Psalter used so richly in other Christian traditions to guide worship and prayer. The Psalter can historically take various forms, but the Psalms were organized specifically for liturgical use—that is, use in hymns, prayers, and other such communal efforts. Although members of The Church of Jesus Christ of Latter-day Saints do not have this form of communal worship through the psalmic prayers, it may prove useful to consider the ways that they might evoke the kinds of practices that would aid in Sabbath efforts towards holiness.

One example that highlights religious innovation as a means of greater observance comes from the Catholic church. After the reforms of Vatican II in the 1960s, an effort began to speak again to the souls of congregants through a revitalization and application of the liturgy to local demographics. The liturgy began to include the language of the community in large degree rather than strictly using Latin. By enlivening the language of the service through familiarity, the idea of community worship became a way to encourage Sabbath participation in greater numbers. The *Mundelein Psalter*'s "Introduction," which focuses on communal religious practice from the Catholic Church and Vatican II, is another inspirational example of the place of prayer in human life and might therefore aid us in our pursuit of pathways to greater holiness.[48] This text was designed to bring into clearer relief the importance of the Psalms as the central feature of the prayer within the storied history of the Church. As a text "with its roots sunk deep in the daily prayer of Judaism, the diurnal, public recitation of the Psalms has been the daily companion of Christians through the history of the Catholic church. The structuring of the liturgical year, of the week, and of the day give a profound meaning and stability to the church's desire to keep the mysteries of faith ever before us."[49] Seeing these examples, one might seek ways of invoking a similar spirit through a common reading of scripture. Perhaps elements of this effort may emerge locally, at the initiative of individuals and families that invite others to join for a conversation focused on a passage of scripture. The possibilities are, at least locally, endless given a desire to find avenues that build individuals and communities through worship. This pursuit of the divine mysteries is often aligned with unique qualities of a well-reverenced Sabbath, and the expansion of the human soul leads to a more engaged spirituality.

One of the great hallmarks of the Eastern Christian tradition is its deep mystery and reverence for prayer. The purpose of prayer is to transform the relationship of self-will to divine will. As the Russian religious philosopher Berdyaev so keenly noted, "In the relation between man and God an infinite spiritual experience is possible."[50] For many in the Christian world, the biblical injunction to maintain prayer as a constant in one's life leads to high dependence on and joyful celebration in Sabbath worship services and unlocks the mystery of the Sabbath. The Psalms centrality in Psalters and books of hours in Catholicism is one such manifestation to keep prayer active in the life of the believer. The eastern tradition has a similar focus that goes beyond the desire to maintain a prayer-filled service.

The words of 1 Thessalonians 5:17 call Christians to this kind of commitment to prayer in the words "pray without ceasing." The possibility of praying in all contexts internally opens one up to a kind of meditative engagement with the divine will in the Orthodox tradition, made possible through the unique encounter with Jesus. For the Latter-day Saint community, the dictate to "pray always to the Father" (3 Nephi 18:19) often speaks to a symbolic rather than a physical manifestation of persistent prayer. In the Orthodox faith, however, the hesychast tradition of interior prayer offers an alternative practice that seeks to accomplish this idea in a more tangible way. Hesychasm in the Eastern Rite is a practice of perpetuating prayer throughout the day by means of a discipline that allows one to internalize the prayer in the way that breathing is autonomously perpetuated.[51] Though the history of the hesychast tradition has its own complex and controversial history, it has remained an Eastern Orthodox practice that is both valid and encouraged.[52] The Jesus Prayer, or "Prayer of the Heart," seeks to accomplish the "infinite spiritual experience" Berdyaev mentions above.[53] Practices such as these likely will not be adopted into Latter-day Saint communal life in any concrete form, but their existence in other traditions might cause us to pause and see what we could draw upon to help strengthen our own worship practices and rituals as instruments for greater holiness. There may well be reasons that Latter-day Saints do not participate in traditional Christian practices that involve liturgy, prayer life, and communal celebrations; however a greater awareness of the ways in which other people of faith have sought to find God in the modern world can help build a greater respect for others' deep love of the Sabbath and the value of tradition as a form of communal continuity.

Again from the Russian Orthodox Christian tradition, we might learn from the twentieth-century martyr Father Alexander Men how to increase our capacity for "rest" in the modern world.[54] In the 1970s and 1980s, Father Men often held clandestine meetings, or *besedy*, with Christians in the Soviet Union and taught them how to live out their religious life with conviction even in antagonistic settings. In one such *besedy*, he taught, "We each have our own external and internal reasons for tiredness that has built up within us. We hope that our situation will somehow radically change when vacation comes. This hope is in vain, however, because we have already been on vacation numerous times and continued to hobble along in the same way. . . . This means that tension weighs upon us a like a rock." His prescribed remedy to this hopeless pursuit of rest depended upon a "lever" that included "six to ten minutes per day for prayers from the prayer book, which we read regardless of our mood," and "prayerful fellowship with God" in addition to scripture reading and the Eucharist.[55] Such systematic approaches suggested by Father Men emerge out of the very oft-prayed prayer of Saint Ephraim the Syrian (AD 306–373), who pleaded for such divine intervention in transforming his own self:

> Lord and Master of my life, Take from me the spirit of laziness, despair, lust of power and idle conversation.
>
> Rather give me the spirit of chastity, humility, patience, and love to Your servant. Indeed,
>
> O Lord, King, allow me to see my own sins and to not judge my brother, for blessed are you from ages to ages.[56]

Father Men believed that the humble stance of despondency shown in the prayer could lead one to a remembrance of the salvation afforded through Jesus. The human being, according to Father Men and Saint Ephraim, seems prone toward idleness or laziness, both qualities that miss the aspirations of Christian discipline. The turn to prayer as a system of discipline, connected to intentional study of scripture and the Lord's Supper, bears the potential to alter the human relationship to the divine and to the world. As the Communion Antiphon for Ash Wednesday suggests, "He who ponders the law of the Lord day and night will yield fruit in due season."[57] Like the hesychasts who pray the Jesus Prayer and the priests who pray the daily offices of the church have shown, intentional building of rituals and disciplines into daily life provides opportunities for greater holiness and further personal growth. Practices such as increased emphasis on prayer and scripture study have been increasingly encouraged as part of Sabbath worship for Latter-day Saints in recent years, though the paucity of liturgical instruments makes it far less clear on how to achieve such aims. The *Mundelein Psalter* reminds us that "it is the essence of the Church to be visible yet endowed with invisible resources, eager to act yet intent on contemplation, present in this world yet not at home in it."[58] As parishioners, members, and believers, perhaps such a stance is one that we all might hope to find through a greater emphasis on devotional discipline. The lessons that might be drawn from other religious faiths can only serve to benefit earnest seekers of truth and broaden their capacity toward creative reengagement through ritual and study. Latter-day Saint tradition will need to be creative in how it builds stronger connections to the Sabbath ideals of rest and holiness, but these examples can serve as a starting point to open up the conversation in directions that may lead to that end goal. Indeed, the active development of religious literacy about people and traditions often provides greater affinity for and common values found between people, forming a deep well of inspiration that bolsters the lives of people of faith.

Latter-day Saints should take comfort in knowing that other traditions look to capture this sense of rest through all kinds of religious festivals, yet it is really the act of stepping out of the mundane temporarily that illuminates the hidden spaces of eternity. For thousands of years the Sabbath as an institution has remained a core aspect of religious life, and people have constantly fought to keep it holy, often failing, but sometimes capturing glimpses of true rest. While doing so, they reengage the divine through efforts to approximate, envision, and embody holiness. Holiness has never been easy, but it is possible, at least in a limited, human form through the rituals of Sabbath observance. We may need to remake them and reimagine them for our modern world again and again, but this is not new. We need not fear the erosion of the Sabbath. The Sabbath day can continue to be a source of strength if we intentionally learn to remember it, postpone work, and seek holiness in everyday life.

Endnotes

1. It is important to register here the fact that for many Jews today, religion is but one nonessential part of a complicated set of contributing elements to Jewish identity, which includes political, ethnic, and cultural factors. Several examples of scholarship that helps expand the concepts of how Jews identify their being "Jewish" and the variations within modern Jewish society are Eugene B. Borowitz, *Choices in Modern Jewish Thought: A Partisan Guide* (New York: Behrman House, 1983); Zvi Gitelman, *Jewish Identities in Postcommunist Russia and Ukraine: An Uncertain Ethnicity* (Cambridge: Cambridge University Press, 2012); Benjamin Harshav, "Theses on the Historical Context of the Modern Jewish Revolution," in *The Polyphony of Jewish Culture* (Stanford: Stanford University Press, 2007), 3–22; and Michael A. Meyer, *The Origins of the Modern Jew: Jewish Identity and European Culture in Germany, 1749–1824* (Detroit: Wayne State University, 1967).
2. Samuel M. Brown, *Where the Soul Hungers: One Doctor's Journey from Atheism to Faith* (Provo, UT: Neal A. Maxwell Institute for Religious Scholarship; Salt Lake City: Deseret Book, 2021), 2.
3. Charles Taylor, *A Secular Age* (Cambridge, MA: Harvard University Press, 2007), 27.
4. The Four Horsemen contributed many books and articles to the New Atheism movement. The core of their thinking individually and as a collective project can be found in the following books: Richard Dawkins, *The God Delusion* (Boston: Houghton Mifflin, 2006); Daniel Dennett, *Breaking the Spell: Religion as a Natural Phenomenon* (New York: Penguin Books, 2006); Sam Harris, *The End of Faith: Religion, Terror, and the Future of Reason* (New York: W. W. Norton, 2004); and Christopher Hitchens, *God is Not Great: How Religion Poisons Everything* (Toronto: Emblem, 2007). A good history of why these voices have become so dominant in many circles is found in Stephen LeDrew, *The Evolution of Atheism: The Politics of a Modern Movement* (Oxford: Oxford University Press, 2016).
5. Tim Crane, *The Meaning of Belief: Religion from an Atheist's Point of View* (Cambridge, MA: Harvard University Press, 2017), 3–4.
6. The term "New Atheists" refers to those writers and thinkers who are highly combative against religion and religious belief; see note 4.
7. Crane, *Meaning of Belief*, 8.
8. Crane, 8.
9. Elsie Talmage Brandley, "The Religious Crisis of Today," in *At the Pulpit: 185 Years of Discourses by Latter-day Saint Women*, ed. Jennifer Reeder and Kate Holbrook (Salt Lake City: Church Historian's Press, 2017), 139.
10. Steven L. Peck, *Evolving Faith: Wanderings of a Mormon Biologist* (Provo, UT: Neal A. Maxwell Institute, 2015), xi.
11. James K. A. Smith, *How (Not) To Be Secular: Reading Charles Taylor* (Grand Rapids, MI: Eerdmans, 2014), vii.
12. The challenge of placing modern concepts of religion in the ancient past is not a new problem, and scholars have not spared much ink in discussing this topic. For more on why this can be a challenging conceptual space, see Brent Nongbri, *Before Religion: A History of a Modern Concept* (New Haven, CT: Yale University Press,

2013); and Jonathan Z. Smith, "Religion, Religions, Religious," in *Relating Religion: Essays in the Study of Religion* (Chicago: Chicago University Press, 2004), 179–96.

13. Taylor, *Secular Age*, 5.
14. Marvin J. Ashton, "A Yearning for Home," *Ensign*, October 1992, 23.
15. James K. A. Smith, *On the Road with Saint Augustine: A Real-World Spirituality for Restless Hearts* (Grand Rapids, MI: Brazos, 2019), 4–5.
16. Cecil Roth, *The Jewish Contribution to Civilisation* (Oxford: East and West Library, 1943), 158. So intense is the human self and human existence that in our refinement we need rest, realignment, and renewal.
17. *The Zohar: Pritzker Edition*, trans. Daniel C. Matt (Stanford: Stanford University Press, 2004), 101.
18. Mishnah Shabbat 7.2 says:

    > The main classes of work are forty save one: sowing, ploughing, reaping, binding sheaves, threshing, winnowing, cleansing crops, grinding, sifting, kneading, baking, shearing wool, washing or beating or dyeing it, spinning, weaving, making two loops, weaving two threads, separating two threads, tying [a knot], sewing two stitches, hunting a gazelle, slaughtering or flaying or salting it or curing its skin, scraping or cutting it up, writing two letters, erasing in order to write two letters, building, pulling down, putting out a fire, lighting a fire striking with a hammer and taking out aught from one domain into another. These are the main classes of work: forty save one.

    The Mishnah, trans. Herbert Danby (London: Oxford University Press, 1954), 106. All passages from Mishnah refer to Danby's translation. See also Avram R. Shannon, "The Sabbath in Rabbinic Judaism: Exploring the How of Keeping the Commandments," in this volume.
19. What this past engagement by Christians has done with this example has not always been productive or entirely helpful, but there have been wonderful aspects that have bolstered Christian behavior in the past without doing harm to Judaism or Jewish communities. It is these kinds of generous engagements that I hope to draw out here.
20. Rascal Flatts, "Mayberry," track 4 on *Melt*, Lyric Street, 2002.
21. John Bowker, ed., *The Oxford Dictionary of World Religions* (Oxford: Oxford University Press, 1997), 830.
22. Anne McCue, "Stupid," track 3 on *Roll*, Messenger Records, 2003.
23. Russell M. Nelson, "The Sabbath Is a Delight," *Ensign* or *Liahona*, May 2015, 129.
24. Mark S. Diamond, "Shabbat in Jewish Thought and Practice," in *Understanding Covenants and Communities: Jews and Latter-day Saints in Dialogue*, ed. Mark S. Diamond and Andrew C. Reed (Provo, UT: Brigham Young University Religious Studies Center and Central Conference of American Rabbis, 2020), 195–226.
25. Roth, *Jewish Contribution*, 159.
26. See Jason Robert Combs, "Christian Anti-Sabbath Polemic and the Textual Transmission of Luke 4:16 and 23:56," *TC: A Journal of Biblical Textual Criticism* 26 (2021): 29–46; and Combs, "Sabbath and Sunday in Ancient Christianity: Second through Sixth Centuries," in this volume.

27. *The Babylonian Talmud: A Translation and Commentary*, trans. Jacob Neusner et al., 22 vols. (Peabody, MA: Hendrickson, 2011), Shabbat 119a.
28. *Babylonian Talmud*, Neusner translation, Shabbat 118b.
29. Danby, *Mishnah*, 100.
30. For a critical recent study of the various ways that communities read the biblical text and find purpose and meaning that can appear at odds with other readers, see Esau McCaulley, *Reading While Black: African American Biblical Interpretation as an Exercise in Hope* (Downers Grove, IL: InterVarsity, 2020), 1–24; and Jordan T. Watkins, *Slavery and Sacred Texts: The Bible, the Constitution, and Historical Consciousness in Antebellum America* (Cambridge, MA: Cambridge University Press, 2021). Taken together, these books examine how readers of the Bible can find useable narratives from the text that inform how they see themselves and others, and how those various interpretations shape our current perceptions of ourselves over and against others.
31. Hellmut Wilhelm, "The Concept of Time in the Book of Changes," in *Man and Time: Papers from the Eranos Yearbooks*, vol. 3, ed. Joseph Campbell (Princeton, NJ: Princeton University Press, 1983), 214.
32. Dan Bellm, "Sabbath," *Image Journal*, 71.
33. Mohammad Ben Ismaïl Al'Bukhari, *Al' Bukhari's Sahih*, trans. Mohammad Mahdi Al'Sharif (Beirut: Dar al-Kotob al-Ilmiya, 2003), 1:205. This text is viewed by Sunni Muslims as one of the six hadith (that is, accounts of sayings of the Prophet Muhammad) collections, and it dates from around AD 846.
34. Colin Turner, *Islam: The Basics* (London: Routledge, 2011), 144.
35. A. J. Droge, trans., *The Qur'ān: A New Annotated Translation* (Sheffield, UK: Equinox, 2017).
36. Al'Bukhari, *Sahih,* 1:205, 209–210. At least some of the hadith literature indicates that the Prophet Muhammad also taught that it is not out of the question to brush one's teeth (as an act of purification) before enjoining in prayer.
37. Emmanuel Levinas, *Time and the Other*, trans. Richard A. Cohen (Pittsburgh: Duquesne University Press, 1987), 32.
38. Levinas, *Time and the Other*, 32.
39. N. T. Wright, *The Case for the Psalms: Why They Are Essential* (New York: HarperOne, 2013), 74–75.
40. Craig Harline, *Sunday: A History of the First Day from Babylonia to the Super Bowl* (New York: Doubleday, 2007), 4.
41. Abraham Joshua Heschel, *The Sabbath: Its Meaning for Modern Man* (New York: Farrar, Strauss, and Giroux, 2005), 15.
42. Heschel, *Sabbath*, 3.
43. Wright, *Case for the Psalms*, 75.
44. Heschel, *Sabbath*, 14.
45. Matthew B. Crawford, *Shop Class as Soulcraft: An Inquiry into the Value of Work* (New York: Penguin, 2009), 21.
46. Saint Augustine, *Confessions*, edited and translated by Carolyn J. B. Hammond (Cambridge, MA: Harvard University, 2014), 1:5.
47. Augustine, *Confessions*, 13:37.
48. Douglas A. Martis, ed., *The Mundelein Psalter* (Chicago: Hillenbrand, 2007).
49. Martis, *Mundelein Psalter*, 43.

50. Nicolas Berdyaev, *The Divine and the Human* (London: Geoffrey Bles, 1949), 183.
51. Vladimir Lossky, *The Mystical Theology of the Eastern Church* (Crestwood, NY: St. Vladimir's Seminary Press, 1976), 209.
52. Timothy Ware, *The Orthodox Church* (London: Penguin, 1997), 64–65.
53. There are various versions of this prayer, but the commonly accepted version of the prayer in the Eastern Church is as follows: "Lord Jesus Christ, Son of God, have mercy on me, a sinner."
54. The September 1990 murder of Father Alexander Men outside of Moscow remains unsolved today, though many in the Orthodox community continue to observe this as a martyrdom. For more on the remarkable life of Alexander Men, see Wallace L. Daniel, *Russia's Uncommon Prophet: Father Alexander Men and His Times* (DeKalb, IL: Northern Illinois University Press, 2016).
55. Alexander Men, *An Inner Step Toward God: Writings and Teaching on Prayer by Father Alexander Men*, ed. April French, trans. Christa Belyaeva (Brewster, MA: Paraclete, 2018), 13–14.
56. Saint Ephraim, "Lenten Prayer of Saint Ephraim the Syrian," in *Pravoslavnyi tokovyi molitvoslov s kratkimi katikhizicheskimi svedeniiami*, ed. Vilenskago Sviato-Dukhovskago Bratstva (St. Petersburg: Sinodal'naia Tipografiia, 1907), 139. Saint Ephraim's "Lenten Prayer" is recited at Vespers, Matins, and other prayers, especially during the Great Fast (Lent).
57. Samuel F. Weber, *Proper of the Mass: Entrance, Offertory and Communion Antiphons for Sundays and Solemnities* (San Francisco: Ingatius Press, 2014), 146. The scriptural text for this antiphon is Psalms 1:2–3.
58. Martis, *Mundelein Psalter*, 11.

Chapter Thirteen

The Decline of Sabbath Observance in an Increasingly Secular Society: Twenty-First Century Efforts to Reclaim the Lord's Day

Brent L. Top

The latter part of the twentieth century brought major developments affecting not only American society and institutions in general but also individuals and families in particular. The post–World War II booming economy enabled millions to realize the "American Dream"—moving to the quiet, clean suburbs and into modern, comfortable single-family houses. Soon every home had a color television and many people had extra money in their pockets, allowing them more time for leisure, recreation, and travel. Supermalls competed for those extra dollars of virtually every person, not just the uber-rich. This growing middle class had a new view of shopping. No longer was it merely what their parents and grandparents had done at the neighborhood grocery store for those commodities needed to sustain life. Shopping became more than just necessity or even luxury; it was a new form of entertainment. In addition to commerce, the advancements of the past century in the fields of medicine, communication, travel, and information have been mind-boggling. Quality of life and standard of living have risen dramatically, and with more disposable income and leisure time available, families and individuals have more freedom to look to the many available entertainment and recreation options. With all these improvements to life, what possible downside could there be?

There is, as it turns out, at least one major drawback. The dawning of the twenty-first century saw a rising level of secularism in American society. Although it is difficult, if not impossible, to draw exact cause-and-effect conclusions, the decline of religiosity in society certainly follows the trends of rising consumerism, leisure, entertainment, and recreation. Arguably the most significant "downside" of the advancements of the late twentieth and early twenty-first centuries has been the decline of faith, as evidenced by decreased religious affiliation in general and regular attendance at church meetings specifically.[1] Research conducted by the Barna Group found that in the last twenty years the percent of US adults that identify as Christians has declined by 20 percent. Barna further reported that in 2020, 36 percent fewer Americans regularly attended religious services than in 1993.[2] In the annual "Ten Today" survey that examines the relevance of the Ten Commandments in modern life, Americans likewise reported a dramatic decline in church attendance and Sabbath day observance since 1978. Yet even with the decline, 62 percent of respondents felt that a day of "religious rest" is important to society.[3]

In a "Saturday Essay" for the *Wall Street Journal*, noted author Sohrab Ahmari stated:

> The 20th century saw the death of the American Sabbath by a thousand cuts. . . . Judaism, Christianity and Islam all appreciated the bond between Sabbath restrictions and human freedom, even as they designated different days to be holy. Across the West today, however, the drive toward maximal market liberty has squeezed out the liberty of the Sabbath. We have banished it in the name of "choice." And some choice we have: Working-class families are denied even a half-day of rest together, yet we are puzzled by astronomical divorce rates, abysmally low rates of family formation, alienation and drug abuse. We have cashiered the Sabbath for algorithmic human-resources scheduling—computer code designed to minimize labor costs, regardless of the impact on families and communities.[4]

No wonder one American noted, "Our forefathers called it the Holy Sabbath; our fathers called it Sunday; we call it the week-end."[5] In a more serious vein, in his book *The Day of Worship*, Calvinist pastor Ryan M.

McGraw raised an alarm concerning secularism's "war" with faith, worship, and observance of the Sabbath day: "We live in a time of crisis with respect to Sabbath-keeping."[6] More recently, President Dallin H. Oaks expressed similar concerns about the secularization of society and the decline of Sabbath observance:

> Today, my message concerns such good and religious-minded people who have stopped attending or participating in their churches. When I say "churches," I include synagogues, mosques, or other religious organizations. We are concerned that attendance in all of these is down significantly, nationwide. If we cease valuing our churches for any reason, we threaten our personal spiritual life, and significant numbers separating themselves from God reduce His blessing to our nations.[7]

Theological Factors Contributing to the Decline of Sabbath Observance in Contemporary Christianity

Undoubtedly there are many factors at play in the decline of religiosity and Sabbath observance in contemporary society generally and Christianity specifically, but they all seem to fall into two main categories: cultural and theological. Many of the cultural factors within the United States have already been discussed.[8] In many respects, Christian theology has sown the seeds for the cultural decline of attitudinal and behavioral commitment to keeping the Sabbath day holy. Two general examples can highlight this.

The Law of Moses versus "Christian Liberty"

Many theologians throughout the history of Christianity have taught that the Old Testament laws and commandments (including the Ten Commandments) are superseded by Christ and, thus, keeping a formal Sabbath day constitutes a "work" that minimizes the grace of Christ.[9] This view can be traced to the writings of second-century Christian leaders and thinkers who sought to more clearly differentiate Christianity from Judaism.[10] A previous chapter in this volume more fully recounts this movement and cites many of these early Christian sources.[11] It is important, however, for this present discussion, to cite Justin Martyr, who taught that there was no "keeping" of the Sabbath by Old Testament patriarchs and peoples prior to Moses.[12] Thus the Sabbath, as a commandment of the Law of Moses, was fulfilled in Christ's death and resurrection:

> Is it not evident to you that the elements do not refrain from work, and that they do not observe the Sabbaths? Stay as you were at birth. For if circumcision was not required before the time of Abraham, and if there were no need of Sabbaths, festivals, and sacrifices before Moses, they are not needed now, when, in accordance with the will of God, Jesus Christ, his Son, has been born of the Virgin Mary, a descendant of Abraham.[13]

Like many of the early Christian fathers before them, many Protestant theologians today point to the New Testament teachings of the Apostle Paul regarding what has been called "Christian liberty." They use the "deadness" of the Mosaic law as evidence that keeping the Sabbath is not a requirement of the Christian faith.[14] This theological teaching has produced a "casualty" in contemporary Christianity and has influenced the decline of the spiritual significance of the sacrament of the Lord's Supper in formal worship. Since the Eucharist or Communion (other words for the sacrament) is not viewed by Protestants as a salvific ordinance essential to the faith, it need not be observed weekly or regularly. The less frequent celebration of Communion became much more common in Protestant churches in the twentieth century. Different denominations adopted their own approach to the frequency of the administration of Communion. While for centuries it was common for Christians to partake of the Eucharist regularly as part of their weekly (and sometimes more frequent) worship service, today it is less so. Some churches have moved toward a monthly or quarterly Communion. Others celebrate the sacrament of the Lord's Supper only at Easter and Christmas. Still others have completely abandoned the practice as part of their worship.

Sabbath as Perpetual Worship of Christ, Not a Weekly Day of Rest

A second theological teaching that affects the decline of Sunday worship is that the Sabbath day is not a "day" of rejoicing in Christ but a perpetual daily praise of the Lord. As has been addressed in previous chapters, in their effort to distinguish themselves from Jews, Christians of the first and second centuries viewed the Jewish Sabbath "day of rest" as idleness.[15]

Thus rejoicing in Christ replaced rest from labors, and by extension, such rejoicing and worship could be done at any time and in any place. In fact, according to this view, any devoted Christian who loved the Lord was keeping the Sabbath holy continuously.

In his work *A Brief History of Sunday from the New Testament to the New Creation*, Justo L. González identifies some of the key passages from the Church Fathers that suggest this move away from the Sabbath as a specific day to an emphasis on the relationship a person has with God.[16] According to González, in the second century, early Christian father Irenaeus "would say that a Christian who speaks directly with the Father, does not need to be reminded of what they ought to do."[17] Then, quoting Irenaeus, "nor will he be commanded to leave idle one day of rest, who is constantly keeping sabbath, that is giving homage to God in the temple of God, which is man's body, and at all times doing works of justice."[18]

Other early theologians and Christian leaders, such as Ambrose and Augustine, likewise spoke of a "second Sabbath" that was "kept holy" through one's relationship with God. According to González, Ambrose viewed the Sabbath "as being superseded, not by another weekly observance, but rather by a different relationship with God."[19] He said, "Thus, the work of the Sabbath is the sign of a future, because all who have fulfilled the Law and Grace are stripped of the vexations of corporeal frailty through the mercy of Christ."[20]

Years later Augustine wrote:

> Afterall, Christ removed from us that very heavy burden with its many prescriptions so that we are not circumcised in the flesh, we do not sacrifice animal victims, and we do not rest even from necessary work on the Sabbath every seven days, and all the many other things like these. But we are to keep them when they are understood spiritually, once the shadows which served as signs have been removed. . . . The carnal observance of the Sabbath, which is a sign of spiritual sanctification and rest, is an exception.[21]

For centuries Christians viewed the "day of rest" as a symbol of the liberation from sin afforded mankind through Christ's atoning sacrifice. Christians did not interpret it as physical rest, as practiced in Judaism; instead they viewed it as a type and shadow of the ultimate "day of rest" with Christ. González writes, "The day of rest was often seen as a sign and a reminder that no human work can merit the grace of God. By resting from all our works we acknowledge that even our best works of charity and obedience are nothing compared to the work of God's grace. Luther and others feared that too much stress on the legal observation of Sunday rest would lead to legalism, and therefore back again to salvation by works."[22] Ironically, today "rest"—be it mental, physical, or emotional—is viewed even among devout Christians as the primary reason for their allowance of Sunday recreation, sports, shopping, and so on.

So how have these centuries-long theological discussions and debates affected contemporary Christian views and practices regarding the Sabbath day? One major evangelical leader bemoaned that the evangelical church has "capitulated to the marketing model"—the need to attract "modern church goers" and particularly millennials who are more interested in inclusivity and connection than doctrinal "purity" and traditional religious practices. In his estimation, the rise of the "contemporary church," or what is sometimes referred to as "relevant worship" with its "come as you are" and "come when you can" approach to religion, is a major factor in the decline of Sunday worship.[23]

The twentieth-century rise of Evangelicalism, with its transdenominational nature, has had a cultural impact on the very nature of what constitutes worship. Arguably, the typical evangelical churchgoer today has little knowledge of or attachment to the rich traditions and Sabbath theology of the past. As a result, there is a growing trend toward a more "casual Christianity," as evidenced in the ministry, music, and approach to religious teaching in Sunday worship services. While such an approach is very appealing to some, others long for more formality and tradition. But a growing number view Sunday as the last day of the weekend, where play has replaced prayer and work has replaced worship.

Institutional Efforts to "Reclaim" the Sabbath as the Lord's Day

Although it may seem like they are swimming upstream against the strong currents of secularism, many Christian institutions and their respective religious leaders have been seeking to reenthrone Sunday as a holy day, one that is a sacred time dedicated to God[24] and not just a holiday.[25] During the last decades of the twentieth century and now in the new century, efforts by Catholics, Protestants, and Latter-day Saints, in their own unique ways and within their own congregations, have placed greater emphasis on keeping the Sabbath day holy.

The *Catechism of the Catholic Church* teaches that "on Sundays and other holy days of obligation, the faithful are to refrain from engaging in work or activities that hinder the worship owed to God, the joy proper to the Lord's Day, the performance of the works of mercy, and the appropriate relaxation of mind and body."[26] The rise of secularism in society in the latter half of the twentieth century, and its accompanying decline of attendance at Sunday worship services, affected not only Catholics but also many other religious communities. Efforts both large and small, local and from the Vatican, were made to stem the tide of religious decline, as manifested by the growing disregard for the "obligations" of proper Sunday worship. The Second Vatican Council, convened by Pope John XXIII in 1962 and culminating in 1965 with sixteen monumental documents intended to reform and "renew" the Catholic Church, did much to revitalize and refocus worship within Catholicism. As González writes:

> In brief, the [second Vatican] council emphasized the renewal of worship—particularly Sunday worship—by encouraging the participation of the laity. This was done, first, by the use of the vernacular; second, by giving the laity an active role in worship; third, by providing a homily which would connect the biblical text with the sacrament itself; fourth, by encouraging the use of music and other cultural elements that are expressive of the idiosyncrasies and experiences of the people; and finally, by recalling that Sunday is a feast day, and that therefore the Mass, rather than a lugubrious remembrance of the death of Christ, is a celebration of his victorious resurrection.[27]

Subsequent popes John Paul II, Benedict XVI, and Francis have likewise called upon believers to more fully return to what has been characterized as "divine worship" on Sunday. In 1998, in an apostolic letter entitled *Dies Domini* (on keeping the Lord's day holy), Pope John Paul II wrote that "Sunday is a day which is at the very heart of the Christian life."[28]

> The disciples of Christ . . . are asked to avoid any confusion between the celebration of Sunday, which should truly be a way of keeping the Lord's Day holy, and the "weekend," understood as a time of simple

> rest and relaxation. This will require a genuine spiritual maturity, which will enable Christians to "be what they are," in full accordance with the gift of faith, always ready to give an account of the hope which is in them (cf. 1 *Pt* 3:15). In this way, they will be led to a deeper understanding of Sunday, with the result that, even in difficult situations, they will be able to live it in complete docility to the Holy Spirit.[29]

The pope further warned that "when Sunday loses its fundamental meaning and becomes merely part of a 'weekend,' it can happen that people stay locked within a horizon so limited that they can no longer see 'the heavens.'"[30]

Pope Benedict XVI in his 2007 Apostolic Exhortation *Sacramentum Caritatis* likewise taught Catholics that participating in the Eucharist at Sunday Mass and maintaining the proper approach to the Lord's Day is the means whereby one can have a regular "encounter" with Christ, which can fortify believers and keep them on the path of Christian discipleship.[31]

The extensive teachings of these respective pontiffs and other clergy and scholars remind Catholics of their fundamental obligations of "divine worship" as stated in the Catholic *Catechism*—first, devoutly and regularly partaking of Communion; second, refraining from "activities that hinder the worship owed to God" on Sunday; and third, reflecting on the mercy and grace of Christ, which is what is to be commemorated at Mass and in one's Sunday worship, by rendering greater compassionate service and mercy toward others. [32]

With the secularization of society has come the "casualization" of religion and Sunday worship. Some Catholic leaders (as well as leaders from other denominations) have called for a return to "Sunday best" in both attire and attitude. "Dressing up," wrote Monsignor Francis Mannion of Salt Lake City, "will help Christians recognize their baptismal dignity. It will say that the presence of God in our midst is worth our best."[33]

Founded in 1888 by representatives of several mainline Protestant denominations, the Lord's Day Alliance (originally known as the American Sabbath Union) sought to "maintain and cultivate the first day of the week as a time for rest, worship, Christian education and spiritual renewal."[34] Today the Lord's Day Alliance (hereafter LDA) is a national organization that boasts representation from clergy and laity all across the spectrum of Christianity, including Orthodox, Catholics, Baptists, Episcopalians,

Lutherans, Methodists, Presbyterians, nondenominational churches, and reformed traditions. One of the stated purposes of the LDA is to "gather and diffuse information, to publish documents, to use the press, to cause public addresses to be made and to use other means as shall be expedient and proper to the end that the blessings of the Lord's Day and the benefits of Sabbath rest shall be secured for all people."[35] The flagship publication of the LDA is *Sunday Magazine*, which is published twice yearly and contains articles and perspectives from a wide array of scholars, clergy, and believers who are united in the mission of encouraging "all people to recognize and observe a day of Sabbath rest" and "to worship the risen Lord Jesus Christ, on the Lord's Day, Sunday."[36] In addition to *Sunday Magazine*, the LDA promotes conferences, lectures, and programs to emphasize "keeping the Sabbath Day holy" as a means of spiritual, physical, and emotional renewal. At its nineteenth-century founding, the LDA sought to promote change in the public sphere by lobbying for "Sunday-rest laws." The original purpose was to benefit postal unions specifically, but it expanded to include all workers who were compelled to work on Sundays.[37]

Today, however, the LDA seeks to promote change in personal lives rather than in societal laws, advocating the importance of the Sabbath as a means of "spiritual renewal and personal well-being in this fast-paced 24/7, 21st century."[38] There has been somewhat of a Sabbath reawakening. Many books now found in Christian bookstores speak of the Sabbath day, and numerous homilies have been delivered by priests and pastors at pulpits across the land on the importance of the third of the Ten Commandments. It is difficult, if not impossible, to fully assess the impact of this reawakening. Although church attendance numbers continue to trend downward, internal belief is harder to measure empirically.

The Church of Jesus Christ of Latter-day Saints, like its Catholic and Protestant counterparts, has also felt the impact of modern-day secularism. In 2015, the Pew Research Center reported that there was a marked decline in religious affiliation and intensity of religious beliefs and practices.[39] The Church doesn't publish statistics of those who stop participating on Sundays with their local congregations or those who lose their faith and leave the Church altogether. Yet much anecdotal evidence at the end of the twentieth and into the twenty-first century has caused concern among the leading quorums of the leadership of the Church. One prominent Latter-day Saint leader observed that "attrition [those leaving the Church and abandoning religion in general] has accelerated in the last five to ten years, reflecting the greater secularization in society."[40]

Understandably, Church leaders have looked for ways to stay the tide of secularism and promote greater faith and devotion. The primary focus of the training meetings of Church general authorities and officers associated with the general conferences of the Church in 2015 was honoring the Sabbath day. "Of all the organization or policy changes or doctrinal training that could hasten the work of salvation at this time," said Elder M. Russell Ballard, speaking on behalf of the senior leadership of the Church, "elevating the spirit and power of the Sabbath day would be most influential in drawing members and families to the Lord Jesus Christ."[41]

This renewed emphasis on the Sabbath as a means of spiritual strength, given in the general conference leadership training meeting, was delivered to local congregations throughout the world. Videos of the training meetings were shown to local leaders and members. Making the Sabbath a delight, as Isaiah admonished anciently (see Isaiah 58:13–14), became the topic for sermons in worship services and conferences, instruction in classes and groups, and discussions among members and families. Six months later additional training was provided to Church leaders and members in the same manner. The focus on keeping the Sabbath holy was sharpened: "In the natural revelatory process the Lord made known His wish that His ancient commandment regarding the Sabbath, or as the scriptures describe, 'His perpetual covenant with His people,' be brought to the fore," Elder D. Todd Christofferson stated on behalf of the First Presidency and Quorum of the Twelve Apostles.[42] He further stated:

> We realize that a deeper understanding of the meaning and purposes of the Sabbath day would bring to the Latter-day Saints a profound faith in God and in His Son Jesus Christ, and the Atonement of Christ. This would build strength in the members of the Church far greater than could be achieved by any programmatic means. We saw that observing the Sabbath could lead to full conversion and spiritual resilience in the Saints.[43]

Other important changes to the Church meeting structure and gospel-study curriculum, coupled with renewed emphasis on Sabbath observance, came in the October 2018 General Conference. In his talk announcing these changes, Elder Quentin L. Cook stated:

> World conditions increasingly require deepening individual conversion to and strengthening faith in Heavenly Father and Jesus Christ and His Atonement. . . . What do these adjustments mean for members of The Church of Jesus Christ of Latter-day Saints? We are confident that members will be blessed in extraordinary ways. Sunday can be a day of gospel learning and teaching at church and in the home. As individuals and families engage in family councils, family history, ministering, service, personal worship and joyful family time, the Sabbath day will truly be a delight.[44]

Another change was implemented in 2019: the reduction of the Sunday meeting schedule from the three-hour block established in 1980 to a two-hour block—one hour for a worship service and one hour for instruction. This development, President Russell M. Nelson explained, was a direct outgrowth from and augmentation of "our efforts over these recent years to hallow the Sabbath—to make it a delight and a personal sign to God of our love for Him."[45]

In many ways this intensive emphasis on honoring, remembering, and keeping the Lord's day spiritually prepared members of the Church for the effects of the COVID-19 worldwide pandemic on religious institutions, which included temporary suspension of in-person worship services and the normal routine workings of ministry and fellowship. Almost immediately upon receiving governmental and health organizations' warnings concerning the seriousness of the coronavirus, the Church suspended all religious gatherings. Sacrament meetings and other Church meetings were cancelled. Many of the typical Sunday (and weekday) activities suddenly ceased, but God's commandment to keep the Sabbath day holy was not "put on hold." The Lord's expectation that disciples remember him on that sacred day remained in force. With the worldwide pandemic, however, obeying that commandment required *internal* worship and devotion, not just *external* observance such as attending church meetings. Church leaders not only clearly taught this principle in the five years prior to the pandemic but also made curricular and organizational changes that placed greater responsibility for Sunday worship on individuals and families instead of solely on congregations and their leaders.

Certainly the consequences of the pandemic on the Church were less than desirable. Yet there were indeed many opportunities to learn from and adapt to these challenges. Many anecdotal accounts highlight that individuals and families felt closer to the Lord and that their Sunday worship was more meaningful during the "lockdown" months of the pandemic. One important anecdotal account is that of Elder Ulisses Soares of the Quorum of the Twelve Apostles. He stated that the challenges posed by the COVID-19 pandemic forced him to look at the Sabbath day in a new way—a holier way—and explained that the pandemic can give us the opportunity "to elevate the power of the Sabbath day in our lives."[46] The full story of the impact of the pandemic on Latter-day Saint Sundays—both empirical and anecdotal—is yet to be told. But it does appear that attendance at Sunday meetings, whether they be in person or via online streaming, has not yet rebounded to prepandemic levels. Certainly this is not unique to The Church of Jesus Christ of Latter-day Saints. Virtually all denominations are facing similar challenges in getting congregants back in the pews. As noted above, President Dallin H. Oaks called upon all people, not just Latter-day Saints, to recognize the individual and institutional benefits of regular attendance at worship services and to return to church, synagogue, mosque, and other places of worship. Then he continued:

> Attendance and activity in a church help us become better people and better influences on the lives of others. In church we are taught how to apply religious principles. We learn from one another. A persuasive example is more powerful than a sermon. We are strengthened by associating with others of like minds. In church attendance and participation, our hearts are, as the Bible says, "knit together in love" (Colossians 2:2). . . . Church attendance can open our hearts and sanctify our souls.[47]

Conclusion

González perhaps best captured the "state of affairs" concerning the challenges facing Christians today and their efforts to keep the Sabbath day holy. There are dark clouds, so to speak, with regards to religious worship in an increasingly irreligious contemporary society. Yet González identifies a silver lining in those dark clouds that gives hope to believers for some degree of a "Sabbath-day renaissance." He wrote:

> Seventeen centuries after Constantine, Christians find themselves once again in the midst of a society that is indifferent and sometimes even hostile to their values and beliefs, and have to find ways to live

> those values, proclaim those beliefs, and worship their God with diminishing support. For all but them, Sunday is just another day—a day of leisure, and football, and trips to the beach.
>
> But despite their nostalgic yearning for a bygone time of legal and social support, many Christians have responded to the secularization of Sunday in society at large with a renewed and deeper understanding of Sunday and its meaning.[48]

Although the conditions of an increasingly secular society have taken and will continue to take a toll on religious institutions and individuals, it is heartening to see the many efforts of Catholics, Protestants, and Latter-day Saints in congregations around the world to reclaim the Sabbath as a day of worship, rest, service, and sacramental communion with God. These efforts may seem like a drop in the bucket in comparison to the secular tsunami of today's society; yet each drop in the bucket is vital. Each drop of faith in an individual's heart yields more light in a darkening world. McGraw wrote beautifully of why the Sabbath is worth remembering, honoring, observing, and defending:

> If a man spent one-seventh of his life in a foreign culture, eventually aspects of that culture would become indistinguishable from his own customs, clothing, speech, and thoughts. He could not return to his own country without weaving something foreign into all he said and did. We ought to regard the Sabbath in the same manner. By virtue of our citizenship in heaven, we are pilgrims and strangers on the earth. On the Lord's Day, our transactions should be almost exclusively with the heavenly country to which we belong. As we engage in the joys of worship for one whole day in seven, we will live in this world, bringing something "foreign" into everything we do. If heaven consists primarily of communion with God, then to the extent that we enjoy communion with God on earth, we have already begun to enjoy the glories of heaven. On the Sabbath day, God has commanded us to spend the whole day in heaven, so to speak. While we are at home in the body, we are absent from the Lord (2 Cor. 5:6). We have not yet received our permanent dwelling place in our eternal homeland, yet on the Sabbath God allows us to visit heaven and return to this world with the glory of His presence shining from our faces.[49]

Endnotes

1. "America's Changing Religious Landscape," Pew Research Center, May 12, 2015, https://www.pewresearch.org/religion/2015/05/12/americas-changing-religious-landscape.
2. "Signs of Decline & Hope Among Key Metrics of Faith," State of the Church 2020, Barna Group, https://www.barna.com/research/changing-state-of-the-church.
3. Kelsey Davis, "New Poll Finds Americans Less Likely to Keep Sabbath Than in 1978, but Majority Still Say It's Important to Society," *Deseret News*, April 27, 2016, https://www.deseret.com/2016/4/27/20587346/new-poll-finds-americans-less-likely-to-keep-sabbath-than-in-1978-but-majority-still-say-it-s-import. For the original report, see "Sabbath Day Observance in the U.S.," Y2 Analytics, April 2016, https://media.deseret.com/media/misc/pdf/DNN-Ten-Today-Sabbath.pdf.
4. Sohrab Amari, "What We've Lost in Rejecting the Sabbath," *Wall Street Journal*, May 7, 2021, https://www.wsj.com/articles/what-weve-lost-in-rejecting-the-sabbath-11620399624.
5. Anonymous, quoted in Craig Harline, *Sunday: A History of the First Day from Babylonia to the Super Bowl* (New Haven and London: Yale University Press, 2011), 285.
6. Ryan M. McGraw, *The Day of Worship: Reassessing the Christian Life in Light of the Sabbath* (Grand Rapids, MI: Reformation Heritage Books, 2011), 7.
7. Dallin H. Oaks, "The Need for a Church," *Liahona*, November 2021, 24. To support his statement concerning nationwide decline in church attendance he cited Jeffrey M. Jones, "U.S. Church Membership Falls below Majority for First Time," Gallup, March 29, 2021, https://news.gallup.com/poll/341963/church-membership-falls-below-majority-first-time.aspx. The secularization thesis about the decline of the Sabbath day is the overarching claim articulated in Justo L. González, *A Brief History of Sunday from the New Testament to the New Creation* (Grand Rapids, MI: Eerdmans, 2017).
8. Ronald F. Inglehart argues that "from 1981 to 2007, most countries became more religious—but from 2007 to 2020, the overwhelming majority became *less* religious." Inglehart based this conclusion on data collected from the World Values Survey (WVS) and the European Values Study (EVS): "423 surveys [were] carried out in successive waves from 1981 to 2020 in 112 countries and territories containing over 90 percent of the world's population." He argues: "For many years, the U.S. has been cited as the key piece of evidence demonstrating that even highly modernized countries can be strongly religious. But since 2007, the U.S. has been secularizing more rapidly than any other country for which we have data. Its level has fallen substantially by virtually every measure of religiosity, and by one widely recognized criterion it now ranks as the 12th *least* religious country in the world." *Religion's Sudden Decline: What's Causing It, and What Comes Next?* (Oxford: Oxford University Press, 2021), ix, xii, 1.
9. See Ignatius, *To the Magnesians* 8.1, 10.3. For a sample of the various Christian views of the Sabbath, some of which do show supersessionist perspective on the

Sabbath laws, see Christopher John Donato, ed., *Perspectives on the Sabbath: 4 Views* (Nashville: B&H, 2011).

10. Some authors have noted that, particularly in the second-century-AD debates and discussions, much conflict existed within Christianity itself, not just between the Jewish and Christian communities. Many manifestations of anti-Judaism—such as the debates of Justin Martyr, Marcion, and others—were not the result of real issues Christians had with Jews; rather, they reflected modes of defending particular Christian ideas against other Christians. David Nirenberg, *Anti-Judaism: The Western Tradition* (New York: Norton, 2013), 100. Other studies that offer important insights into the history of Christian thought about the Sabbath include Samuele Bacchiocchi, *From Sabbath to Sunday: A Historical Investigation of the Rise of Sunday Observance in Early Christianity* (Rome: Pontifical Gregorian University Press, 1977); and Willy Rordorf, *Sunday: The History of the Day of Rest and Worship in the Earliest Centuries of the Christian Church*, trans. A. A. K. Graham (London: SCM Press, 1968).
11. See Jason R. Combs, "Sabbath and Sunday in Ancient Christianity: Second through Sixth Centuries," in this volume.
12. Justin Martyr, *Dialogue with Trypho* (*Dial.*) 23.1–2. *Dialogue with Trypho* is an important early Christian text. It was written sometime between AD 160 and 165—a time when Christians were trying to establish their identity vis-à-vis Judaic and Greco-Roman philosophical schools. Although Justin portrays Christianity as a unified group, the reality is that in his time there were many interpretations about what it meant to be a follower of Jesus. Scholars often talk of "Christianities" during this time, rather than a singular Christianity. For some discussions on the complex relationships between Christians and Jews in the early Christian Church, see Matthijs den Dulk, *Between Jews and Heretics: Refiguring Justin Martyr's Dialogue with Trypho* (London and New York: Routledge, 2018); Amy-Jill Levine, *The Misunderstood Jew: The Church and the Scandal of the Jewish Jesus* (New York: HarperOne, 2006), 29–33; and Marcel Simon, *Verus Israel: A Study of the Relations between Christians and Jews in the Roman Empire AD 135–425*, trans. Henry McKeating (Liverpool, UK: Littman Library of Jewish Civilization in association with Liverpool University Press, 1996), 135–55. In *Dialogue*, particularly for this study, Justin's statements about the Sabbath should be understood as pertaining to his Sabbath experience in Rome rather than as a general description of Christianity.
13. Justin Martyr, *Dial.* 23.3; English translation by Thomas B. Falls in *St. Justin Martyr, Dialogue with Trypho*, ed. Michael Slusser, Selections from the Church Fathers 3 (Washington, DC: Catholic University Press, 2003), 37–38.
14. As examples of some of Paul's teachings that are most often cited in this argument, see Romans 10:3–6; Galatians 3:23–25; and Ephesians 2:14–15.
15. Roman texts also described the Jewish Sabbath as a time of laziness. For examples, see Juvenal, *Satires* 14.96, 106; Tacitus, *History* 5.4; and Cassius Dio, *Roman History* 37.17.3. See also Gaye Strathearn, "Keeping the Sabbath Relevant in Some Late Second Temple Jewish Texts," in this volume.
16. González, *Brief History of Sunday*, 57–66.
17. González, 59. See also Irenaeus, *Proof of the Apostolic Preaching*, trans. Joseph P. Smith (New York: Newman, 1952), 106.

18. Irenaeus, *Proof of the Apostolic Preaching*, 106.
19. González, *Brief History of Sunday*, 63.
20. Ambrose of Milan, *Exposition of the Holy Gospel According to Saint Luke with Fragments on the Prophecy of Isaias*, trans. Theodosia Tomkinson, 2nd ed. (Etna, CA: Center for Traditionalist Orthodox Studies, 2003), 306. See also González, *Brief History of Sunday*, 63.
21. Augustine, *Answer to the Pelagians, II: Marriage and Desire, Answer to the Two Letters of the Pelagians, Answer to Julian*, trans. Roland J. Teske, ed. John E. Rotelle (Hyde Park, NY: New City Press, 1990), 167. See also González, *Brief History of Sunday*, 63–64.
22. González, *Brief History of Sunday*, 113.
23. Richard Mouw, personal correspondence to Robert L. Millet, 2015.
24. See Dana M. Pike's chapter in this volume.
25. For a discussion, see Harline, *Sunday*, ix–xv.
26. *Catechism of the Catholic Church*, 3.2.1.3.2185, https://www.vatican.va/archive/ENG0015/__P7O.HTM.
27. González, *Brief History of Sunday*, 145.
28. John Paul II, *Dies Domini*, apostolic letter, May 31, 1998, 7, https://www.vatican.va/content/john-paul-ii/en/apost_letters/1998/documents/hf_jp-ii_apl_05071998_dies-domini.html.
29. John Paul II, *Dies Domini*, 4.
30. John Paul II, *Dies Domini*, 4.
31. Benedict XVI, *Sacramentum Caritatis*, post-synodal apostolic exhortation, https://www.vatican.va/content/benedict-xvi/en/apost_exhortations/documents/hf_ben-xvi_exh_20070222_sacramentum-caritatis.html.
32. *Catechism of the Catholic Church*, 3.2.1.3.2182, 2185–86.
33. M. Francis Mannion, "In Favor of the Restoration of 'Sunday Best,'" blog post, *Pray Tell*, February 3, 2014, https://www.praytellblog.com/index.php/2014/02/03/viewpoint-in-favor-of-the-restoration-of-sunday-best.
34. "About," Lord's Day Alliance of the U.S., http://ldausa.org/about.
35. "About," Lord's Day Alliance.
36. "About," Lord's Day Alliance.
37. Richard R. John, "Taking Sabbatarianism Seriously: The Postal System, The Sabbath, and the Transformation of American Political Culture," *Journal of the Early Republic* 10, no. 4 (Winter 1990): 517–67; Wayne E. Fuller, *Morality and the Mail in Nineteenth-Century America* (Urbana and Chicago, IL: University of Illinois Press, 2010), 93.
38. "About," Lord's Day Alliance.
39. "America's Changing Religious Landscape," Pew Research Center.
40. "Elder Marlin K. Jensen Questions and Answers," interview by Philip Barlow, November 11, 2011, https://archive.org/details/ElderMarlinJensenQuestionsAndAnswers.
41. M. Russell Ballard, "Sabbath Day Observance" (general conference leadership training meeting, April 2015), https://churchofjesuschrist.org/broadcasts/archive/general-conference-leadership-training/2015/04; see also "Church Leaders Call for Better Observance of Sabbath Day," *Church News*, July 15, 2015.

42. D. Todd Christofferson, "Sabbath Day Observance" (general conference leadership training meeting, October 2015), https://churchofjesuschrist.org/broadcasts/archive/general-conference-leadership-training/2015/10.
43. Christofferson, "Sabbath Day Observance."
44. Quentin L. Cook, "Deep and Lasting Conversion to Heavenly Father and the Lord Jesus Christ," *Ensign* or *Liahona*, November 2018, 10–11.
45. Russell M. Nelson, "Opening Remarks," *Ensign* or *Liahona*, November 2018, 8.
46. Quoted in Lindsey Williams, "Making the Sabbath a Delight, Even during a Pandemic: Counsel from Elder Soares," *LDS Living*, July 8, 2020, https://www.ldsliving.com/making-the-sabbath-a-delight-even-during-a-pandemic-counsel-from-elder-soares/s/93104.
47. Dallin H. Oaks, "The Need for a Church," *Liahona*, November 2021, 24–25.
48. González, *Brief History of Sunday*, 141.
49. McGraw, *Day of Worship*, 145.

Index

D

E

S